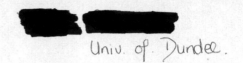

EMPLOYMENT LAW

AUSTRALIA
The Law Book Company Ltd.
Sydney : Melbourne : Brisbane

CANADA AND U.S.A.
The Carswell Company Ltd.
Agincourt, Ontario

INDIA
N. M. Tripathi Private Ltd.
Bombay

ISRAEL
Steimatzky's Agency Ltd.
Jerusalem : Tel Aviv : Haifa

MALAYSIA : SINGAPORE : BRUNEI
Malayan Law Journal (Pte.) Ltd.
Singapore

NEW ZEALAND
Sweet & Maxwell (N.Z.) Ltd.
Wellington

PAKISTAN
Pakistan Law House
Karachi

Employment Law

*Being the Second Edition of Individual
Employment Law*

By

B. A. HEPPLE, M.A., LL.B.

*of Gray's Inn, Barrister; a Chairman of Industrial Tribunals
(England and Wales); Professor of Comparative Social and
Labour Law, University of Kent at Canterbury*

and

PAUL O'HIGGINS, M.A., PH.D.

*of the King's Inns and Lincoln's Inn, Barrister;
Fellow of Christ's College; University Lecturer in Law,
Cambridge and Lecturer in Labour Law at the Inns of Court
School of Law*

LONDON

SWEET & MAXWELL

1976

First Published 1976
Second Impression 1978

Published by
Sweet & Maxwell Limited of
11 New Fetter Lane, London
and printed in Great Britain
by J. W. Arrowsmith Ltd.,
Bristol BS3 2NT

ISBN 0 421 20800 7

PREFACE

The aim of this book, like that of its predecessor *Individual Employment Law* (1971), is to provide an introduction to the law affecting the employment relationship.

Our aim now, as then, has been to provide a systematic and integrated view of common law and statutory duties in place of the old " law of master and servant " in which statutes were regarded as anomalous exceptions or appendices to the judge-made law. Moreover, one of the key problems with which this book, like the earlier version, is concerned is the way in which industrial practices, crystallised in works rule books, collective agreements and the like, are recognised and enforced by law. In this we have been able to draw upon our collection of labour law materials deposited in the Squire Law Library, Cambridge.

However, the changes in this new edition are sufficiently great to have demanded a change of title to *Employment Law*. Not only have we added new chapters on Collective Labour Relations, International Employment Contracts, and the practice and procedure of Industrial Tribunals, but there is scarcely a page of the original which has not required alteration in the light of the fundamental statutory changes since 1971: in particular, the repeal of the Industrial Relations Act 1971, and the enactment of the Trade Union and Labour Relations Acts 1974 and 1976, the Employment Protection Act 1975, the Sex Discrimination Act 1975 and forthcoming race relations legislation. In addition we have had to take account of the rapidly developing case law. Several chapters have been retitled, rearranged, and expanded in the light of these developments while, at the same time, attempting to keep the length within reasonable limits. The emphasis is still on the individual relationship between employer and worker—that is, the matters central to the jurisdiction of the industrial tribunals—but much greater emphasis than before has been placed on the collective framework because it is impossible to understand individual employment rights without reference to collective labour relations, and the latter, in turn, utilise the individual contract as the legal model for the creation, interpretation and enforcement of collective rights, immunities and obligations.

The law is stated, as far as possible, as at May 21, 1976, although it has been possible to insert a few later references usually in footnotes. Since the Employment Protection Act 1975 is being implemented in stages, we have written the text as if all the provisions were already in force. A note of the commencement dates of individual provisions will be found in Appendix 2. We have also written on the assumption that the Race Relations Bill as introduced in the House of Commons in February 1976, will become law in that form some time in 1976.

This text is also published as Part I of the *Encyclopedia of Labour Relations Law*, where it is kept up to date. The first-named author is primarily responsible for Chapters 1–12, 17, 21 and 22, and second-named author for Chapters 13–16, 18, 19 and 20.

B. A. H.

P. O'H.

CONTENTS

PART ONE: THE FRAMEWORK

PART TWO: TERMS AND CONDITIONS OF EMPLOYMENT

PART THREE: DISCIPLINE AND LOSS OF EMPLOYMENT

TABLE OF STATUTES

TABLE OF STATUTORY INSTRUMENTS

TABLE OF CASES

Abbreviations Used in this Book

Code   —Code of Industrial Relations Practice.

C.E.A.   —Contracts of Employment Act 1972.

E.A.T.   —Employment Appeal Tribunal.

E.P.A.   —Employment Protection Act 1975.

R.P.A.   —Redundancy Payments Act 1975.

S.D.A.   —Sex Discrimination Act 1975.

T.U.L.R.A.   —Trade Union and Labour Relations Act 1974.

T.U.L.R.A. (Amdt.)—Trade Union and Labour Relations (Amendment) Act 1976.

Part One

THE FRAMEWORK

CHAPTER 1

COLLECTIVE LABOUR RELATIONS

1. GENERAL FEATURES

The nature and development of the law

1   The most significant feature of labour relations in Great Britain is that
there has generally been a preference for *collective bargaining* between
trade unions and employers over *legislation* as a method of regulating jobs.
The explanation for this does not rest upon some philosophical basis, such
as " the abstention of the law " or " voluntarism," but simply on practical
experience. During the critical periods of their development British trade
unions have found that they could win more economic gains through collective industrial strength than through reliance upon the law. Professor Kahn-
Freund [1] has pointed out that the unions had obtained minimum labour
standards, without the aid of legislation, before the franchise was extended
to the town artisan in 1867 and to the country operative and miner in 1885.
To this Dr. Pelling [2] has added the historical fact of the class antagonism
of workers towards the judiciary. The justices of the peace, who fixed wages
for nearly 500 years and fined and imprisoned workers for breach of
contract until 1875, were nearly always landowners and employers. The
social origins and judicial attitudes of the High Court Bench were also
perceived as being fundamentally anti-trade union. This hostility to the
ordinary courts is reflected, even at the present day, in the establishment
of tripartite industrial tribunals, consisting of a lawyer, an employer and
a trade unionist, to deal with legal disputes in this field.

2   Closely connected with this phenomenon is the fact that the courts
have had a relatively small share in the evolution of the rules which
regulate jobs.[3] The great success of collective bargaining in laying down the
" normal " conduct expected of the employer and worker in matters of
wages and conditions of work has meant that the courts have been concerned only with extreme situations. Moreover, the common law rules laid
down by the judges did little to redress the basic inequality of the individual
employment relationship, in which the property rights of the employer far
outweigh the bargaining power of the individual worker who owns nothing
except his ability to work. Where legislation has intervened it has either
been to grant organised labour *immunities* from the rules hostile to collective bargaining, laid down by the judges, or to *regulate* specific features of
the employment relationships of those whom collective bargaining could
not help.

3   Legislation of the first type need be traced no further back than the
Combination Laws Repeal Act 1824 as substantially modified by Peel's
Combination Act of 1825. In effect this legislation established limited freedom of association, by neutralising the common law of criminal conspiracy
and confirming the repeal of earlier statutory prohibitions against com-

---

[1] *Law and Opinion in England in the 20th Century* (ed. M. Ginsberg) (London, 1959).
[2] *Popular Politics and Society* (1968), Chap. 4.
[3] O. Kahn-Freund, *Labour and the Law* (1972), pp. 21–29.

3

binations; but by the creation of a number of undefined criminal offences such as intimidation, molestation and obstruction, it precluded the freedom to strike. Freedom of association was, however, threatened by what had long been debated and was eventually made clear in 1867, namely, that the purposes of most trade unions were unlawful as being in restraint of trade at common law.[4] The outcry led to the establishment of the Erle Royal Commission on Trade Unions (1867–69) whose members divided between the majority who wanted to impose various obligations on unions in return for conferring fairly extensive legal rights upon them, and the minority who wanted protection for the unions from the common law, but no state supervision of their activities. It was the minority who won. Their proposals were incorporated in Gladstone's Trade Union Act 1871. This Act, the bedrock of trade union freedom for a century, partially legalised unions by removing the consequences of their purposes being in restraint of trade and precluded any of their agreements from being " directly enforceable." This was in order to prevent judicial supervision of their rules. There was a system of voluntary registration (which most major unions utilised) carrying some small advantages.

4   Freedom to strike, however, was not secured until 1906 and then only by Parliament rendering ineffective repeated judicial " re-interpretations " of the common law. The Criminal Law Amendment Act 1871 had ameliorated the judge-made law (interpreting the Act of 1825) under which a mere threat to strike was a statutory offence; but by now defining offences such as intimidation, molestation and obstruction the Act made it clear that even the most elementary forms of picketing were illegal. The Act did not remove other grounds of common law liability, and in *R*. v. *Bunn*[5] London gas workers who threatened a strike unless a colleague dismissed for union activities was reinstated were convicted of a common law conspiracy by threatening to break their contracts (the breach being criminal at the time under the Master and Servant Acts) and by " their unjustifiable annoyance and interference with the masters in the conduct of their business." Trade union agitation led to the appointment of the Cockburn Royal Commission on the Labour Laws (1875) and to the passing of the Conspiracy and Protection of Property Act 1875 which Disraeli told Queen Victoria would "help to soften the feelings of the working multitude."[6] The Act, most of which is still in force, repealed the Master and Servant Acts, codified the crimes relating to molestation and picketing, provided criminal liability for certain strikes in breach of contract in essential services, and, in section 3, reversed the effect of *Bunn's* case in trade disputes.

5   Between 1891 and 1906, however, the judges outflanked the Act of 1875 by developing the *tort* (*i.e.* civil wrong) of conspiracy,[7] by applying and expanding the tort of inducement of breach of contract to labour disputes[8] and by holding, in the *Taff Vale* case,[9] that a trade union registered under the Act of 1871, although not a corporate body, could be made civilly

---

[4] *Hilton* v. *Eckersley*, 106 R.R. 5071; *Hornby* v. *Close* (1867) 2 Q.B. 153.
[5] (1872) 1 Cox 316.
[6] Quoted by R. Harrison, " Practical capable men," *New Reasoner* (Autumn 1958), p. 115.   [7] *Quinn* v. *Leathem* [1901] A.C. 495 (H.L.) was the leading case.
[8] *Temperton* v. *Russell* [1893] 1 Q.B. 715.
[9] *Taff Vale Ry. Co.* v. *A.S.R.S.* [1901] A.C. 426.

responsible for the torts of its officials. The trade unions turned this into what became an historical turning point, leading to the formation of the Labour Party. More directly, the Liberal Government elected in 1906, adopting the minority report of the Dunedin Royal Commission on Trade Disputes and Trade Unions (1906), secured the passing of the Trade Disputes Act 1906. This Act excluded the new tort of "simple" civil conspiracy in respect of acts done "in contemplation or furtherance of a trade dispute" (which was now defined for the first time) (s. 1), permitted peaceful picketing in trade disputes (s. 2), excluded the torts of inducing breach of employment contracts or interference with business in trade disputes (s. 3), and gave complete immunity in actions in tort to trade unions (s. 4), so overcoming the effect of the *Taff Vale* decision without facing the issue whether trade unions were corporate bodies.

6   It was these developments which established what has been described as the age of "collective *laissez faire*," that is managerial freedom, on the one hand, and the freedom of organised labour to secure the terms on which labour-power is bought and sold, on the other hand. The most striking feature of this legal framework of collective labour relations is the relative absence of a collective labour law. The circumstances under which trade unions could operate, when and how they could seek recognition by employers, the subjects of their bargaining with employers and the effect of collective agreements, as well as the legality of strikes, were left undefined. The subject was mainly one of academic disputation based upon a few obscure judicial dicta. Unions and management for their part, encouraged by Government, established, particularly in the years between the Wars, a predominantly "voluntary" industry-wide system of collective bargaining institutions such as the Joint Industrial Councils. By 1965 there were estimated to be some 500 separate industry-wide negotiating agreements covering 14 million of the 16 million manual workers in Great Britain and 4 million of the 7 million non-manual workers.[10] Legislative intervention was limited [11] to the extension of statutory minimum wage legislation (first introduced by the Trade Boards Act 1909) for those industries where collective bargaining was weak or non-existent, and the provision of permanent state machinery (under the Conciliation Act 1896 and the Industrial Courts Act 1919) for encouraging voluntary conciliation and arbitration. When peace-time conditions were finally restored in 1959 all that remained of war-time compulsory arbitration was section 8 of the Terms and Conditions of Employment Act 1959, designed to deal with employers in otherwise well-organised industries who failed to observe employment terms established by collective bargaining for the industry.

7   By the 1960s there was considerable political pressure to deal with what were then perceived as the major problems of British labour relations, namely, the relatively large number of unofficial, unconstitutional strikes, wages drift, alleged oppressive union conduct (such as the well-publicised E.T.U. ballot-rigging and the case of *Rookes* v. *Barnard*) [12] and the

---

10 Ministry of Labour, Memorandum of Evidence to the Donovan Commission (1965).

11 Apart from the Trade Disputes Act 1927 (repealed, without ever being used, in 1946) which in effect outlawed political strikes and prevented affiliations by civil service unions.

12 [1964] A.C. 1100 (H.L.) in which a draughtsman who had left the A.E.S.D. because of policy disagreements lost his job through the operation of a 100 per cent. union membership agreement.

inefficient use of manpower, blamed in part on "restrictive practices" of unions. The Donovan Royal Commission on Trade Unions and Employers' Associations (1965–68) reported that the root cause of these problems was the "irreversible shift" in power from the relatively formal industry-wide level to the relatively informal shop floor. One indication of this shift was that, in comparison with only 3,000 full-time union officials there were some 200,000 shop stewards (by 1973 the latter figure had been raised to 350,000). Research done for the Commission showed that five out of six stewards discussed and settled issues with management, and that most managers preferred to deal with stewards rather than with full-time officers. The majority view of the Donovan Commission was that existing institutions were incapable of dealing with this "challenge from below." Their solution was the reform of rules to encourage more plant and company bargaining, to reduce the fragmentation of bargaining and to widen the subject-matter of bargaining. The Commission wanted more formal, written agreements at plant and company level and the revision of rule books of unions to describe the powers and functions of stewards.

8   The Donovan Commission was "not in principle opposed to the use of legal sanctions"[13] to achieve these reforms but thought that the law would be ineffective unless based upon a consensus. However, the Conservative Government, which took office in 1970, took the view that "legislation had an essential and positive role to play in the improvement of industrial relations."[14] The result was the Industrial Relations Act 1971 which, as McCarthy and Ellis[15] have pointed out, reflected in part the traditional philosophy that "responsible" trade unions should not harm the public interest; in part it implemented proposals of the Donovan Commission; and, in part it attempted to reconcile Conservative policy and Donovan proposals. The traditional philosophy was reflected first in those provisions of the Act which were directed towards changing the strike pattern (the emergency provisions taken from the U.S. Taft-Hartley Act, the "unfair industrial practices," and the imposition of responsibility on unions for the actions of shop stewards); and, secondly, in those provisions aimed at restricting the closed shop. The Donovan proposals which were implemented (some in modified form) included the establishment of the Commission on Industrial Relations on a statutory basis, provisions for the disclosure of information for bargaining purposes to unions (these were never brought into force), for the notification of procedure agreements, and for the extension of individual rights in particular against unfair dismissal. The attempted reconciliation of Conservative and Donovan policies was seen in the complex provisions of the Act designed to encourage legally enforceable collective agreements, to reform bargaining structures and to grant unions recognition rights, to reform union rules, and to give rights to individual members.

---

[13] Cmnd. 3623, paras. 502–503.
[14] Consultative Document on the Industrial Relations Bill (1970); *Fair Deal at Work* (Conservative Political Centre, 1968) and *A Giant's Strength* (Inns of Court Conservative and Unionist Assn., 1958).
[15] *Management By Agreement* (London, 1973).

Trade Union and Labour Relations Acts 1974 and 1976

9   It lies beyond our scope to consider why the Industrial Relations Act failed,[16] but we must note that, despite the repeal of the Act (and the abolition of the National Industrial Relations Court established under the Act) by the Trade Union and Labour Relations Act 1974, a number of the 1971 Act's provisions have been retained or reintroduced in revised form. The Act of 1974 re-enacted (as Schedule 1) the unfair dismissals provisions of the Industrial Relations Act with some important amendments.[17] It abolished the system of trade union registration instituted by the 1971 Act, but created a " list " of trade unions.[18] It restored, with minor improvements, the pre-1971 framework of collective labour law, in particular, reversing the presumption in the 1971 Act that collective agreements were to be enforceable as contracts,[19] clarifying the effect of " no-strike " clauses in agreements, granting immunity to trade unions in tort,[20] redefining the area of protected action in " trade disputes," curbing the use of injunctions in trade disputes [21] and conferring immunity from civil action in respect of certain torts in trade disputes.[22] The Trade Union and Labour Relations (Amendment) Act 1976,[23] reversing the effect of a number of amendments to the 1974 Bill inserted by the House of Lords, broadened the protection in respect of acts in contemplation or furtherance of a trade dispute, removed certain statutory safeguards given by the 1974 Act to trade union members and requirements as to trade union rules, and made dismissal automatically fair in nearly all closed shop situations.[24]

Employment Protection Act 1975

10   The Employment Protection Act 1975 has completed the new structure of collective labour law, as well as considerably extending the range and detail of individual employment rights. It establishes, on a statutory basis, the independent Advisory Conciliation and Arbitration Service (A.C.A.S.) which has been operating since September 1974 as the successor to the Commission on Industrial Relations and to the Department of Employment's conciliation and arbitration service.[25] It also replaces the Industrial Court, established under the Industrial Courts Act 1919, and renamed the Industrial Arbitration Board in 1971, with the independent Central Arbitration Committee, and confers a number of new jurisdictions upon it.[26] The industrial tribunals, first established in 1964, are given a vastly extended jurisdiction and their decisions are made subject to appeal to a new Employment Appeal Tribunal (E.A.T.).[27] A Certification Officer takes

---

16 For illuminating accounts see B. Weekes *et al.*, *Industrial Relations and the Limits of the Law* (Oxford, 1975); and A. W. J. Thompson and S. R. Engelman, *The Industrial Relations Act, A review and analysis* (London, 1975).
17 The amendments included a reduction in the qualifying period for presenting a complaint from 2 years' continuous employment to 6 months. See Chap. 17.
18 T.U.L.R.A., ss. 2–12. See below.
19 T.U.L.R.A., s. 18. See Chap. 8.
20 T.U.L.R.A., s. 14. See below.
21 *Ibid.*, s. 17.
22 *Ibid.*, s. 13.
23 This Act came into operation on March 23, 1976.
24 See Chap. 17.
25 See Chap. 4.
26 See Chap. 4.
27 See Chap. 4.

over from the Registrar of Friendly Societies the task of keeping the "list" of trade unions and he has the vitally important role of certifying "independence" which is the key to a number of new rights for unions and individuals.[28] The 1975 Act reintroduces and improves earlier measures for the unilateral compulsory arbitration of employment terms, for example, as the ultimate sanction for refusal to recognise a recommended independent trade union, or for refusal to disclose information to a recognised independent trade union; and it enlarges, in Schedule 11, the procedures for extending established terms and conditions of employment to all employers in an industry. Apart from improving the unfair dismissal provisions of the 1974 Act, the 1975 legislation implements an EEC directive on collective redundancies by imposing procedural limitations on the employer's power to dismiss by reason of redundancy.[29]

11   It will be observed that there is a close link between the framework of collective labour law and the rights of individual workers. Broadly speaking, the principal aim of recent legislation has been to expand the area of collective bargaining. Trade unions have been provided with negative immunities from common law restrictions on the freedom to associate and the freedom to strike and have been given positive legal rights to organise, to seek recognition and disclosure of information from employers. The actual subject-matter of bargaining and its legal effects have, by and large, been left to autonomous regulation by unions and employers. In the past the subjects to which regulatory legislation was applied were limited to those thought inappropriate for collective bargaining, such as the employment of children and women, safety and health and a few aspects of payment of wages. More recently regulatory legislation has been extended to limit the power of management in matters of termination of employment (in particular the Contracts of Employment Act 1963, re-enacted in 1972, the Redundancy Payments Act 1965 and the unfair dismissals legislation of 1971, re-enacted in 1974 with further modifications in 1975); and to deal with unfair discrimination on grounds of race, sex or marital status.[30] In addition some measures to maintain workers' income have been introduced to complement the social security system, by casting an increased burden on employers (*e.g.* guarantee payments during periods when work is not available; maternity pay; and protection of wages on insolvency of the employer).

12   Labour relations law has changed with breathtaking and bewildering speed since 1971, after two generations of relative stability, and in this it has reflected changing power relations at the place of work. Yet in the collective field it appears at first sight to have gone almost full circle, back to the framework of pre-1971 collective *laissez-faire*. This would be a deceptive characterisation of the post-1974 period, however, because the legislation has been only one side of a so-called "social contract" between the Trades Union Congress and the Government through which the unions have become closely involved in formulating and maintaining a national policy of wage restraint and industrial strategy.

---

[28] See below.
[29] See Chap. 18.
[30] See Chap. 11.

2. EMPLOYERS AND THEIR ASSOCIATIONS

Establishment and undertaking

13   Labour relations may take place at the level of a single establishment, of a business or undertaking, of a company or an industry. There are no universal legal definitions of these bargaining levels; but there are definitions in specific statutory contexts conferring individual rights. More precise definition of certain concepts is bound to become necessary if Great Britain adopts a legislative scheme to institutionalise worker participation in management decision-making.

14   The concept of an " establishment " is important, for example, for the purposes of the Sex Discrimination and Equal Pay Acts.[31] There is no definition, except that " where work is not done at an establishment it shall be treated for the relevant purposes as done at the establishment from which it is done or (where it is not done from any establishment) at the establishment with which it has the closest connection." [32] The old law on Selective Employment Tax gave rise to a case law on the meaning of " establishment " which may be of some guidance, although the Divisional Court has warned against any attempt to lay down an exclusive or comprehensive test.[33] Among the relevant factors in determining the scope of an establishment may be the geographical separation of the premises from other premises owned by the employer, the separation of management, the separation of financial accounting, the separation of services, and the separation of profits.[34]

15   While a law which defines rights by reference to the establishment is concerned only with standards for a particular production unit, a law which utilises the broader notion of a " business " or " undertaking " (what is in Continental Europe generally called the " enterprise ") seeks to regulate the whole body of operations carried on by the employer. For example, for purposes of claiming a redundancy payment an employee may have to show that the requirements of a " business " for work of a particular kind have ceased or diminished [35]; and to maintain his continuity of employment on a change of ownership he may seek to establish a " transfer of the business." [36] The Redundancy Payments Act defines " business " so as to " include a trade or profession and . . . any activity carried on by a body of persons whether corporate or unincorporate " a concept wide enough to cover the activities of charitable bodies, schools and other bodies which are of a non-commercial nature.[37] Moreover, a " business " is a going concern, including the goodwill, and not merely the physical assets upon which employees are engaged.[38] The concept of an

---

31 See Chap. 11.
32 S.D.A., s. 10 (4).
33 *Secretary of State for Employment* v. *Vic Hallam* (1969) 8 K.I.R. 623.
34 See *e.g. Secretary of State for Employment* v. *Hallam* (above); *May & Robertson Ltd.* v. *Minister of Labour* [1967] I.T.R. 607; *Lord Advocate* v. *Babcock & Wilcox* [1970] I.T.R. 69; *Minister of Labour* v. *Tyne Tugs Ltd.* [1969] I.T.R. 17; *United Dairies (London) Ltd.* v. *Minister of Labour* [1967] I.T.R. 596.
35 R.P.A., s. 1 (2) (*b*); see Chap. 18.
36 C.E.A., Sched. 1, para. 9; see Chap. 5.
37 *Dallow Industrial Properties Ltd.* v. *Else* [1967] 2 Q.B. 449.
38 See Chaps. 5 and 18.

"undertaking," where not statutorily defined, has been given a wide con-notation in the case of *Kapur* v. *Shields*.[39] The employer was a company director and property owner who, with his wife, had the sole or a con-trolling shareholding in a number of companies. He dismissed a house-keeper whom he had personally employed as the sole employee in one of his properties. The question arose whether the housekeeper was barred from presenting a complaint of unfair dismissal on the ground that there were less than four employees in the "undertaking." Phillips J. held that in determining this question the identity of the employer was immaterial. The question was whether the distinct but similar activities of the employer, his wife, and their various companies constituted a single undertaking. On the particular facts he found that the industrial tribunal had been justified in deciding that they were a single undertaking. One sees, there-fore, that a number of employees may work in the same "undertaking" while each having different formal employers.

The Employer

16   The definition of employment rights by reference to an "establish-ment" or "undertaking" corresponds to the reality of collective bargaining at these levels between management and trade unions. Unfortunately, however, most of the existing law of employment focuses legal rights and obligations on the "employer." Where defined[40] an "employer" is simply the converse of either the "employee," *i.e.* a person working under a contract of service, or a "worker," *i.e.* anyone who undertakes personally to perform some work or labour.[41] The employer may be an individual proprietor or a partnership or some other body of persons whether corporate or unincorporate. In public companies, the ownership of the capital employed in the business has become separated from management. So while labour relations are in fact carried on between managers and workers or their representatives, the legal theory is that managers, like all others working for the company, are simply employees. Although all these employees form an integral part of the undertaking, they are not members of the company unless they are also shareholders. Even the sole managing director of a company, who beneficially owns all the shares, can also be regarded as an employee of the company because of the doctrine of com-pany law that the company is an entity distinct from its members.[42] For example, in *Lee* v. *Lee's Air Farming Ltd.*,[43] Lee formed a company, of which he was sole governing director and beneficially owned all the shares, in order to carry on his business of aerial top-dressing. He was also chief pilot. He was killed in a flying accident and the question arose whether his widow was entitled to compensation from the company's insurers under the New Zealand Workmen's Compensation Act. This

---

[39] [1976] I.C.R. 26 (Q.B.D.). This particular bar to a complaint of unfair dismissal was removed by E.P.A., Sched. 16, but the general comments on the nature of an "under-taking" retain their interest.

[40] *e.g.* R.P.A., s. 25; T.U.L.R.A., s. 30 (1), as inserted by E.P.A., Sched. 16, Pt. III, para. 7.

[41] See Chap. 3.

[42] *Salomon* v. *Salomon & Co.* [1897] 2 A.C. 22 (H.L.).

[43] [1961] A.C. 12 (P.C.); see too *Ferguson* v. *Telford Grier Mackay & Co. Ltd.* [1967] I.T.R. 387; *Robinson* v. *George Sorby Ltd.* [1967] I.T.R. 148; *Road Transport I.T.B.* v. *Readers Garage Ltd.* [1969] I.T.R. 195. But note that partners are not themselves employees of the partnership: *Palumbo* v. *Stylianou* [1966] I.T.R. 407.

depended upon whether Lee was a "worker" within the meaning of the Act. The Privy Council held that since Lee had a contract of service with the company as chief pilot his relationship with the company was that of employer and employee (*i.e.* within the meaning of "worker"). The "magic or corporate personality" in Gower's words, "enabled him to be master and servant at the same time and to get all the advantages of both —and of limited liability." [44]

17 It is obvious that if a working director is an "employee" of the company, conflicts of interest may arise between the fiduciary duty which company law imposes upon him *qua* director, towards the shareholders, and the obligations of loyalty which he may feel towards his fellow-employees. These obligations may, in some situations, be legal ones such as where, under his contract of membership of a trade union, the managerial employee is obliged to follow the instructions of his union. The problem of workers on both sides of the bargaining table have not yet been squarely faced by either company law or labour law. For example, in *Boulting* v. *A.C.T.T.*[45] the well-known Boulting brothers were managing directors of a film company and were also active in the management and technical side of production. Until 1950 they had been members of A.C.T.T. but they paid no subscriptions from 1950 to 1959. In 1959 the union claimed the arrears of subscriptions. They sought a declaration that they were ineligible for membership and an injunction restraining the union from taking industrial action to compel them to join. The rules of the union said that "all employees engaged on the technical side of film production" were eligible. A majority of the Court of Appeal held that the brothers were employees for the purposes of this rule because they exercised employee functions on the shop floor. A conflict of interests was not inevitable, in the view of the majority, and, even if it was, it was for the company and not the directors to complain. The notion that only the company could complain was a mere fiction in this case because it was, after all, a two-man company. Lord Denning (dissenting) took, it is submitted, a more realistic view when he said that the brothers were in fact the "directing mind and will of the company" and as such employers who should not be forced to join an employee's union. The problem is not limited to small companies. It will arise sharply if any legislative scheme for worker-directors emerges in Great Britain.[46] In the public services the problem is to some extent averted by voluntary arrangements for the fixing of senior civil servants' salaries by a review body outside the normal collective bargaining machinery.

Changes in the undertaking

18 The identity of the employer may change while the employee remains working in the undertaking. In the case of an individual proprietor who is made bankrupt, or who dies, or a partnership which changes composition, or a company which is voluntarily or compulsorily wound up, the contracts of employment of those who work in the undertaking may come to an end

---

[44] *Modern Company Law*, 3rd ed. (1969), p. 202.
[45] [1963] 2 Q.B. 606 (C.A.).
[46] See *e.g. Parke* v. *Daily News Ltd.* [1962] Ch. 927 (scheme to distribute proceeds of sale of business among redundant employees *ultra vires*); and generally N. Bastin (1976) 126 New L.J. 271.

by operation of law in some circumstances, or the employee may treat the change as one which entitles him to treat the contract as at an end by virtue of the employer's repudiation.[47] But the employee may agree to continue working for the new employer. In that case the new owner, or the trustee in bankruptcy, or personal representative, or liquidator, may in law become the employer.

19   The most difficult situations arise in cases of takeover, merger or amalgamation of companies. In some instances the identity of the formal employer remains intact. This would happen where the company's shares are vested in the acquiring company of which it becomes a subsidiary; or the shares may be taken over by the shareholders of the acquiring company; or the undertaking may now be managed by the acquiring company while the undertaking remains nominally the property of the company taken over. In these cases the identity of the employer, for purposes of the collective agreement and the contract of employment, remains the same. But the repercussions for the trade unions and employees may be considerable. At present, labour law provides no protection in these cases. This is likely to change, however, when the draft EEC directive on the protection of acquired rights on mergers and takeovers [48] is implemented. The draft directive provides protection in the case of " concentrations " where a person or undertaking, a group of persons or undertakings, acquire *control* of one or several undertakings.

20   In other cases, however, the takeover, merger or amalgamation may involve acquisition of the ownership of the undertaking in a way that there is a change of identity of the employer. It may be brought about by the winding-up or dissolution of the old company. The fundamental principle of English law is that the dissolution of the company terminates the contract of employment and that the new company does not automatically succeed to the old employer's rights and obligations.[49] It is because of this doctrine that legislation has had to devise complicated rules to safeguard the continuity of employment and other statutory rights of employees in the event of the transfer of a business [50] or the transfer of an employee to an associated employer.[51] Once again, the draft EEC directive on mergers and takeovers may force a fundamental rethinking of the doctrine of non-transferability of employment rights and obligations. The draft directive aims to ensure the automatic transfer of the old employment relationship to the new employer and this applies as well to " customary industrial practice " which, in the British context, would presumably include collective agreements.[52]

21   Since is it not infrequently a matter of difficulty to identify the actual employer, the Contracts of Employment Act 1972, s. 4, requires the

---

47 See Chap. 14.
48 O.J. 1974, C104/1. See further Chap. 20.
49 *Nokes* v. *Doncaster Amalgamated Collieries Ltd.* [1940] A.C. 1014, 1018, 1020.
50 R.P.A., s. 13; C.E.A., Sched. 1, para. 9. See Chap. 5.
51 C.E.A., Sched. 1, para. 10. The standard definition of an " associated employer " now is that " two employers are to be treated as associated if one is a company of which the other (directly or indirectly) has control, or if both are companies of which a third person (directly or indirectly) has control " (*ibid.*); and R.P.A., s. 48 (4), as amended by E.P.A., Sched. 16, Pt. I, para. 18. This differs significantly from the former limitation to an " associated company."
52 See Hepple (1975) 1 Poly L.R. 50 at p. 57.

employer to " identify the parties " in the written statement of employment terms given to the employee.[53] If the name of the employer (whether an individual or partnership or body corporate) is changed without any change in the identity of the employer, or if the identity of the employer is changed without any break in continuity of employment, then the person who is the employer immediately after the change must inform the employee of the change within one month.[54] If he fails to do so the employee may refer the matter to an industrial tribunal.[55] In some circumstances, a person who has misled an employee into believing, to his detriment, that he is that person's employer may be estopped from denying that he is the employer.[56]

Worker participation in the undertaking

22   There has been a plethora of research and proposals in recent years about " worker participation." This is generally understood as a situation in which workers have the right to take part in management decision-making. Those who see collective bargaining as a rule-making or legislative process, a form of " industrial government," and not simply the collective equivalent of individual bargaining over employment terms,[57] do not draw any clear line between collective bargaining and other forms of " worker participation." But " worker participation " has come to have a rather narrower connotation as some form of institutional participation along the lines of the works council, at the level of the establishment, or the two-tier managerial and supervisory board, at the level of the undertaking, such as exists in a number of other European countries. The draft fifth directive on company law of the EEC, which aims to co-ordinate the company laws of Member States by allowing a choice between the German and Dutch models of participation, and the European company statute (which may be used by companies operating in two or more Member States) make it almost inevitable that some reform of the law in Great Britain will take place.[58] A Committee of Inquiry, under the Chairmanship of Lord Bullock, was established in 1975 to consider how an extension of industrial democracy in the control of companies by means of representation on boards of directors could best be achieved.[59]

Employers' associations

23   There is no precise information available about the size or membership of employers' associations in Great Britain, although it seems clear

---

[53] See Chap. 7.   [54] C.E.A., ss. 5 (1) and 5 (4).
[55] Ibid., s. 8.
[56] Smith v. Blandford Gee Cementation Ltd. [1970] 3 All E.R. 154. See Chap. 7.
[57] The view expressed by A. Flanders (1968) 6 B.J.I.R. 1, in criticism of the Webbs' classic formulation in Industrial Democracy (1898), p. 193. But A. Fox (1975) 13 B.J.I.R. 151, argues that Flanders' criticisms are based on a fundamental misconception of the bargaining process.
[58] The literature is vast and rapidly expanding. C.I.R. Study No. 4, Worker Participation and Collective Bargaining in Europe (H.M.S.O., 1974), may be especially recommended; and for critical accounts of the German system T. Ramm, " Co-determination and the German Works Constitution Act 1972 " (1974) 3 I.L.J. 20; W. Daubler, " Co-determination: the German Experience " (1975) 4 I.L.J. 218; and generally S. Simitis, " Workers' Participation in the Enterprise-Transcending Company Law " (1975) 38 M.L.R. 1, and E. Batstone and P. L. Davies, Industrial Democracy: European Experience (H.M.S.O., 1976).
[59] The terms of reference require the committee to investigate " in the light of " the T.U.C.'s proposals in Industrial Democracy (1974). For a current survey of company practice, see I.D.S. Study No. 104, Worker Participation (1975).

that only a minority of them can claim to organise the overwhelming proportion of the employers in the industry for which the association caters.[60] The legal definition of an employers' association, now contained in section 28 (2) of the Trade Union and Labour Relations Act 1974, is identical to the definition of a " trade union " save that the organisation must consist "wholly or mainly of employers or individual proprietors of one or more descriptions." The legal status of such associations differs from trade unions, however, to the extent that an employers' association may be either a body corporate or an unincorporated association.[61] In the latter case, the association possesses the same quasi-corporate attributes as a trade union.[62] Employers' associations which were incorporated under the Industrial Relations Act 1971 lost that status six months after the 1974 Act came into force, unless they acquired corporate status in some other way such as under the Companies Acts.[63] The Certification Officer maintains a list of employers' associations,[64] upon which an association may claim to have its name entered, provided that it is an "employers' association " as defined by the statute and that it complies with certain formalities. Its name must not be the same as that of another listed association or so nearly resemble that name as to be likely to deceive the public.[65] An employers' association (whether listed or not) is under the same duties as a trade union to keep accounting records,[66] to make annual returns and to have its accounts audited.[67] An employers' association is granted immunity in respect of the doctrine of restraint of trade, and in actions in tort.[68]

3. TRADE UNIONS

Legal definition of a trade union

24   Workers' organisations are of many types, but all that matters in order to acquire various rights under current legislation is whether the organisation falls within the definition of a "trade union" in section 28 of the Trade Union and Labour Relations Act 1974. The organisation, which may be temporary or permanent (and so may include an *ad hoc* committee) must :

(1) *consist wholly or mainly of workers* [69] *of one or more descriptions.*[70] The effect of this is to exclude organisations of those working for professional clients, such as solicitors [71]; and of those who simply sell a work of some kind, such as authors writing for the BBC.[72]

---

[60] H. A. Clegg, *The System of Industrial Relations in Great Britain* (Oxford, 1970).
[61] T.U.L.R.A., s. 3 (1).
[62] *Ibid.,* s. 3 (2); and s. 4 regarding property.
[63] *Ibid.,* s. 3 (3).
[64] *Ibid.,* s. 8.
[65] *Ibid.,* s. 8 (5).
[66] *Ibid.,* s. 10.
[67] *Ibid.,* s. 11; and s. 12 for offences.
[68] *Ibid.,* ss. 3 (5) and 14. In the case of incorporated employers' associations the immunity extends only in connection with the regulation of labour relations.
[69] Def. in T.U.L.R.A., s. 30 (1). See Chap. 3.
[70] " Descriptions " leaves the organisation free to prescribe the particular grade or class or occupation or industry it wishes to cover.
[71] *Carter* v. *Law Society* [1973] I.C.R. 113.
[72] *Writers Guild of G.B.* v. *B.B.C.* [1974] I.C.R. 334.

(2) *be an organisation whose principal purposes include the regulation of relations between workers of that description or those descriptions and employers or employers' associations.* It is the principal purposes which must be looked at [73] and it seems that the organisation must be *directly* regulating relations and not simply engaging in, say, political activities which *may* influence labour-management relations.[74] It has been suggested that before an organisation can be said to have the purpose of " regulating " relations with employers it must, at least, have sought recognition from employers. If the sole activity of an organisation is to take or abandon industrial action and it does not enter into negotiations with employers but leaves this to the established union machinery it is, apparently, not a " trade union." [75]

Political objects

25   A fundamental question is whether this statutory definition is an enabling or limiting provision. Does it have the effect that anything done outside these purposes, or not incidental to them, is *ultra vires* the Act? The answer today is that a trade union may include in its rule book any lawful purposes at all, including political objects. This is because the definition in the 1974 Act (unlike that in the Trade Union Act 1871) says that the organisation need only *include* the regulation of labour-management relations among its principal purposes.[76]

26   There is, however, a statutory limitation on the expenditure of funds on certain political objects. The Trade Union Act 1913 lays down a fairly complicated set of conditions which must be observed in order to protect political dissentients within the union. These conditions cannot be fully considered here,[77] but the main points are: (a) there must be a secret ballot of the membership to approve the setting up of a political fund; (b) once approved the union must incorporate political fund rules approved by the Certification Officer; (c) the political fund, and only the fund, can be used to promote those political objects which are set out in section 3 (3) of the Act; (d) individuals must have the right to contract out and to suffer no discrimination by doing so, except in the control and operation of the political fund [78]; (e) any breach of the political fund rules is dealt with

---

[73] *Performing Rights Society* v. *London Theatre of Varieties* [1924] A.C. 1.

[74] See Grunfeld, *Modern Trade Union Law* (London, 1966), p. 7; but the legal precedent is slender, see *Gozney* v. *Bristol Trade & Provident Society* [1909] 1 K.B. 901.

[75] This was suggested by Sir John Donaldson, in relation to the Joint Shop Stewards' Committee of the Workers of the Port of London, in *Midland Cold Storage Ltd.* v. *Turner* [1972] I.C.R. 230 at p. 248 (N.I.R.C.); *cf.* Megarry J. in *Midland Cold Storage Ltd.* v. *Steer* [1972] I.C.R. 435 at p. 443 (Chancery Division).

[76] The Trade Union Acts 1871 to 1940, define a trade union in terms of " the principal objects which are under its definition the ' statutory objects '." In *Amalgamated Society of Railway Servants* v. *Osborne* [1910] A.C. 87, the House of Lords held that this definition was a limiting one; accordingly, it was *ultra vires* the Act for a union to levy a contribution on members to support the Labour Representation Committee, later the Labour Party. The Trade Union Act 1913, s. 1 (1), effectively overruled this by permitting a trade union to have any lawful objects. Although s. 1 (1) was repealed by the Industrial Relations Act 1971, Sched. 9, the definition of " trade union " in the 1971 Act, like that in the 1974 Act, was made to depend only on the *inclusion* of certain principal purposes. The argument that a trade union, with a political objects clause in its rules, cannot call a " political " strike did not find favour in *Sherard* v. *A.U.E.W.* [1974] I.C.R. 421 (C.A.).

[77] See Grunfeld, *op. cit.*, Part Four, for an extensive analysis.

[78] Trade Union Act 1913, ss. 3 (1) (*b*) and 5. A contracted-out member cannot be prevented from holding a district office: *Birch* v. *N.U.R.* [1950] Ch. 602, but the position may be different in regard to national office: see Grunfeld, pp. 305, 306.

by the Certification Officer with a right of appeal on questions of law to the Employment Appeal Tribunal.[79]

Legal classifications of trade unions

(1) Listed unions

27   The Certification Officer maintains a list of trade unions. An organisation of workers which is a trade union within the meaning of section 28 of the 1974 Act and which complies with certain formalities[80] is entitled to have its name entered on the list. Unions registered under earlier legislation or otherwise affiliated to the TUC were automatically placed on the list provided they appeared to be trade unions.[81] The Certification Officer may prevent the use of misleading names.[82] A listed trade union is entitled to a certificate that its name is included on the list.[83] The advantage of such a certificate is that it enables the trade union to provide proof of its status for purposes of income tax relief on its provident fund income,[84] and it is the necessary first stage to obtaining a certificate of independence (see next paragraph). The Certification Officer may remove a trade union from the list if it appears to him that it is not a trade union (after allowing representations to be made), or if he is requested by an organisation to remove its name, or if he is satisfied that it has ceased to exist.[85] There is a right of appeal on questions of fact or law against the Certification Officer's decision to the Employment Appeal Tribunal.[86]

(2) Independent unions

28   An " independent trade union " is, according to section 30 (1) of the Trade Union and Labour Relations Act 1974, one which

" (a) is not under the domination or control of an employer or a group of employers or of one or more employers' associations;
(b) is not liable to interference by an employer or any such group or association (arising out of the provision of financial or material support or by any other means whatsoever) tending towards such control."

The Employment Protection Act vests the decision whether or not a trade union is independent in the hands of the Certification Officer,[87] subject to a right of appeal on a question of fact or law to the Employment Appeal Tribunal.[88] If a question arises in any legal proceedings as to whether a trade union is independent, those proceedings must be stayed until a certificate of independence has been issued or refused by the Certification Officer.[89] The certificate is conclusive evidence that the trade union is

---

[79] Trade Union Act 1913, s. 3 (2); E.P.A., ss. 7 and 88 (2) (a).
[80] T.U.L.R.A., s. 8 (4). These include payment of a fee, sending in a copy of its rules, a list of officers and its address and name.
[81] T.U.L.R.A., s. 8 (2).
[82] Ibid., s. 8 (5).
[83] Ibid., s. 8 (10).
[84] Income and Corporation Taxes Act 1970, s. 338, as modified by Finance Act 1974, s. 28 (1).
[85] T.U.L.R.A., ss. 8 (6) and 8 (6A).
[86] Ibid., s. 8 (7) as amended, and E.P.A., s. 88 (3).
[87] E.P.A., s. 8.
[88] Ibid., ss. 8 (9) and 88 (3). Only the organisation aggrieved may appeal.
[89] Ibid., s. 8 (12).

independent.[90] Any listed trade union may apply for a certificate of independence (it will be noted that listing does not imply independence),[91] provided it complies with certain formalities and pays a fee.[92] The Certification Officer is under a duty to act "fairly" in the sense that he must take into account relevant information submitted to him by any person. This, in effect, gives trade unions an opportunity to challenge before the Certification Officer the independence of other organisations seeking a certificate as a preliminary to invoking various legal rights to recognition and the like. The certificate of independence is, indeed, required by a trade union in order to (a) refer recognition issues to A.C.A.S. and the C.A.C.[93]; (b) enforce rights to information [94]; (c) allow individuals to claim protection for trade union membership and activities [95]; (d) allow individuals to claim time off for union activities [96]; (e) be consulted in respect of redundancies [97]; (f) make union membership agreements in a form which allows the employer fairly to dismiss non-members [98]; (g) obtain planning information under the Industry Act 1975.

(3) Special register bodies

29 These are organisations whose names were, immediately before the commencement of the Trade Union and Labour Relations Act 1974 (September 16, 1974) entered on the special register maintained under section 84 of the Industrial Relations Act 1971 and which are companies registered under the Companies Act or are incorporated by charter or letters patent.[99] The special register was created in 1971 for organisations, such as the Royal College of Nursing and the British Medical Association, whose principal purposes are the advancement of professional standards or training but which have come to include among their activities the regulation of labour-management relations. These bodies are not willing to alter their constitutions in order to become trade unions because they would thereby endanger their corporate status. The main legal distinction between special register bodies and other trade unions is that the former are corporate bodies while the latter cannot register under the Companies Act.[1] The 1974 Act equates special register bodies, in so far as they regulate labour-management relations, with trade unions by conferring on them immunity from the doctrine of restraint of trade [2] and immunity from actions in tort.[3] However, unlike other trade unions, a special register body is not obliged to keep accounting records, submit annual returns and have accounts audited (it may have corresponding obligations to do so under the Companies Act); and those whose *principal* purposes do not

---

90 *Ibid.*, s. 8 (11).
91 *Ibid.*, s. 8 (4).
92 *Ibid.*, s. 8 (2).
93 *Ibid.*, s. 11.
94 *Ibid.*, ss. 17–21.
95 *Ibid.*, ss. 53–56 and 78–80.
96 *Ibid.*, ss. 57–60.
97 *Ibid.*, Pt. IV.
98 T.U.L.R.A., Sched. 1, para. 6 (5), and definition in s. 30 (1) as amended.
99 T.U.L.R.A., s. 30 (1).
1 *Ibid.*, s. 2 (2), which re-enacts corresponding provisions of the Industrial Relations Act 1971, s. 157, and the previous Trade Union Act 1871, s. 5 (3).
2 *Ibid.*, s. 2 (5).
3 *Ibid.*, s. 14 (1) (*b*) (*c*).

include labour-management relations cannot be listed or seek a certificate of independence. The effect is to exclude a number of special register bodies from many of the rights conferred on trade unions and their members by legislation.[4]

Legal status of trade unions

30   Although a trade union which is not a special register body " shall not be, or be treated as if it were a body corporate," it is given a number of attributes of quasi-corporateness by the Trade Union and Labour Relations Act 1974. In particular:

(a) it is capable of making contracts [5];

(b) all property belonging to the union must be vested in trustees in trust for the union [6];

(c) it is capable of suing and and being sued in its own name [7]; and it is amenable to criminal prosecution in its own name [8];

(d) judgments, awards and orders may be enforced against any property held in trust for the union.[9]

31   In addition, trade unions are given statutory protection against the common law doctrine of restraint of trade, both in respect of their purposes and their rules,[10] and are immune from actions in tort.[11]

Liability for the acts of officials

32   There is a wide array of union officials, elected, appointed, full-time and part-time. Some are employees of the union while others are not.[12] The definition of an " official " in the Trade Union and Labour Relations Act 1974 covers " any person who is an officer of the union or a branch or section of the union or who (not being such an officer) is a person elected or appointed in accordance with the rules of the union to be a representative of its members or of some of them, including any person so elected or appointed who is an employee of the same employer as the members, or one or more of the members, whom he is to represent." [13]

---

[4] An account of the legal problems of some of these bodies will be found in Hepple & O'Higgins, *Public Employee Trade Unionism in the United Kingdom: The Legal Framework* (Ann Arbor, 1971), pp. 48 *et seq.*

[5] T.U.L.R.A., s. 2 (1).

[6] T.U.L.R.A., s. 2 (1) (*b*), and s. 4 for detailed provisions in transfer of property.

[7] *Ibid.*, s. 2 (1) (*c*).

[8] *Ibid.*, s. 2 (1) (*d*).

[9] *Ibid.*, s. 2 (1) (*e*).

[10] In *Hornby* v. *Close* (1867) L.R. 2 Q.B. 153 it was held that the *purposes* of a union, whose rules enabled a majority to control the terms on which all members disposed of their labour, were unlawful. This was reversed by s. 3 of the 1871 Act, as re-enacted by Industrial Relations Act 1971, s. 135. In *Edwards* v. *S.O.G.A.T.* [1971] Ch. 354, it was suggested that this did not protect a *rule* in restraint of trade. S. 2 (5) of the 1974 Act accordingly covers both the *purposes* and *rules* of a trade union.

[11] T.U.L.R.A., s. 14, broadly re-enacting Trade Disputes Act 1906, s. 4, which had nullified the effect of the *Taff Vale* case (above). However, the 1974 Act is both clearer and narrower in scope than the 1906 Act. In particular a trade union is not immune in respect of acts of negligence, nuisance or breach of duty resulting in personal injury, nor in connection with the ownership, occupation, possession, control or use of property, unless the act was done in contemplation or furtherance of a trade dispute: s. 14 (2).

[12] See Chap. 3. There was said to be sufficient control under the rules to make a " sick steward " an employee of the union in *A.E.U.* v. *Minister of Pensions and National Insurance* [1963] 1 W.L.R. 441.

[13] T.U.L.R.A., s. 30 (1). See too, definition of " officer " inserted by E.P.A., Sched. 16, Pt. III, para. 7 (5).

The shop steward, not defined as such in any legislation, would clearly fall within this definition which is important for a variety of purposes such as the right to time off to participate in the activities of an independent trade union.[14]

33   The authority of an official, including a shop steward, to bind the trade union depends on two sources: (1) the written rule book of the union; and (2) the custom and practice of the union. In the words of Lord Wilberforce in the case of *Heatons Transport (St. Helens) Ltd.* v. *T.G.W.U.*,[15] which is still of fundamental importance on this point:

> " The original source of a shop steward's authority is the agreement entered into by each member on joining the union. By that agreement each member joins with all other members in authorising specified persons or classes of persons to do particular kinds of acts on behalf of all the members, who are hereafter collectively referred to as the union. The basic terms of that agreement are to be found in the union's rule book. . . . [I]t is not to be assumed, as in the case of a commercial contract which has been reduced into writing, that all the terms of the agreement are to be found in the rule book alone: particularly as respects the discretion conferred by the members upon committees or officials of the union as to the way in which they may act on the union's behalf. What the members understand as to the characteristics of the agreement into which they enter by joining a union is well stated in the section of the TUC Handbook on the Industrial Relations Act which gives advice about the content and operation of unions' rules. Paragraph 99 reads as follows: ' . . . Custom and practice may operate either by modifying a union's rules as they operate in practice or by compensating for the absence of formal rules . . . . ' "

The major premise of this approach is that " if the authority to take a particular type of action is not excluded by the rules, and if such authority is reasonably to be implied from custom and practice, such authority will continue to exist until unequivocally withdrawn." [16]

34   Since trade unions are, in general, not liable in tort (and the unfair industrial practices for which unions incurred responsibility for the acts of officials under the Industrial Relations Act 1971 have been repealed) questions of legal responsibility of unions for industrial action taken by officials do not now arise. However, the approach in the *Heatons'* case may still be of importance in relation to the acts of officials purporting to make or break contracts on behalf of a trade union. Even if an official has no authority under the rule book or by custom and practice, his unauthorised action may be subsequently ratified by the union which will then be legally responsible for the official's act.[17] The main importance of the judicial remarks in the *Heatons* case is in indicating that it is justifiable for lawyers

---

14 E.P.A., s. 56. See Chap. 10.

15 [1972] I.C.R. 308 (H.L.) at p. 393; see Hepple (1972) 1 I.L.J. 197 and Davies (1973) 36 M.L.R. 78; *Howitt Transport Ltd.* v. *T.G.W.U.* [1973] I.C.R. 1; comment (1973) 2 I.L.J. 102; *General Aviation Services (U.K.) Ltd.* v. *T.G.W.U.* [1976] I.R.L.R. 224 (H.L.).

16 [1972] I.C.R. at 394.

17 *Bonsor* v. *Musicians' Union* [1956] A.C. 104 (H.L.).

to regard trade union written rules as "the tip of the iceberg," [18] beneath which lies the reality of industrial custom and practice.

Control of internal trade union activities

35 Since March 1976 [19] legal control over the internal affairs of trade unions has depended almost entirely upon the common law. The exceptions to this are the various statutory rights not to be discriminated against, as a non-contributor to the political fund,[20] or on racial grounds,[21] or on grounds of being an EEC national,[22] or on grounds of sex.[23]

Common law control is based on the court's assumption of a power to supervise the contract of association. Becoming a union member involves, in law, becoming a party to such a contract and the member is bound by the rules whether or not he reads them personally or approves of them. The contract is subject to the same general rules as other contracts, but it may be noted that two principal devices have been used by the courts to determine the rights of individual members.

36 (1) *Interpretation of the contract.* We have seen that not only the written rules but also "custom and practice" must be looked at. Moreover, it has come to be recognised that the rules themselves "are not so much a contract, but they are much more a legislative code laid down by some members of the union to be imposed on all members of the union. They are more like by-laws than a contract. In those circumstances the rules are to be construed not only against the makers of them, but, further, if it should be found that if any of these rules is contrary to natural justice . . . the courts would hold them to be invalid." [24]

37 (2) *Public policy.* This judicially assumed power to strike out rules in the contract which are contrary to natural justice has, in most cases, not had to be directly exercised because the courts have generally been able to " interpret " rules so as to operate in a way which does not offend natural justice. However, there can be little doubt that a rule which stipulates for *automatic* loss of membership will be treated as invalid, apparently even if loss of membership does not result in loss of job.[25]

38 Another rule of public policy is that the jurisdiction of the courts as final arbiters on questions of law cannot be ousted by the contract of association. Two general principles seem to emerge from the decided cases. First, even where there is an express requirement in union rules that

---

[18] Kahn-Freund (1974) 3 I.L.J. at pp. 186–191. However, it must be said that the alleged custom was not satisfactorily proved in the *Heatons'* case: (1972) 1 I.L.J. at p. 208.

[19] Following the repeal of ss. 5 and 6 of T.U.L.R.A. by T.U.L.R.A. (Amdt.). However, s. 7 of T.U.L.R.A. has been amended by TU.L.R.A. (Amdt.), s. 2 (1), so as to improve the member's right to terminate his membership, on giving reasonable notice and complying with reasonable conditions.

[20] Trade Union Act 1913, s. 3. See above.

[21] At present the Race Relations Act 1968, s. 4; now see Race Relations Bill 1976 (discussed in Chap. 11).

[22] E.E.C. Reg. 1612/68, art. 8 (equality of treatment in trade union membership and activities).

[23] Sex Discrimination Act 1975, s. 12. See Chap. 11.

[24] *Bonsor* v. *Musicians' Union* [1954] Ch. 479 at p. 485, *per* Lord Denning M.R.

[25] *Edwards* v. *S.O.G.A.T.* [1971] Ch. 354. Generally on the meaning and scope of natural justice (which means, broadly, the right to a fair hearing before an unbiased tribunal), see De Smith, *Judicial Review of Administrative Action*, 3rd ed. (1973), Chaps. 4 and 5, esp. pp. 198–200.

internal remedies in the rules must be exhausted before a member can go to court the court is not bound by such a requirement. However, it is for the plaintiff member to show why he should not first exhaust domestic remedies. Secondly, where there is no express requirement in the rules that domestic remedies must first be exhausted, the court will more readily interfere without recourse to those remedies being first required. In deciding whether or not to intervene the court will have regard to the nature of the point at issue. If it is one of fact and discretion, it will generally be left to the union's domestic appeals procedure in the first instance; but if it is a question of law the court is likely to agree to intervene at any stage.[26]

39   One other attempted basis of common law control in closed shop situations has been the so-called " right to work." This is discussed briefly in Chapter 5.

40   Through these methods the courts have worked out a number of detailed rules relating to union discipline and also to the right of individual members to participate in union activities. The courts have insisted that powers must arise under the rules (express or implied),[27] that procedural requirements in the rules must be adhered to,[28] and that rules of natural justice must be observed.[29] A particularly important development in recent years, on the analogy of judicial control of administrative authorities, has been the doctrine that discretions conferred on officials and committees of a union must be exercised for proper purposes.[30]

Trades Union Congress

41   Trade unions representing over 10 million of Great Britain's 11 million organised workers are affiliated to the TUC, which, itself, falls within the statutory definition of a " trade union." [31] It is an open question whether the TUC constitution is directly legally enforceable between its affiliated organisations,[32] but TUC committees will probably be restrained by the courts from acting in excess of their powers.[33]

---

[26] These principles emerge from the judgment of Goff J. in *Leigh* v. *N.U.R.* [1970] Ch. 326, adopted by Plowman J. in *Radford* v. *N.A.T.S.O.P.A.* [1972] 1 Ch. 484. See too, *Lawlor* v. *U.P.W.* [1965] 1 All E.R. 353. It appears from *Esterman* v. *N.A.L.G.O.* [1974] I.C.R. 625 that the courts will intervene even before disciplinary proceedings have begun if it is shown that " no reasonable tribunal acting bona fide could uphold the complaint." This is a long way from *White* v. *Kuzych* [1951] A.C. 585, where the Privy Council required exhaustion of domestic remedies.

[27] *e.g. McClelland* v. *N.U.J.* [1975] I.C.R. 116 (rule strictly interpreted so as not to require member to remain in attendance throughout mandatory meeting).

[28] *e.g. Yorkshire Miners' Association* v. *Howden* [1905] A.C. 256; *Edwards* v. *Halliwell* [1950] 2 All E.R. 1064 (C.A.).

[29] See above, note 25.

[30] Esp. *Breen* v. *A.E.U.* [1971] 1 All E.R. 1148 at pp. 1153, 1158, 1162 (C.A.); *Hodgson* v. *N.A.L.G.O.* [1972] 1 W.L.R. 130; *Esterman* v. *N.A.L.G.O.* [1974] I.C.R. 625 at p. 632.

[31] T.U.L.R.A., s. 28 (1) (*b*).

[32] The view usually taken is that there is no " intention to create legal relations " (*e.g.* Grunfeld, *op. cit.*, p. 219, and cases on the Bridlington principles, below). However, in *McCluskey* v. *Cole* [1922] 1 Ch. 7, the Court of Appeal treated a federal trade union constitution as a contract and said that (apart from a statutory restriction under s. 4 of the 1871 Act then in force) " there would have been no objection to enforcing " it (at pp. 15, 18).

[33] The appropriate remedy to prevent a private arbitrator from hearing a case in which he has no jurisdiction, or to prevent action being taken on an arbitrator's decision in such a case, is a declaration.

42   Two areas in which TUC committees are most likely to become involved
with the law are, first, the independent review of complaints by trade
union members, and, secondly, the application of principles for the
avoidance of inter-union disputes. As regards the first the TUC has set up
an independent review body with three members, including a legal chairman, appointed in consultation with the Secretary of State and the A.C.A.S.
The committee's functions will be limited to cases where a person has been
expelled from a trade union affiliated to the TUC and has lost his job
because the union operates a closed shop. Problems may arise if the courts
do not require exhaustion of appeals to this body before legal proceedings
are instituted.

43   A set of principles for the avoidance of inter-union disputes was first
laid down by the TUC in 1924 (the Hull Main Principles) and revised
at the Bridlington Conference in 1939.[34] The so-called "Bridlington
Principles" advise unions to reach agreement on spheres of influence,
recognition of cards and transfers of members. They provide that no
affiliated union should accept a member of another affiliated union into
membership without inquiry. If the reply shows he is under discipline,
in arrears or engaged in a trade dispute, the application should not be
accepted. They also provide that an affiliated union should not begin
recruitment among a grade of workers in an establishment where another
union already has a majority of such workers and negotiates for them,
except with that union's consent. The TUC Disputes Committee deals
with complaints from affiliated unions concerning a breach of Bridlington
principles. These principles have been described as a "morally binding
code of conduct between persons of similar views" without legal force.[35]
Legal problems do, however, arise if an affiliated union is required to
expel a member who has been recruited contrary to Bridlington principles.[36]
At common law, the union may expel a member so long as the rules permit
this. Most unions now incorporate a model rule, drafted by the TUC, that
"notwithstanding anything in these rules the Executive Committee may by
giving six weeks' notice in writing terminate the membership of any member
if necessary to comply with a decision of the Disputes Committee of the
TUC." However, the case of *Rothwell* v. *A.P.E.X.*[37] shows that such a rule
implies that there must be a *valid* decision of the Disputes Committee, and
the General Council of the TUC must act within its powers in enforcing
that decision.

---

[34] The text is to be found in the T.U.C. pamphlet, *A Guide to the Avoidance of
Disputes Between Unions and the Settlement of Disputes with Employers* (1972). For
discussion see John Hughes, *Trade Union Structure and Government* (R.C. on Trade Unions
and Employers Assns., Research Paper 5, 1967), pp. 27–30; and S. W. Lerner, *Breakaway
Unions and the Small Trade Union* (London, 1961).

[35] By Mr. Vic Feather (as he then was) in evidence, described as "accurate" by Sir
Leonard Stone V.-C., in *Spring* v. *N.A.S.D.S.* [1956] 1 W.L.R. 585. For this reason, it
was held that the principles were not an implied term of the individual member's contract
of membership of his union.

[36] An expulsion in compliance of a Bridlington award was held void in *Spring* v.
N.A.S.D.S. (above); see too *Andrews* v. *N.U.P.E.*, *The Times*, July 9, 1955. However,
this protection of individual rights does appear to conflict with the guidance in the Code
of Practice, para. 11 (4), which states that "trade unions should . . . make full use of the
procedure established by the T.U.C. for settling inter-union disputes."

[37] [1975] I.R.L.R. 375.

Trade union amalgamations

44   Legislation has existed since 1876 to facilitate mergers between trade
unions. The present statute is the Trade Union (Amalgamations) Act
1964.[38] This provides for mergers in two ways, by amalgamation and by
transfer of engagements. The former method requires the consent of the
majority of those voting in each amalgamating union, whereas the latter
requires a vote only of the members of the transferor union. The Act lays
down a number of minimum standards for the ballot designed to ensure
that every member has an opportunity to vote and that he has full
knowledge of the terms. Complaints may be made to the Certification
Officer with a right of appeal on questions of law to the Employment
Appeal Tribunal.[39]

4. LEGAL SUPPORT FOR COLLECTIVE BARGAINING

45   The legal framework gives support to collective bargaining in various
ways.[40] The most obvious is by giving legal effect to the agreements reached
between employers and their associations and trade unions. We shall see,
in Chapter 8, that the substantive terms of collective agreements as to
wages, hours and other conditions of employment may be incorporated
into individual contracts of employment. Another way in which the law
helps the bargaining process is by providing guarantees for workers who
wish to form, or to participate in the activities of trade unions. The
existence of strong and representative trade unions is a *conditio sine qua
non* of collective bargaining. Freedom of association can also be considered
an individual civil liberty. The law in Great Britain has emphasised this
latter function by establishing three *individual* rights to organise : the right
not to be unfairly dismissed, the right not to have action taken short of
dismissal, and the right to time off for trade union activities. These will be
considered in Chapters 6, 10 and 17. In this chapter we shall discuss four
other statutory supports for collective bargaining which are essentially
collective rather than individual in nature.

The right to recognition for collective bargaining

46   Recognition problems are generally of three kinds: (1) where an
employer refuses to recognise any union; (2) where he bargains with some
unions but excludes others; and (3) where he recognises a union but fails
to bargain genuinely with it. These problems are generally resolved without
the aid of the law by voluntary arrangements. However, in the public
corporations and the education service *legal* duties to bargain have existed
for some time. Most of the post-war nationalisation statutes required the
boards of directors of the new corporations to consult with " any organisation appearing to the Board to be appropriate " to establish negotiating
machinery.[41] Similarly, the Secretary of State for Education was given the

---

[38] For a detailed discussion of the experience under this Act, see Elias (1973) 2 I.L.J.
125; see too Grunfeld, *op. cit.*, Chap. 13.
[39] Trade Union (Amalgamations) Act 1964, s. 4, as amended by E.P.A., Sched. 16, Pt.
IV, para. 10.
[40] Kahn-Freund, *Labour and the Law* (1972), pp. 76–123, 165–210.
[41] *e.g.* Transport Act 1962, s. 72. For further examples, see Hepple & O'Higgins,
Public Employee Trade Unionism in the U.K.: The Legal Framework (1971), p. 57.

duty to consult those associations " which appear to him to represent teachers." [42] The remarkable feature of this type of legislation is that it does nothing to resolve the second and third types of recognition problem mentioned above. No statutory criteria are laid down as to how the discretion of the employing authority is to be exercised. Administrative law remedies might be available for abuse of discretion (although the scope of remedies would be limited in the case of independent public corporations),[43] but it has not proved possible for unions denied recognition to mount successful legal actions either on this basis or by alleging a breach of individual rights to have the union to which an employee belongs recognised.[44]

47   The Industrial Relations Act 1971 provided the first general statutory procedure to enable trade unions and employers and the Government to refer recognition problems to an independent public authority (in this case the Commission on Industrial Relations) for investigation and ultimately for enforceable orders granted by a court (the National Industrial Relations Court). Most unions, being unregistered, could not use the complicated procedures of the Act, and employers with multi-union problems were apparently not keen to invoke the law.[45] After the repeal of the Industrial Relations Act there was still felt to be a need to implement the proposals of the Donovan Royal Commission on Trade Unions and Employers' Associations that statutory recognition procedures should be used to create " orderly " bargaining structures. The Employment Protection Act 1975, ss. 11–16, creates a procedure for obtaining recognition which is tortuous, although not as legally oriented as the Industrial Relations Act.

48   The Act allows only an independent trade union [46] to refer a recognition issue to the A.C.A.S. There is no right for employers to refer multi-union problems. The issue may concern the recognition of an unrecognised union, or it may be a request by an already recognised union for " further recognition." It is the claims for " further recognition " which are likely to produce the most difficult issues; but one extremely important limitation is that only the issue of recognition or further recognition " for the purpose of collective bargaining " may be referred. " Collective bargaining " means negotiations related to or connected with one or more of the matters which can form the subject of a " trade dispute " as set out in section 29 (1) of the Trade Union and Labour Relations Act 1974. This effectively rules out, for example, negotiations about investment plans or those pension schemes which are not of a contractual nature.[47]

49   The A.C.A.S. is obliged to examine the issue, to consult all the parties whom it considers will be affected, and it may make such inquiries as it

---

[42] Remuneration of Teachers Act 1965, s. 1. There is corresponding legislation in Scotland which overcomes the difficulties in *Cameron* v. *Secretary of State for Scotland*, 1964 S.L.T. 91.

[43] Mandamus would not be available in the case of these corporations. Lord Pearson in a report on the British Steel Corporation in 1968 (Cmnd. 4754) described the problems as being " in the sphere of administration not adjudication."

[44] *Gallagher* v. *Post Office* [1970] 3 All E.R. 712.

[45] See Weekes *et al., Industrial Relations and the Limits of the Law* (1975), Chap. 5.

[46] Defined in T.U.L.R.A., s. 30 (1). See above.

[47] See below.

thinks fit.[48] It must try to settle the matter by negotiation, and if this fails it must prepare a written report containing a recommendation and the reasons for it.[49] The requirement that reasons be given will help to build up a body of principles, but at the same time it will make it easier for the superior courts to review the operative recommendations of the A.C.A.S. on grounds of error of law. The recommendation will contain a choice of bargaining unit, bargaining agent and subjects of bargaining,[50] and it is in these respects that its reports can be expected to have the most significant impact on the range of collective bargaining. Collective bargaining is in effect mandatory in respect of the subjects listed. The A.C.A.S. has a free hand as to the means it uses to ascertain the opinions of workers to whom the issue relates but if it decides to take a formal ballot, it must comply with certain rules in particular the " need for securing that every worker invited to take part has an equal right and a fair opportunity of voting, and that the vote cast by any individual in the ballot will be kept secret." [51] Interesting questions may arise whether attempts by employers to influence the outcome by propaganda have influenced the " fair opportunity of voting "; a narrow reading of the Act would lead to the interpretation that it is concerned only with physical facilities, a wide interpretation that it is concerned with the psychological conditions in which voting occurs as well.

50 The A.C.A.S. recommendation becomes *operative* (this word was preferred to " legally enforceable " but it may amount to much the same thing) 14 days after it is received by the employer. It can be superseded only by (1) an agreement between the employer and the union; (2) another recommendation by A.C.A.S.; or (3) revocation by the A.C.A.S. either on the joint application of the parties or by any trade union or employer to whom it relates.[52]

51 Legal enforcement of an operative recommendation is by means of unilateral compulsory arbitration. " Unilateral " arbitration describes a situation in which one of the industrial parties can seek arbitration against the will of the other party. As such it is distinguishable from compulsory arbitration imposed against the will of both parties (unknown in Great Britain in peace-time) or voluntary arbitration to which both parties must consent (the usual form of arbitration allowed for in many collective bargaining arrangements as the last stage in the event of failure to agree).[53] In this case only the recommended union may complain of a breach of the recommendation. It must wait two months after it became operative before taking the matter to the Central Arbitration Committee. The union will have to show that the employer " is not then taking such action by way of or with a view to carrying on negotiations as might reasonably be expected to be taken by an employer ready and willing to carry on such negotiations as are envisaged by the recommendation." [54] If the C.A.C. finds that the complaint is well-founded it must make a declaration to that

---

48 E.P.A., s. 12 (2).
49 *Ibid.*, s. 12 (3) (4).
50 *Ibid.*, s. 12 (5).
51 *Ibid.*, s. 14 (2).
52 *Ibid.*, ss. 13 and 15 (1).
53 For an account of the development of arbitration, see Hepple, Chapter on " Great Britain " in Loewenberg *et al.*, *Compulsory Arbitration: An International Comparison* (Lexington, forthcoming 1976).
54 E.P.A., s. 15 (2).

effect, giving reasons, and it may make an award specifying the terms and conditions which the employer must observe in respect of those workers who are employees.[55] The way in which such an award is incorporated in individual contracts is discussed in Chapter 8. It is significant that the ultimate sanction is an attenuated one; there is no enforceable right for the union to be recognised, only a determination by arbitration, instead of by collective bargaining, of employment terms.

The right to disclosure of information

52   The Industrial Relations Act 1971 contained provisions to oblige employers to disclose certain information to recognised registered trade unions and to employees. These provisions were never brought into operation.[56] The Employment Protection Act, ss. 17–21, obliges an employer to make disclosure to an independent trade union [57] which is already recognised for collective bargaining. The information must be such as is in the possession of the employer or an associated employer.[58] It must *both* be information without which the union would be impeded in collective bargaining to a " material extent " *and* which the employer should disclose in accordance with good industrial relations practice.[59] The A.C.A.S. is to issue a Code giving a guide to this practice. As with recognition, disclosure is limited to the subject-matter of " collective bargaining " listed in section 29 (1) of the Trade Union and Labour Relations Act 1974. Moreover, it is only on those subjects in respect of which the union is already recognised that information need be given. A union seeking information on other listed subjects will need first to seek " further recognition." There is no legal right under the Employment Protection Act to information on non-listed subjects such as investment plans. This kind of information for longer-term planning and national economic policies will have to be obtained by the Secretary of State in the exercise of his powers under Part IV of the Industry Act 1975. The Secretary of State may obtain information of this kind for his own use by following a procedure which is subject to parliamentary scrutiny; and he may require an employer to disclose some or all that information to relevant independent trade unions, after reference to an advisory committee. Refusing to furnish information required under the Industry Act is an offence punishable on summary conviction by a fine of up to £400.[60]

53   There is a complicated enforcement procedure where an employer fails to disclose information in accordance with the Employment Protection Act. An independent trade union may present a complaint to the C.A.C., which has to refer it to A.C.A.S. for conciliation. If it is not settled, the C.A.C. must make a declaration whether it finds the complaint well founded and stating its reasons.[61] The employer is then given an opportunity

---

[55] There is no obvious reason why workers on the " lump," *e.g.* in the construction industry, should be excluded from the benefits of unilateral compulsory arbitration, but this is the policy of the E.P.A.: see further examples below in respect of disclosure and extension of terms; on the definition of employee, see Chap. 3.
[56] There was an inconclusive C.I.R. Report, No. 31, on Disclosure of Information.
[57] T.U.L.R.A., s. 30 (1). See above.
[58] For " associated employer," see above.
[59] E.P.A., s. 17 (1) (*a*) (*b*).
[60] For further details, see Tinnion (1976) 5 I.L.J. 80 at pp. 87–88.
[61] E.P.A., s. 19.

to comply with this declaration. If he fails to do so, a "further complaint" may be presented to C.A.C. by the union.[62] The C.A.C. again makes a declaration whether the complaint is well-founded, giving its reasons, and it may then determine a claim by the union for the determination of the terms and conditions of workers (but not workers who are not employees) [63] specified in the claim. The way in which the award of the C.A.C. becomes part of individual contracts is discussed in Chapter 8.

54   As with recognition, the ultimate right is one to have terms and conditions determined by arbitration. But it is arguable that the C.A.C. could order that each employee should have a contractual right to have the information disclosed to his trade union.[64] There seems to be no legal objection to this type of award which would force disclosure. However, serious limitations on disclosure are to be found in section 19 of the Employment Protection Act. Among a number of exceptions to the information which must be disclosed are "any information communicated to the employer in confidence" [65] and "any information the disclosure of which would cause substantial injury to the employer's undertaking, for reasons other than its effect on collective bargaining." [66] Both these exceptions are likely to give rise to a case law because the C.A.C. must give reasoned decisions which will presumably be amenable to review by superior courts on grounds of error of law.

Extension of terms and conditions

55   One of the symptoms of the relative absence of collective labour law in Great Britain is that collective agreements are usually not regarded as contracts between the collective parties,[67] and the employer is free to contract out of the collectively agreed terms with individual workers.[68] The only way in which an employer can be prevented from getting his own workers to *agree* to terms of employment which are below the minimum standards laid down in a collective agreement is by means of the procedure previously contained in section 8 of the Terms and Conditions of Employment Act 1959, and now to be found in modified form in Schedule 11 of the Employment Protection Act 1975. This particular procedure originates in war-time legislation for the unilateral compulsory arbitration of employment terms.[69] Its purpose has been to prevent recalcitrant employers in otherwise well-organised industries from failing to observe the terms and conditions established by collective bargaining.[70]

56   In addition to this policy of extending "established" terms there has long existed the "fair wages policy," expressed in the Fair Wages Resolutions 1891 to 1946 of the House of Commons and in a number of "fair wages" statutes applicable to particular industries (see Chapter 8 for

---

62 *Ibid.*, s. 20.
63 *Ibid.*, s. 21.
64 This is suggested by K. W. Wedderburn (1976) 39 M.L.R. at p. 179.
65 E.P.A., s. 19 (1) (*c*). For the developing law of confidence, see Chap. 9.
66 E.P.A., s. 19 (1) (*e*).
67 See Chap. 8.
68 *Hulland* v. *Saunders* [1945] K.B. 78 (C.A.).
69 Industrial Disputes Order 1370 of 1951 which itself replaced Order 1305 of 1940: see further Hepple, *op. cit.* (note 53 above).
70 It is by no means clear that it has achieved this objective: see Latta (1974) 3 I.L.J. 215 for an analysis.

details). In addition to requiring government contractors to pay wages not less favourable than those established by collective bargaining, the Resolution of 1946 obliged them to observe terms of employment "not less favourable than the general level of wages, hours and conditions" in the trade or industry. Schedule 11 of the 1975 Act has now in effect, made the "general level" claim applicable to all employers and not only government contractors. The Schedule is, accordingly, an amalgam of section 8 of the Terms and Conditions of Employment Act 1959 (with some modifications), and clause 1 (*b*) of the Fair Wages Resolution 1946.

57   The procedure is available only to independent trade unions,[71] or employers' associations. Either may report a claim to A.C.A.S. that an employer is not observing "recognised terms and conditions" or, if there are no recognised terms and conditions, that he is not observing the "general level of terms and conditions." [72] The former means the *minimum* terms and conditions of workers in "comparable employment in the trade or industry or section of the trade or industry, in which the employer in question is engaged either generally or in the district in which he is so engaged" which have been settled by collective agreement or arbitration award. The agreement or award must be one to which the parties are employers' associations and independent trade unions which represent "a substantial proportion of the employers and of the workers in the trade, industry or section, being workers of the description to which the agreement or award relates." [73] Only one or both of the parties to the agreement or award are entitled to report a claim.[74]

58   A claim founded on the "general level of terms and conditions" may be reported by either an employers' association having members engaged in the trade, industry or section in the district to which the claim relates, or a trade union of which any worker concerned is a member. But where an employer recognises a trade union in respect of that description of worker only the recognised union may report a claim.[75] The "general level" means the terms and conditions observed for comparable workers by employers (i) in the trade, industry or section in which the employer in question is engaged in the district in which he is so engaged; and (ii) whose circumstances are similar to those of the employer in question.[76] The employer's terms must be judged as a whole.[77]

59   If the A.C.A.S. is unable to settle the claim it must refer it to the C.A.C.[78] It is for the party making the claim to show that there are recognised terms and conditions and what they are, or what the general level of terms and conditions is. It is for the employer to satisfy the C.A.C. that he is observing terms not less favourable than the recognised terms or general level.[79] If the claim is upheld, wholly or partly, the C.A.C. must make an award of terms and conditions of employment conforming to the

---

[71] Defined in T.U.L.R.A., s. 30 (1). See above.
[72] E.P.A., Sched. 11, para. 1. See the detailed analysis by Bercusson, *The Employment Protection Act 1975* (London, 1976).
[73] *Ibid.*, para. 2 (*a*).
[74] *Ibid.*, para. 4.
[75] *Ibid.*, para. 5.
[76] *Ibid.*, para. 2 (*b*).
[77] *Ibid.*, para. 9.
[78] *Ibid.*, para. 7.
[79] *Ibid.*, para. 8.

recognised terms or to the general level as the case may be.[80] This award is incorporated in the individual contracts of those workers to whom the claim relates who are employees (but not of those workers who are not employees). The legal effect of this is discussed in Chapter 8.

60 In the past the procedure for the extension of terms established by collective bargaining did not apply to certain low-paid industries where wages are determined by Wages Councils or the Agricultural Wages Board. This restriction is removed in Schedule 11. In addition, independent trade unions are now allowed by Schedule 11 to claim the extension of collective agreements under the different criteria laid down in Part II of the Schedule. In particular it needs to be shown that the union's agreement or agreements cover a " significant number of establishments " within the field of operation of the Wages Council or Board either generally or in the district in which the worker is employed; that the circumstances in those establishments are similar; and that the employer is paying less than " the lowest rate of remuneration " payable to workers of that description under any of those agreements.[81] In most cases, the union is likely to find it more advantageous to invoke the " general level."

Wages Councils and Statutory Joint Industrial Councils [82]

61 Wages Councils are important for $3\frac{1}{4}$ million workers (and a further 400,000 in agriculture). They are statutory bodies continued or established under the Wages Councils Act 1959 by the Secretary of State for Employment. A Wages Council consists of equal numbers of members representing employers and members representing workers in relation to whom the Council operates, together with not more than three independent persons (usually lawyers, university teachers or social workers), one of whom is appointed by the Secretary of State to act as Chairman. Before 1976 the main function of a Wages Council was to prepare and submit to the Secretary of State proposals for fixing the statutory minimum remuneration and the holidays and holiday pay to be paid by all employers to workers in relation to whom the Council operated. When embodied in a wages regulation order by the Secretary of State these proposals were legally enforceable. The Employment Protection Act 1975 [83] has enhanced the powers of Wages Councils by enabling them to make their own wages regulation orders and by widening the terms of reference and the ambit of their orders to cover terms and conditions of employment generally and not only remuneration and holidays. Moreover, employers' associations and trade unions have been enabled to appoint their own representatives to a Wages Council, instead of the appointment being made by the Secretary of State. The independent members continue to be appointed by the Secretary of State.

---

[80] *Ibid.*, paras. 10–12.

[81] *Ibid.*, para. 15.

[82] For an account of the history and operation of these bodies, see C. W. Guillebaud, *The Wages Councils System in Great Britain*, 2nd ed. (London, 1962), and Steve Winyard, *Policing Low Wages* (Low Pay Unit, London, 1976).

[83] By s. 89 and Sched. 7, Pts. I–IV; and the Agricultural Wages Act 1948 and Agricultural Wages (Scotland) Act 1949, respectively, are amended by s. 97 and Scheds. 9 and 10. The E.P.A. also permits the use of the " extension " procedure (above) even where a Wages Council or S.J.I.C. exists: Sched. 11, paras. 3, 5, 16.

62   The Wages Councils are the modern successors to the Trade Boards which were first established in 1909, on the basis of a model established in the Australian State of Victoria, to prevent "sweated labour" in a limited number of trades. In 1918 their function, and the number of Boards, was enlarged to provide wage-fixing machinery where collective bargaining was weak or non-existent. The Trade Boards were converted into Wages Councils in 1945; separate Agricultural Wages Boards were first set up in 1924 for England and Wales and in 1937 for Scotland and are now regulated by the Agricultural Wages Act 1948 and the Agricultural Wages (Scotland) Act 1949; a special Act passed in 1938 provides what is now a Wages Council for the road haulage industry.[84] The Donovan Royal Commission on Trade Unions and Employers' Associations (1968) reported [85] that these Councils were doing little to help the growth of collective bargaining. Although the number of Councils has declined (from 60 in 1959 to 48 in 1975) organisation has remained weak in the industries they cover and these industries are generally ones in which pay is low.

63   In order to accelerate the growth of collective bargaining in these industries, the Employment Protection Act 1975 [86] gives the Secretary of State power, at the request of one side or after consulting both sides, to convert a Council into a Statutory Joint Industrial Council (S.J.I.C.). An S.J.I.C. will have no independent members. It has power to make an order regulating minimum terms and conditions. A deadlock between the two sides can be resolved by unilateral reference to the A.C.A.S. for conciliation, and if this fails, to the C.A.C. for arbitration. The S.J.I.C. is bound by the arbitration award and must make an order in its terms.[87]

64   A Wages Council or an S.J.I.C. may be abolished by the Secretary of State if he considers that voluntary collective bargaining machinery will be established within the Council's field of operation. The S.J.I.C. is seen as a half-way stage towards full collective bargaining.

5. INDUSTRIAL ACTION

Freedom or right?

65   The "right to strike" was described by Lord Wright in a leading case as "an essential element in the principle of collective bargaining." [88] In some countries this is a right specifically bestowed by the Constitution as a fundamental right of the individual citizen. In Great Britain, however, this is not the case. The right is seen simply as "a right to withdraw labour in combination without being subject to legal consequences." [89] In this sense the "right" in Britain is no more than a freedom without which workers could not bargain collectively. This freedom derives from the language of statutes which protect those who act "in contemplation or furtherance of a trade dispute" from judge-made liabilities for tort and crime.

---

[84] Road Haulage Wages Act 1938, as amended (most recently by E.P.A., s. 125 and Sched. 16). Separate Catering Wages Boards were brought under the Wages Councils Act in 1959.

[85] Cmnd. 3623, para. 234.   [86] ss. 90–96 and Sched. 8.

[87] See Chap. 8 regarding enforcement of orders.

[88] *Crofter Harris Tweed Co.* v. *Veitch* [1942] A.C. 435 at p. 463.

[89] Cmnd. 3623, para. 935; and see generally Kahn-Freund, *Labour and the Law* (London, 1972), Chap. 7, and Kahn-Freund and Hepple, *Laws Against Strikes* (Fabian Research Series 305, 1972).

66   There are two particularly important consequences of the absence of a positive "right" to strike. The first is that there is, in Britain, no such phenomenon as a "lawful" strike or an "unlawful" strike.[90] Individuals who participate in, or counsel, a strike or other industrial action may commit crimes, torts or breaches of contract; the strike itself is neither lawful nor unlawful. So much so, that there is not even a definition of a "strike" or "industrial action" in the 1974 legislation. In common understanding, a strike involves two essential ingredients: a complete cessation of work, and concerted action. The Trade Union and Labour Relations Act 1974 (in relation to unfair dismissal) speaks of a "strike *or other industrial action*"[91] and this latter concept plainly covers concerted action short of a complete cessation of work, such as picketing, a go-slow, a work-to-rule, "working without enthusiasm" or the *grève du zèle* (extreme attention to detail) made famous by French customs officers. None of these forms of action is *ipso facto* illegal; but individuals may commit crimes or civil wrongs in preparation for or in the course of such action.

67   The second consequence of the absence of a "right" to strike is that the freedom to strike is strictly limited to those circumstances in which Parliament has granted immunity for acts "in contemplation or furtherance of a trade dispute." Although immunities have been granted in respect of certain crimes and certain torts there is no protection in respect of breaches of contract as such. These breaches, which usually occur in strikes and industrial action short of a strike,[92] may give rise to disciplinary action by the employer (considered in Chapter 13) or, if sufficiently serious, to the dismissal of the strikers. We shall see, in Chapter 17, that the non-selective dismissal of those who are on strike or who are locked-out by the employer falls outside the scope of the law on unfair dismissal. The common law right of the employer to replace a striking labour force by "blacklegs" remains an essential feature of the framework of collective labour relations.

The definition of acts " in contemplation or furtherance of a trade dispute "

68   This formula is of fundamental importance in determining the boundaries of protection for individuals from liability in tort[93] from liability for criminal conspiracy[94]; and for participation in peaceful picketing.[95] The definition of a "trade dispute," now considerably wider and clearer than when first delimited in 1906, is to be found in the Trade Union and Labour Relations Act 1974, s. 29 (1). The courts have traditionally taken the view that the words of the definition must be construed with reasonable strictness because of the immunities from the common law which they confer. The following points in the definition may be noted.

---

[90] But see the argument in *Sherard* v. *A.U.E.W.* [1973] I.C.R. 428 at p. 430.

[91] T.U.L.R.A., Sched. 1, para. 7 (as amended by E.P.A., Sched. 16). In *Thompson* v. *Eaton Ltd.* [1976] I.C.R. 336, the E.A.T. held that workers who were physically preventing their employers from testing new machines were engaged in " other industrial action."

[92] The effect of a go-slow and work-to-rule on the individual contract are considered, in connection with the duty of fidelity, in Chap. 9 below.

[93] T.U.L.R.A., ss. 13 and 14 (2).

[94] Conspiracy and Protection of Property Act 1875, s. 3.

[95] T.U.L.R.A., s. 15.

69   (1) *The parties.* There must be a dispute between "employers" and "workers."[96] The workers need not be employed by the employer in dispute.[97] The parties may be a trade union or employers' association.[98] The parties may also be "workers" and "workers," the effect of this being to include inter-union disputes in which the employer is found to be wholly neutral.[99] On the other hand disputes between employers are not covered.[1] Disputes with the Government are not covered unless the Government is the employer of the workers in dispute or the employer of workers with whom the strikers are taking sympathetic action.[2]

70   (2) *The subject-matter.* The dispute must be "connected with" one or more of the subjects listed in section 29 (1):

"(a) terms and conditions of employment or the physical conditions in which any workers are required to work[3];

(b) engagement or non-engagement, or termination or suspension of employment or the duties of employment of one or more workers[4];

(c) allocation of work or the duties of employment as between workers or groups of workers[5];

(d) matters of discipline;

(e) the membership or non-membership of a trade union on the part of a worker[6];

(f) facilities for officials of trade unions[7];

(g) machinery for negotiation or consultation, and other procedures, relating to any of the foregoing matters including the recognition by employers or employers' associations of the right of a trade union to represent workers in any such negotiation or consultation or in the carrying out of such procedures."

71   (3) *Purposes of the dispute.* The dispute must be "connected with" one or more of the above subjects. This means that if the predominant motive

---

[96] See Chap. 3.

[97] T.U.L.R.A., s. 29 (6), removing doubts expressed in *Torquay Hotel Co. Ltd.* v. *Cousins* [1969] 2 Ch. 106 at p. 148.

[98] T.U.L.R.A., s. 29 (4).

[99] The Trade Disputes Act 1906, s. 5 (3), also covered these disputes: see *White* v. *Riley* [1921] 1 Ch. 1; *Hodges* v. *Webb* [1920] 2 Ch. 70. A majority of members of the Donovan Commission commented that it was difficult to find any inter-union or demarcation dispute in which the employer is wholly neutral (para. 120), but the Industrial Relations Act 1971, s. 167 (1), removed the express coverage of "worker/worker" disputes. This did not prevent the courts from finding that sympathy strikes were still protected: *Midland Cold Storage Ltd.* v. *Turner* [1972] I.C.R. 230; *Same* v. *Steer* [1972] I.C.R. 495; *Sherard* v. *A.U.E.W.* [1973] I.C.R. 421 at p. 433.

[1] *Larkin* v. *Long* [1915] A.C. 814; *cf. Brimelow* v. *Casson* [1924] 1 Ch. 302.

[2] *Sherard* v. *A.U.E.W.* [1973] I.C.R. 421 at pp. 433, 436; *G.A.S.* v. *T.G.W.U.* [1974] I.C.R. at pp. 35–36 (N.I.R.C.); [1975] I.C.R. 276 at pp. 289, 299–300 (C.A.). See too, T.U.L.R.A., s. 29 (2), which brings in disputes where a Minister is represented on a J.I.C. or exercises some statutory authority.

[3] A dispute connected with trading hours may not be the same as one connected with working hours: *Esplanade Pharmacy Ltd.* v. *Larkin* [1957] I.R. 285; *cf. Brendan Dunne* v. *Fitzpatrick* [1958] I.R. 29. "Psychological" conditions (*e.g.* barrack-room language) are not mentioned: *cf.* Grunfeld, *op. cit.*, p. 340.

[4] The words "or the duties of employment" overcome the difficulties expressed in *Cory Lighterage Ltd.* v. *T.G.W.U.* [1973] I.C.R. 339 at pp. 357–358; *cf. Langston* v. *A.U.E.W.* [1974] I.C.R. at pp. 191, 192, 193–194, 519–520.

[5] In the *Langston* case (above, at p. 520) Sir John Donaldson said this was intended (in the corresponding provisions of the Industrial Relations Act 1971) to cover demarcation disputes but it could also cover closed shop disputes.

[6] This issue could also arise under (b) and (c) above.

[7] "Official" is defined in T.U.L.R.A., s. 30 (1), and see above.

of the person claiming the immunity was the furtherance of a personal grudge or a desire to punish the plaintiff there will be no protection. For example, where the district committee of a trade union, in defiance of national instructions, treated a member as expelled and prevented him from getting jobs in order to punish him for his conduct, the members of the district committee were held to be unprotected.[8] Moreover, in order to gain protection the act in question must have been done " in contemplation or furtherance " of a trade dispute. This means not only that the predominant purpose must be the advancement of one of the listed subjects, but also that the dispute must either exist or be imminent. For example, when a union official circularised members who were managers of public-houses with a questionnaire for confidential information about their employers' businesses thereby inducing breaches of contract, it was held that the official was unprotected because the questionnaire was designed to " obtain information which after consideration might lead to a request which, if not granted, might lead to a dispute." The trade dispute was neither imminent nor impending.[9]

72   The effect of the definition is to provide a large measure of protection for non-violent action in most labour-management disputes. However, acts in particular disputes, when subjected to judicial interpretation, may be found to be in furtherance of *personal* rather than *trade* purposes.[10] Most difficult of all are those disputes in which, directly or indirectly, the Government or Parliament are involved.[11] There is a trade dispute even though it relates to matters outside Great Britain.[12]

Torts connected with industrial action

73   We have already noted that the Trade Union and Labour Relations Act 1974, s. 14, re-establishes and clarifies the rule than no action in tort shall lie against a trade union or employers' association. This immunity applies whether or not there is a trade dispute, subject to certain exceptions.[13] However, other persons (including officials) may be personally

---

[8] *Huntley* v. *Thornton* [1957] 1 W.L.R. 321; see too *Conway* v. *Wade* [1909] A.C. 506; but it must be the *predominant* purpose: *Dallimore* v. *Williams* (1912) 29 T.L.R. 67; (1914) 30 T.L.R. 432.

[9] *Bent's Brewery Co. Ltd.* v. *Hogan* [1945] 2 All E.R. 570; for other aspects of this case, see Chap. 9. T.U.L.R.A., s. 29 (5), overcomes the strange dicta in *Cory Lighterage Ltd.* v. *T.G.W.U.* [1973] I.C.R. 197, 339 at p. 362, by providing, in effect, that the mere fact that a party does not resist a demand or threat does not prevent that demand or threat from being made " in contemplation " of a dispute. However, action taken *after* a dispute is settled is not " in furtherance " of that dispute. This, it is suggested, is the *ratio decidendi* of *Stratford* v. *Lindley* [1965] A.C. 307, esp. at p. 341; see too *Stewart* v. *A.U.E.W.* [1973] I.C.R. 128.

[10] As in *Torquay Hotel Co. Ltd.* v. *Cousins* [1969] 2 Ch. 106 (C.A.).

[11] The dangers of using the label " political strike " were explained by Roskill L.J. in *Sherard* v. *A.U.E.W.* (above) at p. 435. A day of protest against the Industrial Relations Bill was " purely political " and the tortfeasors were unprotected in *Associated Newspapers Ltd.* v. *Flynn* (1971) 10 K.I.R. 17; but a dispute about nationalisation is capable of being a trade dispute: *G.A.S.* v. *T.G.W.U.* [1974] I.C.R. at pp. 36–37. The decision of Astbury J. in *National Sailors' and Firemen's Union* v. *Reed* [1926] 1 Ch. 536, that the general strike of 1926 was illegal may one day have to be reconsidered in the light of Goodhart's comments in (1927) 36 Yale L.J. 464 (see Roskill L.J. in *Sherard* v. *A.U.E.W.* at p. 436).

[12] T.U.L.R.A., s. 29 (3), as amended by T.U.L.R.A. (Amdt.), s. 2. This protection may be important where sympathy action is taken in Great Britain in respect of action in another country or on an oil-rig on the Continental shelf: see K. W. Wedderburn (1972) 1 I.L.J. 12 at pp. 15–18; and *Hanseatic Ship Management Ltd.* v. *I.T.W.F.* [1974] I.C.R. 112 at p. 116.

[13] See above, under " Trade Unions."

liable in tort if acting outside the "trade disputes" protection. It is important to note that the protection granted is in respect of *specific* torts listed in the Trade Union and Labour Relations Acts 1974 and 1976. So far as individuals are concerned there is no general immunity.[14]

74 It is beyond our scope to expound the various torts which may be of importance in the course of industrial action.[15] We simply note that the protection granted to "any person" acting "in contemplation or furtherance of a trade dispute" is limited to the following torts:

(1) Inducing another person to break a contract or interfering or inducing any other person to interfere with its performance.[16]

(2) Threatening that a contract (whether one to which he is a party or not) will be broken or its performance interfered with, or that he will induce another person to break a contract or to interfere with its performance.[17]

(3) Interfering with the trade, business or employment of another person, or with the right of another person to dispose of his capital or labour as he wills.[18]

(4) Conspiracy to injure another without unlawful means (so-called "simple" conspiracy)[19] or a conspiracy to use unlawful means, where the means are either a breach of contract in contemplation or furtherance of a trade dispute or an act falling within (1) or (2) above.[20]

75 It will be seen that although peaceful primary and secondary labour boycotts are generally protected, a number of torts which involve injuries

---

[14] There is no vicarious immunity: *Vacher* v. *London Society of Compositors* [1913] A.C. 107 at pp. 120, 131; *London Motor Cab Proprietors* v. *20th Century Press* (1917) 34 T.L.R. 38 at p. 39; *Eglantine* v. *Smith* [1948] N.I. 29 at p. 36.

[15] For a full account, see K. W. Wedderburn in *Clerk & Lindsell on Torts*, 14th ed. (London, 1975); see too Heydon, *Economic Torts* (London, 1972).

[16] T.U.L.R.A., s. 13 (1) (*a*), as amended. This is wider than the protection afforded by the Trade Disputes Act 1906, s. 3, which was limited to inducement of breach of contracts of *employment*. T.U.L.R.A.(Amdt.) removed this limitation from the 1974 Act; it also extended immunity to "interference with performance" so as to overcome the dicta in *Torquay Hotel Co. Ltd.* v. *Cousins* [1969] 2 Ch. 106 on this point.

[17] T.U.L.R.A., s. 13 (1) (*b*). The Trade Disputes Act 1965, reversing the effect of the decision in *Rookes* v. *Barnard* [1964] A.C. 1129 covered only a threat to break a contract of *employment*. T.U.L.R.A.(Amdt.) extends this to *any* contract and also covers threats to interfere with performance.

[18] T.U.L.R.A., s. 13 (2). This provision is "for the avoidance of doubt." In *Allen* v. *Flood* [1898] A.C. 1, the House of Lords decided there was no such tort; but the point has been much debated (see *e.g.* Lord Denning M.R. in *Torquay Hotel Co. Ltd.* v. *Cousins* (above) at p. 138).

[19] T.U.L.R.A., s. 13 (4). This was originally enacted in the Trade Disputes Act 1906, s. 1, to overcome *Quinn* v. *Leathem* [1901] A.C. 495, but the common law concept of "legitimate interests" which would justify a simple conspiracy was subsequently expanded to cover much the same ground as s. 1 in trade disputes (*e.g. Reynolds* v. *Shipping Federation Ltd.* [1924] 1 Ch. 28 and the *Crofters'* case [1942] A.C. 435 in which securing and maintaining the advantages of collective bargaining were treated as legitimate interests). In two respects the common law defence is *wider* than T.U.L.R.A., s. 13 (4): there is no list of legitimate subjects at common law, *cf.* s. 29 (1), and the parties are not limited at common law as they are by s. 29 (1). Moreover, s. 13 (4) does not cover conspiracies where unlawful means are used.

[20] T.U.L.R.A., s. 13 (3). The tort of intentionally causing loss by unlawful means is of uncertain scope. Not all illegal means suffice, and s. 13 (3) avoids doubts by declaring that these two types of illegality will not suffice in trade disputes; but there is no such protection for other wrongs such as nuisance, trespass etc. An allegation of *conspiracy* to intentionally cause loss by unlawful means gives the plaintiff certain evidential advantages and makes it possible to catch persons who are not otherwise joint tortfeasors: see *Rookes* v. *Barnard* (above); *Pratt* v. *B.M.A.* [1919] 1 K.B. 244.

to reputation (such as libel committed by using a defamatory placard) or to property (such as detaining the employer's or a customer's goods) or to land (such as trespass or nuisance) or to the person (such as physically preventing a person from working) are not excluded. One area in which tort liability may arise is where public employees (such as members of fire services) act in breach of a duty laid down in a statute.[21]

76   The most important intervention of the law of tort in labour-management disputes is through the power of the High Court to issue injunctions before, during or after the trial of an action.[22] The injunction may be interim, until a named day which can usually be anticipated by the respondent, or interlocutory, that is until the trial of the action. In collective labour disputes the injunction is commonly issued before trial in either of these forms and the trial does not take place because the party seeking the injunction—usually the employer—secures the desired tactical advantage simply by forcing the lifting of industrial action. Two important statutory limitations have been placed on the High Court's power to grant injunctions in trade disputes. First, section 17 (1) of the Trade Union and Labour Relations Act 1974 precludes *ex parte* injunctions (granted in the absence of the respondent) if the respondent would, in the opinion of the court, be likely to claim a "trade dispute" defence. Secondly, section 17 (2) of the Act (as inserted by the Employment Protection Act 1975)[23] requires the court, in exercising its discretion whether or not to grant an interlocutory injunction, to "have regard to the likelihood of that party's succeeding at the trial" in establishing his claim to a "trade dispute" defence.[24]

Criminal offences connected with industrial action

77   Before 1875, as we noted at the beginning of this chapter, the criminal law intervened through offences such as conspiracy, molestation and obstruction to restrict the freedom to strike. The Conspiracy and Protection of Property Act 1875, s. 3, provides that " an agreement or combination by two or more persons to do or procure to be done any act in contemplation or furtherance of a trade dispute shall not be indictable as a conspiracy if such act committed by an individual would not be punishable as a crime." The effect of this is to protect those acting in "trade disputes" from liability for a criminal conspiracy to "injure or annoy,"[25]

---

21 This will fall within the scope of the tort of intentionally causing loss by unlawful means: *e.g. Cunard Steamship Ltd.* v. *Stacey* [1955] 2 Lloyd's Rep. 247; *Cory Lighterage Ltd.* v. *T.G.W.U.* [1973] I.C.R. at pp. 358–359.

22 For a full discussion, see Anderman & Davies (1973) 2 I.L.J. 213 and (1974) 3 I.L.J. 30.

23 E.P.A., Sched. 16, Pt. III, para. 6; but this does not extend to Scotland (s. 17 (3)). This overcomes, in trade disputes, *American Cyanamid Ltd.* v. *Ethicon* [1975] A.C. 396 as applied *e.g.* in *Hubbard* v. *Pitt* [1975] I.C.R. 308 (C.A.), in which it was held that, if the balance of convenience is for the applicant, all he need show is a "serious issue to be tried." Previously it was thought that the applicant had to show a prima facie case.

24 See *Camellia Tanker Ltd. S.A.* v. *I.T.W.F.* [1976] I.R.L.R. 183, 190 (C.A.), in which it was left open whether the *Ethicon* case had affected the earlier law regarding injunctions in trade disputes.

25 *R.* v. *Bunn* (1872) 12 Cox 316; in *Kamara* v. *D.P.P.* [1974] A.C. 104 at pp. 124–126, 129–130, it was left open whether this was a criminal conspiracy.

or conspiracy to commit a tort,[26] or conspiracy to break contracts, or conspiracy to effect a public mischief.[27] However, it does not protect a conspiracy to commit a criminal offence, whether triable summarily or on indictment. Where individuals participating in industrial action are alleged to have committed criminal offences, the prosecution gains several advantages by alleging a conspiracy. In particular, conspiracy is an inchoate offence which can be proved even if the substantive offence is not carried out; conspiracy is a continuing offence and anyone who joins can be held liable for the acts of his co-conspirators; a charge of conspiracy may be joined with a charge of the substantive offence " where the substantive charges do not reflect the overall criminality " [28]; and the maximum sentence for conspiracy is life imprisonment which is usually far greater than the penalty for the substantive offence.[29]

78   The 1875 Act also created a series of specific criminal offences, in place of the old crimes of molestation, obstruction, etc. These are offences of general application but they are particularly relevant to picketing. Section 7 of the Act makes it a criminal offence for any person " with a view to compel any other person to abstain from doing or to do any act which such other person has a legal right to do or abstain from doing, wrongfully and without legal authority " to commit any one of a number of specified acts. A controversial question, of very great importance, is what significance should be attached to the words " wrongfully and without legal authority." There are now three Court of Appeal decisions [30] in which support can be found for the view, first expressed in 1906, that section 7 " legalises nothing, and it renders nothing wrongful that was not so before." [31] According to this view a criminal prosecution is possible only if in addition to one of the listed acts (such as intimidation, or watching and besetting) there is some extraneous civil wrong committed by the defendant (e.g. an actionable nuisance). However, there is an early Court of Appeal decision,[32] which has never been expressly overruled, in which a majority of the court held that the words " wrongfully and without legal authority " do not make it necessary to establish the illegality of the acts alleged by evidence other than that which proves the acts themselves. According to this latter view a mere " watching and besetting " " with a view to compel " is itself subject to criminal prosecution. It is submitted

---

[26] *Kamara* (above) decides that this is a crime in certain circumstances. Wallington (1975) 4 I.L.J. 69 refers to the *Birmingham Building Workers'* case (1973), in which there was a prosecution for conspiracy to trespass arising from a sit-in at the offices of an employment bureau alleged to be supplying " lump-labour." The acquittal of the defendants on this count was directed by Wien J. since it was conceded that there was an " industrial " dispute (under the Act of 1971).

[27] The scope of this crime is uncertain, and like all the other forms of conspiracy so far mentioned, its abolition has been proposed by the Law Commission.

[28] *R.* v. *Jones* [1974] I.C.R. 310 at p. 316 (the " Shrewsbury " pickets).

[29] This was why, in *Jones* (above), sentences of three years, two years and nine months, respectively, were imposed for conspiracy to intimidate, although the maximum sentence for the substantive offence is three months' imprisonment.

[30] *Ward, Lock & Co.* v. *O.P.A.S.* (1906) 22 T.L.R. 327; *Fowler* v. *Kibble* [1922] 1 Ch. 487; *Hubbard* v. *Pitt* [1975] I.C.R. 308 at pp. 317–319, *per* Lord Denning M.R.

[31] *Ward, Lock & Co.* v. *O.P.A.S.* (above), *per* Moulton L.J.; see too Vaughan Williams L.J. at p. 329.

[32] *Lyons* v. *Wilkins* [1896] 1 Ch. 811; [1899] 1 Ch. 255 at p. 267.

that the more recent judicial dicta, requiring proof of an extraneous wrong, have implicitly overruled the earlier case.[33]

79   The specific acts listed in section 7 include intimidation, which according to recent authority,[34] is not limited to cases of violence or threats of violence to the person; persistently following a person about from place to place; hiding tools, clothes or other property or hindering or depriving a person of their use [35]; watching and besetting the house or other place where a person resides, or works or carries on business or happens to be [36]; and following a person with two or more other persons in a disorderly manner in or through any street or road. The offence is punishable, summarily or on indictment, by a fine of £25 or a term of not more than three months' imprisonment.

Peaceful picketing

80   To a limited extent, legislation has provided protection for peaceful picketing. The word "picket" is nowhere defined in legislation but it is commonly understood to mean persons, either singly or in groups, attending at or near premises connected with a dispute. The aims may be to communicate information, or to persuade others, or to cause a physical obstruction. The lawfulness of the acts of the pickets depends upon the nature of their attendance (e.g. whether or not there was a mass picket and whether or not it was on the highway), their purposes (to communicate information, to obstruct, etc.) and the means used (peaceful or not). There is no "right to picket" in the law in Great Britain.[37]

81   The lawfulness of *attendance* at or near a place depends primarily on the civil law relating to trespass to the highway and nuisance. Picketing usually occurs on the highway (including footpaths and pedestrian pre-cincts) which at common law is a strip of privately owned land dedicated to use by the public for passing and repassing. Any activities not incidental to passing or repassing (including *stationary* pickets) would constitute a trespass to the highway; but only the owner of the subsoil beneath the highway could complain. Another civil wrong which may be committed is private nuisance, that is an unreasonable interference with the enjoy-ment by its owner of an estate in land; pickets who block access to private property, at least if this is deliberate and prolonged, commit a private nuisance. There is a conflict of judicial opinion as to whether peaceful "watching and besetting" of premises is itself a private nuisance. In *Lyons* v. *Wilkins* (1899),[38] Lord Lindley M.R. said that a picket of two men seeking peacefully to persuade workers not to work until a dispute had been settled was conduct " which seriously interferes with the ordinary comfort of human existence and the ordinary enjoyment of the house beset and so would support an action on the case for nuisance at common

---

[33] But it was to set the matter beyond doubt that s. 2 of the Trade Disputes Act 1906 (not T.U.L.R.A., s. 15) was enacted.

[34] *R.* v. *Jones* [1974] I.C.R. 310; and see comment by Wallington (1975) 4 I.L.J. 69.

[35] *Fowler* v. *Kibble* [1922] 1 Ch. 487.

[36] *R.* v. *Wall* (1907) 21 Cox C.C. 401 (walking up and down is watching); *Charnock* v. *Court* [1899] 2 Ch. 35 (watching may be for relatively short time); and see generally *Ward, Lock* v. *O.P.A.S.* (above); *cf. Lyons* v. *Wilkins* (above).

[37] On the problems of mass picketing, see Wallington (1972) 1 I.L.J. 219.

[38] [1899] 1 Ch. at p. 267; in [1896] 1 Ch. at p. 820 the same judge said: " You cannot make a strike effective without doing more than is lawful."

law." This view was not accepted in *Ward Lock & Co.* v. *O.P.A.S.* (1906),[39] and it has been uncompromisingly rejected by Lord Denning M.R.[40]

82 A third wrong which may be committed is public nuisance, which, in this context, would be constituted by an unreasonable obstruction of the highway. Unlike trespass a mere attendance is not a public nuisance; there must be an element of unreasonableness and this involves balancing the interests of highway users against the interests of those causing the obstruction; processions (*mobile* pickets) are generally regarded as reasonable, but stationary pickets are less favoured. Moreover, unlike trespass, a public nuisance requires an actual obstruction; somebody must be seriously inconvenienced. The remedies for public nuisance are prosecution, an action for an injunction at the suit of the Attorney-General; or an action for damages or an injunction by any members of the public who have suffered particular damage. The conclusion one may draw is that peaceful picketing, which does not involve an actionable trespass to the highway or an unreasonable obstruction of the highway or of access to private premises is probably lawful at common law.[41]

83 Section 15 of the Trade Union and Labour Relations Act 1974 (re-enacting with modifications section 2 of the Trade Disputes Act 1906) is of very limited ambit, but it puts at rest certain doubts about peaceful picketing in respect of acts done " in contemplation or furtherance of a trade dispute." The section provides that:

> " It shall be lawful for one or more persons in contemplation or furtherance of a trade dispute to attend at or near—(*a*) a place where another person works or carries on business; or (*b*) any other place where another person happens to be, not being a place where he resides, for the purpose only of peacefully obtaining or communicating information or peacefully persuading any person to work or abstain from working."

84 The effect of this may be summarised as follows: (1) the section codifies the view in the *Ward Lock* case that watching and besetting with a view to compel someone to work or not to work is not in itself unlawful[42]; (2) by protecting *attendance* it provides an immunity in respect of trespass to the highway[43]; (3) however, only *simple attendance* is protected and not attendance accompanied by the detention of persons in order to communicate arguments more effectively,[44] or accompanied by non-obstructive " invitations " to passers-by to stop and listen to the pickets' arguments[45]; (4) it protects informational picketing and persuasion to work

---

[39] (1906) 22 T.L.R. 327.

[40] *Hubbard* v. *Pitt* [1975] I.C.R. at pp. 317–319.

[41] The dicta of Forbes J. in *Hubbard* v. *Pitt* (above), which would in effect destroy this common law freedom, were disapproved by Lord Denning M.R. (at pp. 316–319). Stamp L.J. simply described Forbes J.'s conclusions as " not satisfactory " (at p. 322) while Orr L.J. (at p. 330) says nothing on this aspect of the law.

[42] Dicta in *Lyons* v. *Wilkins* (above) suggest that it is the element of persuasion (as opposed to information) which is the source of the private nuisance.

[43] So avoiding in trade disputes the effect of Forbes J.'s decision in *Hubbard* v. *Pitt* (above).

[44] *Hunt* v. *Broome* [1974] I.C.R. 84 (H.L.) which confirms *Tynan* v. *Balmer* [1967] 1 Q.B. 91.

[45] *Hunt* v. *Broome* (above), *per* Lords Morris, Dilhorne and Salmon (*cf.* Lord Reid). Nothing in s. 15 protects what the pickets say, *e.g.* by way of inducing breaches of contract, libel etc.

or not to work, but it does not protect consumer picketing [46]; (5) it does not grant any immunity in respect of unreasonable obstruction of access to premises or unreasonable obstruction of the highway.

85   The main form of control over picketing is, in fact, by the police. The police have power to issue instructions to pickets either limiting or entirely prohibiting their actions if a breach of the peace is reasonably anticipated.[47] The police have an almost absolute discretion because there is no legal " right to picket."

[The next paragraph is 91.]

---

[46] *Bird* v. *O'Neal* [1960] A.C. 907 (P.C.).
[47] *Piddington* v. *Bates* [1961] 1 W.L.R. 162; *Kavanagh* v. *Hiscock* [1974] Q.B. 600; *Hunt* v. *Broome* (above).

CHAPTER 2

THE INDIVIDUAL EMPLOYMENT RELATIONSHIP

1. SOURCES OF RULES

91 THE rules regulating the relationship between employer and worker are derived from three principal sources: (a) the judge-made common law; (b) legislation; and (c) the practice of work-groups and workers' organisations, employers and employers' organisations, government departments, arbitrators and others concerned with industrial relations.

The common law

92 This is to be found in the reported decisions of the courts of law. Some of the employment cases in the law reports were decided in a pre-industrial society at a time when agricultural and domestic labour were the most common forms of gainful employment. Others were decided in the early stages of the industrial revolution at a time when the judiciary was anxious to allow entrepreneurs freedom to trade without interference from combinations of workmen and with little regard for the safety, health and welfare of children, let alone of women and men. These decisions and the social philosophy which guided them have little relevance to a modern industrial society. Yet the orthodox legal view in England and Wales is that a proposition of law which forms the basis of the decision in a case cannot be held to have lost its force simply because it has become obsolete. This approach is particularly noticeable in the treatment, by some authors, of the grounds for summary dismissal of an employee. Most of the nineteenth century cases which are cited in text-books to illustrate specific grounds for summary dismissal were decided at a time when breach of a contract of service was a criminal offence. The Conspiracy and Protection of Property Act 1875 abolished nearly all forms of criminal liability flowing from breach of contract. This " funda-mental revolution in the law " (as the Webbs called it [1]) meant that thenceforward master and servant became, as employer and employee, two equal parties to a civil contract.[2] Accordingly, it is misleading to rely on the older cases in which the judges were strongly influenced by the requirements of the criminal law. Modern courts should be invited to distinguish or not follow the older cases on summary dismissal for this reason. Indeed, the courts have shown some willingness to develop new rules to meet changed conditions.[3]

Legislation

93 There are over seventy major Acts of Parliament and numerous pieces of subordinate legislation made by Ministers, wage-regulating bodies,

---

[1] S. & B. Webb, *History of Trade Unionism* (rev. ed., London, 1919), p. 291. For another reason why the old decisions on summary dismissal are dangerous precedents, see para. 501.

[2] This was the theory of the new law. In reality, not only are the economic powers of capital greater than those of the individual worker but, we believe, the legal duties imposed on the employee are more onerous than those of the employer at common law.

[3] *e.g. Hill* v. *C. A. Parsons & Co. Ltd.* [1972] Ch. 305; *Langston* v. *A.U.E.W.* [1974] I.C.R. 180, 190, 192.

local authorities and others, affecting the employment relationship. Much legislation—from the medieval protection of apprentices down on to modern employment protection and anti-discrimination legislation—has aimed to provide workers with protection which the common law had failed to achieve. Yet, in interpreting statutes, the judges read them in the light of the common law. Fine legal distinctions are drawn based on common law concepts. For example, an employee's right to compensation for redundancy and unfair dismissal may turn on whether the employer's action is treated as a "termination" or a "variation" of the contract at common law.[4] The rigid literal approach of the courts, excluding relevant explanatory materials such as White Papers and parliamentary debates, leads the draftsman of a new statute, in turn, to over-refinement. This results in unintelligibility. Difficulties are also caused by the inconsistent and incorrect use by draftsmen of concepts, such as "employee," "dismissal," etc. Sometimes Parliament itself complicates matters by inserting clauses in a Bill during its passage without sufficient regard to the overall structure of the measure. Recently, there has been some judicial recognition of the need to avoid strict legal interpretations of employment statutes,[5] but this is simply a straw in the wind when so many cases turn on hair-breadth legal distinctions.[6] It was plainly the intention of Parliament in setting up specialised tribunals in which legally qualified chairmen are assisted by those with knowledge and experience in industrial matters, that the employment statutes dealt with by those tribunals should be interpreted in the light of practical experience.[6a] However, a member of an industrial tribunal cannot make good from his own experience a deficiency of evidence. The court must reach decisions on the evidence before it, but it can weigh that evidence and assess its cogency in the light of the special knowledge of its appointed members.[6b]

Practice

94 This is the most difficult and nebulous source of rules. It consists of written ageements, arbitration awards and works rules as well as informal arrangements and understandings. Not all the formal practices of industry, and very few of the informal ones, give rise to legal obligations which the individual employer or worker can enforce. The usual test of enforceability is whether the particular practice forms an express or implied term of the individual's contract. We shall later investigate in detail how terms of the contract are proved, and indicate how far the courts are prepared to go in filling in the unspoken terms in the light of practice.[7] We shall also be concerned with the conflict between two levels of practice: the formal practices embodied in industry-wide collective agreements and

---

[4] See below, Chap. 18.

[5] *Secretary of State for Employment* v. *Maurice & Co. Ltd.* [1969] 2 A.C. 346, *per* Lord Guest at p. 359, and Lord Pearson at p. 363.

[6] See *e.g.* the remarks of Viscount Dilhorne, Lord Hailsham of St. Marylebone and Lord Salmon concerning the obscure wording of the Redundancy Payments Act 1965, in *Lord Advocate* v. *de Rosa* [1974] I.C.R. 480 at pp. 487, 490, 500.

[6a] *Ioannou* v. *British Broadcasting Corpn.* [1974] I.C.R. 414, at pp. 417–418, *per* Sir John Donaldson (" reality should prevail over technicality ").

[6b] *Heatons Transport (St. Helens) Ltd.* v. *Transport & General Workers Union* [1972] 2 All E.R. 1214 (C.A.) *per* Buckley L.J. at p. 1248, and Roskill L.J. at p. 1263. For example, see *Cole* v. *Midland Display Ltd.* [1973] I.R.L.R. 62 (construction of contract).

[7] See below, para. 221.

awards, and the informal practices created by the actual behaviour of managers, shop stewards and workers. This conflict creates special problems for the lawyer. For example, is a worker entitled to be paid at local rates informally agreed with shop stewards where these rates are at variance with the formal nationally agreed rates? We shall see that the courts have so far given few answers to important questions such as this.[8]

The Codes of Practice

95   A Code of Industrial Relations Practice was issued under the Industrial Relations Act 1971, and, when that Act was repealed, it was retained in force by the Trade Union and Labour Relations Act 1974.[9] This Code will remain in force until superseded by Codes of Practice to be issued by the Advisory, Conciliation and Arbitration Service (below, Chap. 4). A failure to observe the provisions of a Code does not " of itself " render a person liable to any legal proceedings; but the Code is admissible in evidence in proceedings before an industrial tribunal or the Central Arbitration Committee (C.A.C.) and any provision of a Code which appears to the tribunal or C.A.C. to be relevant to any question arising in the proceedings *shall* be taken into account by the tribunal or C.A.C. in determining that question." [10] The description of the documents as a " code " is a misnomer because they do not " codify " the existing practices of industry. They aim to guide management and unions into practices which have been imperfectly observed in the past.[10a]

96   It is debatable, however, what the precise legal effect will be of a breach of the provisions of a Code in any particular case. The difficulty arises from the provision that a breach " shall not *of itself* render him liable to any proceedings." [11] In dealing with cases of unfair dismissal, the National Industrial Relations Court said that " the Code is, of course, always one important factor to be taken into account in the case, but its significance will vary according to the particular circumstances of each individual case." [12] The Code may also be relevant to the construction of employment legislation.[13]

2. THE SIGNIFICANCE OF CONTRACT

97   The legal basis of the employment relationship is usually the exchange of a promise to work in return for a promise to pay wages. The element of bargain, that is an agreement exchanging promises, means that " contract " appears to be the most appropriate legal category in which to place the

---

[8] See below, para. 252.

[9] Trade Union and Labour Relations Act 1974 (hereafter T.U.L.R.A.), s. 1 (2) (*a*), Sched. 1, Pt. I, paras. 1–3.

[10] Employment Protection Act (hereafter E.P.A.) 1975, s. 6; *cf.* E.P.A., s. 17 (4) (Code not conclusive evidence of good industrial relations practice on disclosure of information). Italics added.

[10a] Note in particular C.I.R. Report (No. 69) *Small Firms and the Code of Industrial Relations Practice* (H.M.S.O., 1974) which suggests a revised version for small firms.

[11] s. 6 (11).

[12] *Lewis Shops Group* v. *Wiggins* [1973] I.C.R. 335 at p. 338, *per* Sir Hugh Griffiths; *cf. Earl* v. *Slater & Wheeler (Airlyne) Ltd.* [1972] I.C.R. 508 at pp. 511–512; see further Chap. 16 on unfair dismissal.

[13] *Cf. Post Office* v. *Ravyts* [1972] 3 All E.R. 485 at p. 491 (although in this case the N.I.R.C. was not persuaded that the Code favoured the construction contended for).

relationship of employer and worker. This legal model of an individual bargain has been criticised on two grounds, which we must examine.

Collective bargaining and the individual

98   The first criticism is that the legal model conflicts with reality because the main terms and conditions of employment of over two-thirds of the working population of Britain are resolved, not by individual bargaining, but by collective bargaining between employers and their associations and organisations of workers. The legal model has its roots in the nineteenth century before the rise of modern collective bargaining had helped redress the economic inequality between the employer and individual worker. The logical answer to this objection would be to replace the individual contract entirely with a collective contract enforceable between the collective parties. This is the solution adopted, for example, in the U.S.A. where it is an unfair (*i.e.*, unlawful) labour practice for employers to negotiate directly with individual members of a bargaining unit. This solution is not without its problems, however, because it exposes the individual, who is in opposition to the majority union or otherwise vulnerable because he belongs to some ethnic, political or other minority, to unfavourable discrimination by the union which is designated as bargaining agent for that unit. Labour law in the U.S.A. has struggled to provide protection to the individual through devices such as the duty of the union to represent all employees fairly, and the right of the individual to enforce a collective agreement if the union unfairly declines to do so.

99   This is not the way in which British labour law has dealt with the problem. In this country, the individual contract has been skilfully refashioned by the courts to take collective bargaining into account while leaving the individual free to negotiate and enforce his own contract, which may be either more or less advantageous to him than the terms of the collective agreement. We shall examine the ways in which this has been done—through express and implied incorporation—in Chapter 8.

Contract and status

100   The second criticism is based on the apparent conflict between the insistence on agreement as the legal basis of the obligation to work and to pay wages, and the growing number of statutes which lay duties on the parties (usually designed to protect the worker) which cannot validly be set aside by agreement. This led Dicey, in a statement often repeated today, to say that " the rights of workmen . . . have become a matter not of contract but of status." [14] There is a difference between Dicey and the modern proponents of the concept of status. He deduced that the statutory rights conferred on workmen were, legally speaking, a regression, since, in Maine's famous words, " the movement of the progressive societies has hitherto been a movement from status to contract." [15] The modern advocates of status deduce from this concept a means to enforce extended rights for the worker in his job and to develop new remedies such as

---

[14] *Lectures on the Relation between Law and Opinion in England in the 19th Century* (London, 1926), p. 284.
[15] *Ancient Law* (London, 1927, reprint), p. 174.

reinstatement.[16] Both deductions rest upon a misuse of the term " status " by which Maine meant " the sum total of the powers and disabilities which society confers or imposes on individuals irrespective of their own volition." [17] Apart from minority and mental disorder, the only important modern example of status of this kind is " non-patriality." Special restrictions are imposed on the freedom of movement and of work of those United Kingdom and Commonwealth citizens and aliens who do not have the right of abode in the United Kingdom.[18] This is quite different from the kind of restrictions on freedom of contract imposed by other statutes which are said to confer " status " on certain workers. These statutes regulate the legal relationship between the parties, but the existence and the termination of that relationship still depends, in the last resort, on the volition of the parties. So even a dockworker who, by registering under a statutory scheme, loses his freedom to contract or not contract (in the sense that he must accept an offer of employment by a registered employer) still retains the ultimate freedom whether to register or not.[19] In this sense his " status," which the courts will protect, derives not from a characteristic imposed on him by law but from his own volition in registering.

Contract and statutory regulation

101   The confusion about the various meanings of status really springs from the difficulty which English lawyers have in classifying the legal duties imposed by statutes. Many of these duties are compulsory in the sense that they are expressed in imperative form and it is expressly forbidden to contract out of them.[20] This makes it difficult to treat those duties as *implied* terms in the individual contract. An implied term cannot oust an express term and this is precisely what compulsory statutory duties purport to do. No consistent solution has been applied to this dilemma.

102   (a) Some compulsory duties are regarded, not as part of the employment contract, but as giving rise to extra-contractual rights and duties. For example, the duties of the occupier of a factory under the Factories Act 1961 are usually, although not inevitably, treated as statutory torts, whereas the employer's common law duty of care in relation to his employees may be classified as contractual or tortious.[21]

---

[16] R. W. Rideout, " The Contract of Employment " (1966) 19 *Current Legal Problems* 111.

[17] *Op. cit.* p. 9. Professor O. Kahn-Freund develops this point forcefully in his " Note on Status and Contract in British Labour Law " (1967) 30 M.L.R. 635, on which this section draws extensively.

[18] Immigration Act 1971, s. 2. See below, para. 186.

[19] Under the Docks and Harbours Act 1966, ss. 1–12, and the Orders made thereunder (based on recommendations of the Committee of Inquiry under the Rt. Hon. Lord Devlin, Cmnd. 2734 (1965)).

[20] *e.g.* the prohibition on contracting-out in Trade Union and Labour Relations Act 1974, Sched. 1, Pt. II, para. 32, the Redundancy Payments Act 1965 (hereafter R.P.A.), s. 25 (4), and E.P.A., s. 118. In *Lumsden* v. *Harry Price (Haulage) Ltd.* (1970) 5 I.T.R. 92 an Industrial Tribunal (Shrewsbury) left open the question whether the latter provision also rendered void a *collateral* agreement between employers to grant an indemnity on a change of business.

[21] *Matthews* v. *Kuwait Bechtel Corporation* [1959] 2 Q.B. 57 (a case concerning jurisdiction in actions arising out of contract); but *cf. Davie* v. *New Merton Board Mills Ltd.* [1959] A.C. 604. See too, *Quinn* v. *Burch Bros. (Builders) Ltd.* [1966] 2 Q.B. 370; *Sole* v. *W. J. Hallt Ltd.* [1973] Q.B. 574.

103   (b) Some statutes expressly provide that the duties they impose are to take effect as terms in the individual contract. Because of the imperative language in which these duties are couched, the terms expressly or impliedly agreed by the parties must bow to these compulsory statutory duties. For example, the Equal Pay Act 1970 provides that an "equality clause" is deemed to be included in the terms of the contract of a woman (or man) employed at an establishment in Great Britain.[22] This device aids the enforcement process by enabling the woman to enforce her right to equal pay through an action on the contract.

104   (c) Some statutes are silent as to whether actions for breach of the compulsory duties which they impose are to be regarded as founded in contract, yet the courts have been prepared to interpret them in this way. For example, in *Gutsell* v. *Reeve*[23] it was held that an action by an agricultural labourer, claiming the difference between the amount of wages received by him under his contract and the amount of minimum wages to which he was entitled in terms of an order by an Agricultural Wages Board, was one based on the contract as amended by substituting for the amount provided by the contract the amount of the minimum wages provided by statute. The important practical effect of this classification was that his action was not barred by lapse of time, as it would have been had it been founded upon a statute.[24]

105   (d) Some statutory rights remain distinct from contractual rights but overlap is avoided by express provision in the statute, either for the set-off of amounts awarded under the statute against amounts due under the contract and *vice versa*, or by the creation of "composite" rights enabling the employee to claim those features of the contractual and statutory rights which are more favourable. Examples are to be found in the provisions of the Employment Protection Act 1975, for guarantee payments,[25] medical suspension payments,[26] maternity pay[27] and payment for time off.[28]

106   (e) The statutory machinery for extending terms and conditions of employment in a particular trade or industry rests, for its ultimate sanction, on the implication into the individual contract of an award of the Central Arbitration Committee.[29] The same applies to the enforcement of operative recommendations for trade union recognition[30] and disclosure of information.[31]

Contract and remedies

107   These classifications into contractual and extra-contractual duties are not simply a matter of idle academic speculation. We have observed that

---

[22] Equal Pay Act 1970, s. 1 (3), as substituted by Sex Discrimination Act 1975 (hereafter S.D.A.), Sched. 1.

[23] [1936] 1 K.B. 272 (C.A.); distinguishing *Aylott* v. *West Ham Corporation* [1927] 1 Ch. 30.

[24] The Limitation Act 1623 provided that an action for debt upon a statute was barred after six years, whereas an action for a simple contract debt could be brought for up to 20 years. These particular limitation periods no longer apply.

[25] E.P.A., s. 26 (2).   [26] *Ibid.*, s. 31 (4).

[27] *Ibid.*, s. 37 (4).

[28] *Ibid.*, ss. 57 (7), 61 (13).

[29] *Ibid.*, Sched. 11, para. 11.

[30] *Ibid.*, s. 16.   [31] *Ibid.*, s. 21.

the contractual analysis gives rise to peculiar problems about contracting out of statutory duties. In passing we have noticed that it may affect the *way* in which a particular duty is enforced (*e.g.*, equal pay) or whether there is some procedural bar (*e.g.*, lapse of time) on the action. The classification of a duty as contractual may also affect the jurisdiction of a particular tribunal to hear a dispute arising out of that duty.[32] In a few cases it may actually affect the scope of the duty itself.[33] But perhaps the most important practical effect is on the nature of the remedies available.

108   The ordinary common law remedy for breach of the contract of employment is a claim for damages. For at least 100 years the courts have refused to grant injunctions which, in effect, would require specific performance of contracts of employment. The reason is to be found in the classification by the judges of the employment relationship as being between two equal contracting parties. Since, it is said, it would "turn contracts of service into contracts of slavery"[34] if employers could compel their employees to continue in service, therefore, on the principle of reciprocity between contracting parties, and the need to maintain mutual confidence, the employee should not be able to compel the employer to keep him in service. By classifying the relationship as "contractual" the judiciary has rendered itself incapable of protecting the worker's "property" in his job, that is such valuable assets as his seniority and pension rights. Where reinstatement does occur in practice it is always (apart from statute) with the consent of the employer.[35]

109   A special, and very limited, exception to the general rule against reinstatement as a legal remedy seems to have been created by the Court of Appeal in *Hill* v. *C. A. Parsons & Co. Ltd.*,[36] the facts of which occurred before Part II (Rights of Workers) of the Industrial Relations Act 1971 came into force. A professional engineer was wrongfully dismissed without reasonable notice for refusing to join the Draughtsmen's and Allied Technicians Association as required by a collective agreement between the employer and the Association. A majority of the Court of Appeal (Lord Denning M.R. and Sachs L.J.; Stamp L.J. dissenting) granted an interlocutory injunction restraining the employer from treating a notice of less than reasonable length as having determined the engineer's contract of employment. Three reasons were given for this indirect enforcement

---

[32] *e.g. Treganowan* v. *Robert Knee & Co. Ltd.* [1975] 10 I.T.R. 121 (irrelevant in case of unfair dismissal that employer acted in breach of contract). As regards jurisdiction of industrial tribunals, see para. 155 below.

[33] *e.g.* at common law (before the passing of the Employer's Liability (Defective Equipment) Act 1969) an employee's claim against his employer for damages in respect of personal injuries caused by a defective tool supplied by the employer and obtained from a reputable dealer or manufacturer failed simply because the House of Lords treated the alleged duty as one in tort; had it been regarded as contractual the employee would have succeeded: see *Davie* v. *New Merton Board Mills Ltd.* [1959] A.C. 604, and comment by C. J. Hamson [1959] C.L.J. 157 and J. A. Jolowicz [1959] C.L.J. 163.

[34] *Per* Fry L.J. in *De Francesco* v. *Barnum* (1890) 45 Ch.D. 430, 438, and *Fry on Specific Performances*, 6th ed., p. 50. This rule is now enshrined in the Trade Union and Labour Relations Act 1974, s. 16.

[35] In cases of voluntary arbitration, reinstatement is sometimes awarded (*e.g.*, *T.G.W.U.* v. *Silcock & Colling Ltd.*, I.C. Case 3081, in which the dismissed employee was not in fact reinstated but the former Industrial Court indicated a willingness to make such an award). In the last resort, the employer would be free to disregard such an award.

[36] [1972] Ch. 305; *cf. Keetch* v. *London Passenger Transport Board, The Times,* September 20, 1946; Howells (1972) 35 M.L.R. 310; Hepple (1972) 30 C.L.J. 37.

of a contract for personal services, each of which is open to serious question. First, it was said that damages would not have been an adequate remedy, apparently because the employee could not have been compensated for his loss of pension rights.[37] This seems to have rested on a special finding that his entitlement to a pension was purely within the employer's discretion and not a term of his contract. Stamp L.J. (dissenting) pointed out that damages do not always provide full compensation, yet this is no reason for specifically enforcing an employment contract.[38] Secondly, it was said that " personal confidence " between employer and employee had not been lost; it was a third party (the Association) which was insisting upon the dismissal.[39] This (as Stamp L.J. indicated) confuses desire with the possibility of fulfilment. What was the employer expected to do if all the union members walked out in protest against the continued employment of the engineer and 37 others who refused to join the union? [40] Finally, the court was most anxious that the engineer should be able to remain in his employment until Part II of the Industrial Relations Act came into force, when remedies would be available to him to protect his right not to belong to an organisation.[41] In this regard, it should be noted that the Industrial Relations Act itself did not give an unfairly dismissed employee any legal right to reinstatement. The Act simply provided for a tribunal to *recommend re-engagement* (*i.e.* a new contract, which may involve loss of pension rights, etc.), or, if such a recommendation is not complied with, to grant compensation.[42] So the Court of Appeal's extraordinary decision to grant an interlocutory injunction, could not prevent the employer from dismissing the engineer by giving him reasonable notice nor could it protect an unfairly dismissed employee after the Act came into force because his remedies for unfair dismissal (as defined in the Act) were limited to those stated in the Act. No reference was made in the judgments in *Hill* v. *C. A. Parsons & Co. Ltd.* to section 128 (1) of the Industrial Relations Act, which codified the former practice of the courts, by providing that " no court shall, whether by way of (*a*) specific performance . . . of a contract of employment or (*b*) an injunction . . . restraining a breach or threatened breach of such contract compel an employee to do any work or to attend at any place for the purpose of doing any work." [43] This means, for example, that strikers who are in breach of their employment contracts cannot be ordered back to work. The majority in the Court of Appeal showed a willingness to abandon the principle of reciprocity which would have precluded the court from compelling the employer to retain the employee in service. Sachs L.J. apparently recognised the difficulty of fitting this new approach into a contractual analysis and remarked that, as a result of recent legislation,

---

[37] [1972] Ch. at 314, 316, 320.
[38] *Ibid.* at p. 324; *cf. Giles & Co. Ltd.* v. *Morris* [1972] 1 All E.R. 960 (order of specific performance to *enter into* service agreement as promised).
[39] *Ibid.* at p. 320. This point emphasised in *Chappell* v. *Times Newspapers Ltd.* [1975] I.C.R. 145 at pp. 159, 173–174, 176, 178–179.
[40] *Ibid.* at p. 323, *per* Stamp L.J.: " the court will not exercise its discretion where the order will be nugatory, uncertain, or as a practical matter, impossible to enforce." Even Lord Denning M.R. at p. 314 seems to concede that the order he proposed to make could not be enforced by writ of sequestration if the company refused to comply with it.
[41] *Ibid.* at pp. 315, 317, 321.
[42] See below, Chap. 17. The E.P.A. permits an order of reinstatement.
[43] s. 16 of the Trade Union and Labour Relations Act 1974 is in identical terms.

the employee "may now be said to acquire something akin to a property in his employment." [44]

110 This conceptualisation of " job-property " rights has not, however, been developed by the judiciary. *Hill* v. *C. A. Parsons & Co. Ltd.* has been treated as a " highly exceptional case " [45] which arose in the special circumstances that both the employers and the employee had complete confidence in each other.[46] In *Chappell* v. *Times Newspapers Ltd.*[47] six printing workers who had been threatened that they would be treated as having terminated their own contracts of employment if their union failed to give an undertaking that the union would withdraw instructions for the members to take industrial action, were refused interim injunctions restraining their employers from acting on this threat. The Court of Appeal held that, even if the employers were in breach of the contracts of employment, no ground had been shown for not applying the general rule that a court will not grant an injunction or an order for specific performance of a contract for personal services. If an injunction were to be granted there could be no confidence that the employment would continue peaceably.[48] Moreover, the workers had not come to equity willing to do equity because they were not willing to give an undertaking that they would refuse to obey any instructions from their union, which operated a closed shop, to take industrial action.[49]

111 The courts are sometimes prepared to grant injunctions to restrain the breach of an undertaking not to work for a rival employer. The grant of an injunction is discretionary. It will not be granted to enforce a negative stipulation of this kind if damages would be an adequate remedy or if the employee would be left, as a result of the injunction, with the choice of either being idle or performing his contract. So, on the one hand, an injunction was granted against the actress Bette Davis, when she broke her promise to work only for Warner Bros., since she was able to employ herself remuneratively in other spheres of activity. By means of an injunction she was " tempted," as the judge said, although not " driven " to perform her contract with Warner Bros.[50] On the other hand, an injunction was refused against the " Troggs " pop-group to restrain them from breaking their promise to employ a particular person as their manager. The reasons given were two-fold : (a) to be successful pop-groups need managers (a fact of which judicial notice was taken!), so that the grant of an injunction would have compelled the " Troggs " to employ the plaintiff; and (b) unlike a film actress, a manger has duties of " a personal and fiduciary nature to perform " and these could not be continued where the " Troggs " had lost confidence in him.[51]

---

[44] At p. 321.
[45] *Per* Sachs L.J. at p. 321. In *Sanders* v. *Ernest A. Neale Ltd.* [1974] I.C.R. 565 at p. 571, Sir John Donaldson described the *Hill* v. *Parsons* exception as being of " unusual, if not unique, character."
[46] *Chappell* v. *Times Newspapers Ltd.* [1975] I.C.R. 145 at pp. 173, 176, 178.
[47] [1975] I.C.R. 145.
[48] *Ibid.* at pp. 158, 174, 179.
[49] *Ibid.* at pp. 161, 174, 177, 179.
[50] *Warner Bros. Pictures Inc.* v. *Nelson* [1937] 1 K.B. 209.
[51] *Page One Records* v. *Britton* [1968] 1 W.L.R. 157; see too, *Whitwood Chemical Co.* v. *Hardman* [1891] 2 Ch. 416, and Trade Union and Labour Relations Act 1974, s. 16.

112   Another remedy which is affected by the " contractual " classification of the relationship is that of the declaration. This remedy simply determines the rights of the parties without any order of court for their fulfilment. Despite the absence of a sanction, a declaratory judgment is usually obeyed in practice. However, this remedy is not available to an ordinary employee who is wrongfully dismissed in breach of his contract. This is because dismissal terminates the contract of employment, however wrongful that dismissal may be in law. The justification for this is that the contract, being of a personal nature, requires the co-operation of both parties for its continuance.[52] If one party decides to bring it to an end, the other is not entitled to regard himself as still being a party to that contract. In other words he may have a right to claim damages if the termination has been in breach of contract but he cannot obtain a declaration that his status is still that of an employee (or employer, if it is the employee who has repudiated the contract).[53] Recent statements by Lord Denning M.R. and Sachs L.J. in *Hill* v. *Parsons & Co. Ltd.*,[54] that a declaration of rights may be granted to an ordinary employee in (undefined) " special circumstances " cannot be reconciled with these general principles and, it is submitted, run contrary to the general trend of the authorities.

However, the employee who is fortunate enough to enjoy a special statutory status may be able to obtain a declaration or even an injunction (in some cases) restoring him to that status. An example is a registered dockworker whose status will be protected by means of a declaration.[55] If he is wrongfully dismissed the removal of his name from the statutory register is in law a nullity and he is entitled to a declaration to the effect that he is still entitled to all the benefits which, by statute, that status confers on him.

113   There is some doubt as to the precise limits of this judicial power to grant declaratory relief to protect status. In one case the House of Lords (by a 3–2 majority) granted a declaration to a senior hospital clerk to the effect that her dismissal from a " permanent and pensionable " post was invalid.[56] The remarkable feature of the decision is that their lordships apparently regarded the employment as being based on contract only and did not refer to any statutory status. In fact (although this was not referred

---

[52] It is controversial whether this is a legal rule or simply a practice, and, in either event whether it is open to exceptions, below para. 509.

[53] *Taylor* v. *N.U.S.* [1967] 1 W.L.R. 532, 551–553. Special considerations arise where a full-time trade union official, in addition to being an employee of the union, is also a member. In his capacity as member (but not employee) he may be able to protect his status by means of a declaratory judgment: *ibid. Quaere*: does an *elected* union official unlike an ordinary employee have a status which will be protected by declaration or injunction?: see the remarks of Megarry J. in *Leary* v. *N.U.V.B.* [1971] Ch. 34, and now *Stevenson* v. *U.R.T.U.* [1976] 3 All E.R. 29 (Ch.D.).

[54] [1972] Ch. 305, 314, 319 (C.A.).

[55] *Vine* v. *National Dock Labour Board* [1957] A.C. 488, *per* Viscount Kilmuir L.C. at p. 490 and Lord Keith at p. 507. Similar considerations apply to the holder of a common law office, *e.g.*, the chief constable in *Ridge* v. *Baldwin* [1964] A.C. 40 (H.L.), who was granted a declaration that his dismissal without a hearing was null and void (and so was able to protect his pension rights).

[56] *McClelland* v. *N.I. General Health Services Board* [1957] 1 W.L.R. 594, esp. *per* Lord Goddard at p. 601, and Lord Evershed at p. 612; but contrast *Barber* v. *Manchester Regional Hospital Board* [1958] 1 W.L.R. 181 with this case and *Palmer* v. *Inverness Hospitals Board*, 1963 S.L.T. 124 (hospital doctors); and see *Vidyodaya University of Ceylon* v. *Silva* [1965] 1 W.L.R. 77 (university teacher an ordinary employee: no declaration). *Francis* v. *Kuala Lumpur Councillors* [1962] 1 W.L.R. 1411 (council clerk: no declaration).

to in the speeches of their lordships) the plaintiff's terms of employment had to be approved by the Northern Ireland Minister of Health and Local Government. This may indicate that the decisive factor was that the plaintiff held a public post which carried with it a permanent status. The question which arises, as one commentator has said, " is whether the special features of public employment are important enough to justify special rules as to dismissal therefrom." [57] The real difficulty is that the line between public and private employees is not clearly drawn in England. Nor is it certain that the lower grades of public employees would be treated in the same way as the higher grades.[58] This problem really brings us to the definition of an " employee," a question to be considered in the next chapter.

Relevance of general principles of contract

114   How far is the law governing the individual employment relationship an application of the general principles of the law of contract, and how far is it a separate and distinct body of legal rules? This is an extremely difficult question to answer. On the one hand, the common law concept of bargain is essential to the formation of the legal employment relationship. In other words, there must be an agreement supported by consideration. Moreover, the techniques of the common law for filling in the unspoken terms of the contract are applied, and indeed developed with considerable subtlety, in this area. On the other hand, there are a number of special common law rules applicable only to the employment contract (or to a class of contracts, involving the implied duty of co-operation, to which the employment contract belongs), particularly in regard to the termination of the contract.[59] Above all else, as we have seen, there are many statutory rights and duties governing the employment relationship, only some of which can be fitted into a " contractual " analysis. In this book we shall have little to say about general contractual principles applicable to the employment contract (*e.g.*, the doctrine of consideration, the law of mistake, etc.). Instead, we shall concentrate on those rules which are special to the individual employment relationship.

[The next paragraph is 121.]

---

[57] I. Zamir, *The Declaratory Judgment*, pp. 146–148.
[58] Note the remarks of Lord Reid in *Malloch* v. *Aberdeen Corporation* [1971] 1 W.L.R. 1578, 1582, and Lord Wilberforce, *ibid.* p. 1596.
[59] See below, Chap. 15.

CHAPTER 3

THE CONTRACT OF EMPLOYMENT

Terminology

121   The last statute to use the words "master and servant" in its title
was enacted in 1867[1] and repealed in 1875.[2] Since then Parliament has
used the words "employer" and "workman"[3] and, more recently,
"employer" and "employee"[4] to describe the parties to the contract of
employment. The change reflected the new conception of legal equality
between parties to a civil contract. Nevertheless, some judges and textbook writers persist in the use of the archaic terminology when expounding
the common law. We shall follow Parliament's example.

Purposes of definition

122   Despite the fact that the contract of employment is the "corner-stone
of the edifice" of labour law,[5] there is no uniform or consistent statutory
definition of an "employee" or a "contract of employment." A person's
rights under particular statutes will be vitally affected by the question
whether or not he is an "employee" or "workman" for the purposes of
that statute. For example:

123   (a) *The Truck Act 1831* (which prohibits payment of wages otherwise
than in cash) originally applied to "artificers,"[6] a term which was
undefined until an Act of 1887[7] said it was to be construed as referring
to "workmen" as defined in the Employers and Workmen Act 1875.

124   Although the latter Act has now been repealed,[8] the definition of "workman" is still limited to those engaged in manual labour and working
under a contract with an employer "whether the contract be . . . express
or implied, oral or in writing, and be a contract of service or a contract
personally to execute any work or labour."[9] This originally brought within
the scope of the Truck Acts the "self-employed" butty on the collieries
and the gangers and their men at work on the railways and would today
include "self-employed" men on the "lump" in the building industry.[10]

---

[1] Master and Servant Act 1867.

[2] Conspiracy and Protection of Property Act, 1875.

[3] *e.g.* Employers and Workmen Act, 1875, s. 10 (continued by Statute Law (Repeals)
Act 1973, Sched. 2, para. 2); Trade Disputes Act 1906, s. 5 (3) (repealed by Industrial
Relations Act 1971, Sched. 9); Industrial Courts Act 1919, s. 8; Wages Councils Act 1959,
s. 24 (uses expression "worker").

[4] Contracts of Employment Act 1972, s. 11; Prices and Incomes Act 1966, s. 34; Redundancy Payments Act 1965, s. 25; Industrial Relations Act 1971, s. 167 (repealed by Trade
Union and Labour Relations Act 1974, which uses definitions of "employee" and "worker"
identical to those in the 1971 Act). E.P.A., s. 126, adopts the T.U.L.R.A. definitions.

[5] O. Kahn-Freund in *The System of Industrial Relations in Great Britain* (London,
1954), p. 45.

[6] ss. 1–4.

[7] Truck Act (Amendment) Act, s. 2. The Truck Act 1896, s. 1 (3), applies s. 1 of that
Act (deductions for fines) to "shop assistants" as well as workmen. See below, paras.
344–347 and 451–461.

[8] Statute Law (Repeals) Act 1973, s. 39.

[9] *Ibid.*, Sched. 2, para. 2, amending Truck Amendment Act 1887, s. 2.

[10] *Stuart* v. *Evans* (1883) 49 L.T. 138 (slater working for builder). Provided that the
individual must be doing at least part of the work personally: *Ingram* v. *Barnes* (1857)
7 E. & B. 115. See below, para. 136 on modern problems of labour-only sub-contracting.

The words "manual labour" are restrictively interpreted. Among those who have been held *not* to be engaged in *manual* labour are: a hairdresser,[11] the guard of a goods train,[12] and a man employed to make chemical inventions.[13] The exclusion of *domestic* servants has been held to exclude those "whose main or general function is to be about their employer's persons, or establishments, residential or quasi-residential, for the purposes of ministering to their employer's needs or wants, or to the need or wants of those who are members of such establishments, or of those resorting to such establishments, including guests." [14]

125 (b) *The Contracts of Employment Act 1972* (which provides for written particulars of employment contracts and minimum periods of notice) [15] defines "employee" as "an individual who has entered into or works under (or, where the employment has ceased, worked under) a contract with an employer, whether the contract be for manual labour, clerical work or otherwise, be expressed or implied, oral or in writing, and whether it be a contract of service or of apprenticeship." [16] This definition does not include an individual under a contract "personally to execute any work or labour," [17] *i.e.*, the "self-employed." As a result of an amendment in 1971 it does include ex-employees.[18] A number of categories of "employees" are, however, excluded from the Act's operation: registered dockworkers,[19] certain seamen,[20] certain close relatives,[21] those working wholly or mainly outside Great Britain unless the employee ordinarily works in Great Britain and the work outside Great Britain is for the same employer [22] and certain casual and part-time employees working less than 16 hours weekly (or in some cases 8 hours weekly).[23]

126 (c) *The Redundancy Payments Act 1965* has a similar definition (also covering ex-employees) [24] but with far wider exceptions: registered dockworkers, share fishermen, the spouse of an employer, employees in public office, in the civil service and the National Health Service,[25] domestic servants in private households who are close relatives,[26] and certain employees who have agreed in writing to exclude their rights to redundancy payments.[27]

---

[11] *R.* v. *Louth Justices* (1900) 2 I.R. 714.

[12] *Hunt* v. *G.N. Ry.* [1891] 1 Q.B. 601.

[13] *Bagnall* v. *Levinstein* [1907] 1 K.B. 531. See Fridman, *Modern Law of Employment,* pp. 374–375, for further examples.

[14] *Cameron* v. *Royal London Ophthalmic Hospital* [1941] 1 K.B. 350 (stoker employed in hospital a domestic servant) at p. 357 quoting *Re Junior Carlton Club* [1922] 1 K.B. 166, 170.

[15] ss. 1–4.

[16] s. 11 (1).

[17] These words do not appear in s. 11 (1) of the Act.

[18] But in this case a reference to an industrial tribunal as to particulars of terms must be made within three months of termination: Contracts of Employment Act 1972 (hereafter C.E.A.), s. 8 (8).

[19] Contracts of Employment Act 1972, s. 9 (1).

[20] *Ibid.* s. 9 (2).

[21] *Ibid.* s. 9 (3).

[22] *Ibid.* s. 12 (1).

[23] E.P.A., Sched. 16, Pt. II, paras. 8–11.

[24] s. 25.

[25] *Ibid.* s. 16. (For these public employees there are parallel voluntary and, in some cases, statutory arrangements.)

[26] *Ibid.* s. 19.

[27] *Ibid.* ss. 15, 20 (and those covered by collective agreements on redundancy payments, which have received ministerial approval: s. 11).

127   (d) *The Trade Union and Labour Relations Act 1974* makes a distinction between a " worker " and an " employee." [28] Some provisions of the Act are confined to the latter. These include the rights in respect of unfair dismissal (although even this does not cover all classes of " employees ").[29] Others apply to the wider class of " workers." [30] The term " employee " is limited to an individual who has entered into or works under (or, where the employment has ceased, worked under) a contract of employment otherwise than in police service.[31] A contract of employment may be one of service or of apprenticeship, express or implied, and (if it is express) oral or in writing.[32] The definition of " worker " (too lengthy to be set out here) seems wide enough to cover an individual who is temporarily unemployed, or who is seeking work, as well as one who is actually working. He may be under a " contract of employment " (as defined above) or " under any other contract . . . whereby he undertakes personally to perform any work or services." [33] However, the contract must not be with " a professional client " of his. This vague phrase is not defined in the Act. The *Oxford English Dictionary* indicates that " professional " may have either a narrow or wide meaning. The former confines the word to being engaged in " the learned or skilled professions, or in a calling considered socially superior to a trade or handicraft." The latter extends it to cover anyone who " follows an occupation as his profession, life-work, or means of livelihood," and if this meaning were accepted a self-employed businessman could not be regarded as a " worker " for the purposes of the Act. Difficult questions are bound to arise, however, over the word " client," the use of which seems to strengthen the case for attributing the narrow meaning to the word " professional." Parliament has expressly provided that one group of persons with " professional clients " are to be regarded as " workers." These are individuals providing general medical, pharmaceutical, dental or ophthalmic services under the National Health Service Act.[34] The term " worker " also embraces those in employment under or for purposes of a government department, except for the armed services.[35]

128   (e) *The Employment Protection Act 1975,* adopts the same definitions of " employee " and " worker " as those in the Trade Union and Labour Relations Act 1974.[36] Nearly all the individual rights granted by the Act are confined to employees [37] (and certain classes of employees are excluded from particular rights).[38]

---

[28] s. 30.

[29] Sched. 1, Pt. II, para. 4 (on which see below, Chap. 17).

[30] Note the special definition for trade disputes, s. 29 (6).

[31] s. 30 (1).

[32] *Ibid.*

[33] s. 30 (1). The contract must involve *personal* performance by the " worker ": *Broadbent* v. *Crisp* [1974] I.C.R. 248. There must also be an undertaking to work and not simply to sell a completed work: *Writers' Guild of G.B.* v. *British Broadcasting Corpn.* [1974] I.C.R. 234, 240, 243–245.

[34] s. 30 (2).

[35] s. 30 (1). Policemen are excluded from the definition of " employee " and " worker ": *ibid.*

[36] E.P.A., s. 126.

[37] *e.g.* E.P.A., ss. 22–28, 29–33, 34, 35–52, 53–56, 57–60, 63–69, 70, 81–84, 99–107; *cf.* s. 12 (5) (*b*).

[38] E.P.A., s. 119.

129 (f) *The Sex Discrimination Act 1975* makes discrimination on grounds of sex and marital status unlawful in respect of " employment," which is defined as " employment under a contract of service or of apprenticeship or personally to execute any work, or labour." [39-40]

130 (g) *The Social Security Act 1975* distinguishes between " employed earners " and " self-employed earners " for purposes of contributions to the National Insurance Fund and entitlement to benefits. The former are those gainfully employed under a contract of service, or in an office (including an elective office) with emoluments chargeable to income tax under Schedule E. The latter is the residual category. [41]

131 Apart from statute, it is also important to identify the contract of employment for purposes of certain common law rights and duties. There are many obligations which are imposed on an employer or employee by the courts as an *implied* incident of the contract of employment. For example, in *Lister* v. *Romford Ice and Cold Storage Co. Ltd.*,[42] it was held by the House of Lords that there was an implied obligation upon an employee to indemnify his employer in respect of negligence, only because of the employee's status under the contract of employment. It does not follow that a similar term would be implied in every contract between an independent contractor and an employer, where the former could reasonably assume that the latter had effected insurance. Another example is the fourfold common law duty imposed on an employer to take reasonable steps to provide an employee with safe plant, a safe system of work, safe premises and safe fellow-employees. Although a *general* duty of care is owned by an employer to his self-employed workers, the standard of care and the degree of advice and supervision which he is expected to give them may be significantly lower than in the case of his employees.[43] The distinction between an " employee " and an " independent contractor " is also important in regard to the imposition of vicarious liability on an employer.[44]

Identifying a contract of employment [45]

132 Most statutes do not offer any definition at all of the " contract of employment " (or " service ") as such. Those which do simply indicate that the expression includes both oral and written and express and implied

---

39-40 s. 82 (1). See Chap. 11, below.

41 Social Security Act 1975, s. 2 (1). The Secretary of State (in practice an inspector appointed by him) determines the class into which a person should be placed. At one time these decisions were issued as pamphlets by H.M.S.O., but this practice has now stopped: see, *e.g.* M. 38 (cricket umpire not " employed "); M. 48 (B.B.C. interviewer not " employed ") but this may have been implicitly overruled by *Market Investigations Ltd.* v. *Minister of Social Security* [1969] 2 Q.B. 173; M. 64 (jobbing gardener " employed ") but *cf. Braddell* v. *Baker* (1911) 27 T.L.R. 182 (jobbing gardener not employee); M. 67 (*au pair* girls " employed " by their hosts). On appeals against such decisions, see below, para. 163. See, too, below, para. 632.

42 [1957] A.C. 555, esp. *per* Viscount Simonds at pp. 576–579.

43 *Inglefield* v. *Macey* (1967) 2 K.I.R. 146; *Baxter* v. *Central Electricity Generating Board* [1965] 1 W.L.R. 200.

44 See Atiyah, *Vicarious Liability in the Law of Torts* (London, 1967) p. 6; but for a different approach Street, *Law of Torts* (Chap. 27).

45 Where a court has determined whether there is a contract of service, this will not be set aside on appeal unless no person acting judicially and properly instructed as to the relevant law could reach such a decision: *Global Plant Ltd.* v. *Secretary of State for Health and Social Security* [1972] 1 Q.B. 139 (D.C.); *Maurice Graham* v. *Brunswick* (1974) 16 K.I.R. 158.

contracts. It is left to the courts to decide what a " contract of employment " is. Three main tests have been expounded : control, organisation and a multiple or mixed test.

133   The traditional test is *control*.[46] An employee works under the control of another, not only as to *what* he must do but also *how* and *when* he must do it. This test has been used to distinguish an employee from an agent (who brings his principal into contractual relations with a third party but the manner in which he does so is usually in the agent's discretion). It has also been used to distinguish an employee from an independent contractor or self-employed person, *i.e.*, one who works under a " contract for services," who is engaged to produce a particular result but who is entitled to use his own discretion as to *how* and *when* to do that work, subject to the terms of his contract. A chauffeur is an employee under orders; a taxi-driver merely contracts to drive his " employer " from one place to another.[46a] The mere fact that an individual is given some freedom of action, however, does not necessarily remove the element of control.[47] Other relevant factors are the nature of the task, the magnitude of the contract amount, the manner in which it is to be paid, the powers of dismissal, and the circumstances in which rewards may be withheld.[48]

134   The control test assumes that the employer is both a manager and a technical expert; in other words, it reflects a stage of society in which the employer could be expected to be superior to the employee in skill and knowledge. It is still a useful test when dealing with simple relationships such as those between a factory owner and an unskilled labourer, a craftsman and a journeyman or a householder and his domestic staff. However, as Professor Kahn-Freund has pointed out, " to say of the captain of a ship, the pilot of an aeroplane, the driver of a railway engine, of a motor-vehicle or of a crane that the employer ' controls ' the performance of his work is unrealistic and almost grotesque." [49] In these cases the employer is in no position to instruct the skilled worker *how* to do his job. Indeed, a skilled worker who simply relied on his employer's directions without exercising his own professional judgment might actually be in breach of his contract. It is no wonder, therefore, that the courts have found it increasingly difficult to apply the " control " test to modern industrial relationships. At first an attempt was made to stretch the " control " test to its limits, by making control of the *manner* in which the work was to be done the decisive test (rather than simply control of *what* the worker did). In particular, Lord Simon said in *Mersey Docks and Harbour Board* v. *Coggins and Griffiths Ltd.*[50] that the test should turn " on where the authority lies to direct or to delegate to, the workman, the manner in which

---

46 Described by McCardie J. in *Performing Right Society Ltd.* v. *Mitchell and Booker Ltd.* [1924] 1 K.B. 762 as the " final test."
46a Some taxi-drivers are employees of taxi-owners, while others are not: *Challinor* v. *Taylor* [1972] I.T.R. 104 (N.I.R.C.) (" off-the-clock " driver not employee).
47 *Walker* v. *Crystal Palace Football Club* [1910] 1 K.B. 87 (footballer a " workman," although entitled to use initiative in playing game); *cf. R.* v. *Negus* (1873) L.R. 2 C.C.R. 34, 37 (commission agent not a " clerk or servant "), and *Re Ashley and Smith* [1918] 2 Ch. 378 (newspaper contributors not " servants ").
48 *Performing Right Society Ltd.* v. *Mitchell and Booker Ltd.* at p. 767.
49 (1951) 14 M.L.R. 504, 505–506.
50 [1947] A.C. 1 at p. 12; see, too, Lord Porter at p. 17, Lord Simonds at p. 18, Lord Uthwatt at p. 23; and comment by C. Grunfeld (1947) 10 M.L.R. 203, 205.

[the work is to be done]." Subordination to the employer's managerial power was thus made the criterion. A further step in this direction was made in *Cassidy* v. *Minister of Health* [51] (in which a hospital authority was held to be vicariously liable for an injury suffered by a patient following negligent treatment by full-time medical staff). Two of the Lord Justices of Appeal based their decision on the fact that the doctors and nurse involved were on the permanent establishment subject to the standing orders of the hospital authority which was in a position to make rules concerning the organisation of the medical staff's work, as opposed to the manner in which it was done. This led Professor Kahn-Freund to suggest that the decisive test might be "Did the alleged servant form part of the alleged master's organisation." [52] Lord Justice Denning (as he then was) later developed this test as follows:

> "Under a contract of service, a man is employed as part of the business, and his work is done as an integral part of the business; whereas under a contract for services, his work, although done for the business, is not integrated into it but is only accessory to it." [53]

135   Unfortunately, "organisation" or "integration" does not provide a clear answer in many situations, particularly where the worker provides some tools or equipment himself, or is paid on a productivity basis. In such cases the courts have come, in recent times, to prefer a more flexible "multiple" or "mixed" test. At its most casuistic level, this is simply said to be a "common-sense" approach of the "reasonable man." [54] At other times various criteria are mentioned, such as the employer's power of selection and dismissal, the form of payment of wages, and, in addition, the employer's right to control the method of doing the work. [55] Most recently, it has been suggested that a "multiple" test should be applied in two stages. First, it must be asked whether there is control. This is a necessary but not a sufficient test. Secondly, it must be asked whether the provisions of the contract are "consistent with its being a contract of service." [56] In other words, are there indications that the worker is an entrepreneur rather than an employee? For example, has he invested in tools and taken the chance of profit or the risk of loss? On the other hand, the mere fact that he is paid on an incentive basis, [57] or that he is expressly declared to be "self-employed" [58] is not conclusive. The entrepreneurial

[51] [1951] 2 K.B. 343, in *Roe* v. *Minister of Health* [1954] 2 Q.B. 66 an anaesthetist providing a regular service for a hospital, but also engaged in private practice, was regarded as part of the "organisation" of the hospital (at pp. 79, 91).

[52] *Loc. cit.* at pp. 505–506; but *cf. Labour and the Law* (London 1972), p. 9, where the same author emphasises that "there can be no employment relationship without a power to command and a duty to obey."

[53] *Stevenson, Jordan and Harrison Ltd.* v. *Macdonald and Evans* [1952] 1 T.L.R. 101, 111. So a regular contributor to a newspaper would not be an employee, but a full-time journalist relying on the organisation's resources would: *Re Ashley and Smith* [1918] 2 Ch. 378; *Beloff* v. *Pressdram Ltd.* [1973] 1 All E.R. 241.

[54] *Cassidy* v. *Minister of Health*, at 352–353, *per* Singleton L.J.; *Whittaker* v. *Minister of Pensions* [1967] 1 Q.B. 156; *Challinor* v. *Taylor* [1972] I.C.R. 129 (N.I.R.C.).

[55] *Short* v. *J. and W. Henderson Ltd.* (1946) 62 T.L.R. 427, 429; *Morren* v. *Swinton and Pendlebury B.C.* [1965] 1 W.L.R. 576.

[56] *Ready-Mixed Concrete (S.E.) Ltd.* v. *Minister of Pensions* [1968] 2 Q.B. 497; discussed by G. de N. Clark (1968) 31 M.L.R. 450; C. Drake (1968) 31 M.L.R. 408; B. A. Hepple [1968] C.L.J. 227.

[57] *Tucker* v. *Axbridge Highway Board* (1888) 5 T.L.R. 26; but contrast the *Ready-Mixed* case, at p. 526.

[58] *Ready-Mixed* case at p. 513, *cf. Inglefield* v. *Macey* (1967) 2 K.I.R. 146.

element is clearly of importance. But it begs the question to ask whether the contract is " consistent with a contract of service." Had it been asked whether the contract was consistent with a contract for services, precisely the opposite result would have been reached. In other words, the form of the question will dictate the answer given.

Labour-only sub-contracting

136   None of the tests in vogue for identifying a contract of employment has been able to deal adequately with the legal problems associated with " self-employment " and sub-contracting for labour supply. Sub-contracting is older than the industrial revolution, but in recent times it has become rife, particularly in the building industry (where it is known as " the lump "). The practice takes many different forms. For example, a gang of labourers, all in partnership, and all " self-employed "; or a number of individuals, claiming to be " self-employed " although working more or less permanently for the same employer; a group of self-employed men, in contract with a sub-contractor, who in turn contracts to make their labour available to the main contractor; or a specialist trade sub-contractor (a company) whose workers are under contracts of employment with it, but are then " loaned " or " hired," with or without equipment (such as cranes), to a main contractor. Men often move backwards and forwards between work under a contract of employment and self-employment in one of these forms. One of the reasons for " self-employment " may be a desire by an employer or worker to avoid certain statutory imposts,[59] for example, national insurance contributions,[59a] redundancy payments,[60] industrial training levies,[61] compulsory liability insurance,[62] preferential claims on liquidation,[63] the extension of terms and conditions of employment [64] and

---

[59] Another reason is the avoidance of collective bargaining obligations, *e.g.* holidays, sick pay, pensions, wages.

[59a] Social Security Act 1975, s. 2; *Marley Tile Co. Ltd. and J. Clark* (Minister's decision, reported in Wedderburn, *Cases and Materials on Labour Law* (1965), p. 10). But *cf. Rennison and Son* v. *Minister of Social Security* (1970) 114 S.J. 952; [1970] C.L.Y. 1755.

[60] Redundancy Payments Act 1965, s. 25.

[61] In terms of orders made under the Industrial Training Act 1964, s. 4. See *Construction Industry Training Board* v. *Labour Force Ltd.* [1970] 3 All E.R. 220 (labour-only supplier not an " employer " because its 50,000 employees not under a " contract of service " and accordingly not liable to pay £12,000 training levy: the " multiple " test applied); and see, too, *Emerald Construction Co. Ltd.* v. *Lowthian* [1966] 1 W.L.R. 691.

[62] Under the Employers' Liability (Compulsory Insurance) Act 1969, s. 2; *cf.* Employer's Liability (Defective Equipment) Act 1969, s. 1, which further restricts " employee " to those employed for purposes of the employer's business.

[63] Companies Act 1948, s. 319 (4); Bankruptcy Act 1914, s. 33; *Re C. W. and A. L. Hughes Ltd.* [1966] 1 W.L.R. 1369 (gang-leaders and members not in employment of company: control test applied); this is consistent with *Westall Richardson Ltd.* v. *Roulson* [1954] 1 W.L.R. 905.

[64] Claims may be reported as regards " workers " under E.P.A., Sched. 11, a term which includes the self-employed other than casuals. But an award can have effect only as regards " employees," which means that the self-employed worker gets no legally enforceable right. But the former Industrial Court has been prepared to " pierce the veil of self-employment " (as Wedderburn, *op. cit.* p. 15n. says), so as to treat " self-employed " tilers as " employees " for purposes of this and other statutes and the agreements of the N.J.C. for the Building Industry: *W. Creighton and Co. Ltd. and Amalgamated Slaters, Tilers and Roofing Operatives Society*, I.C. Casee No. 3107. But the opposite conclusion was reached in *Amalgamated Society of Woodworkers, Painters and Builders and C. E. Barden and Sons Ltd.*, I.A.B. Case No. 3256. See, too, the provisions regarding recognition of trade unions (E.P.A., s. 16) and disclosure of information (E.P.A., s. 21) which are enforceable only in respect of " employees."

Contracts of Employment Act,[65] and the remedies for unfair dismissal,[66] as well as certain common law duties, in particular regarding safety.[67] The former Industrial Court, and some Commonwealth courts, however, have shown that it is possible to prevent the evasion of statutory duties by giving an extended meaning to the term "employee."[68] An alternative approach is to be found in some legislation which "deems" the worker, however recruited or paid, to be the "employee" of the head contractor for all purposes.[69]

Casual or temporary employees

137   At common law the duration of a person's employment is not directly relevant to the question whether or not he has a contract of employment. Moreover, so long as he is an "employee" a part-time or casual worker has the same common law rights and obligations as a full-time employee. Indeed, many workers enter a series of separate contracts of employment with their employer, each time they take on a fresh assignment, like the research interviewer in a case in 1968 who could work when she wanted, within the time specified for completion of the market survey, and was free to undertake similar work at the same time for other organisations.[70] On the other hand, the fact that a person has a full-time job elsewhere may indicate that he is to be regarded as "self-employed."[71]

138   Many statutory protections, however, do not apply to temporary or casual employees. In each case it is necessary to examine the particular statute: for example, the rights to minimum periods of notice under the Contracts of Employment Act do not apply to those who have worked for less than four weeks[72]; the right to a written statement of employment terms under that Act do not apply to a person who works less than 16 hours (or in some cases 8 hours weekly)[72a]; entitlement to redundancy payments depends on length of service which must be of at least two

---

65 Above, para. 125.

66 Above, para 127. *Cf.* S.D.A., s. 9, which covers "contract workers."

67 Occasionally the courts have held employers liable for breach of statutory safety regulations to labour-gang workers: *e.g., Donaghey* v. *Boulton and Paul Ltd.* [1968] A.C. 1. But in *Alderton* v. *Richard Burgon Associates (Manpower)* [1974] Crim.L.R. 318 (D.C.) an employment agency was able to avoid liability for drivers, under the Transport Act 1968, s. 98.

68 Above, note 64; and *D. C. Dewan, Mohideen Sahib* v. *United Beedi Workers' Union,* A.I.R. 1966, S.C. 370 (S.Ct. India). The Fair Wages Resolution has been used to secure observance of " recognised terms and conditions " by " labour-only " cleaning companies employed by government departments, where the workers were " employees " of the contract-cleaners: *Civil Service Union against Cleaners Ltd. and others* (I.C. Cases Nos. 3206, 3212, 3216–3219, 3242, 3243).

69 *e.g.,* Wages Councils Act 1959, s. 18 (1). National Insurance Act 1965, s. 16 (1); and the recommendations of the Report of the Committee of Inquiry under Professor E. H. Phelps-Brown into Certain Matters concerning Labour in Building and Civil Engineering, Cmnd. 3714, paras. 448–457 (not so far implemented). The Finance Act 1971, ss. 29–31, and the Finance (No. 2) Act 1975, ss. 68–71, attempt to deal with evasion of income tax and social security deductions in the construction industry.

70 *Marker Investigations Ltd.* v. *Minister of Social Security* [1969] 2 Q.B. 173; *Greater London Council* v. *Ministry of Social Security* [1971] 1 W.L.R. 641; *Global Plant Ltd.* v. *Secretary of State for Health and Social Security* [1972] 1 Q.B. 139.

71 *Argent* v. *Minister of Social Security* [1968] 1 W.L.R. 1749; *Hammett* v. *Livingstone Control Ltd.* (1970) 5 I.T.R. 136 (D.C.).

72 Contracts of Employment Act 1972, s. 1 (1). This period also applies to the rights to guarantee pay and medical suspension pay under E.P.A. See Chap. 10.

72a C.E.A., s. 4 (7), subject to ss. 4 (8)–(10), as amended by E.P.A., Sched. 16, Pt. II, paras. 8–11.

years' duration[73]; and remedies in respect of unfair dismissal are available only to those who have been continuously in that employment for a qualifying period before the date of dismissal.[74]

Borrowed employees

139 An employer sometimes " lends " or " hires " an employee, with or without equipment, to another employer. Two questions may then arise: (a) who is responsible for the torts of that employee (*e.g.*, negligence) committed in the course of his employment, the general employer or the temporary employer? (b) Who is, in law, the employer of the borrowed employee, and so responsible for various statutory or common law obligations? The first question is one of vicarious liability: in nearly all cases the general employer will be held responsible to third parties for the borrowed employee's torts.[75] The answer to the second question is that the contract of employment cannot be transferred from one employer to another without the employee's consent.[76] This consent will not be readily inferred; there must be clear evidence of real consent to the change on the part of the employee. If that consent is obtained then the employee starts a fresh contract of employment with the new employer.[77] As we shall see when dealing with loss of employment, this may vitally affect the employee's rights to redundancy payments and minimum periods of notice.[78]

Public employees

140 Over one-quarter of the working population of Britain are in public employment. These include the following:

(a) Those in " Crown employment," that is, employment under or for the purposes of a government department—in practice those who are not in the armed forces or holders of judicial or political posts are divided into two broad classes, the non-industrial civil service who carry out the executive functions of government, and the industrial civil service, *e.g.*, civilian defence employees, others employed in government industrial establishments, and by bodies such as the Forestry Commission.

(b) National Health Service employees, whose formal employer may be a Regional, Area, or Local Health Authority.[78a]

(c) Local authority employees.[79]

---

[73] Redundancy Payments Act 1965, s. 8.

[74] 26 weeks in respect of dismissals after March 16, 1975: T.U.L.R.A., Sched. 1, Pt. II, para. 10. There is a six-month qualifying period under the Equal Pay Act, but none in respect of other forms of sex discrimination under S.D.A. See Chap. 11.

[75] *Mersey Docks and Harbour Board* v. *Coggins and Griffith (Liverpool) Ltd.* [1947] A.C. 1, and generally Atiyah, *op. cit.* p. 432.

[76] *Smith* v. *Blandford Gee Cementation Ltd.* [1970] 3 All E.R. 154, 164; approving *Denham* v. *Midland Employers' Mutual Ass. Ltd.* [1955] 2 Q.B. 437, 443; *Savory* v. *Holland* [1964] 1 W.L.R. 1158, 1165.

[77] And see, *Nokes* v. *Doncaster Amalgamated Collieries Ltd.* [1940] A.C. 1014, 1018 (on amalgamation of two companies, employee of one of those companies did not automatically become an employee of the new company). The common law rules are sometimes altered by statute, *e.g.* Atomic Energy Authority Act 1971, ss. 8–10, which provides that certain employees of the Authority are to be transferred to two new companies, and that this transfer is not to be regarded as a termination of their contracts of employment by the Authority.

[78] Below, Chaps. 16 and 18.

[78a] National Health Service Reorganisation Act 1973, and Orders made thereunder.

[79] Local Government Act 1972 and regulations made thereunder.

(d) The police, who are not " employees " at all, but are appointed by and subject to dismissal by the local police authority (Metropolitan Police Commissioner in case of the metropolis) and subject to central administrative control by the Home Secretary.

(e) Employees of public corporations, e.g., the Post Office,[79a] British Rail, London Transport, British Steel Corporation, National Coal Board, etc.

141   Each of these categories is subject to certain special legal rules. For example, the remuneration and conditions of health service employees are governed by statutory regulations binding on all employing authorities,[80] as is the remuneration of teachers.[81] The remuneration and conditions of police officers are also regulated by statutory provisions,[82] as is the question of discipline and dismissal in fire services.[83] A problem common to all these cases is whether an individual employee can enforce the statutory terms and conditions as part of his employment contract. The wording of the relevant regulations for the health service indicates that this is possible. In the case of teachers, the model agreement adopted by education authorities contains an express clause which makes this possible. The position is dubious, however, in relation to the police.[84]

142   In the case of those in Crown employment, the legal rules are to be found in the regulations and instructions issued by the Civil Service Department. There are also statutes applying specially to Crown employment, such as the restrictions on the employment of aliens,[85] and there are the rules of the common law.

In practice, those in Crown employment enjoy considerable security of tenure. In law, however, it has been a matter of doubt whether a civil servant has a contract of employment.[86] The balance of authority is now clearly in favour of the view that there is a contract,[87] and earlier cases [88] which had denied the right of a civil servant to recover arrears of pay must now be taken to have been wrong.[89] The contract is subject to an implied term that the civil servant is dismissable at any time at the will

[79a] Post Office employees now derive their status solely from contract and so cannot seek the protection of administrative law remedies: R. v. Post Office, ex p. Byrne [1975] I.C.R. 221; cf. Malins v. Post Office [1975 I.C.R. 60.

[80] National Health Service (Remuneration and Conditions of Service) Regulations, S.I. 1974 No. 296.

[81] Remuneration of Teachers Act 1965 and Remuneration of Teachers (Scotland) Act 1967. Terms other than remuneration are laid down by the Secretary of State in regulations of national application: Schools Regulations, S.I. 1959, No. 364, as amended. The general powers of appointment and dismissal of teachers are to be found in the Education Act 1944, s. 24 (1) (2); Education (Scotland) Act 1962, ss. 82, 85.

[82] Police Act 1964, ss. 44 and 46, Police Act 1969, s. 4, and regulations made thereunder.

[83] Fire Services Act 1947, ss. 17, 18, and 1959, ss. 5, 14, and regulations thereunder.

[84] This and related problems are discussed in B. A. Hepple and P. O'Higgins, *Public Employee Trade Unionism in the United Kingdom: The Legal Framework* (Ann Arbor, 1971), pp. 150–151.

[85] Aliens Employment Act 1955.

[86] See generally S. A. de Smith, *Constitutional and Administrative Law*, 2nd ed. (London, 1973), pp. 192–196.

[87] Brandy v. Owners of SS. Raphael [1911] A.C. 413; Sutton v. Att.-Gen. (1923) 39 T.L.R. 294; Reilly v. The King [1934] A.C. 176; Kodeeswaran v. Att.-Gen. Ceylon [1970] 2 W.L.R. 456; Att.-Gen. for Guyana v. Nobrega [1969] 3 All E.R. 1604.

[88] e.g., Lucas v. Lucas [1943] P. 68.

[89] Kodeeswaran v. Att.-Gen. Ceylon [1970] 2 W.L.R. 456.

of the Crown, with or without notice.[90] Under the Trade Union and Labour Relations Act, however, those in Crown employment, like other employees, are given a right of appeal against unfair dismissal,[91] and most of the rights under the Employment Protection Act 1975 apply to those in Crown employment.[91a]

143 The Contracts of Employment Act 1972, the Redundancy Payments Act 1965 and much other protective labour legislation, however, does not bind the Crown either expressly or by necessary implication. It has been held that employees of area health authorities are not protected by legislation not binding on the Crown.[92] However, it has been held that the commercial nationalised corporations are not acting on behalf of the Crown and are not entitled to immunity from statutes not binding on the Crown.[93] Their employees, accordingly, are entitled to the protection of labour legislation like other " employees," unless expressly excluded.

Office-holders

144 The label of " office " is sometimes used to describe those in positions of authority in a variety of public and private institutions.[94] Historically the concept of " office " was distinguished from that of a " contract of service." There were public office-holders, with duties concerning the public, most of which were created by the Crown. These offices were included in the class of freeholds and could be bought and sold and were subject to the law of property. There were also private offices such as the steward and bailiff appointed by the lord of the manor. The proprietary rights attaching to these public and private offices was specially protected by the common law. In modern times many of those who are dignified with the title of " officer " are, on analysis, no more than employees and, as such subject to the same rights and obligations as other employees. Some legislation makes it quite clear that it applies to " officers "[95]; in other cases it is a question of mixed fact and law whether the officer is employed under a contract of employment or, where this is relevant, under a contract personally to perform any work or labour. There is little guidance in the

---

[90] *Shenton* v. *Smith* [1895] A.C. 229; *Gould* v. *Stuart* [1896] A.C. 575; *Riordan* v. *War Office* [1961] 1 W.L.R. 210; *cf. Reilly* v. *The King* [1934] A.C. 176, 179–180; *Rodwell* v. *Thomas* [1944] K.B. 596.

[91] Trade Union and Labour Relations Act 1974, Sched. 1, Pt. II, para. 33; see below, Chap. 16; the definition in para. 33 (2) excludes those in the armed forces.

[91a] E.P.A., s. 121, House of Commons staff are also protected: E.P.A., s. 122.

[92] *Wood* v. *Leeds Area Health Authority* [1974] I.C.R. 535 (technical assistant employed by health authority acting on behalf of Minister of the Crown, could not bring complaint under s. 8 of the 1972 Act). For the earlier position, see D. Foulkes, " Are Hospital Officers Crown Servants?" (1964) 114 New L.J. 703 and " Crown Servants in the National Health Service " (1965) 115 New L.J. 689, 703. Mr. Foulkes' discussion is based on the decision in *Pfizer Corporation* v. *Minister of Health* [1965] 1 All E.R. 450. Sched. 1, Pt. II, para. 33 (4) of the Trade Union and Labour Relations Act expressly provides that for the purpose of that Act employment by a national health service employer shall not be regarded as Crown employment.

[93] *e.g.*, *Tamlin* v. *Hannaford* [1950] K.B. 18.

[94] *e.g.*, Companies Act 1948, s. 74; Friendly Societies Act 1896, s. 36 (2); County Courts Act 1959, s. 201. There is an important category of elective offices, such as those in a trade union, where special protection against removal is granted by the courts: *e.g. Taylor* v. *N.U.S.* [1967] 1 W.L.R. 532; *Leary* v. *N.U.V.B.* [1971] Ch. 34.

[95] *e.g.* Income and Corporation Taxes Act 1970 (Schedule E tax chargeable on emoluments of any " office or employment "); Social Security Act 1975 (any person in an office, including an elective office, with emoluments chargeable under Schedule E is an " employed earner ").

case law as to the modern distinction between an officer and an employee but it is suggested that some relevant criteria may be whether the office is a permanent one, created by an enactment, which continues to exist whether or not it is occupied at any particular time; whether the holder is a member of the corporation in question; and whether there is some special statutory or common law method applicable to his removal.[96] The most important practical example is the director of a company who is an " officer " but may also have a service contract if he is a working director.[97]

[The next paragraph is 151.]

---

[96] *Forbes* v. *Eden* (1867) L.R. 1 Sc. & Div. 568, H.L., at p. 576. Most of the cases are concerned with vicarious liability which does not arise if the duties were performed in pursuance of a statutory duty, *e.g. Stanbury* v. *Exeter Corporation* [1905] 2 K.B. 838; but will arise if the duties are of a general nature, *e.g. Ormerod* v. *Rochdale Corporation* (1898) 62 J.P. 153. The suggestion by Lord Goddard in *I.R.C.* v. *Hambrook Bros.* [1956] 2 Q.B. 641 that a public officer does not have a contract must be regarded as erroneous. The criteria suggested here are among those proposed by Dr. Brian Napier in *The Contract of Service: The Concept and its Application* (unpublished Ph.D. dissertation, Cambridge, 1975) to whom we are grateful for permission to draw on his conclusions.
[97] Companies Act 1948, s. 184. See above Chap. 2.

CHAPTER 4

LEGAL MACHINERY FOR RESOLVING
EMPLOYMENT CLAIMS

Importance of voluntary procedures

151   Most disputes arising out of employment contracts are not processed through machinery provided by law. They are settled informally on the works or office floor between line management and the worker or his shop steward or trade union official. There is a wide diversity of company and plant procedures for dealing with matters such as discipline, redundancy and work practices. These procedures consist largely in tacit arrangements and understandings and in custom and practice. The distinction between disputes over the interpretation of existing contracts (disputes of right) and the negotiation of new concessions (disputes of interest) is blurred; often one kind of procedure will be used to resolve both types of dispute. The major advantage claimed for these informal procedures is their flexibility, but this very advantage carries with it an imprecision which makes it difficult to know what procedures are to be followed in particular circumstances. Even where workplace procedures take a written form, as one writer says, " they are seldom implemented in the precise form laid down." [1]

152   Although a growing number of disputes is settled through these workplace procedures, use is also made in some industries of national procedures for resolving disputes. Here, too, there is a great diversity of bodies: Joint Industrial Councils and similar institutions, Whitley councils, and direct negotiations between employers or their organisations and one or more organisations of workers. Each of these industry-wide machineries has its own disputes procedures. Again, the same procedure may be used to deal with disputes of right and disputes of interest. This is because of the prevalence of " custom and practice," which makes it difficult to distinguish between the interpretation of an existing unwritten and imprecise understanding and the claim for some new concession. Another reason is that collective agreements often run for an indefinite period; it is far easier to distinguish a dispute of right from a dispute of interest where an agreement runs for a stipulated period, because matters of interpretation would tend to be raised during the period, and new claims on its expiry.

153   The Code of Industrial Relations Practice lays down the essentials of a model procedure for settling disputes.[2] It describes two different kinds of dispute—those of right " which relate to the application or interpretation of existing agreements or contracts of employment," and disputes of interest " which relate to claims by employees or proposals by management about terms and conditions of employment." [3] The Code does not, however, define the different ways of dealing with the two different types of dispute.

---

[1] A. I. Marsh, *Disputes Procedures in British Industry*, R.C. Research Paper No. 2 (London, 1968), pp. 18–19.

[2] Code of Practice, para. 126.

[3] *Ibid.* para. 129. See too Contracts of Employment Act 1972, s. 4 (2) (below, para. 231), which requires employees to be informed of grievance and disciplinary procedures.

All it says is that arbitration, while it can be used to settle all types of dispute, is particularly suitable for settling disputes of right, and its wider use for that purpose is desirable. Moreover, where it is used, the parties should undertake to be bound by the award. We have already observed some of the impediments to the development of any clear distinction between the two kinds of dispute, but it is possible that there will be an increasing use of voluntary arbitration to settle disputes over matters such as the interpretation of agreements.

Parliament has followed an active policy of encouraging the growth of voluntary procedures for dealing with certain disputes of right. For example, the statutory rights and procedures in respect of unfair dismissal,[4] redundancy payments [5] and guarantee payments [6] may be replaced with approved voluntary procedural agreements when certain conditions are satisfied.

Statutory bodies in general

154   It has been said that " the success of the British legal machineries is to be measured by the infrequency with which they are used." [7] This is certainly true of those bodies set up to provide means of inquiry, investigation and voluntary arbitration. The thousands of cases dealt with each year by voluntary disputes procedures in industries, such as building, engineering and coal-mining, may be favourably compared with the relative paucity of cases brought before the statutory bodies. At the same time it can be said that some legal machineries are little used because of expense and ignorance. Even a claim in a county court for £40 damages for wrongful dismissal might result in considerable costs.[8] These might be recoverable from the defendant by a successful plaintiff, who might, in any event, be assisted by his trade union or the Legal Aid scheme. But not all plaintiffs are this lucky. When it comes to statutory claims before the industrial tribunals or National Insurance tribunals, there is no legal aid at all.[8a] This means that, unless a worker is made aware of his rights by a trade union or other organisation and given assistance by them, he is unlikely to make use of the available legal machinery.

Industrial tribunals

155   These were established under the Industrial Training Act 1964 to determine appeals by employers against levies imposed on them by industrial training boards. Subsequently a variety of other questions were allotted to them.

Their jurisdiction [9] is as follows:

---

[4] Trade Union and Labour Relations Act 1974, Sched. 1, Pt. II, para. 13. Below, Chap. 17.

[5] Redundancy Payments Act 1965, s. 11. Below, Chap. 18.

[6] E.P.A., s. 28. See Chap. 10.

[7] K. W. Wedderburn and P. L. Davies, *Employment Grievances and Disputes Procedures in Britain* (Berkeley, 1969), p. 160; O. Kahn-Freund, *Labour and the Law* (London, 1972), pp. 56 *et seq.*

[8] *Ibid.* p. 38.

[8a] However, the " Green Form " Legal Advice and Assistance Scheme may be used to give advice, write letters etc., and prepare a " brief " for the tribunal (usually not exceeding a cost of £25).

[9] Trade Union and Labour Relations Act 1974, Sched. 1, Part III, para. 16. For the commencement date of each jurisdiction, see Part II, under the relevant statute.

(a) under the Industrial Training Act 1964 (appeals against levies) [10];

(b) under the Contracts of Employment Act 1972 (questions regarding written particulars of employment under section 4) [11];

(c) under the Redundancy Payments Act 1965 (right to payment, amount of payment and employer's right to rebate) [12];

(d) under twenty-three statutes listed in sections 41 and 42 read with Schedule 7 to the Redundancy Payments Act (payments similar to redundancy payments for persons such as civil servants and employees of nationalised industries) [13];

(e) under the Docks and Harbours Act 1966 (disputes about meaning of " dock-work ") [14];

(f) under the Sex Discrimination Act 1975 (complaints of unlawful discrimination) [15];

156

(g) under the Equal Pay Act 1970 (disputes in respect of equality clause) [16];

(h) under the Local Government Act 1972 and Water Act 1973 (compensation to employees on reorganisation);

(i) under Schedule 1, Part III, paragraph 17 of the Trade Union and Labour Relations Act 1974 (complaint of unfair dismissal);

(j) under the Health and Safety at Work, etc. Act 1974, s. 24 (improvement and prohibition notices appeals) [16a];

(k) under the Employment Protection Act 1975, s. 27 (guarantee payments);

(l) under the Employment Protection Act 1975, s. 32 (medical suspension payments);

(m) under the Employment Protection Act 1975, s. 38 (maternity pay) [16b];

(n) under the Employment Protection Act 1975, s. 46 (maternity pay rebates);

(o) under the Employment Protection Act 1975, s. 54 (trade union rights);

(p) under the Employment Protection Act 1975, s. 57 (time off for trade union officials);

(q) under the Employment Protection Act 1975, s. 58 (time off for trade union members);

(r) under the Employment Protection Act 1975, s. 59 (time off for public duties);

(s) under the Employment Protection Act 1975, s. 61 (time off to look for work or training);

---

[10] Industrial Training Act 1964, s. 12.

[11] Contracts of Employment Act 1972, s. 8.

[12] Redundancy Payments Act 1965, ss. 9, 42, 44; under s. 11 tribunals also have jurisdiction in respect of disputes arising under collective agreements providing for redundancy payments if these have been granted exemption from the Act by the Secretary of State.

[13] Previously these disputes were referred to referees or boards of referees.

[14] Docks and Harbours Act 1966, s. 51.

[15] Sex Discrimination Act 1975, s. 63.

[16] Equal Pay Act 1970, s. 2, as substituted by Sex Discrimination Act 1975, Sched. 3.

[16a] See Industrial Tribunals (Improvement and Prohibition Notices Appeals) Regulations 1974 (S.I. 1974 No. 1925).

[16b] The enforcement of the right to return to work after confinement is through a complaint of unfair dismissal: E.P.A., s. 50.

(t) under the Employment Protection Act 1975, s. 66 (employee's rights on insolvency);

(u) under the Employment Protection Act 1975, s. 70 (refusal to provide written statement of reasons for dismissal);

(v) under the Employment Protection Act 1975, s. 84 (failure to provide itemised pay statement);

(w) under the Employment Protection Act 1975, s. 101 (protective award for failure to observe redundancy procedures) and s. 103 (claim for remuneration under protective award).

The Lord Chancellor has the power (not yet exercised) to confer jurisdiction upon the tribunals (under Employment Protection Act 1975, s. 109) in respect of claims for damages for breach of the contract of employment and other contracts connected with employment.

The regulations governing the tribunals [17] allow for the appointment of a President (a barrister or solicitor of at least seven years' standing) by the Lord Chancellor. The Lord Chancellor nominates a panel of barristers and solicitors (also of at least seven years' standing) from whom the President (or, since 1967, a regional chairman) selects a chairman for a sitting of a tribunal. Similarly, panels of persons have been appointed by the Secretary of State for Employment " after consultation with such organisation or association of organisations representative of employers or of employed persons as [he] considers to be appropriate," [18] and from each of these panels the President (or regional chairman) appoints a member to make up a tribunal of three.

157   The proceedings before tribunals are governed by regulations made in terms of Schedule 1 to the Trade Union and Labour Relations Act.[19] The Act provides for a right of representation by counsel or a solicitor or by a representative of a trade union or an employers' association " or by any other person whom he desires to represent him." [20] An award of compensation made by a tribunal may be registered, in accordance with regulations, and, if a county court so orders, be recoverable by execution issued from the county court, as if it were payable under an order of the county court.[21] Tribunals are bound by decisions of the superior courts and the Employment Appeal Tribunal (below), but no doubt should heed the warning given by the Court of Appeal to another tribunal, not to develop a rigid body of case law of their own.[22] Indeed, one of the frequently voiced criticisms of the right of appeal from their decisions to the ordinary courts has been that this severely limits their flexibility.[23]

Employment Appeal Tribunal

158   This Tribunal has been established to hear appeals on questions of law arising from the decisions of industrial tribunals under the Redundancy

---

[17] Industrial Tribunals (England and Wales) Regulations, S.I. 1965 No. 1101, as amended by S.I. 1967 No. 301. There are corresponding regulations for Scotland.

[18] Industrial Tribunals (England and Wales) (Amendment) Regulations 1971, S.I. 1971 No. 1660.

[19] Industrial Tribunals (Labour Relations) Regulations 1974, S.I. 1974 No. 1386 (Scotland S.I. 1974 No. 1387), as amended, see Chap. 22.

[20] Sched. 1, Pt. III, para. 24.

[21] *Ibid.* para. 25 (with corresponding proceedings for Scotland).

[22] *Merchandise Transport Co.* v. *British Transport Commission* [1962] 2 Q.B. 173, 186, 192–193.   [23] Wedderburn and Davies, *op. cit.* p. 274.

Payments Act 1965, Equal Pay Act 1970, Contracts of Employment Act 1972, Trade Union and Labour Relations Act 1974, Sex Discrimination Act 1975 and Employment Protection Act 1975, and from decisions of the Certification Officer under the Trade Union Act 1913, and the Trade Union (Amalgamations etc.) Act 1964. It may also hear appeals on questions of fact or law from decisions of the Certification Officer under section 8 of the Trade Union and Labour Relations Act 1974 and section 8 of the Employment Protection Act 1975 (listing and independence of trade unions). There is a further appeal on questions of law from decisions of the Tribunal, with the leave of the Tribunal or of the Court of Appeal (Court of Session in Scotland), to those Appeal Courts.[24]

The Tribunal consists of High Court and Court of Session judges (one of whom is President) and " appointed " members. The latter must have special knowledge or experience of industrial relations, either as representatives of employers or of workers.[25] It is a superior court of record with a central office in London but with power to sit at any time and any place in Great Britain. Appeals must be heard by a judge and two to four appointed members, so that in any case there is an equal number of persons whose experience is as employers' or workers' representatives. However, both parties may consent to a hearing before a judge and one appointed member. Rules as to representation and costs are the same as in proceedings before industrial tribunals.[26]

Appeals on questions of law under any of the other jurisdictions of the industrial tribunals are to the High Court (Court of Session in Scotland),[27] again with a further appeal to the Court of Appeal (Court of Session in Scotland) and thence to the House of Lords, but only with leave.

The civil courts

159 The ordinary civil courts continue to exercise a jurisdiction to the *exclusion* of the industrial tribunals in the following main respects:

(a) actions for damages in respect of personal injuries to any person or in respect of a person's death;

(b) actions for damages, injunctions (or declaration, the latter being available only in the High Court) arising out of the breach of a contract of employment;

(c) actions for any remedy arising out of the breach of a contract other than a contract of employment (*e.g.*, a labour-only contract);

(d) actions in tort.

The present limit on the jurisdiction of county courts is £1,000 in respect of actions in contract or tort, unless both parties agree that the court shall have jurisdiction for a greater amount. Any claim may be brought in the High Court, but a plaintiff who brings an action there which could have been instituted in a county court may find, if he wins, that he will recover costs only on the much lower county court scale.

---

24 E.P.A., s. 88.
25 E.P.A., s. 87.
26 E.P.A., Sched. 6. Employment Appeal Tribunal Rules 1976 (S.I. 1976 No. 322). See Chap. 22.
27 Tribunals and Inquiries Act 1971, s. 13.

160   A single High Court judge, usually sitting without a jury, hears ordinary actions. In addition, the Divisional Court is the major body through which judicial supervision is exercised over inferior legal bodies, keeping them within the limits of their authority (*e.g.*, by bringing up and quashing by certiorari, or by declaring invalid, a decision that is *ultra vires*, or by restraining by prohibition the performance or continuance of unlawful action, or by securing the performance of a public duty by way of mandamus). This supervisory jurisdiction could be invoked, for example, if an industrial tribunal failed to observe the rules of natural justice, that, if there has been a failure to give a proper hearing before an unbiased tribunal.[28] Appeals lie from the county courts or any Division of the High Court to the Court of Appeal (Civil Division) and, with leave, to the House of Lords.

Magistrates' courts

161   Apart from their extensive criminal jurisdiction, which may be important in regard to the punishment and remedying of offences relating to the employment of women and young persons and to the breach of certain other statutory duties, both stipendiary and lay magistrates continue to possess jurisdiction, rendered obsolete by inflation, in certain civil matters relating to employment. For example:

(a) under the Metropolitan Police Courts Act 1839 (disputes about wages for labour done on the river Thames where the amount does not exceed £5) [29];

(b) under the Apprentices Act 1814 (certain complaints respecting apprentices).[30]

Social security tribunals

162   In this book we are concerned with certain parts of the machinery for the determination of social security benefits related to employment. Rights to social security benefits (in particular unemployment and sickness benefits) are determined in the first instance by an insurance officer.[31] There is an appeal from his determination to a local tribunal and a further appeal to a National Insurance commissioner, whose decisions are final.[32] There is no further appeal to the ordinary courts, except by way of judicial review through the prerogative orders.[33] The Chief Commissioner may direct that an appeal involving a question of law of special difficulty should be dealt with by a tribunal of three commissioners, who decide by a majority.[34] Selections of the decisions of the commissioners are published as pamphlets and are on sale through H.M.S.O. Bound volumes are available once every four years. Unreported decisions are not infrequently relied upon by the commissioners, tribunals and insurance officers. These are available for

---

[28] For an introductory account of judicial review on these and other grounds, see S. A. de Smith, *Constitutional and Administrative Law* (2nd ed., 1973), Chaps. 26, 27.

[29] s. 37.

[30] s. 3.

[31] Social Security Act 1975, s. 97 *et seq.*

[32] In decisions C.S. 414/50 and C.S.G. 9/49 the Commissioner decided that his decisions would be binding on local tribunals and insurance officers.

[33] Above, para. 160; but not by way of declaration: *Punton* v. *Ministry of Pensions (No.* 2) [1964] 1 W.L.R. 226.

[34] Social Security Act 1975, s. 116.

inspection on request. Decisions are numbered in six series. Those relevant to employment are: U—unemployment benefit; S—sickness benefit; P—retirement pensions; I—industrial injuries benefits.[35]

The Supplementary Benefits Act (formerly Ministry of Social Security Act) 1966 established the Supplementary Benefits Commission to administer a system of supplementary benefits, in place of national assistance.[36] Supplementary benefits tribunals deal with appeals from decisions of the Commission on a variety of matters such as the entitlement to benefit and the recovery of payments made in certain urgent cases. A tribunal's decisions are conclusive: the only avenue for challenge being by way of the prerogative orders. Sittings are in private and rights of representation are limited.[37]

163 Mention must also be made of the determination of certain questions by the Secretary of State for the Social Services.[38] These include the question whether contribution conditions have been satisfied and as to the class of insured persons in which a person is to be included. The Secretary of State may appoint someone (usually a solicitor) to hold an inquiry and report to him. Any person aggrieved by his decision may appeal to the High Court (a single judge) whose decision is final.[39] The Secretary of State himself may refer a question of law to the High Court, and has power in some circumstances to review his own decisions. Selected decisions (numbered as M.) as to classification and insurability were reported and sold as separate pamphlets until 1958.

Advisory, Conciliation and Arbitration Service (A.C.A.S.)

164 This Service, originally established on a non-statutory basis from September 2, 1974,[40] is charged with the general duty of promoting the improvement of industrial relations and, in particular, of encouraging and extending collective bargaining,[41] and where necessary reforming collective bargaining machinery.[42] The Service is directed by a tripartite Council consisting of a full-time Chairman and nine others, three from among employers, three from workers' organisations, and three independent members.[43] The Service must report annually to the Secretary of State.[44]

The Service has seven principal functions:

---

[35] For a full explanation of the numbering and reporting of these decisions, see *Index and Digest of Decisions given by the Commissioner under the National Insurance Act etc.* (ed. E. Jenkins) (London 1964, with supplements).

[36] Supplementary Benefits Act 1966, s. 18.

[37] Supplementary Benefit (Appeal Tribunal) Rules, S.I. 1971 No. 680. An interested person is entitled to be accompanied by not more than two persons.

[38] Social Security Act 1975, ss. 93–94.

[39] The appeal lies in respect of points of law only. Accordingly, the court will be concerned only with the questions whether the Minister's decision contained a false statement of law *ex facie*, whether it was supported by no evidence, and whether the facts found were such that no person acting judicially and properly instructed as to the relevant law could have come to the determination under appeal: *Global Plant Ltd.* v. *Secretary of State for Health and Social Security* [1972] 1 Q.B. 139, at pp. 154–155 (*per* Lord Widgery C.J.).

[40] It now functions under E.P.A., s. 1 and Sched. 1. The whole of the Conciliation Act 1896 and the relevant parts of the Industrial Courts Act 1919 have been repealed: Sched. 18 to E.P.A.

[41] Defined in E.P.A., s. 126.

[42] E.P.A., s. 1 (2).

[43] E.P.A., Sched. 1, Pt. I, para. 2.

[44] *Ibid.*, para. 13 (1).

(1) *Conciliation in trade disputes* [45]

165   Where a trade dispute exists or is apprehended, the Service may offer to assist in bringing about a settlement either with or without the consent of the parties. The assistance may be by the use of the Service's conciliation officers " or otherwise " and may include bringing in outside help.[46] The traditional principle of the autonomy of collective bargaining institutions is respected: the Service must have regard to the " desirability of encouraging the parties . . . to use appropriate agreed procedures for negotiation or settlement of disputes." [47]

(2) *Conciliation in proceedings before industrial tribunals*

166   Conciliation officers designated by the Service are required to endeavour to promote a settlement of any complaint presented to an industrial tribunal in respect of unfair dismissal,[48] discrimination on grounds of sex or marital status in employment,[49] and the various statutory claims (to which others may be added) [50] under the Employment Protection Act 1975.[51] A conciliation officer must be kept informed of tribunal proceedings and proceedings may be adjourned to permit parties to avail themselves of his services.[52] An officer may be requested to intervene before a complaint has been presented [53] and he may intervene once proceedings have begun even in the absence of a request if he considers that he could act with a reasonable prospect of success.[54] In order to encourage free negotiations, evidence is not admissible in industrial tribunal proceedings of anything communicated to a conciliation officer in connection with the performance of his functions, except with the consent of the person who communicated it to the officer.[55]

(3) *Advice*

167   The Service may provide free advice to employers, employers' associations, workers and trade unions on industrial relations and employment policies.[56] It may also publish general advice.[57]

(4) *Inquiry*

168   The Service may inquire into an industrial relations matter either generally or in a particular industry, undertaking or part of an undertaking.[58] The findings and the advice given may be published but only

---

[45] Defined in T.U.L.R.A., s. 29. This definition is wider than the corresponding definition in the Industrial Courts Act 1919.
[46] E.P.A., s. 2.
[47] E.P.A., s. 2 (3).
[48] T.U.L.R.A., Sched. 1, Pt. IV, para. 26.
[49] S.D.A., s. 64 (this includes complaints in respect of breach of an equality clause under the Equal Pay Act 1970).
[50] E.P.A., s. 108 (2) and (8).
[51] E.P.A., s. 108 (2).
[52] Industrial Tribunals (Labour Relations) Regulations 1974 (S.I. 1974 No. 1386), para. 2 (4).
[53] E.P.A., s. 108 (4); S.D.A., s. 4 (2).
[54] E.P.A., s. 108 (3); S.D.A., s. 64 (2); T.U.L.R.A., Sched. 1, Pt. IV, para. 26 (2).
[55] E.P.A., s. 108 (6); S.D.A., s. 64 (4); T.U.L.R.A., Sched. 1, Pt. IV, para. 26 (5), and see *M. W. Grazebrook Ltd.* v. *Wallens* [1973] I.T.R. 258 (N.I.R.C.).
[56] E.P.A., s. 4 (1).
[57] E.P.A., s. 4 (2).
[58] E.P.A., s. 5 (1).

after sending a draft of the findings to the parties and after taking their views into account.[59] The Secretary of State also has the power to set up courts of inquiry under the Industrial Courts Act 1919, s. 4. These inquiries are designed to inform Parliament and the public about important disputes. Their findings (like those of the A.C.A.S.) have no legally binding effect.

(5) Codes of Practice

169   The Service has general powers to issue Codes of Practice containing practical guidance to promote the improvement of industrial relations.[60] In addition, the Service must, in one or more Codes, provide practical guidance on (a) the disclosure of information for purposes of collective bargaining [61]; and (b) time off for trade union officials [62] and trade union members.[63] Before a Code is issued or revised the Service must publish a draft and consider representations and must subject the Code to parliamentary scrutiny.[64] (The effect of a Code in legal proceedings is discussed in para. 95 above.)

(6) References to arbitration

170   Where a trade dispute [65] exists or is apprehended the Service may refer the dispute to arbitration by one or more ad hoc arbitrators (who are not officers of A.C.A.S.) [66] or to the Central Arbitration Committee (C.A.C.) (below, para. 171). At least one of the parties must request such a reference and all the parties to the dispute must consent.[67] Moreover, agreed disputes procedures must first have been exhausted unless " in the opinion of the Service, there is a special reason which justifies arbitration " as an alternative to the agreed procedures.[68] Awards of ad hoc arbitrators are published only if the parties consent.[69]

(7) Wages councils

171   The Service has miscellaneous duties in connection with wages councils inquiries, disputes of statutory joint industrial councils and the operation of the Wages Councils Act 1959.[70]

The Certification Officer

172   The functions of the former Registrar of Friendly Societies have been taken over by the Certification Officer appointed under section 7 of the Employment Protection Act 1975. He has duties connected with the listing and certification of independent trade unions and the monitoring of their annual returns and accounts.[71] He also exercises powers under the Trade

---

[59] E.P.A., s. 5 (2) (b).
[60] E.P.A., s. 6 (1).
[61] E.P.A., ss. 6 (2) (a), 17 and 18.
[62] E.P.A., ss. 6 (2) (b), 57.
[63] E.P.A., ss. 6 (2) (b) and 58.
[64] E.P.A., s. 6 (3), (5)–(9).
[65] Defined in T.U.L.R.A., s. 29.
[66] E.P.A., s. 3 (1). Another statutory function of ad hoc arbitrators is in disputes between employers' and workers' representatives on statutory joint industrial councils (s. 92 (2) (a)).
[67] E.P.A., s. 3 (1).
[68] E.P.A., s. 3 (2).
[69] E.P.A., s. 3 (3).
[70] E.P.A., ss. 89, 92, 96.
[71] E.P.A., ss. 7, 8, and T.U.L.R.A., s. 8.

Union Act 1913, approving the political fund rules of trade unions and dealing with complaints of discrimination against non-contributors to the political fund.[72] He handles complaints relating to amalgamations under the Trade Union (Amalgamations, etc.) Act 1964. Appeals from certain of his decisions go to the Employment Appeal Tribunal (para. 158 above).

Central Arbitration Committee (C.A.C.)

173　　This Committee has replaced the Industrial Arbitration Board (first established under the Industrial Courts Act 1919 under the name of the Industrial Court and later the Industrial Arbitration Board) as a permanent arbitration body maintained at state expense.[73] It is independent of the A.C.A.S. and is not subject to governmental directions of any kind.[74] The Committee consists of a Chairman and members, some with experience as employers' representatives, and others with experience as workers' representatives.[75] For each hearing the Committee is composed of the Chairman (or his Deputy) and such of the members as he directs.[76] Assessors may be used.[77] The Committee may sit in public or private [78] and where a unanimous decision cannot be reached the Chairman has the powers of an umpire.[79] The Committee must hear the parties (unless they consent to no hearing) and, in addition to being notified to the parties, decisions made under any of the Committee's statutory jurisdictions must be published.[80] The Committee may be asked to interpret its own awards.[81] It determines its own procedure and the provisions of the Arbitration Act 1950 (which is designed for commercial arbitrations) do not apply.[82] Like its predecessors the C.A.C. has no power to compel the attendance of witnesses to take evidence on oath or to punish for contempt. There is no appeal from its awards, but it is subject to judicial review if it acts in excess of its statutory powers.[83] Its main importance in relation to individual employment rights is that its awards usually take effect as terms of individual contracts of employment (see Chap. 8 below). The general practice of the predecessors of the C.A.C. was not to give reasons for their awards. The C.A.C. is likely to follow this practice, but in two of its statutory jurisdictions it is required to give reasons, namely: (a) when making a declaration on a complaint of failure to comply with an A.C.A.S. recommendation for union recognition,[84] and (b) when making a declaration stating whether it has found a complaint of failure to disclose information for purposes of collective bargaining well-founded.[85]

The main statutory jurisdictions of the Committee are:

---

[72] Trade Union Act 1913, ss. 3, 4, 5.
[73] E.P.A., s. 10 and Sched. 1, Pt. II.
[74] E.P.A., Sched. 1, Pt. II, para. 27.
[75] *Ibid.*, para. 14 (2). 　　　　　　　　　　　　　　[76] *Ibid.*, para. 17 (1).
[77] *Ibid.*, para. 17 (3).
[78] *Ibid.*, para. 18. 　　　　　　　　　　　　　　　　[79] *Ibid.*, para. 19.
[80] *Ibid.*, paras. 23 (2), 24.
[81] *Ibid.*, para. 23 (1). 　　　　　　　　　　　　　　[82] *Ibid.*, para. 26.
[83] There are ambiguous judicial dicta on this point as far as the " voluntary " jurisdiction is concerned: *R.* v. *Industrial Court, ex p. A.S.S.E.T.* [1965] 1 Q.B. 377; *R.* v. *N.J.C. for Crafts of Dental Technicians* [1953] 1 Q.B. 704. Presumably, if the A.C.A.S. referred a matter under s. 3 (1) (*b*) of the E.P.A. without the consent of all the parties or which was not a " trade dispute," for example, orders of certiorari or prohibition would be granted by the High Court.
[84] E.P.A., s. 15 (4).
[85] E.P.A., ss. 19 (4), 20 (2).

174 (a) under Schedule 11 to the Employment Protection Act 1975 (claim for extension of terms and conditions of employment) (below, Chap. 8);

(b) under the Fair Wages Resolution 1946 (claims for observance of fair wages and conditions and freedom of association by government contractors) (below, Chap. 8);

(c) under various statutes which provide assistance to industries or public authorities by way of grant loan, subsidy or licence (claims similar to those under Fair Wages Resolution) (below, Chap. 8);

(d) under the Equal Pay Act 1970, as amended by the Sex Discrimination Act 1975 (amendment of collective agreements, employers' pay structures, wages regulation orders and agricultural wages orders which contain any provision " applying specifically to men only or to women only ") (below, Chap. 11);

(e) under the Employment Protection Act 1975, s. 16 (application arising from non-compliance with A.C.A.S. recommendations for trade union recognition);

(f) under the Employment Protection Act 1975, ss. 19–20 (complaint and further complaints of failure to disclose information for purposes of collective bargaining);

(g) under the Employment Protection Act 1975, s. 92 (2) (disputes between employers' and workers' representatives on statutory joint industrial councils).

In addition the C.A.C. has an important " voluntary " jurisdiction, now embodied in the Employment Protection Act 1975, s. 3 (1) (*b*). Where a trade dispute [86] exists or is apprehended the A.C.A.S. may at the request of one or more parties to the dispute, and with the consent of all the parties, refer the dispute to the arbitration of the C.A.C. (The legal effect of the awards made under these various jurisdictions is discussed below, Chap. 8.)

Civil Service Arbitration Tribunal

175 This body does not owe its existence to any statute, but to a National Whitley Council agreement on arbitration in the non-industrial civil service. Between 1925 and 1936 the Industrial Court (as it then was) served as the arbitration body under this agreement, but it was replaced by this tribunal. Arbitrable claims are expressly limited to " emoluments, weekly hours of work and leave." Cases involving individual civil servants are expressly excluded (disciplinary matters being regulated by another procedure). Awards are published. A variety of other specialised arbitration bodies exist in the public services; and in the non-industrial civil service, the National Health Service, fire service, and local government services the Central Arbitration Committee is available for voluntary arbitration.

[The next paragraph is 181.]

---

[86] Defined in T.U.L.R.A., s. 29.

Part Two

TERMS AND CONDITIONS OF EMPLOYMENT

CHAPTER 5

FORMATION OF THE CONTRACT AND CONTINUITY OF EMPLOYMENT

The individual bargain

181　The basic requirement for an enforceable contract is that there must be an agreement supported by consideration. In the employment context the usual situation is that a promise to pay wages is "bought" either by the actual performance of work, or by a promise to work. The act or return promise constitutes the consideration. The promises on either side may be express or implied, and the exchange is invariably analysed as a process of offer and acceptance. In employment, the offer is usually made by the prospective employer, but it could equally be made by the employee. A recent House of Lords decision [1] illustrates that the offer need not be addressed specifically to each worker. It may be posted on a notice-board or otherwise addressed to a large group. The acceptance may be by word of mouth, or in writing (or both) or by conduct. For example, simply reporting for work may be construed as acceptance of the conditions offered. The actual moment at which the contract comes into existence may be important. For example, in *Taylor* v. *Furness, Withy & Co. Ltd.*,[2] a dockworker was given a letter by dock employers welcoming him to their employment and an identity card which he signed. Later the same day, it was discovered that his membership of the union had lapsed and the employers returned him to the Dock Labour Board which had allocated him to the employers under a statutory scheme. It was held that the employers had broken their contract with the worker. This had been formed when they handed him the documents.

182　The agreement must be sufficiently certain for the courts to be able to give it a meaning. The courts have, in recent times, shown a willingness to uphold even fairly ambiguous terms. For example, in *National Coal Board* v. *Galley*,[3] a promise to work "such days or part days in each week as may reasonably be required by the management" was held to mean that the men would work a reasonable number of days, and their refusal to work on Saturdays (which they had thought, when entering into the agreement, would soon become unnecessary) was held to be unreasonable and so in breach of contract.

The requirement of consideration means that a promise to perform gratuitous services is not enforceable. Nor will a volunteer be entitled to remuneration. So a quarryman who helped during the harvest, and was sometimes given beer and supper when the work was over, had no

---

[1] *McCreadie* v. *Thomson & Macintyre (Patternmakers) Ltd.* [1971] 1 W.L.R. 1193; *Lonmet Engineering Ltd.* v. *Green* [1972] I.T.R. 86 (N.I.R.C.).

[2] (1969) 6 K.I.R. 488, in which it was left open whether the "allocation" of the worker in itself constituted acceptance of a continuing offer by a registered dockworker to work for a registered employer.

[3] [1958] 1 W.L.R. 16; *cf. Flood* v. *Coates Bros. Australia Ltd.* [1968] 3 N.S.W.R. 646; *Farelee Motors (Gosport) Ltd.* v. *Winter* (1971) 6 I.T.R. 57. See below Chap. 10, regarding ambiguous terms about pay.

contract [4]; nor did an officer who had a "relationship of a spiritual character" with the Salvation Army. [5]

Variation

183   An employer may, after the employment has commenced, attempt to introduce changes in working conditions, gradings, rates of remuneration or other employment terms. The effect of this on the contract varies according to the precise circumstances. There are at least three possibilities.

(a) The change is made unilaterally by the employer after giving the employee lawful notice to terminate the existing contract. [6] In this case the change will be construed as an offer of re-engagement which the employee may accept, for example by reporting for work on the new terms.

(b) The change is made unilaterally by the employer without giving the requisite notice to terminate. [7] In this case the employer will be liable in damages for breach of contract. The contract itself will come to an end and the employee may accept the change as an offer of re-engagement.

(c) The change is made by mutual agreement between employer and employee, but without notice to terminate the contract. In this case the contract will be varied, provided either (i) the variation is supported by consideration (which may include compliance with a request to work on a different job); or (ii) the employee is estopped from asserting his rights under the original contract (for example, because his promise to work under new conditions has led the employer to reorganise working arrangements for other employees). In practice, it may be difficult to distinguish between these situations. The issue is important under various statutes which require proof of a "dismissal" as a condition for payment of compensation. In the context of the Redundancy Payments Act, the courts have recently asserted their dislike of an employer's attempt to make "use of the employee's willingness to work, and work for a lower wage" as a means of avoiding a dismissal and re-engagement which might result in a redundancy payment. [8] The courts will be "slow to find that there has been a consensual variation where the employee has been faced with the alternative of dismissal and where the variation has been adverse to his interest." [8a] In practice, however, a worker (*e.g.* one whose sick pay is reduced while he is absent from work) may be in no position to contest an unlawful variation.

Minors

184   At common law, minors (since 1970, those under 18) [9] have limited contractual capacity. A minor may always enforce an employment contract to which he is a party. But the general legal rule is that he is bound

---

[4] *Kemp* v. *Lewis* [1914] 3 K.B. 543; *Bromiley* v. *Collins* [1936] 2 All E.R. 1061.
[5] *Rogers* v. *Booth* [1937] 2 All E.R. 751; *Parker* v. *Orr* [1966] I.T.R. 488 (congregational minister).
[6] *e.g. Spelman* v. *George Garnham* (1968) 3 I.T.R. 370 (lesser hours).
[7] *Gresham Furniture Ltd.* v. *Wall* (1970) 5 I.T.R. 171 (lower wages). *Hill* v. *C. A. Parsons & Co.* [1971] 3 W.L.R. 995, 999, 1002.
[8] *Saxton* v. *National Coal Board* (1970) 5 I.T.R. 196; *Marriott* v. *Oxford & District Co-operative Society Ltd.* [1970] 1 Q.B. 186; *Armstrong, Whitworth, Rolls Ltd.* v. *Mustard* (1971) 6 I.T.R. 79. See further Chap. 14.
[8a] *Sheet Metal Components Ltd.* v. *Plumridge* [1974] I.C.R. 373, 376 (N.I.R.C.); *Shields Furniture Ltd.* v. *Goff* [1973] I.C.R. 187, 190 (N.I.R.C.).
[9] Family Law Reform Act 1969, ss. 1, 9.

by a contract of employment only if it is on the whole beneficial to him. He may be bound although some terms are to his disadvantage.[10] This has been extended to other contracts which enable a minor to earn a living, such as between a boxer who is a minor and the Board of Boxing Control,[11] and between an under-age author and his publisher.[12] In this, the courts have strayed a little from the original rationale of making minors liable, namely, that the contract enabled them to gain vocational experience, rather than simply to make money. There is, in any event, a need to show that the contract is " beneficial ": money gain seems, on recent authority, to be sufficient.[13]

185   These common law rules have been supplemented by many statutory restrictions on the employment of children, who are defined as those under school-leaving age (16, since September 1, 1972).[13a] The Children Act 1972 provides that the minimum age at which children may be employed is not affected by further changes in the school-leaving age and will remain at thirteen years.[13b] Children may not be employed in industrial undertakings, unless only members of the same family are employed there.[14] Nor may they be employed in any United Kingdom registered ship,[15] nor in any factory,[16] nor mine,[17] nor transport [18] (other than air transport). The employment of children in entertainment is strictly regulated.[19] Previously, local authorities had power to regulate the employment of children under the upper limit of school age, but this has now been replaced by an enlarged power for the Secretary of State to restrict their employment.[20] Local authorities have power to require information concerning children's employment and may prevent the employment of a child in ways or at times or for periods which are unsuitable in relation to that child although not otherwise unlawful.[21] The employment of children in the last year of compulsory schooling in work experience schemes is regulated by an Act of 1973.[22] Restrictions on the hours of other minors, described as " young persons " in legislation, are discussed briefly in para. 360.

Aliens and other non-patrials

186   Although aliens have full contractual capacity, there are a number of statutory restrictions on their employment. An alien may not hold a pilotage

---

[10] Compare, *Clements* v. *L. & N.W. Ry.* [1894] 2 Q.B. 482 with *De Francesco* v. *Barnum* (1889) 43 Ch.D. 165.
[11] *Doyle* v. *White City Stadium* [1935] 1 K.B. 110.
[12] *Chaplin* v. *Leslie Frewin (Publishers) Ltd.* [1966] Ch. 71.
[13] *Chaplin's* case (above), *per* Danckwerts and Winn L.JJ. at p. 95; *contra* Lord Denning M.R. at p. 88.
[13a] Raising of the School Leaving Age Order 1972, S.I. 1972 No. 444.
[13b] Children and Young Persons Act 1933, s. 18 (1).
[14] Employment of Women, Young Persons and Children Act 1920, s. 1. As to the duty of a factory occupier to give notice of employment of a young person to the local careers office, see Employment Medical Advisory Service Act 1972, s. 5.
[15] Merchant Shipping Act 1970, s. 51 (subject to regulations).
[16] Factories Act 1961, s. 167.
[17] Mines & Quarries Act 1954, s. 124 (applies to all females, and male young persons under 16), and s. 160.
[18] Employment of Women, Young Persons and Children Act 1920, Sched., Pt. II (definition of " industrial undertaking ").
[19] Children and Young Persons Act 1963, ss. 37–44 (under 16).
[20] Employment of Children Act 1973, s. 1.
[21] *Ibid.*, s. 2.
[22] Education (Work Experience) Act 1973.

certificate,[23] nor be employed in the civil service without certificate,[24] nor hold public office,[25] and is subject to restrictions in regard to military employment.[26] Any employment restrictions which by virtue of section 34 (3) of the Immigration Act 1971 and the Aliens Order 1953 applied to an alien who is a national of a state which is a member of the European Economic Community have been revoked.[26a] An alien promoting industrial unrest in an industry in which he has been bona fide engaged for less than two years is liable, on conviction, to up to three months' imprisonment.[27] These provisions are unimportant to the majority of immigrants to this country, who are, however, affected by the provisions of the Immigration Act 1971. All non-patrials (a term which includes aliens, many citizens of Commonwealth countries, and some United Kingdom citizens)[28] may, on being given leave to enter the country, have restrictions placed on their right to accept and change employment.[29]

Formal validity

187   There are only two types of employment relationship in which writing is essential to the effectiveness of the contract.

(a) *The Merchant Shipping Act 1970* requires an agreement, in writing, signed by both parties, for the engagement of a seaman on a ship registered in the United Kingdom. The provisions of the " crew agreement " and its form must be approved by the Department of Trade and Industry. Breach of the regulations is a criminal offence but, it is submitted, would not prevent the seaman from enforcing his rights under it.[30]

(b) *A contract of apprenticeship.* This is dealt with in Chapter 12. Under the Contracts of Employment Act 1972, the employer is obliged to provide the employee with written particulars of certain terms of employment. Failure to comply with this obligation does not, however, invalidate the contract itself. These provisions are discussed in Chapter 7.

Continuity of employment

188   In order to qualify for most statutory employment rights the employee must have a stated period of " continuous employment." For example, unless an employee has been continuously employed for at least two years there is no right to any maternity pay under the Employment Protection Act or redundancy payment under the Redundancy Payments Act[31]; the amount of any redundancy payment, as well as of a basic award of compensation for unfair dismissal, is measured according to his length of continuous employment[32]; he does not get the right to the statutory

---

[23] Aliens Restriction (Amendment) Act 1919, s. 4.
[24] Aliens Employment Act 1955, s. 1. The Civil Service Nationality Rule (see below Chap. 10) also restricts the employment of some British subjects.
[25] Act of Settlement, 1700.
[26] Army Act 1955, s. 21; Air Force Act 1955, s. 21.
[26a] Immigration (Revocation of Employment Restrictions) Order 1972 (S.I. 1972 No. 1647).
[27] Aliens Restriction (Amendment) Act 1919, s. 3.
[28] Immigration Act 1971, s. 2.
[29] *Ibid.*, s. 3 (1) (c). The immigration rules are contained in House of Commons Papers 1973, Nos. 79, 80, 81, 82 (as amended).
[30] Merchant Shipping Act 1970, s. 1. There are a number of special regulations relating to seamen.
[31] See Chaps. 10 and 18 respectively. - S 81 Emplt Protn. (London) Act 1978
[32] See Chaps. 17 and 18 respectively.

minimum periods of notice prescribed by the Contracts of Employment Act 1972, as amended, unless he has been continuously employed for the requisite period [33]; and he cannot complain of unfair dismissal, in most cases, unless he has 26 weeks' continuous employment.[34]

189 The method of determining whether an employee has been continuously employed is so set out in the first Schedule to the Contracts of Employment Act 1972, as amended by the Employment Protection Act 1975, Schedule 16, Pt. II, that there are many difficulties of interpretation.[35] However, we believe that the essential foundations of the concept of continuous employment can be understood as follows. One can regard " continuous employment " as having two elements. The first is *continuity of employment, i.e.* the existence of an employment relationship based on a contract of employment (or series of contracts of employment) over a period of time. The second element necessary to an employee being continuously employed for the requisite period is that he must have been credited with the requisite number of weeks, or *periods of employment.* For a week to count it must be a week during which the employee has been employed, *i.e.* has worked for 16 hours or more,[36] or alternatively, it must be a week for part or all of which the employment relationship was governed by a contract " which normally involves employment for 16 hours or more weekly." [37] This presumably has the effect that if the employee is off work due to sickness, provided his contract is one which normally involves him in working for 16 hours or more, he will be credited with that week. Special rules apply to protect the continuity of employment of an employee whose normal working hours are reduced below 16 but whose contract normally involves employment for eight hours or more.[38] In this case not more than 26 weeks count between any two periods of employment for 16 hours or more.[39] Moreover, an employee with at least five years' continuous service, governed by a contract or series of contracts normally involving eight hours or more weekly, can count, from the beginning of the employment, all those weeks normally involving eight hours or more but less than 16 hours weekly.[40]

190 The general rule is that if a week occurs which cannot be credited to an employee, then not only does that week not count as a period of employment, but also it destroys continuity of employment,[41] with the

---

[33] See Chap. 16.

[34] See Chap. 17.

[35] For a more sanguine view, see Grunfeld, *Law of Redundancy,* Chap. 7. The Schedule forms a comprehensive definition of what is continuous employment: *Lee and Utting* v. *Barry High Ltd.* [1971] I.T.R. 3 (C.A.). But since the Schedule is, in our view, unclearly expressed, we have set out *our interpretation,* rather than the precise words of the Schedule.

[36] C.E.A., Sched. 1, para. 3, as amended. Where an employee is required to live on the premises where he works, his hours are " the hours during which he is on duty or during which his services may be required " (para. 11 (2)).

[37] C.E.A., Sched. 1, para. 4, as amended; and see *Parkes Classic Confectionery Ltd.* v. *Ashcroft* [1973] I.T.R. 43, 44 (D.C.); *cf. Gascol Conversions Ltd.* v. *Mercer* [1974] I.T.R. 282 (C.A.).

[38] C.E.A., Sched. 1, para. 4A, inserted by E.P.A., Sched. 16, Pt. II, para. 14.

[39] *Ibid.,* para. 4A (2).

[40] *Ibid.,* para. 4B. Note, too, that an employee whose period of continuous employment has, at any time, been long enough to qualify him for a particular right does not lose the benefit of that qualifying period unless his normal working hours under his contract are reduced to less than eight hours weekly *and* he is employed for less than 16 hours in a week after he qualified for the right: para. 4C.

[41] *Ibid.,* para. 2.

consequence that any weeks credited to the employee towards the requisite period of continuous employment are wiped out and the employee has to start from week one all over again when he returns to work. There is, however, a presumption of continuity of employment,[42] and this applies, unless it is rebutted, not only where there has been one employer but also where there has been a change of employer.[43] The presumption is based on the premise that the employee does not know the details of a transfer of business but the owner knows and should be able to prove it.[44] Hearsay evidence produced by the employer has been regarded as insufficient to rebut the presumption.[45] It is necessary for the written statement under section 4 of the Contracts of Employment Act 1972 to include particulars of any period of continuity of employment with a previous employer which counts as a period of employment with the present employer.[46] The effect of this, or of any other representation made by the employer, would seem to be to estop the employer who made the representation of continuity from contending that there has been a break in continuity.[47]

191   There are, however, two broad categories of exceptions to the general rule we have stated. First of all there are weeks which are not credited but which do not have the effect of destroying continuity, so that after a return to work following such a week, although the employee cannot count that week as a period of employment he is still entitled to be credited with the weeks of continuous employment before work was interrupted. Secondly, there are weeks during which, although there was in fact no contract in existence governing the employment relationship, the worker is nevertheless entitled to have such periods (1) treated as not breaking continuity, and (2) counted as periods of employment.

Periods which are not credited but which do not destroy continuity

192   There are two situations where a week does not count as a period of employment but does not destroy continuity either:

(1) Any week during any part of which the employee took part in a strike, *i.e.* a five-minute strike will prevent that week being credited[48];

(2) any week during all or part of which the employee is absent from work because of a lock-out by the employer.

---

42 R.P.A., s. 9 (2).
43 *Evenden* v. *Guildford City Assn. F.C. Ltd.* [1975] I.C.R. 367 (C.A.).
44 *Ibid., per* Lord Denning M.R. at p. 373.
45 *Etherington* v. *Henry J. Greenham* (1929) *Ltd.* [1969] I.T.R. 226 (D.C.).
46 See Chap. 7.
47 *Evenden* v. *Guildford City Assn. F.C. Ltd.* (above).
48 It is perhaps worth noting that the complications which flow from the fact that strike action takes many different forms (see Chap. 1) have not been judicially considered. But the point should be made that it is likely that, if a strike took place after an un-equivocal notice to terminate, that continuity would probably be lost. The provisions of the Act regarding strikes were certainly based on the erroneous assumption that notice to strike means notice to suspend the contract, and therefore it may be that the provision of the Act which preserves continuity, which would otherwise be lost because the week on strike does not count as a period of employment, applies only to cases where the strike involves either a suspension or a breach of the contract. *Contra,* Grunfeld, *op. cit.,* p. 215. Further, it should be noted that the Industrial Court has held the *dismissal by an employer* of a striker does not destroy continuity of employment if the striker is subsequently re-engaged: *Bloomfield* v. *Springfield Hosiery Finishing Co. Ltd.* [1972] 1 W.L.R. 386. See also *Clarke Chapman & John Thompson* v. *Walters* [1972] 1 W.L.R. 378 and *McGorry* v. *Earls Court Stand Fitting Co. Ltd.* [1973] I.C.R. 100; [1973] I.T.R. 109 (N.I.R.C.).

Periods which count but during which there is no contract [49]

193   Certain periods may occur during which there is no contract in existence, but which may still be credited as periods of continuous employment, provided that the employee returns at some stage to the employment of the employer in respect of whom he has already been credited with so many weeks of continuous employment. These are any week:

(1) during all or part of which the employee is incapable of work in consequence of sickness or injury [50]; or

(2) during which the employee is absent from work on account of a temporary cessation of work [51]; or

(3) during which the employee was absent from work " in circumstances such that *by arrangement or custom* [52] he is regarded as continuing in the employment of his employer for all or any purposes " (italics added). This would apply, where, although the employee has been dismissed, there is a custom or agreement in the industry that if such an employee is subsequently re-engaged for, say, pension purposes or for seniority purposes he is to be treated as though he had been employed throughout;

(4) during which the employee is absent from work wholly or partly because of pregnancy or confinement. [53]

Change of employer

194   Where an employee has received and accepted an offer of renewal or of suitable alternative employment from another employer then, in certain circumstances, the period of employment with the old employer and the new employer are counted as a single period of continuous employment.

The main instances are as follows:

(1) If a trade, or business or undertaking is transferred the period of employment in that trade, business or undertaking at the time of the transfer counts as a period of employment with the transferee and the

---

[49] C.E.A., Sched. 1, para. 5, covers these cases.

[50] Such weeks may count up to a maximum of 26: para. 5 (2) as amended.

[51] " The decided cases have established that para. 5 (1) (b) poses three questions: was there a cessation of the employee's work or job, was the employee absent on account of that cessation, and (which is perhaps the most important question in this case) was the cessation a temporary one "; *per* Phillips J. in *Bentley Engineering Co. Ltd.* v. *Crown* [1976] I.C.R. 225 at p. 228. " Whether the cessation of work was temporary or permanent has been construed retrospectively from the time when the employee returned to his work in the light of all the circumstances of the cessation "—Grunfeld, *op. cit.*, p. 207, explaining *Hunter* v. *Smith's Docks Ltd.* [1968] I.T.R. 198, and *Fitzgerald* v. *Hall, Russell Ltd.* [1970] I.T.R. 1. The " work " is the work of the employee, rather than of the employer: *Fitzgerald* v. *Hall, Russell Ltd.*

[52] The words in italics have been interpreted as implying that the custom or arrangement must predate the absence from work. A subsequent agreement will not do: see *Murray* v. *Kelvin Electronics Ltd.* [1967] I.T.R. 622; *cf. Cann* v. *Co-operative Retail Services Ltd.* [1967] I.T.R. 649. The paragraph was found to apply when the employee was retained as a member of a pension scheme: *Wishart* v. *N.C.B.* [1974] I.T.R. 320; *cf. Southern Electricity Board* v. *Collins* [1969] I.T.R. 277.

[53] C.E.A., Sched. 1, para. 5 (1) (d), as inserted by E.P.A., Sched. 16, Pt. II, para. 15. Moreover if an employee returns to work in accordance with E.P.A., s. 49 (see Chap. 17), after pregnancy or confinement, every week of absence occasioned by pregnancy or confinement counts: *ibid.*, para. 5A.

transfer does not break continuity.[54] The business must be sold as a going concern, a mere sale of the physical assets of the business being insufficient.[55]

(2) If the employee is taken into the employment of an associated employer the period of employment with the old employer counts as a period of employment with the associated employer and the change of employer does not break continuity.[56]

(3) If on the death of an employer the employee is taken into the employment of the personal representatives or trustees of the deceased, periods of employment at the time of the death count as periods of employment with the personal representatives or trustees and the death does not break continuity.[57]

(4) If there is a change of partners, personal representatives or trustees who employ any person, the employee's period of employment at the time of the change count as periods with the new partners etc. and the change does not break continuity of employment.[58]

[The next paragraph is 201.]

---

[54] *Ibid.*, para. 9 (2). Note that R.P.A., ss. 3 (2) and 13 (2) (see Chap. 18), have no relevance to the computation of the period of continuous employment which depends entirely on para. 9 (2): *Lord Advocate* v. *De Rosa* [1974] I.T.R. 357 (H.L.).

[55] *e.g. Woodhouse* v. *Peter Brotherhood Ltd.* [1972] I.T.R. 263; but regard must be had to the substance rather than the form of the transaction so that where farm land and buildings are sold the business would necessarily be sold with it in a case of mixed farming: *Lloyd* v. *Brassey* [1969] I.T.R. 100 (C.A.); and see *Crompton* v. *Truly Fair* (*International*) *Ltd.* [1975] I.T.R. 114.

[56] C.E.A., Sched. 1, para. 10. " Associated employer " is defined in para. 10 (2). See Chap. 1.

[57] *Ibid.*, para. 9 (4).

[58] *Ibid.*, para. 9 (5). If the employee is employed by two persons as partners and then by one of them alone, para. 9 (5) is inapplicable because there is no partnership after the change. There is a new business. See *Harold Fielding Ltd.* v. *Mansi* [1974] I.T.R. 208.

CHAPTER 6

FREEDOM OF ASSOCIATION AND THE RIGHT TO WORK

Managerial freedom

201 FREEDOM of contract implies, as its correlative, freedom not to contract. Accordingly, it is a basic tenet of the common law that there is no legally enforceable right to work. As Lord Davey said in the House of Lords in *Allen* v. *Flood* [1]:

> "An employer may refuse to employ [a workman] for the most mistaken, capricious, malicious or morally reprehensible motives that can be conceived, but the workman has no right of action against him . . . A man has no right to be employed by any particular employer, and has no right to any particular employment if it depends on the will of another."

This is simply an application of the general principle of English law that the exercise of a right (in this case, not to enter into contractual relations) will not be rendered unlawful only because of the bad motives of the person exercising that right. There are advocates of a new legal rule which would render unlawful all intentionally inflicted harm, unless justified.[2] This would give rise to a legal remedy for those refused a job for ulterior motives of the kind mentioned by Lord Davey. However, so long as *Allen* v. *Flood* remains authoritative, this development is not possible at common law.

Workers' freedom of association

202 In the period of collective *laissez-faire* (see Chapter 1) it came to be recognised that the workers' defence against this unbridled freedom of management was the freedom to associate for trade union purposes. This freedom has been internationally recognised in the twentieth century, for example in Conventions Nos. 87 (1948) and 98 (1949) of the International Labour Organisation, in article 11 of the European Convention on Human Rights and Fundamental Freedoms, and in article 5 of the European Social Charter. (These are discussed in Chapter 20.) Governments in the United Kingdom have accepted these obligations and have encouraged their own employees to join trade unions. Since 1946 the Fair Wages Resolution of the House of Commons has, in effect, recommended government departments to include in their contracts with suppliers a clause along the lines of paragraph 4 of the Resolution, that "the contractor shall recognise the freedom of his workpeople to be members of trade unions." A breach of this clause may be reported to the Secretary of State and, if not otherwise disposed of, he will refer the dispute to an independent tribunal which, in the past, was the Industrial Court set up under the Industrial Courts Act 1919 and, in future, is likely to be the

---

[1] [1898] A.C. 1. The only examples in the common law of refusal to contract being tortious are the cases of the common carrier and common innkeeper.

[2] Lord Devlin in his *Samples of Lawmaking* (London 1962), pp. 11–12, expressed the view that *Allen* v. *Flood* had "dammed a stream of thought that I believe would have had a beneficial effect on the law of tort," but added "there is no going back now."

C.A.C. It is a striking fact, however, that the clause has been used only eight times in 29 years and in every case the contractor has been found to be blameless.[3] The Industrial Court took the view that the Resolution covered only freedom to belong to a trade union and not the freedom to belong to the union of one's choice.[4] The Court also decided that freedom of association did not involve any duty to negotiate with trade unions.[5]

203   It was not until the passing of the Industrial Relations Act 1971 that a legal right to belong to a trade union was introduced in Great Britain. Section 5 of the 1971 Act, however, led to a number of clashes between trade unions and the National Industrial Relations Court because it also gave a legal right *not* to belong to an organisation of workers, and the right to belong was a right to belong to any registered trade union of *one's choice*. Since there was competition for membership and for recognition by employers between registered unions and organisations affiliated to the TUC, whose policy was not to register, some disruption of stable bargaining relationships was threatened by the operation of section 5 of the 1971 Act.[6]

204   The Trade Union and Labour Relations Acts 1974 and 1976 and the Employment Protection Act 1975 have laid the foundation of a *right* to associate out of three separate types of individual employment rights. Before examining these rights, it is worth noting that in one vital respect they are narrower than the rights conferred by the 1971 Act. The rights are conferred only on *employees*, whereas the rights under the 1971 Act were given to *workers*. The result is that not only are workers on the " lump " excluded (see Chapter 3) but also an employer still has the common law freedom, enunciated in *Allen* v. *Flood,* to refuse to *engage* a workseeker on grounds of his trade union membership or activities. In this respect the 1974–76 legislation has not gone beyond the proposals of the Donovan Commission [7] and, in our view, the United Kingdom must, in this respect be considered to be in breach of its international obligations.

205   The three individual rights are as follows. First, the dismissal of an employee by reason of membership of, or activities, at an appropriate time, in an independent trade union, are automatically unfair and " interim relief " to continue the employee's contract of employment until the case is finally determined may be obtained. (This is discussed in Chapter 17.) Secondly, " officials " and members are given the right to time off to participate in the activities of an independent trade union. (This is discussed in Chapter 10.) Thirdly, every employee has the right " as an individual " not to be penalised for, or deterred or prevented from, joining an independent trade union [8] or taking part in its activities at

---

[3] I.C. Award Nos. 2481, 2672, 3009, 3039, 3079, 3212, 3267. (We are indebted to Dr. B. Bercusson for this information from his unpublished paper on The Fair Wages Resolution 1946.)

[4] I.C. Award 3009.

[5] I.C. Awards 3039, 3071, 3212.

[6] See in particular *Post Office* v. *Union of Post Office Workers* [1974] I.C.R. 378 (H.L.); *cf. Howle* v.*G.E.C. Power Engineering Ltd.* [1974] I.C.R. 13 (N.I.R.C.).

[7] Report of the Royal Commission on Trade Unions & Employers' Assns., Cmnd. 3623, 1968, paras. 213–215, 242–252, which pointed out various instances in which the so-called " yellow-dog " contract persists.

[8] Defined in E.P.A., s. 126, which refers to T.U.L.R.A., s. 30 (1). See Chap. 1.

an appropriate time,[9] by sanctions short of dismissal imposed by the employer.[10]

206   Some features of this third individual right should be noted. First, as has already been observed, it is a right limited to those with existing contracts of employment. It also excludes members of the police [11] and armed forces.[12] Secondly, there is not an unlimited right to belong to the trade union of one's choice. It must be an independent trade union (and so not a special register body or employer-dominated "house union "),[13] and where it is "the practice" for employees to belong to a specified independent trade union or unions, under a "union membership agreement" it must be that trade union or one of those unions.[14] If there is no "union membership agreement" then, it appears, the employee has freedom of choice among all independent trade unions and does not have to show that the union which he seeks to join or in whose activities he wishes to participate is the union recognised for collective bargaining by his employer.

207   A third point to note is that the right is one against the employer only, and not against a trade union exerting pressure on the employer to penalise the employee for membership or activities in another union.[15] No account is to be taken of the pressure put on the employer by workers,[16] and the burden is on the employer to prove the purpose of his penalising the employee and that it did not contravene the Act.[17] The employee's remedy is to make a complaint to an industrial tribunal within three months of the act complained of.[18] The tribunal may grant a declaration and also award compensation. The tribunal must have regard, in assessing compensation, not only to the loss sustained but also to "the infringement of the complainant's rights" (a statutory penalty of unspecified amount).[19]

Right not to belong

208   The Benthamite reformers who secured some protection for freedom of association in 1825 were firmly of the view that this freedom was

---

[9] Defined, in similar terms to the Industrial Relations Act 1971 definition, in E.P.A., s. 53 (2); see *Post Office* v. *U.P.W.* [1974] I.C.R. 378 at pp. 398–399. In effect this limits the right to participate in activities to time outside working hours, or times when the employee is on his employer's premises with permission but not required to be *at work* (*e.g.* tea breaks). While he is at work the employer's permission is required.

[10] E.P.A., s. 53 (1).

[11] The Police Act 1964, s. 47, makes it unlawful for a member of a police force to belong to any trade union. In exceptional circumstances a person who belonged to a union before joining the police may be permitted to continue (s. 47 (1)). Certain classes of employee are excluded from the protection of s. 53: the husband or wife of an employer (s. 119 (2)), share fishermen (s. 119 (4)), those ordinarily working outside G.B. (s. 119 (5)).

[12] E.P.A., s. 121 (3).

[13] See Chap. 1.

[14] E.P.A., s. 53 (4). The meaning of a "union membership agreement" for purposes of s. 53 (3) and (5) is as defined in T.U.L.R.A., s. 30 (1). The new definition was to some extent anticipated by E.P.A., s. 126 (4), which was passed before the T.U.L.R.A.(Amdt.). See the discussion of the corresponding provisions of T.U.L.R.A., Sched. 1, para. 6 (5), on unfair dismissal in Chap. 17.

[15] E.P.A., s. 53 (1).

[16] ss. 55 (2) and 56 (4).

[17] *Ibid.*, s. 55 (1).

[18] *Ibid.*, s. 54.

[19] *Ibid.*, s. 56 (1), but the amount may be reduced for contributory action of the employee: s. 56 (5).

tolerable only if there was also a freedom not to associate. The 1971 Act accepted this doctrine and established a legal right not to belong. The legislation of 1974–76, however, grants only two legally protected rights not to belong. First, there is a right for an employee not to be compelled to be or to become a member of a trade union which is not independent.[20] Secondly, an employee who genuinely objects on grounds of religious belief to being a member of any trade union whatsoever is protected from compulsion by an employer to join.[21] Other " conscientious " objectors are not protected. Nor is there any remedy under the legislation against trade unions exerting pressure on workers to join.

209   Some attempts have been made, notably by Lord Denning M.R., to create a legal " right to work " in the situation where a professional body or trade union controls the right of entry to a profession or trade. The difficulty which the applicant for membership faces, if he is blackballed by the organisation, is that he cannot establish that any legal right of his has been infringed. No tort has been committed (thanks to *Allen* v. *Flood*) unless there is a conspiracy to use unlawful means (*e.g.*, violence or a threat to break contracts). So long as the organisation is pursuing what it conceives to be its own legitimate interests there will be no tortious conspiracy to injure the work-seeker. Nor will the work-seeker be able to establish a breach of contract by the organisation if he is not yet a member of it. In *Nagle* v. *Feilden*,[22] these difficulties were overcome. It was held that a declaration could be granted to a woman trainer that the unwritten rule of the Jockey Club (which controls horseracing on the flat) of refusing to grant licences to women was void as in restraint of trade. This has been criticised as bad law, because adhering to an unlawful restraint is not itself a legal wrong. And it is difficult to reconcile with an earlier House of Lords decision in which it was held that the London Stock Exchange was entitled to exercise a discretion " honestly and in good faith " to refuse a broker readmission on grounds of his German origin.[23] In any event, it seemed that *Nagle* v. *Feilden* could have little effect on trade union closed shops because, since 1871, statute has expressly protected them from the doctrines of restraint of trade.[24] Nevertheless in *Edwards* v. *S.O.G.A.T.*[25] Lord Denning asserted that all union rules which impose " an unwarranted encroachment on the right to work " are *ultra vires* and void. The statutory protection was said to be inapplicable because, according to Sachs L.J., " it cannot be that a rule which enabled such capricious and despotic action is proper to the 'purposes' of this or indeed any trade union." This blatant judicial legislation runs counter to an earlier House of Lords decision, virtually

---

[20] E.P.A., s. 53 (1) (c).

[21] *Ibid.*, s. 53 (6).

[22] [1966] 2 Q.B. 633. The action was eventually settled on the basis that the trainer was granted her licence, but the " absolute and unfettered discretion " to refuse a woman a licence was to be retained.

[23] *Weinberger* v. *Inglis* [1919] A.C. 606. This conduct might now be unlawful by virtue of the Race Relations Act 1968, s. 4.

[24] Trade Union Act 1871, s. 3; now Trade Union and Labour Relations Act 1974, ss. 2 (5) (trade unions) and 3 (5) (employers' associations).

[25] [1971] Ch. 354, 376, 382.

ignored by Lord Denning and distinguished by Sachs L.J., which denied the courts the power to strike down union eligibility rules on grounds of unreasonableness or as being in unlawful restraint of trade.[26]

210   The novel dicta in *Edwards* v. *S.O.G.A.T.* have now been blocked by section 2 (5) and 3 (5) of the Trade Union and Labour Relations Act 1974, which protect not only the purposes but also the *rules* of a trade union or unincorporated employers' association [27] from the doctrine of restraint of trade.[28]

Statutory restrictions

211   The attempted restrictions on trade union control over job entry have not been matched by similar limitations on the employer's freedom to refuse employment. Lord Davey's remarks are as true today as they were at the end of the nineteenth century. There are only five noteworthy statutory controls over the power of capital in labour recruitment.

(a) *The Disabled Persons (Employment) Act 1944* obliges an employer who has more than a certain number of employees (usually 20) to employ a quota of 3 per cent. or more handicapped persons and reserves certain vacancies such as lift attendants and car park attendants for the disabled. The quota may be reduced with special permission and, under section 11, a special permit may be obtained to employ less than the quota of disabled persons. Breach of the Act's provisions is punishable by a fine.

212   (b) *The Dock Workers Employment Scheme 1967*,[29] obliges a registered dock employer to employ a registered dockworker allocated to him by the Dock Labour Board. The scheme is designed to overcome the evils of casual labour on the docks.

(c) *The Rehabilitation of Offenders Act 1974*, makes it unlawful to exclude (or to dismiss) a rehabilitated offender from any office, profession, occupation or employment by reason that he has a conviction that is spent.[30] A conviction becomes " spent " after a period varying in length according to the gravity of the sentence (*e.g.* for a sentence of 30 days' imprisonment the rehabilitation period is 7 years). Where the sentence is imprisonment for life or for a term exceeding 30 months the conviction can never be spent. No civil remedy is provided by the Act for unlawful exclusion, so it would appear that the only remedy would be to obtain a declaration of unlawfulness. There is, however, no way of compelling the employer to engage the rehabilitated offender. The Act also relieves a rehabilitated offender of any legal or contractual obligation to disclose a spent conviction.[31] Since, it would appear, there is no obligation at common

---

[26] *Faramus* v. *Film Artistes Association* [1964] A.C. 925. The distinction drawn by Sachs L.J. between " eligibility " and expulsion rules is illogical, once the rule book can be opened. *Cf. Breen* v. *A.E.U.* [1971] 2 Q.B. 175, at pp. 189–190, 194–195.

[27] The terms are defined in s. 28. For purposes of s. 2 (5) this includes a body on the " specal register," and for purposes of s. 3 (5) a corporate employers' association, so far as their purposes relate to the regulation of relations between employers and workers. See Chap. 1.

[28] For the circumstances in which union purposes may not be in restraint of trade, see O. Kahn-Freund (1943) 7 M.L.R. 625.

[29] The text of the whole scheme is set out in Sched. 2 to the Dock Workers (Regulation of Employment) (Amendment) Order 1967, S.I. 1967 No. 1252.

[30] s. 4 (2).

[31] s. 4 (3).

law to disclose a conviction [32] (apart from a contractual undertaking to do so) the Act does not seem to make much difference in this respect. Moreover, the application of the Act has been severely limited by an Order made by the Secretary of State excluding a number of professions, offices and employments from its scope.[33] (The effect on unfair dismissal is dealt with in Chapter 17.)

(d) *The Sex Discrimination Act 1975*, makes it unlawful to discriminate on grounds of sex or marital status against a workseeker. (The Act is discussed in Chapter 11.)

(e) *The Race Relations Bill 1976* (replacing the Race Relations Act 1968) makes it unlawful to discriminate on racial grounds against workseekers and others. (See Chapter 11.)

The "right to work" discussed in this chapter must be distinguished from a possible "right," which it has been suggested arises as an implication of law in a contract of employment, of doing work when it is there to be done. This "right" is considered in connection with terms of employment, in Chapter 9.

[The next paragraph is 221.]

---

[32] *Hands* v. *Simpson, Fawcett & Co. Ltd.* (1928) 44 T.L.R. 295.
[33] Rehabilitation of Offenders Act 1974 (Exemption) Order 1975 (S.I. 1975 No. 1023).

CHAPTER 7

PROOF OF TERMS

Express and implied terms

221   The terms of the contract may be express or implied. Apart from those exceptional circumstances in which the contract must be written (Chap. 5), the express terms may be written or oral, or partly written and partly oral; they may even be established by conduct. The written parts may be embodied in various pieces of paper including correspondence, works rules, collective agreements or even the back of an envelope. However, even if the parties have drawn up a lengthy written contract, they will not have directed their minds to many matters. They may have omitted to mention some of these because they are governed by a collective agreement, arbitration award or wages council order. The way in which those " collective " terms become incorporated into the individual contract will be considered in Chapter 8. The way in which the employer's works rules affect the contract is dealt with below in paragraph 225. Apart from these matters, there are terms which will be implied into the contract in order to make the contract between the parties a workable one. These implied terms are sometimes treated as resting on the presumed intention of the parties, and sometimes as being duties imposed by the law. Those which will be implied into every contract of employment, such as co-operation, care and fidelity, have more of the appearance of general legal duties than those which necessarily vary from employment to employment, such as rates of remuneration, hours and holidays. Whichever theory is preferred, it is clear that implied terms play a vital part in shaping the contract of employment.

222   No less than four different approaches have been adopted by the courts in deciding whether to imply terms in particular contracts. First, there is the principle stated by Bowen L.J. in *The Moorcock* [1] :

> " What the law desires to effect by the implication is to give such business efficacy to the transaction as must have been intended at all events by both parties who are businessmen." [2]

This shades off into the second approach, that most clearly expressed by MacKinnon L.J. in *Shirlaw* v. *Southern Foundries Ltd.* [3] :

> " Prima facie that which in any contract is left to be implied and need not be expressed is something so obvious that it goes without saying; so that if, while the parties were making their bargain, an officious bystander were to suggest some express provision for it in their agreement, they would testily suppress him with a cry of ' Oh, of course!' " [4]

Thirdly, there is the so-called " status " approach. This was favoured by the House of Lords in *Lister* v. *Romford Ice and Cold Storage Co.*

---

[1] (1889) 14 P.D. 64.
[2] *Ibid.*, at p. 68.
[3] [1939] 2 K.B. 206.
[4] *Ibid.* at p. 227.

Ltd.,[5] when deciding (by a majority) to imply a term that an employer who was insured, or could reasonably have been insured, was nevertheless entitled to claim an indemnity from his negligent lorry driver who had rendered the employer liable in damages to a fellow-employee.[6] Viscount Simonds said:

> " We are concerned with a general question, which if not correctly described as a question of status, yet can only be answered by considering the relation in which drivers of motor vehicles and their employers generally stand to each other." [7]

Lord Tucker, in the same case, required " very compelling evidence " to add as an implied term " some quite novel term into the relationship outside the duties which have already been recognised in earlier cases." [8] This approach regards implied terms as general rules of law attaching to particular kinds of relationship. Although this at first sight appears to be more realistic than the invocation of the fictitious " intention " of the parties through the " business efficacy " and " officious bystander " tests, it does not necessarily yield any more satisfactory results. Indeed, the majority decision in *Lister's* case has been criticised by many as implying a term which ran contrary to the *actual* contemplation of motor-vehicle drivers and their employers, so much so that insurance companies have agreed not to act upon the decision in future without the consent of the employer concerned.[9]

223   Fourthly, the courts may accept as an implied term one which is proved as a custom. To constitute a custom it must be " reasonable, certain and notorious." For example, in *Sagar* v. *Ridehalgh,*[10] the Court of Appeal allowed customary deductions for bad workmanship from a weaver's wages. " A Lancashire weaver knows and has for very many years past known," said Lawrence L.J., " precisely what his position was as regards deductions for bad work in accepting employment in a Lancashire mill." [11] The question whether knowledge of the custom is required by the particular employee is uncertain. In *Sagar* v. *Ridehalgh*, it was said that knowledge was immaterial because the weaver had accepted employment " on the same terms for deductions " as the other weavers at the mill. On the other hand, in *Meek* v. *Port of London Authority,*[12] Astbury J., in refusing to imply as a term a usage that the employers were to pay their employees' tax for them, seems to have regarded it as important that when the employees entered the employment they had not heard of the usage, and that they had not contracted " on the faith and in consideration of " the existence of the usage. Perhaps the crucial, and distinguishing, fact about *Meek's* case was that the employees were seeking to impose the usage on the new employer to whom they had been transferred under the Port of London Act 1908. In *Sagar's* case the employee had joined an

---

5 [1957] A.C. 555.
6 Below, para. 278.
7 *Ibid.* p. 576.
8 *Ibid.* p. 594.
9 Below, para. 280.
10 [1931] 1 Ch. 310.
11 *Ibid.* at p. 336.
12 [1918] 1 Ch. 415 (affirmed [1918] 2 Ch. 96 on other grounds); *Petrie* v. *MacFisheries Ltd.* [1940] K.B. 93.

operating enterprise. In the latter situation, the courts will be more inclined to dispense with the requirement of knowledge and to hold that the employee must be taken to know of the local customs. By his conduct he may have led the employer to believe that he was accepting employment on the basis of those practices.

224   Finally, the optional nature of implied terms (including custom) must be stressed. A term will not be implied if it is contrary to an express term; and a custom may not be proved if it would be inconsistent with either an express or an implied term. These principles of the common law give a feature to labour law in England which distinguishes it sharply from other European legal systems. This is that, apart from statutory protection, there are no *imperative* terms in the legal relationship between employer and employee. In particuar, implied terms can always be replaced by express ones, even if these are less favourable to the employee. So individual bargaining may oust the results of collective bargaining. In practice, however, workers' organisations do not permit this to happen.

Works rules

225   Many employers issue their employees with a book of rules, or some other document, either at the time of engagement or subsequently. Some display notices at the workplace. These contain regulations which are often drawn up by the employer without the aid of collective bargaining. The rules laid down are frequently of a disciplinary nature, such as a right to " suspend " without pay or summarily dismiss the worker for a wide variety of offences such as bad timekeeping, drunkenness, gambling and other misconduct " likely to be prejudicial to the employer." The rules may prescribe methods of payment or mention restrictions, such as a duty to wear clean overalls or protective clothing, to work overtime as required, and not to engage in spare-time work. Grievance and disciplinary procedures may also be set out.

These rules may become part of the contract of employment on ordinary principles of contract law. First, they may be made *express* terms by requiring the worker to sign an acknowledgment, at the time of entering employment, that they form part of his contract. For example, the worker will be bound by the rules if he signs a document (even without reading it) which states : " I have read the foregoing rules and regulations and accept the conditions of employment as set out in this booklet." If the worker makes this acknowledgment only *after* the formation of his contract, he may nevertheless be bound by the rules either because his acceptance of them amounts to a " variation " of his contract (on which see para. 183) or because his conduct will estop (*i.e.*, preclude) him from denying that these rules form part of his contract (on which see further below, para. 236).

226   Secondly, they may become *express* terms of the contract, even without a signature, if reasonable notice of their existence is given to the worker. Three factors must be taken into account in deciding whether the notice given is reasonable. The first is the nature of the document. Would the ordinary reasonable worker regard the displayed notice or booklet as one likely to contain contractual conditions? Some examples may be given. A notice posted in a mill setting out the conditions relating to termination of contract and which workers had to pass on their way to work has been regarded as of a contractual kind.[13] So has a notice in a mill setting out provisions for sick pay.[14] A safety notice, requiring the wearing of spats by metal-spinners, was said, in one case, to be "almost compulsory." [15] The second factor is the extent of the steps taken to bring the rules to the notice of the worker. It seems that the illiteracy of the worker is immaterial,[16] and it is enough that a notice is displayed in a prominent place, or handed personally to the worker. It is unlikely that the handing of the notice or document to an official or shop steward of the union to which the worker belongs would be regarded as reasonable.[17] The third factor is the time at which the notice is given. For the rules to become part of the contract, notice of them must be given either before or at the time of the formation of the contract. It may be that a worker has been previously engaged by the same employer, and re-engaged on various occasions. If at some stage on one or more of these engagements reasonable notice of the rules has been given, the worker may be bound by them on a later engagement even without fresh notice, simply because of the long and consistent course of dealings between the parties. Moreover, despite these general principles about notice, there is always the possibility that, by acting on the rules for some time without demur, the worker may be held to have agreed to a contractual "variation" (above, para. 183) or be estopped from denying that they form part of his contract (below, para. 236).

227 Finally, some or all of the contents of works notices and rule books may become *implied* terms of the contract, in accordance with any one or more of the tests mentioned earlier. For example, the worker may be said to have accepted employment "on the usual conditions" (which would include the ordinary works rules) or the rules may be proved as a custom of the district or the works.[18]

228 It needs to be emphasised, however, that works rules are of so many different kinds that not all of them are contractual in character. For example, in *Secretary of State for Employment* v. *A.S.L.E.F.* (*No.* 2) [19] Lord Denning M.R. stated that the British Railways Rule Book 1950, "Rules for Observance by Employees," although signed by every employee, were "in no way terms of the contract of employment." They were "only instructions to a man as to how he is to do his work." The importance of this finding in relation to a work to rule situation is discussed in para. 225, above; in the present context its significance is that, if the rules are simply "instructions to a man as to how he is to do his work," they can be unilaterally altered by the employer without the need for consideration or the consent of the employee. The employee, on the other hand, is bound by the rules, as altered by the employer from time to time, because he is obliged to obey the lawful commands of his employer.[20] The elastic and

---

[13] *Carus* v. *Eastwood* (1875) 32 L.T. 855.
[14] *Petrie* v. *MacFisheries Ltd.* [1940] 1 K.B. 93.
[15] *James* v. *Hepworth and Grandage Ltd.* [1968] 1 Q.B. 94 *per* Davies L.J. at p. 106.
[16] *Carus* v. *Eastwood* (above, note 13) at p. 856; *James* v. *Hepworth and Grandage Ltd.* (above, note 15) at p. 103.
[17] This might be argued by analogy with *Morris* v. *Bailey* [1969] 2 Lloyd's Rep. 215 (notice of dismissal to union, not notice to individual employees).
[18] As happened in *Carus* v. *Eastwood* (above, note 13).
[19] [1972] 2 All E.R. 949 (C.A.), at p. 965, and *per* Roskill L.J. at p. 979.
[20] See para. 225, above.

varied nature of rule books makes it impossible to lay down any general legal principle as to when they will be construed as contractual in character [21] and when they will be treated simply as instances of lawful managerial commands.

Written particulars: Contracts of Employment Act 1972, s. 4

229 We have seen (Chap. 5) that, apart from exceptional cases, the contract of employment need not be in writing. Section 4 of the Contracts of Employment Act 1972 is a curious provision because it does not require a written contract. Instead it obliges the employer to provide the employee with a written statement identifying the parties, specifying the date when the employment began, stating whether any employment with a previous employer counts as part of the employee's continuous period of employment with him, and, if so, specifying the date on which the continuous period of employment began, and giving particulars of certain terms of employment. This written statement must be given to the employee not later than thirteen weeks after the beginning of his period of employment with the employer, and must reflect the terms of his employment as at a specified date not more than one week before the statement is given. In other words, the statement contains particulars of terms which formed part of the contract before notice was given.

230 The terms of which particulars must be given are set out in section 4 (1) [22] as follows:
  (a) the scale or rate of remuneration, or the method of calculating remuneration,
  (b) the intervals at which remuneration is paid (that is, whether weekly or monthly or by some other period),
  (c) any terms and conditions relating to hours of work (including any terms and conditions relating to normal working hours),
  (d) any terms and conditions relating to:
    (i) entitlement to holidays, including public holidays, and holiday pay (the particulars given being sufficient to enable the employee's entitlement, including any entitlement to accrued holiday pay on the termination of employment, to be precisely calculated),
    (ii) incapacity for work due to sickness or injury, including any provisions for sick pay,
    (iii) pensions and pension schemes,[23] and
  (e) the length of notice which the employee is obliged to give and entitled to receive to determine his contract of employment,

---

[21] In the A.S.L.E.F. case (above note 19) itself, two other rule books (the N.U.R. Conditions of Service, June 1959, and the A.S.L.E.F. Rates of Pay and Conditions of Service of Men in the Line of Promotion for Footplate Staff, 1972) were said to be " plainly incorporated " in contracts of employment, " in so far as any of the terms and conditions respectively contained in those books are, on their respective true construction, contractual in character." This was established by the written statements, issued to those members of staff under s. 4 of the Contracts of Employment Act 1963, which expressly referred to those conditions " which are contained in a series of agreements made with the trade unions . . ."; [1972] 2 All E.R. at pp. 977–978 *per* Roskill L.J.

[22] As amended by E.P.A., Sched. 16, Pt. II, para. 4. See, too, Code of Practice, paras. 60–61.

[23] This does not apply to statutory pension schemes which require such information to be given to new employees: Contracts of Employment Act, s. 4 (1), proviso.

   (f) the title of the job which the employee is employed to do,

   (g) (from April 1978) stating whether a contracting-out certificate is in force under the Social Security Pensions Act 1975.[24]

If there are no express or implied terms of the contract about these matters that fact must be stated.[25]

231   In addition, the Act[26] requires the statement given to the employee to include a note:

   " (a) specifying any disciplinary rules applicable to the employee, or referring to a document which is reasonably accessible to the employee and which specifies such rules;

   (b) specifying, by description or otherwise—

      (i) a person to whom the employee can apply if he is dissatisfied with any disciplinary decision relating to him; and

      (ii) a person to whom the employee can apply for the purpose of seeking redress of any grievance relating to his employment,

   and the manner in which any such applications should be made; and

   (c) where there are further steps consequent upon any such application, explaining those steps or referring to a document which is reasonably accessible to the employee and which explains them."

These are particularly significant innovations. Unlike the other particulars in section 4 (1) it is probably not open to the employer to say in his statement that there are no express or implied terms on these matters.[27] The aim is to encourage employers to establish clear procedures. The legal effect of giving a note to each employee will be to facilitate proof that these procedures form part of the individual contract.[28] In general, " the only purpose of section 4 is to ensure for the benefit of an employee that the terms of his contract of employment are set out in writing so that the employee knows his legal rights in terms of the contract and can, if need be, insist upon them by legal action against his employer." [29] But disputes as to the interpretation of those terms must be resolved by the ordinary courts.[30]

232   The obligation to specify disciplinary rules does not extend to rules, disciplinary decisions, grievances or procedures relating to health or safety at work.[31] These matters must be covered in the written statement of general policy regarding health and safety which every employer is required to prepare and bring to the notice of his employees under the provisions of section 2 (3) of the Health and Safety at Work, etc. Act 1974.

---

[24] Social Security Pensions Act 1975, s. 30 (5).

[25] *Ibid.* s. 4 (3).

[26] s. 4 (2), as amended by E.P.A., Sched. 16, Pt. II, para. 5.

[27] It is submitted that this is implicit in s. 4 (2) (*b*), otherwise there would have been no need for the draftsman to have treated the " note " under this subsection differently from the " particulars " of the contract under subs. (1). The Code of Practice, para. 120, supports this view.

[28] *The Darlington Forge Ltd.* v. *Sutton* [1968] I.T.R. 198 (D.C.) (tribunal may treat statement as evidence of contract in absence of objection). See, however, Trade Union and Labour Relations Act 1974, s. 18 (4), which restricts the incorporation of " no-strike " clauses; Chap. 8, below.

[29] *Owens* v. *Multilux Ltd.* [1974] I.R.L.R. 113 at p. 114 (N.I.R.C.).

[30] *Ibid.*

[31] C.E.A., s. 4 (2A), inserted by E.P.A., Sched. 16, Pt. II, para. 6. (The reference to para. (*d*) of s. 4 (2) is obviously a draftsman's slip since there is no such paragraph!)

233   The employer's obligation under section 4 extends only to those who are "employees" for the purpose of the 1972 Act,[32] and excludes those whose normal hours are less than sixteen (and, in some cases eight)[33] weekly. The thirteen-week threshold (above, para. 229) means that casual employees do not usually benefit from the section. Before 1972, an employee whose contract had been terminated could not seek enforcement of his rights under section 4,[34] but section 8 (8) of the Contracts of Employment Act gives the ex-employee three months from the date on which his employment terminates to do so.

Any changes in the terms of which written particulars must be given are required to be communicated[35] to the employee not more than one month after the change. If the employer does not leave a copy of the amendments with the employee, he must preserve the statement and make it reasonably accessible to the employee.[36] It is important to appreciate that any failure on the part of the employer to inform the employee of the change does not itself vitiate the agreed variation of the terms of the contract, which may have been oral.[37]

234   The terms of works rules[38] and collective agreements[39] may have become express or implied terms in the individual contract. Section 4 (5) of the 1972 Act facilitates proof of such incorporation by providing that the written statement may refer the employee to " some document which the employee has reasonable opportunities of reading in the course of his employment, or which is made reasonably accessible to him in some other way."[40] Section 5 (3) makes it unnecessary for the employer to notify the employee of subsequent changes in the terms of employment if he indicates, in advance, that those changes will be entered up in the " document " (*e.g.*, collective agreement). These provisions do not resolve all the problems of incorporation of collective terms, a topic fully examined in Chapter 7.

Effect of conflict between written statement and terms of employment

235   The written statement is supposed to reflect the terms of the contract at a specified date. From the employer's viewpoint this brings home to the employee his obligations; from the employee's viewpoint it provides him with detailed information on his rights.[41] The statement may be useful as evidence in subsequent legal proceedings between the parties, but it cannot be regarded as conclusive. Either party could adduce evidence to prove that the actual terms at the specified date differed from those in the

---

[32] s. 11 (1). See above, para. 125.

[33] C.E.A., s. 4 (8)–(10), as inserted by E.P.A., Sched. 16, Pt. II, paras. 8–10.

[34] *Fountain* v. *Simmons* (1968) 3 I.T.R. 343.

[35] Publication in a house journal may be deemed sufficient communication: *e.g. King* v. *Post Office* [1973] I.C.R. 120 (Post Office *Gazette*).

[36] Contracts of Employment Act, s. 5 (1) (2); *Grantham* v. *Harford* [1968] C.L.Y. 1384 (Woolwich County Court). Under s. 5 (4) a change in the name or identity of the employer is treated as a change of which notice must be given in accordance with s. 5 (1). At the same time the employee must be told when his continuous employment began.

[37] *Chant* v. *Turiff Construction Ltd.* (1966) 2 I.T.R. 380, 383.

[38] Above, para. 229.

[39] Below, para. 245.

[40] See *Camden Exhibition and Display Ltd.* v. *Lynott* [1966] 1 Q.B. 555 on the effect of such a notice.

[41] *Owens* v. *Multilux Ltd.* [1974] I.R.L.R. 113 at p. 114 (N.I.R.C.).

written particulars and failure to give an employee a written statement setting out changes in employment terms does not render those changes ineffectual.[42] However, Parliament has provided a special procedure to enable an employee to obtain a statement which is correct. This procedure was introduced in 1965,[43] in substitution for the criminal penalties originally provided in respect of a breach of section 4. The employee may complain to an industrial tribunal if no statement is given; and either employer or employee may refer the matter to a tribunal if a question arises as to whether the correct particulars, and any changes in them, have been given. The tribunal will determine what the particulars ought to be, but it has no powers to enforce its determination. It is not surprising, therefore, that very little use has been made of this enforcement procedure. The employee who wants convincing, although still not conclusive, evidence of his employment terms must first go to the tribunal and then, if he complains of a breach of those terms, to the ordinary courts.

236   The employer or employee who fails to have an inaccurate statement corrected may find himself at a serious disadvantage in subsequent legal proceedings. Although the written statement does not constitute the contract, reliance on the terms contained in the statement may give rise to an estoppel which prevents the employer from denying that they are the terms under which the employee was engaged.[44] In particular, an employer who states that a period of employment with a previous employer counts as part of the employee's continuous period of employment with him, will not be allowed to contend to the contrary.[45] Likewise, it would appear,[46] acceptance of the written particulars could give rise to an estoppel against the employee. So, for example, if an employee who is required by his terms of employment to give one week's notice to terminate his employment is given, without fault on the employer's part, a written statement which, incorrectly, states that he is to give four week's notice, his conduct in accepting the statement, if that conduct is relied upon by the employer to his detriment, may give rise to an estoppel and, in effect, preclude the employee from setting up his true contractual rights. Thus, it may be one of the remarkable effects of section 4 that the rights of the employee may be restricted if he fails to have inaccurate particulars corrected in good time.

237   Apart from estoppel there is another danger which faces the employee. If he *signs* a receipt for the document handed to him by his employer then, according to the Court of Appeal,[47] the document may be treated as a signed binding contract, and it will be the " sole evidence that is permissible of the contract and its terms." It is submitted that this decision of the Court

---

[42] *Parkes Classic Confectionery Ltd.* v. *Ashcroft* (1973) 8 I.T.R. 43 (Div.Court).

[43] Redundancy Payments Act 1965, s. 38 (as amended by Industrial Relations Act, Sched. 2, para. 4), now replaced by Contracts of Employment Act 1972, s. 8. There is a limitation period of three months from date of termination of employment: *Grimes* v. *London Borough of Sutton* (1973) 8 I.T.R. 217 (N.I.R.C.).

[44] As in *Smith* v. *Blandford Gee Cementation Co. Ltd.* [1970] 3 All E.R. 154.

[45] This seems to be the effect of the additions to the written statement by E.P.A., Sched. 16, Pt. II, para. 4, in the light of *Evenden* v. *Guildford City F.C. Ltd.* [1975] I.C.R. 367 (C.A.).

[46] See P. O'Higgins [1964] C.L.J. 220 for a fuller discussion.

[47] *Gascol Conversions Ltd.* v. *Mercer* [1974] I.C.R. 420. Unfortunately the reports of the case do not make it clear whether the document whose receipt the employee acknowledged was an offer of a new written contract governed by s. 6 (see below) or simply a new written statement. The distinction is crucial as regards the parol evidence rule.

of Appeal was erroneous. Only if the entire contract is *formed* in writing can the parol evidence rule be applied; the rule can have no application to the written statement under section 4, whether signed by the employee or not.[48]

Relation between other documents and written statement

238   We have seen (para. 234) that the written statement may refer the employee to " some document." There are, however, circumstances in which it is not necessary for the employer to provide a written statement at all. This is the case if the following conditions [49] are fulfilled :

(a) the employee's contract of employment has been reduced to writing in one or more documents containing the same particulars as are required in a written statement;

(b) there has been given to the employee a copy of the contract (with variations) or it is made reasonably accessible to him; and

(c) such note as is mentioned in section 4 (2) of the Contracts of Employment Act [50] has been given to him or made reasonably accessible to him.

If, however, there are later oral variations of his written contract, or he otherwise fails to fall within these conditions, a written statement will have to be given to him.[51]

[The next paragraph is 241.]

---

[48] See Hepple (1974) 3 I.L.J. 164 for a fuller discussion.
[49] Contracts of Employment Act, s. 6. The full text is not quoted here.
[50] Above, para. 231.
[51] Contracts of Employment Act, s. 6.

CHAPTER 8

THE INCORPORATION OF COLLECTIVE TERMS, AWARDS AND ORDERS

Nature of collective bargaining

241 Collective bargaining has been defined as "an institution for the joint regulation of labour management and labour markets."[1] The lawyer who comes to analyse the legal nature of collective agreements does well to keep this definition in mind. Collective agreements are not simply the collective equivalents of individual bargains. Collective bargains fulfil two basic purposes. First, they regulate relations between the collective parties, that is the employer or employers' organisation and the trade unions. These arrangements are usually of a procedural or constitutional nature (generically called *procedural* agreements) but they are of infinite varieties, sometimes defining specific stages of procedure to be followed for the resolution of disagreements, sometimes limiting or prohibiting industrial action until the defined procedure has been exhausted, sometimes setting up permanent joint machinery for the negotiation of terms and conditions of employment.[2] Secondly, collective bargaining is a means of regulating individual contracts of employment. This is usually done through *substantive* agreements which cover subjects such as pay-scales, working hours and holidays, shift-work and overtime, conditions of hiring (*e.g.,* limiting the number of apprentices, reserving certain skilled crafts or agreeing to "dilution" or "relaxation" of custom and practice in this regard), and a wide variety of other topics. Occasionally, collective agreements regulate the *procedures* to be followed by individuals with grievances, and section 4 (2) of the Contracts of Employment Act now require every employer to give his employees a "note" of such procedures.[3] In practice, of course, both substantive and procedural provisions (the latter relating either to the collective parties or to the individual employee or to both) may frequently be found in the same agreement, which may also include terms which cannot properly be classified as either procedural or substantive, *e.g.,* an obligation on every employer belonging to an Employers' Federation which is a party to an agreement to provide copies of the agreement to its employees.

Legal enforceability between collective parties

242 One must be careful not to confuse two separate questions. The first is the legal enforceability of collective agreements between the collective

---

[1] A. Flanders, "Collective Bargaining: a theoretical analysis", *Br.Jo.Ind.Rel.*, 6 (1968) 1, reprinted in *Collective Bargaining* (ed. A. Flanders) (Harmondsworth), (1969), p. 1 at p. 37. See Chap. 1.

[2] In 1965, the Ministry of Labour (as it then was) listed 500 pieces of negotiating machinery for manual workers alone, covering 14m of the 16m manual workers in Britain. It is estimated that 4m of the 7m non-manual workers in employment are covered by some sort of voluntary or statutory joint negotiating machinery. It will be noted that the total of 18m covered by machinery is considerably larger than the number (10m) who are trade union members. Most of the machinery has been established by voluntary agreement between the parties themselves, but some are the result of statutory obligations (*e.g.* teachers, and the nationalised industries). In some industries there is statutory minimum wage-fixing machinery (see Chap. 1).   [3] Above, Chap. 7.

parties. As we have seen, this will usually resolve itself into a question about the enforceability between the parties of procedural or constitutional arrangements. The second question is the effect of the collective agreement on individual contracts of employment. Occasionally, the courts confuse these questions, for example, by saying that the agreement will not be incorporated into individual contracts if it is simply a " gentlemen's agreement " between the collective parties.[4] The status of the arrangements between the employer and the union, however, is not relevant to the legal relationship between the employer and his individual workers. In paragraphs 244–253 we shall explain the various ways in which the terms of a collective agreement may become enforceable between the individual parties to the employment relationship, irrespective of the enforceability of the agreement between the collective parties. The enforceability of the agreement between the employer and union does not fall within the scope of this chapter. But, for the sake of setting the individual relationship in its context, we shall briefly mention the legal position in this regard.

243 The law governing the legal status of collective bargains now falls into three parts. First, certain collective agreements [5] made before December 1, 1971, or after July 31, 1974, are conclusively presumed not to have been intended by the parties to be a legally enforceable contract unless the agreement (a) is in writing,[6] and (b) contains a provision which (however expressed) states that the parties intend that the agreement shall be a legally enforceable contract.[7] (It should be noted that it does not necessarily follow that an agreement containing such a provision is a contract.) Secondly, there are those collective agreements [8] which were made between the dates mentioned above and which were conclusively presumed to be legally enforceable unless containing an express exclusion clause.[8a] Most agreements made during that period included such a clause. Thirdly, there are those agreements which are not " collective agreements " as defined by the Trade Union and Labour Relations Act 1974.[8b] These are governed by the common law. There is considerable uncertainty about the legal status of collective agreements at common law. There are now basically two views. The first is that they are not contracts because the parties thereto do not intend them to be legally binding.[9] The second view is that " collective

---

[4] e.g. Loman & Henderson v. Merseyside Transport Services Ltd. (1968) 3 I.T.R. 108, 112; comment by Wedderburn (1969) 32 M.L.R. 99; Gascol Conversions Ltd. v. Mercer [1974] I.C.R. 420, 425; comment by Hepple (1974) 3 I.L.J. 164.
[5] Defined in s. 30 (1) read with s. 29 (1) of the Trade Union and Labour Relations Act 1974.
[6] Trade Union and Labour Relations Act 1974, s. 18 (1). An agreement may be expressed to be enforceable in part only.
[7] Unlike the provisions of the Industrial Relations Act 1971, s. 34, it is not necessary for the agreement to be made in writing, a point which led to some difficulties in National Union of Bank Employees v. Mitsubishi Bank Ltd. [1974] I.C.R. 200, 207, 208, 210 (C.A.).
[8] As defined in the Industrial Relations Act 1971, s. 166.
[8a] Industrial Relations Act 1971, ss. 34, 35.
[8b] ss. 29 (1), 30 (1).
[9] This is based upon the views of Professor Kahn-Freund in his contribution to The System of Industrial Relations in Great Britain (ed. by A. Flanders and H. Clegg, Oxford, 1954), pp. 56–58. For a recent decision applying this view see Ford Motor Co. Ltd. v. A.E.F. [1969] 2 Q.B. 303. The reason given in respect of the agreements before the court in that case not being contracts was an absence of " intention to create legal relations." The decision has been criticised (i) on the ground that this requirement is not essential to the formation of a contract in English law (by B. A. Hepple, " Intention to Create Legal Relations " [1970] C.L.J. 122); and (ii) on the ground that it does not accord with several

agreements " cover so many different kinds of agreement that it is not possible to give a simple answer to the question, " Are collective agreements contracts? " Some agreements are in our opinion contracts. Some are not because they are either so vague and uncertain as not to be capable of taking effect as contracts, others because it is clear that the parties expressly or by their choice of language have indicated that they do not regard them as legally enforceable transactions. Finally, some collective agreements are not contracts because the legislative function they perform is not appropriate to the law of contract.[10]

Legal enforceability between individual parties

244   The terms of a collective agreement can come to be legally enforceable between the individual parties to the employment relationship in the cases which follow (paras. 244–253).

Agency

(1) Where the union, or its officers, act as the agent of their members or some of them for the purpose of making a contract on their behalf with a particular employer. The courts are reluctant to interpret the relationship of a union and its members as the relationship of agent and principal,[11] and in very few cases would it indeed be possible to establish that a union had the authority of its members for the purpose of making contracts on their behalf.[12] Where such is the case, however, the union can make contracts on behalf of its members and such agreements would be legally enforceable as between the individual workers and the employer with whom the union negotiated on their behalf. This is likeliest to occur where the number of workers involved is small.[13]

Express incorporation

245   (2) The individual contract of employment may contain an express provision to the effect that the contract is subject to the terms of a particular collective bargain or bargains.[14] The terms of the Contracts

---

earlier authorities (by N. Selwyn, " Collective Agreements and the Law " (1969) 32 M.L.R. 377). It should be noted that it is still open to a court, in a future case, to decide that at common law a particular collective agreement is legally enforceable between the parties, given the requirement of " intention to create legal relations," because the " climate of opinion " in relation to enforceability had changed or the parties had expressly or impliedly agreed to enforcement. Further consideration of this question lies beyond the scope of this chapter.

[10] See P. O'Higgins, " Legally Enforceable Agreements," *Industrial Relations Review and Report*, No. 12 (July 1971), pp. 3–5.

[11] *Holland* v. *London Society of Compositors* (1924) 40 T.L.R. 440.

[12] *Cf. Rookes* v. *Barnard* [1961] 2 All E.R. 825, where at the trial it had been conceded by the defendants that their union had made an agreement which was contractually binding on them. In the Court of Appeal Lord Donovan made the point that in the absence of such admission the court would have required positive proof that the union had the necessary authority to act in such a way as to bind its members. See [1963] 1 Q.B. 623 at p. 675. Alternatively, a trade union may agree with an employer what are to be the terms of an offer made by the employer to his employees. The terms of the offer are collectively agreed upon but become binding upon individual employees, not because the union is their agent, but only when each individual employee has accepted his employer's offer: see *Edwards* v. *Skyways Ltd.* [1964] 1 All E.R. 494.

[13] An example is *Deane* v. *Craik, The Times*, March 16, 1962; Wedderburn, *Cases and Materials on Labour Law* (Cambridge, 1967), pp. 286 and 459. There are hints of an " agency " approach in *Singh* v. *British Steel Corporation* [1974] I.R.L.R. 131 (Tribunal) (withdrawal of union's negotiating rights by workers).

[14] *National Coal Board* v. *Galley* [1958] 1 W.L.R. 16.

of Employment Act 1972, s. 4, requiring the employer to give a written statement to every employee containing the main terms of his contract or specifying some other document where such terms can be seen, have encouraged the reference to collective agreements.[15] It must be emphasised that the written notice is not the contract itself,[16] and may lawfully contain only terms which have already been agreed upon between the parties. In other words, the parties must have already agreed to the incorporation of the terms of the collective agreement in their contract. The employer cannot unilaterally alter the terms of the contract of employment[17] by referring to a collective agreement as embodying the terms of employment in the absence of such agreement.[18]

Implied incorporation

246   (3) If the contract contains an implied term incorporating the terms of a collective agreement, these terms are then legally binding upon the individual parties. The courts have been very ready to imply such a term since at least as early as the mid-nineteenth century.[19]

247   *Employee's knowledge.* The problem may arise as to whether it is necessary in order to imply the terms of a collective agreement into a contract that the employee should be aware of the content of those terms. The answer to this partly depends upon the way in which the court formulates the term to be implied into the contract. For example, if the court asks, " Was there a term in the contract that any terms not spelt out in the contract shall be filled out by the terms of any relevant collective

---

15 s. 4 (5) of the Contracts of Employment Act provides: " A statement under subsection (1) . . . of this section may, for all or any of the particulars to be given by the statement, refer the employee to some document which the employee has reasonable opportunities of reading in the course of his employment, or which is made reasonably accessible to him in some other way."

16 " The statement made pursuant to section 4 of the 1963 Act is not the contract "— *Turriff Construction Ltd.* v. *Bryant* [1967] I.T.R. 292 at p. 294. See above, paras. 229 and 238.

17 *Cf.* Lord Denning M.R. in *Camden Exhibition & Display Ltd.* v. *Lynott* [1966] 1 Q.B. 555 at p. 557: " In view of that notice these working rules are not only a collective agreement between the union and the employers. They are incorporated into the contract of employment of each man, in so far as they are applicable to his situation." This is not properly to be understood as giving the employer a right to add to the terms of an agreement already reached new terms by reference to a collective agreement; see the remarks of Lawton L.J. in *Gascol Conversions Ltd.* v. *Mercer* [1974] I.C.R. 420, 427.

18 Sometimes provision may be made in a collective agreement for the express incorporation *in the collective agreement* of works rules. Thus for example agreements drawn up under the auspices of the National Joint Council for Civil Air transport sometimes contain the following provision: " The regulations of the Employers concerning conditions of employment are deemed to be incorporated in this agreement." The effect of this would appear to be somewhat circular. If the employer's regulations are already part of individual contracts of employment this would appear to have no particular legal effect where the collective agreement itself in turn is incorporated in the individual contract. It may of course give greater authority to such regulations because they are seen to have the support of the employees' side of the National Joint Council as well as the backing of the employers. On the other hand, if for some reason the employer's regulations were not *per se* terms of individual contracts of employment, their incorporation into a collective agreement, which in turn may be incorporated into the individual contracts, is a long way round to the ultimate end of giving them legal status.

19 *Hill* v. *Levey* (1858) 157 E.R. 366. Watson B.: " For more than fifty years the business of printing in London, as between the master printers and compositors, has been regulated by committees of each body, who have from time to time agreed upon rules, which so long as they remain unaltered are treated and acted upon as binding between master and compositor, and *are incorporated into every engagement to which they are applicable* . . . " (italics added).

bargains? " there is no problem, because clearly the employee's knowledge of the particular terms of particular collective agreements is irrelevant. Alternatively, if the court asks, " Is there a custom in the industry that conditions of employment be regulated by collective bargaining " [20] it may arrive at different conclusions from those it would arrive at if it asked the question, " Have the terms of this particular collective agreement stood for so long and been so universally followed that they have become customary in this industry? " The formulation of the term to be implied into the individual contract is therefore a matter of some importance in relation to the relevance of the knowledge of employees as to the precise details of the content of particular collective agreements.

248   *Appropriateness of terms for incorporation.* There are problems, however, in respect of the incorporation of the terms of a collective agreement. In *Young* v. *Canadian Northern Railway Company* (1931) [21] for example the Privy Council said of the agreement in that case between a trade union and the railway company: " [This agreement] does not appear . . . to be a a document adapted for conversion into or incorporation with a service agreement. . . ." The question then of the appropriateness of the terms of a collective agreement for incorporation into an individual contract of employment sets a limit to the terms which may be incorporated. One may give three kinds of illustration where it may be difficult to incorporate the terms of a collective agreement into an individual contract of employment.

249   First of all, the collective agreement may contain an obligation which is essentially collective in its nature. The agreement may say " There shall be no strikes or lock-out until the procedure for the settlement of disputes has been exhausted." Can this be translated into terms of an individual obligation? If so, what is that obligation? Does this mean that an individual may never withdraw his labour as a means of putting pressure on his employer to improve conditions until procedure has been exhausted? But the procedure for the settlement of disputes may only be open to the union; an individual may not be able to use such procedure. Or does it mean that each worker promised not to withdraw his labour as a means of putting pressure on his employer in conjunction with his fellow workers who are simultaneously withdrawing their labour for the same purpose? What is clear, however, is that some obligations may not be translatable into terms of individual obligations. It must be noted that, in any event, there are now statutory restrictions on the incorporation of " no-strike " clauses (para. 253, below).

250   Secondly, certain terms of collective agreements may not be appropriate for incorporation into a contract of employment between John Brown, a worker, and Peter Smith, an employer, because the collective agreement

---

[20] *Cf. Maclea* v. *Essex Lines* (1933) 45 Ll.L.R. 254 at p. 257, where the court was willing to imply a term that employment " was upon the terms and conditions of the National Maritime Board and upon those conditions as they may from time to time be altered." Here absence of knowledge on the employee's part of the detailed content of agreements negotiated on the National Maritime Board would clearly be irrelevant. *Cf. Spring* v. *National Amalgamated Stevedores & Dockers Society* [1956] 1 W.L.R. 585. The court formulates the question notionally to be asked by the officious bystander as to whether the parties intended a *particular* agreement to govern the contract. See too, above, paras. 221 to 224 and *Joel* v. *Cammell Laird (Ship Repairers) Ltd.* [1969] I.T.R. 206; *Callison* v. *Ford Motor Co. Ltd.* [1969] I.T.R. 74.
[21] [1931] A.C. 83.

imposes an obligation upon a named person other than John Brown or Peter Smith. For example, the agreement between an Employers' Federation and the Proletarian Trade Union may state: " The Employers' Federation shall distribute copies of this agreement to its members." This imposes an obligation upon someone other than Peter Smith or John Brown, and the courts will not permit John Brown to sue Peter Smith because of the failure of someone else, the Employers' Federation, to fulfil an obligation of the collective agreement.

251 Thirdly, the collective agreement may confer rights upon some person other than John Brown or Peter Smith. Thus, the collective agreement may provide that the wages of foremen shall be £30 per week, and the wages of fitters shall be £25 per week. If John Brown is a fitter he may sue Peter Smith for failing to pay him, a fitter, £25 per week, but may John Brown sue Peter Smith, his employer, if the employer fails to pay Mary Green, a foreman, £30 per week? In one case at least an English court doubted if this would be possible.[22] In fact it is possible but the amount of damages recovered would be small. Still there is some doubt as to whether such a term as to the wages of a foreman may be incorporated into the contract of employment of any worker who is not himself a foreman.

There may be reasons therefore why the terms of a collective agreement cannot be incorporated into a contract of employment.

252 *Conflicting collective agreements.* Existing case law gives surprisingly little guidance with respect to the problem which may arise if there are several conflicting collective agreements applicable to the conditions of a particular employee.[23] In *Clift* v. *West Riding County Council*,[24] the claimant was paid in accordance with a local agreement as a result of which over a period of time he received substantially less in wages than he would have received had he been paid in accordance with a national agreement. The court decided that the local agreement prevailed. This could theoretically be justified on the ground that it was later in time; that by its terms it was intended to modify the national agreement. But no clear principle arises out of this case. In somewhat similar circumstances, where the local agreement would have had the effect of making the employee better off financially, it has been held that the national agreement prevailed, for reasons which are even more obscure.[25] Fortunately, some of the more sophisticated modern collective bargains do now make specific provision by their own terms as to what is to happen in case of conflict with other agreements. This of course would not be decisive, but it may help the courts.

253 *Incorporation of no-strike clauses.* The Trade Union and Labour Relations Act 1974 does not directly affect the common law rules we have outlined bearing upon the problems of the incorporation of the terms of a collective agreement into individual contracts. It does, however, define the circumstances in which one particular type of " procedural " clause

---

[22] *Barber* v. *Manchester Regional Hospital Board* [1958] 1 W.L.R. 181 at p. 186.
[23] See K. W. Wedderburn, " The Legal Force of Plant Bargains " (1969) 32 M.L.R. 99–102.
[24] *The Times*, April 10, 1964.
[25] *Loman & Henderson* v. *Merseyside Transport Services Ltd.* (1969) 4 I.T.R. 108. See also Wedderburn, *op. cit.*; *Gascol Conversions Ltd.* v. *Mercer* [1974] I.C.R. 420 (C.A.); Hepple (1974) 3 I.L.J. 164.

may be incorporated. Section 18 (4) of the Act of 1974 provides that any terms of a collective agreement (whether made before or after the Act came into force) which prohibit or restrict the right of workers to engage in a strike or other industrial action [26] or have the effect of prohibiting or restricting that right shall *not* form part of the individual contract, unless five conditions are satisfied: (1) the collective agreement must be in writing; (2) it must contain a provision expressly stating that such terms shall or may be incorporated into the individual contracts; (3) it must be reasonably accessible at the workplace and available during working hours; (4) each trade union party to the collective agreement must be independent [27]; and (5) the relevant individual contract must expressly or impliedly incorporate such terms into the contract. This fifth condition is particularly important because it means that the " translation " problem (*i.e.*, is this " appropriate " for incorporation) must, in each case, be answered affirmatively before the term may be incorporated.[28] The employer cannot contract-out of these provisions either with the union or the individual worker.[29]

Awards of joint negotiating bodies

254   Sometimes joint negotiating machinery is set up of a more permanent kind and the results of their proceedings, sometimes referred to as awards, are in effect collective bargains in another form. They may be incorporated into the individual contracts of employees in the ways indicated already.[30] Dependent upon the particular form of the machinery concerned, there may be problems as to when the awards or agreements settled by such bodies come to be incorporated into individual contracts. Thus in the public sector where such bodies tend to be advisory, in the sense that the implementation of their awards may, in accordance with some statutory provision, require the authority of some other entity such as the Treasury before it can lawfully be implemented, it may be difficult to incorporate the terms agreed upon by the negotiating body before the Treasury has given its authority.[31]

Arbitration awards

Under statutory jurisdictions

255   The Central Arbitration Committee may make an award that an employer observe certain terms and conditions of employment under its various statutory jurisdictions.[32] Any terms which an employer is required to observe in respect of an employee of his under Schedule 11 of the Employment Protection Act 1975 (extension of terms and conditions), section 16 of that Act (arising from non-compliance with A.C.A.S. recom-

---

[26] These terms are not defined. Presumably they include any form of concerted pressure on an employer. The section applies to " workers " (as defined in s. 30 (1) of the Act of 1974) and not only " employees."

[27] Defined in s. 30 (1) of the Act of 1974 so as to exclude employer-dominated or supported organisations.

[28] Above, para. 249.

[29] s. 18 (5).

[30] See paras. 244–246, above.

[31] See *Dudfield* v. *Ministry of Works, The Times,* January 24, 1964. *Cf. Brand* v. *London County Council, The Times,* October 28, 1967.

[32] Above para. 173.

mendation for trade union recognition) and sections 19–21 of that Act (arising from failure to disclose information for collective bargaining), have effect as part of the contracts of employment of those employees.[33] These terms have effect from the date specified in the award.[34] They may be superseded or varied by (a) a subsequent award of the C.A.C.; (b) a collective agreement between the employer and the trade union for the time being representing that employee; or (c) express or implied agreement between the employer and the employee so far as the agreement effects an improvement in any terms and conditions awarded by the C.A.C.[35] The C.A.C. may, in certain circumstances make an award when there is a wages council order, statutory joint industrial council order or agricultural wages order,[36] and in that event the employee is entitled to the composite rights taking whatever is more favourable to him in the award and order respectively.[37] Apart from this no award can be made where terms of employment are fixed by virtue of an enactment.[38]

Under voluntary jurisdictions

Where an *ad hoc* arbitrator or the Central Arbitration Committee acts under a reference made by the A.C.A.S. by virtue of section 3 of the Employment Protection Act 1975 (the so-called "voluntary" jurisdiction) the award can come to be legally enforceable between the individual parties to the employment relationship in any one of the ways set out in paras. 245–253 above. The same applies to any other type of "voluntary" arbitration.

Fair Wages Resolution

256   Although this resolution does not give direct contractual force to the terms of a collective agreement as between the individual employer and employee, it does help to encourage employers who are government contractors to comply with the terms of any applicable collective agreement. The Fair Wages Resolution passed by the House of Commons in 1946 [39] instructs any government department entering into a contract for the supply of goods or services with a private contractor to insert in the contract with such contractor certain terms, the most relevant of which for our purpose is a term imposing an obligation on the contractor to provide his workers with terms and conditions (a) "not less favourable than those established for the trade or industry in the district where the work is carried out by machinery of negotiation or arbitration" to which representative trade unions and employers' organisations are parties; (b) in

---

[33] E.P.A., Sched. 11, Pt. I, paras. 11, 16; E.P.A., s. 16 (7), and E.P.A., s. 21 (6) respectively. Note the difference between these imperative terms and the "implied" terms effect of an award under the former Terms and Conditions of Employment Act 1959, s. 8.

[34] Not earlier than the date on which the employer was first informed of the claim (Sched. 11, para. 10); and note the special limit in s. 21 (4) in disclosure of information complaints.

[35] See note 33 above.

[36] E.P.A., Sched. 11, Pt. II.

[37] E.P.A., ss. 16 (8), 21 (7) and Sched. 11, para. 12.

[38] E.P.A., ss. 16 (9), 21 (8) and Sched. 11, para. 13.

[39] For text of the Resolution, see Wedderburn, *Cases and Materials on Labour Law*, pp. 330–331. Government contracts now also include a clause prohibiting racial discrimination against employees. For proposals to extend the Resolution, see T.U.C. Reports. 1968, p. 433, and 1969, p. 147.

the absence of terms so established, then terms not less favourable than the general conditions observed by other similar employers in the trade or industry. Terms fixed by a national agreement have been held to be terms within (a) above, even though they are not in fact the terms being observed in the district.[40] Any complaint of the employer's non-compliance must be addressed to the department concerned, who in turn can, if they wish, raise it with the employer. If the employer contests the complaint the matter is referred to the Central Arbitration Committee. The Committee has no compulsory power here and merely advises the parties as to whether the contractor is fulfilling the terms of his contract with the government department, including the term relating to the terms and conditions of his employees. The only sanction to encourage a lagging employer to step into line with collectively agreed terms is that the government department may threaten to withdraw its business if the contractor does not give his employees the collectively agreed terms. The employer is obliged to display a copy of the Resolution at the workplace. Arguably, this makes the Committee's award a term in individual contracts.[41]

Statutory " fair wages "

257 Employers in certain industries which have received financial assistance from the state or which are dependent upon a licence from the state for their operation, are usually placed by statute under the same duty to comply with the standards laid down in applicable collective agreements as they would be if they were government contractors. The only difference is that a government contractor owes a contractual duty to the government department, whereas in the case of statutory fair wages the employer is bound by statute. In the case of statutory fair wages the enforcement machinery is essentially the same in most cases as the machinery under the former Terms and Conditions of Employment Act 1959, s. 8.[42]

258 An example of this system may be found in the film industry which in the past has received considerable financial assistance from the state. The wages and conditions of employment of those employed in the industry must be not less favourable than those which government contractors are required to observe. Any disputes must be referred by the Secretary of State to the Central Arbitration Committee for settlement. The Films Act 1960, s. 42 (2), goes on to provide:

"Where any award has been made by the [Central Arbitration Committee] upon a dispute referred to it under this section, then, as from the date of the award or from such other date, not being earlier than the date on which the dispute to which the award relates first arose,

[40] *Racal Communications Ltd.* v. *The Pay Board* [1974] I.C.R. 590, in which Griffiths J. remarked that " the passage of time has rendered the Fair Wages Resolution of 1946 out of date. If it became necessary to invoke it to secure its original objectives it would in many cases be an ineffective instrument." The I.A.B. has, however, adopted a different interpretation: *Desborough Engineering Co. and Mrs. I. Farral*, Award No. 3281 (1973); *Wickman Wimet Ltd. and A.S.T.M.S.*, Award Nos. 3282–3 (1973).

[41] *Cf. Petrie* v. *MacFisheries Ltd.* [1940] 1 K.B. 258, above, para. 226. But see *Simpson* v. *Kodak Ltd.* [1948] 2 K.B. 184.

[42] Films Act 1960, s. 42; Civil Aviation Act 1949, s. 15; Road Traffic Act 1960, s. 152; Road Haulage Wages Act 1938, Pt. II (all four of these Acts are amended by E.P.A., Sched. 16, Pt. IV, to substitute the A.C.A.S. for the D.E. in referring disputes to the arbitration of what is now the C.A.C.).

as the [Committee] may direct, it shall be an implied term of the contract between the employer and the workers to whom the award applies that the rate of wages to be paid, or the conditions of employment to be observed, under the contract shall, until varied in accordance with the provisions of this section, be in accordance with the award."

259 The last point is particularly interesting as it permits the terms of the collective agreement incorporated in the individual contract of employment as a result of the court's order or award to be varied and altered only by negotiation between the employer and " organisations representative of the persons employed."

260 The procedure is not always the same under the different statutes embodying a " fair wages " provision. Usually the person making the complaint must be a trade union, but sometimes an individual worker may complain to the government department. Sometimes the sanctions which may be imposed against an employer who is failing to comply with his statutory duty to comply with the relevant collective bargains are more severe than a mere award of the Central Arbitration Committee. Thus under the Road Traffic Act 1960, s. 178, a person employing workers in connection with public service vehicles may have his licence to run his transport enterprise revoked or suspended. Under the Road Haulage Wages Act 1938, either a trade union or an individual worker may complain; if the complaint is found to be true, not only may there be an award embodying the terms of the relevant collective agreement into the individual contracts of employment, and the employer's licence to run a road haulage business revoked, but the employer may also be convicted of the crime of failing to comply with the collectively agreed terms and conditions of employment.

Wage councils and statutory joint industrial councils orders

261 In employments covered by a wages council, statutory joint industrial council [43] or Agricultural Wages Board, orders laying down minimum standards of pay, holidays and other terms of employment operate to replace any inconsistent terms in the contracts of the workers to whom the orders apply. There is no power given to the parties to contract out of the minimum wages orders. Workers may sue for under-payment of wages for a period of up to six years; if criminal proceedings are brought against the employer, in addition to any criminal penalty imposed, he may be ordered to pay up to two years' arrears to his employees.

[The next paragraph is 271.]

---

[43] Wages Councils Act 1959 as amended by E.P.A. 1975, Sched. 7. The amendments enable the Council itself instead of the Secretary of State to make orders (a power previously exercised by the Agricultural Wages Board) and enables them to fix other terms in addition to pay and holidays, and to specify the date from which remuneration is payable. See para. 255 regarding C.A.C. awards when orders are in force.

CHAPTER 9

CO-OPERATION, CARE AND FIDELITY

1. CO-OPERATION

271 IT is incumbent upon an employer and employee to facilitate performance of their mutual obligations under the contract. This is a general contractual principle, particularly relevant to the employment relationship, which takes effect as an implied term in the contract.[1]

The employer's duty and the provision of work

272 An example is *Shindler* v. *Northern Raincoat Co. Ltd.*,[2] in which a managing director had a ten-year service contract with his company. The share capital of the company was acquired by another company which secured the passing of a resolution which removed him as a director, with the consequence that his tenure as managing director was automatically terminated. It was argued that he had no claim for damages for breach of his service contract because the articles of association of the company allowed a director to be removed in this way. Diplock J., however, held that there was an implied undertaking in the contract of employment that the company would not revoke his appointment. This duty would presumably be implied in any employment contract for a fixed term so as to prevent the employer from depriving the employee of the opportunity to perform his services. This does not mean, however, that the employer is under an obligation to provide work. " It is within the province of the [employer] to say that he will go on paying wages, but that he is under no obligation to provide work." [3] Of course, the provision of work where it is available may be part of the consideration moving from the employer in certain exceptional situations.[4] Three such situations are: (1) contracts, for example with theatrical performers, in which the consideration is a salary plus the opportunity of becoming better known [5]; (2) contracts with commission or piece-workers, in which the consideration is an agreed rate plus an implied obligation to provide a reasonable amount of work [6]; and (3) contracts with skilled workers to pay a salary and to provide a reasonable amount of work to maintain or develop skills. Suggestions [7] that " it is arguable that in these days a man has, by reason of an implication in the contract, a right to work " cannot be reconciled with the weight of authority, nor with other common law rules.[8]

---

[1] J. F. Burrows, " Contractual Co-operation and the Implied Term " (1968) 31 M.L.R. 390 for an account of the general principle.

[2] [1960] 1 W.L.R. 1038.

[3] *Turner* v. *Sawdon* [1901] 2 K.B. 653; *Collier* v. *Sunday Referee Publishing Co. Ltd.* [1940] 2 K.B. 647, 650.

[4] *Langston* v. *A.U.E.W.* (*No. 2*) [1974] I.C.R. 510 at p. 521 (*per* Sir John Donaldson).

[5] *Herbert Clayton and Jack Waller Ltd.* v. *Oliver* [1930] A.C. 209; *Marbe* v. *George Edwardes (Daly's Theatre) Ltd.* [1928] 1 K.B. 269.

[6] *Devonald* v. *Rosser & Sons* [1906] 2 K.B. 729; and see below, para. 324.

[7] *Re Rubel Bronze & Metal Co. and Vos* [1918] 1 K.B. 315, 324.

[8] *Langston* v. *A.U.E.W.* [1974] I.C.R. 180 (C.A.) *per* Lord Denning M.R. at p. 190, with whom Cairns and Stephenson L.JJ. hesitantly agreed (at pp. 192 and 193); see Hepple (1974) 37 M.L.R. 681.

Effect of failure to provide work on contract

273   In those situations where the employer is under a duty to provide work, the failure to do so will constitute a breach of contract. Such a breach may be construed as an instant termination (*i.e.*, a dismissal) if it is construed as a repudiation by the employer of his obligation to maintain the continuing relationship.[9] This, in turn, may have important effects on the employee's contractual and statutory rights (see para. 323 below). Where the employee is not provided with work for a prolonged period this may be the correct inference. In other cases of short-time working it may be more correct to analyse the situation as one of variation of the contract (where the employee has agreed to the change) or as one in which the contract subsists. In a few cases, where the reason for the failure to provide work is due to an occurrence (*e.g.*, destruction of the factory by fire) which substantially deprives the parties of the benefits of the contract, the situation may be regarded as one of frustration (*i.e.*, automatic termination) (see Chap. 14 below).

The employee's duty

274   The employee, as well, must not put it out of his power to do what he has promised to do. An example is *Learoyd* v. *Brook*,[10] in which a pawnbroker, having discovered that his apprentice was an habitual thief, refused to continue the apprenticeship. It was held that he was not liable in damages for breach of the apprenticeship deed because by becoming an habitual thief the apprentice had put it out of his employer's power to perform his basic obligation to teach him how to carry on a pawnbroker's trade honestly. Another example of an employee in breach of the duty to co-operate is one who refuses to travel to a site where the employer is able to provide him with work when, in the circumstances, it would be reasonable for the employee to do so.[11]

275   A group of cases which is traditionally dealt with as laying down an implied duty to obey the lawful and reasonable orders of the employer is probably also better understood, in modern times, as an example of the duty of co-operation. This would help modern courts to avoid treating nineteenth-century cases as laying down a rule that a single act of disobedience of a lawful order must entitle the employer to dismiss, and from engaging in question-begging discussions as to whether the order was " lawful." [12] An employee who refuses to carry out an order is usually making it difficult for the employer to perform his side of the contract. But whether this breach of the duty of co-operation gives rise to a right

---

[9] There is little direct authority, but see *Puttick* v. *John Wright & Sons Ltd.* [1972] I.C.R. 457 (N.I.R.C.).

[10] [1891] 1 Q.B. 431.

[11] Compare *Parry* v. *Holst* (1968) 3 I.T.R. 317; *Briggs* v. *I.C.I. Ltd.* (1968) 3 I.T.R. 276; *Murray* v. *Robert Rowe & Son (Rutherglen)* (1969) 4 I.T.R. 20; *Beale* v. *Great Western Ry.* (1901) 17 T.L.R. 450; with *O'Brien* v. *Associated Fire Alarms Ltd.* [1968] 1 W.L.R. 1916; *Stevenson* v. *Teesside Bridge and Engineering Ltd.* [1971] 1 All E.R. 296; *Mumford* v. *Boulton and Paul (Steel Constructions) Ltd.* (1971) 6 I.T.R. 76; *United Kingdom Atomic Energy Authority* v. *Claydon* [1974] I.C.R. 128.

[12] As in *Turner* v. *Mason* (1845) 14 M. & W. 112; and even in such modern cases as *Laws* v. *London Chronicle Ltd.* [1959] 1 W.L.R. 698 and *Pepper* v. *Webb* [1969] 1 W.L.R. 514 (in which there was a background of insolence and inefficiency). But *Wilson* v. *Racher* [1974] I.C.R. 428, 433, 434 emphasises that the duty is to maintain a co-operative relationship, including in a domestic situation some degree of courtesy.

to dismiss the employee summarily will depend on a variety of other circumstances, in particular the seriousness of the refusal. In other words, not every unco-operative act is necessarily a repudiation of the fundamental terms of the contract.[13]

Work-to-rule and go-slow

276   Certain forms of industrial action may, in some situations, be considered as a breach of the implied duty of co-operation. A go-slow is generally regarded as a breach " of an implied undertaking of the worker that, in so far as he is capable of doing so, he should work at a reasonable speed." [14] A work-to-rule may take many different forms, some of which, but not all, may involve a breach of contracts of employment. The Court of Appeal has stated that a worker is not bound to do more for his employer than his contract requires. He can withdraw his goodwill if he pleases.[15] For example, he is not obliged to work hours longer than those which he has agreed with his employer to work merely because by so doing he will or may make his employer's business more efficient or more profitable or more convenient for his employer's customers.[16] In most cases then, the crucial legal question is what those contractual obligations are. This will depend on the express and/or implied terms of the contract. If a rule book is a part of the contract (on which see Chap. 8 above) then an instruction to " work to contract " may amount to no more than an instruction to withdraw goodwill.[17] On the other hand, a rule book may be construed as containing the lawful instructions of the employer to his workers as to how they are to work.[18] In that event, the Court of Appeal has said a " work to rule " may constitute a breach of each worker's employment contract. In *Secretary of State for Employment* v. *A.S.L.E.F.* (*No.* 2) [19] several justifications were suggested for this view: (1) there is, as a matter of law, an implied term in the contract of service that an employee will not, in obeying lawful instructions, seek to obey them in a wholly unreasonable way which will have the effect of disrupting his employer's business [20]; (2) there is, also as a matter of law, an implied term in the contract of service, that " the employee must serve the employer faithfully with a view to promoting those commercial interests for which he is employed " and so must " perform the contract in such a way as not to frustrate that commercial objective " [21]; (3) that, as a question of fact in the *A.S.L.E.F.*

---

[13] *Cf. Edwards* v. *S.O.G.A.T.* [1971] Ch. 354, 374–375, in which Lord Denning M.R. said that a skilled man was entitled to refuse an order to do labouring work. " But I think he was being very unco-operative." This did not, however, mean that his claim for damages for loss of earnings (against the union which had wrongfully terminated his membership, so depriving him of skilled work) was to be reduced. Nor, it is submitted, would such a refusal give an employer a right of summary dismissal. See generally, Chap. 14.

[14] O. Kahn-Freund, *Labour and the Law* (London 1972), p. 266.

[15] *Secretary of State for Employment* v. *A.S.L.E.F.* (*No.* 2) [1972] 2 Q.B. 455 (C.A.) *per* Lord Denning M.R. at p. 491, Roskill L.J. at pp. 507, 509.

[16] See above, Chap. 8.

[17] In the Court of Appeal, Roskill L.J., *ibid.*, at pp. 504–505, found himself unable to agree with Sir John Donaldson P.'s statement in the court below, [1972] 2 Q.B. at p. 466, that an instruction to work strictly in accordance with contracts of employment " is intended either to be unrealistically construed or is in the nature of ' window dressing '."

[18] See above, Chap. 8.   [19] [1972] 2 Q.B. 455.

[20] *Ibid. per* Lord Denning M.R. at p. 490, Roskill L.J. at p. 508.

[21] *Ibid. per* Buckley L.J., pp. 497–499; *cf.* Roskill L.J. at pp. 508–509 who preferred to rest his decision on the first-mentioned ground rather than this " clearly equally tenable " ground.

case, "each party to each service agreement must, as rational beings, be taken to have assumed as a matter of course, when each service contract was entered into, that the employee would never seek to interpret and act upon the rules so as to disrupt the entire railway system " [22] (the " officious bystander " test : see para. 222 above); (4) that, as a matter of custom and usage in the *A.S.L.E.F.* case, there was a course of dealing and common understanding in the performance of instructions from which each employee was not free arbitrarily to depart.[23] The third and fourth reasons are peculiar to the facts of the *A.S.L.E.F.* case. It should be noted, however, that the application of the " officious bystander " test involves a finding of serious disruption through a work to rule, and that a custom can only be implied to explain or supplement a contract if it does not contradict the express terms of that contract. The first two reasons, the terms said to be implied by law, are differently stated by each of the judges in the *A.S.L.E.F.* case. Lord Denning M.R. emphasised the " wilfulness " of the disruption,[24] while Roskill L.J. expressly disavowed the notion that questions of motive or intent are relevant in the law of contract and preferred to rest his judgment on the *effect* of an unreasonable interpretation of rules.[25] Buckley L.J. stressed the commercial objectives of the contract in a way which, it is respectfully submitted, indicates that a work to rule must result in a very serious disruption—a frustration of the commercial objective—before it will amount to a breach of each employment contract.[26] This formulation, like any other attempt to attach common " commercial objectives " to contracts of employment, does, however, rest on a fundamental fiction which is rejected by most practitioners of industrial relations. As Professor Kahn-Freund has said, " it is . . . sheer utopia to postulate a common interest in the substance of labour relations." [27] To sum up : certain forms of work to rule may be construed as an " unreasonable " interpretation of management instructions. The legal foundation for regarding such an interpretation as a breach of contract may be seen as having an affinity with the implied duty of fidelity or the implied duty of co-operation or as resting in fact or in custom. The social foundation, in regard to the standard of " reasonableness," rests on whatever view the judiciary may take of management prerogatives.

2. CARE

The employer's duty

277   It is the duty of an employer to take reasonable care for the safety of his employees in the course of their employment. For convenience this duty is often split up into different categories, such as safe tools, a safe place of work, a safe system of working and the selection of properly skilled fellow-employees. The employer is under no guarantee to ensure safety. In each case it must be proved that he was negligent, or that some person for whom the employer is vicariously liable was negligent. The

---

[22] *Ibid. per* Roskill L.J. at p. 508. Presumably the " business efficacy " test would lead to a similar result.
[23] *Ibid. per* Roskill L.J. at p. 508, who does not develop this point fully.
[24] *Ibid.* at pp. 491–492: " what makes it wrong is the object with which it is done."
[25] *Ibid.* at p. 508.
[26] *Ibid.* at p. 498.
[27] *Op. cit.*, p. 19.

employer's duty may be regarded as arising in tort or as an implied term of the contract of employment.[28] Since there is a specialised body of law on this topic, well covered in the books, we shall not deal with it.[29] It should be noted, however, that there is no general principle that an employer is liable, at common law, for failing to have a proper system for the protection of his employee's property (e.g., his clothing left in a dressing-room).[30] There are, however, certain statutory duties which oblige the employer to provide adequate and suitable accommodation for clothing not worn during working hours.[31]

The employee's duty

278   An employee must exercise reasonable care and skill in the performance of his services. In deciding what is reasonable one must apply, as Lord Maugham said, " the standards of men, and not those of angels." [32] The decided cases on the application of this duty in particular circumstances are no more than analogies, and it is mistaken to regard them as authorities for more than the existence of a general duty of care. The circumstances in which a breach of this duty (i.e., by unreasonable conduct) will entitle the employer to dismiss the employee summarily, are discussed in Chapter 14. Irrespective of whether a right of summary dismissal exists, the employee is under an implied duty to indemnify the employer in respect of the consequences of his negligent conduct.[33] The precise scope of this implied term in the contract of employment is a matter of controversy. In *Lister* v. *Romford Ice and Cold Storage Co. Ltd.*[34] the House of Lords was unanimous in deciding that there was an implied term in a lorry driver's employment contract that he would exercise reasonable care when about his employer's business. This part of the decision seems to have been misconstrued in the later case of *Harvey* v. *R. G. O'Dell Ltd.*,[35] in which it was held that a storekeeper was not obliged to indemnify his employer in respect of his negligent driving of his own motor-cycle while fetching some spare parts in the course of his employment. A narrow definition of the duty was applied, i.e., not to cause damage by his negligence while doing that which he was actually engaged to do, namely, storekeeping. It has been suggested that a wide definition, i.e., to take reasonable care while about the employer's business, was what the House of Lords intended to lay down in *Lister's* case.[36]

279   Is the employer under a corresponding duty to take out insurance to cover the employee's liability for negligence? In *Lister's* case a majority of their Lordships held that no such duty could be implied into the contract. (A minority took the view that the officious bystander would have been answered " Oh, of course!" if he had asked the parties this question.[37])

---

[28] *Davie* v. *New Merton Board Mills* [1959] A.C. 604; *Matthews* v. *Kuwait Bechtel Corporation* [1959] 2 Q.B. 57; and see above, para. 102.

[29] See especially J. L. Munkman, *Employer's Liability at Common Law*, 8th ed. (London, 1975).

[30] *Deyong* v. *Shenburn* [1946] K.B. 227; *Edwards* v. *West Herts Hospital Committee* [1957] 1 W.L.R. 415.

[31] e.g. Factories Act 1961, s. 59; Offices, Shops and Railway Premises Act 1963, s. 12.

[32] *Jupiter General Ins. Co.* v. *Shroff* [1937] 3 All E.R. 67.

[33] *Lister* v. *Romford Ice and Cold Storage Co. Ltd.* [1957] A.C. 555.

[34] *Ibid.*

[35] [1958] 2 Q.B. 78.

[36] J. A. Jolowicz (1959) 22 M.L.R. 71.   [37] Above, note 33.

There is, however, an earlier case, the validity of which was accepted by both sides in *Lister's* case, in which it was held that an employer is bound to indemnify his employee if the damage occurs in circumstances in which insurance is compulsory, *e.g.*, under the Road Traffic Act.[38] In any event an employee, whose employer's compulsory policy under that Act purports to cover the employee, has an express statutory right to enforce that policy against the insurer.[39] In such a case the employer will not be able to claim an indemnity from the employee, because he will have suffered no damage.

280 The employer will also have suffered no damage if he has an employer's liability policy (which he is obliged to have under the Employer's Liability (Compulsory Insurance) Act 1969)[40] and the negligent employee has caused him to incur liability to a fellow-employee. Then, only if the employer's liability insurance company chooses to exercise its subrogation rights, will the right to an indemnity be enforced. In fact, there is a " gentlemen's agreement " among insurance companies not to enforce their rights of subrogation against employees, where a fellow-employee is injured or killed, except in cases of collusion or wilful misconduct. This agreement, which followed a threat of legislation to protect employees from actions like that in *Lister's* case, applies to all members of the British Insurance Association, Lloyd's underwriters, and nearly all other insurance companies. The nationalised industries and local authorities follow a similar policy, except in respect of claims against negligent doctors and dentists (who usually effect their own insurance) and in cases of gross negligence in coal mines.[41] In any event, it appears that the courts will now not allow the right of subrogation to be exercised in an industrial setting.[42]

3. FIDELITY

281 A term will be implied in every contract of employment that the employee will serve honestly and faithfully. This basic duty may be amplified and extended by express agreement, for example, to restrain competition by ex-employees or to protect trade secrets. We shall discuss the interrelationship of implied and express duties in three situations: handling the employer's property (including the right to search), restraining competition, and protecting confidential information.

Handling the employer's property

282 Any conduct of the employee, in handling his employer's property, which indicates that he is unfit for a position of trust and confidence may

---

[38] *Gregory* v. *Ford* [1951] 1 All E.R. 121; doubted by Glanville Williams (1957) 20 M.L.R. at pp. 225–226. In *Lister's* case the accident occurred in circumstances in which compulsory insurance was unnecessary, *i.e.*, in the employer's yard.

[39] Road Traffic Act 1972, s. 148.

[40] In force on January 1, 1972: Employer's Liability (Compulsory Insurance) Act 1969 Commencement Order, S.I. 1971 No. 1116; see too, Employer's Liability (Compulsory Insurance) General Regulations, S.I. 1971 No. 1117; Employer's Liability (Compulsory Insurance) Exemption Regulations 1971, S.I. 1971 No. 1933.

[41] See Gardiner (1959) 22 M.L.R. 652. Where an employer and employee are joint tortfeasors, the employer is entitled to such indemnity and contribution as the court thinks just under the Law Reform (Married Women and Tortfeasors) Act 1935, s. 6.

[42] *Morris* v. *Ford Motor Co. Ltd.* [1973] Q.B. 792.

justify the employer in dismissing him.[43] However, the common law right to dismiss for dishonesty is now subject to the law of unfair dismissal (Chap. 17); in order to show that the dismissal was not unfair the employer must show that he had reasonable grounds for believing that the employee committed the offence,[44] and generally ought to give him an opportunity to explain his conduct. Where property is entrusted to the employee either by or for his employer, he must render proper accounts for it. Anything which he acquires secretly in the course of his employment (*e.g.* a secret profit or bribe) belongs to his employer, and he must account for it.[45]

Searching employees

283   Some works rules books, which may be incorporated as terms in the individual contract, authorise the employer to search employees when entering or leaving the place of work. In the absence of a contractual right, the employer cannot force an employee to submit to a search. Without the employee's consent, a search of his person, clothing or belongings constitutes an unlawful trespass. Powers of search and seizure, connected with a valid arrest or by warrant, are exercisable only by the police.[46]

Competition: spare-time work

284   In the absence of express agreement, that the worker is employed exclusively by one employer, the courts are reluctant to imply a term which would restrict a worker from utilising his spare-time (*i.e.,* outside the times when he is obliged to work for his employer). On the other hand, as Lord Greene M.R. said, in the leading case,[47] " it would be deplorable if it were laid down that a workman could, consistently with his duty to his employer, knowingly, deliberately and secretly set himself to do in his spare-time something which would inflict great harm on his employer's business." An injunction may be granted to restrain an employee from working for a rival employer during his spare-time if it can be shown that the competition would seriously damage the employer's business. It is not necessary to show that confidential information has actually been divulged.[48] There is one dubious decision in which it was suggested that it is a breach of the implied duty of fidelity if the employee's spare-time work is " a substantial drain " on his time and energies, or is " in the same field of activity " as his employer's business. This wide proposition is clearly in conflict with Lord Greene's remarks quoted above and, it is submitted, should be regarded as erroneous.[49]

---

[43] *Sinclair* v. *Neighbour* [1967] 2 Q.B. 279 (betting shop manager " borrowed " £15, which he replaced later, knowing that had he asked for a loan it would have been refused: held this was incompatible with his duty as manager and he was properly dismissed). See generally, Chap. 14, on summary dismissal.

[44] See *Ferodo Ltd.* v. *Barnes, The Times,* July 3, 1976 (E. A. T.). See generally Chapter 17.

[45] *e.g. Reading* v. *Att.-Gen.* [1951] A.C. 507 and generally Goff and Jones, *Law of Restitution* (London, 1965), p. 457.

[46] A description of these powers falls beyond our scope. See De Smith, *Constitutional and Administrative Law* (2nd ed. 1973), p. 469. It should be observed that some employees are subject to regulations giving powers to special police, *e.g.* docks, railways, etc.

[47] *Hivac Ltd.* v. *Park Royal Scientific Instruments Ltd.* [1946] Ch. 169.

[48] *Ibid.* at p. 175.

[49] *Bartlett* v. *Shoe and Leather Record, The Times,* March 29, 1960 (comment by W. Frank [1960] J.B.L. 362).

Competition: ex-employees

285   As a general rule an ex-employee is free to go into competition with
his former employer. This is subject to two exceptions. The first is that
he may not do anything, while still employed, which is in breach of his
duty of fidelity. So, in *Wessex Dairies Ltd.* v. *Smith*,[50] it was held that
a milk roundsman, who canvassed his employer's customers on his last
day of service to transfer their custom to him from the following day, was
in breach of this duty. Similarly, in *Robb* v. *Green*,[51] it was held that it
was a breach of the duty for a tradesman to copy out a list of his
employer's customers before leaving his service. However, it is perfectly
lawful for an ex-employee to canvass customers of his former employer
after leaving his service. Moreover, he is entitled to make use of the knowledge and skill which he acquired while in his former employer's business,
apart from such information which he obtained in confidence (see below,
para. 288).

286   The second exception is where there is an express clause in the contract
of employment restraining competition by the employee when he leaves
the employer's service. Covenants of this sort are in restraint of trade at
common law and will be treated by the courts as prima facie void. They
will be upheld only if they are shown to be reasonable and not contrary
to the public interest. An employer cannot protect himself, by express
stipulation, against competition as such. He can protect his trade secrets[52]
(which, as we shall see in paragraph 288 below, might be protected even
without an express agreement), and probably his *own* expertise or " know-
how," but he cannot bind an employee not to canvass customers on leaving
the employment, if the employee's work did not bring him into contact
with customers.[53] There may be other, non-proprietary interests which can
be validly protected.[54]

In order to be regarded as reasonable the restraint must go no further
than is reasonable for the protection of the employer's interest. For
example, the courts have been more inclined to uphold covenants which
restrain the employee from soliciting his former employer's customers than
those which simply restrain him from working at all within a specified
area.[55] This does not mean that " area " covenants are invariably unlawful;
it all depends on the size of the area in which the employee worked, the
number of customers he dealt with within it, in comparison with the area
of the restraint. In one case a world-wide restraint may be reasonable,[56]
in another a five-mile restraint may be unreasonable. Equally, the duration
of the restraint will be relevant to its reasonableness. This, too, will depend
on the nature of the business and whether it is of a fluctuating kind.

287   Even if the restraint is reasonable it may still be struck down as unlawful
if it is regarded by the court as being contrary to the public interest. This

---

[50] [1935] 2 K.B. 80.
[51] [1895] 2 Q.B. 315; *Worsley and Co. Ltd.* v. *Cooper* [1939] 1 All E.R. 290.
[52] *Herbert Morris Ltd.* v. *Saxelby* [1916] 1 A.C. 688.
[53] *G. W. Plowman and Son Ltd.* v. *Ash* [1964] 1 W.L.R. 568.
[54] *Eastham* v. *Newcastle United F.C. Ltd.* [1964] Ch. 413, 432.
[55] *S. W. Strange Ltd.* v. *Mann* [1965] 1 W.L.R. 629; *Gledhow Autoparts* v. *Delaney*
[1965] 1 W.L.R. 1366; *Home Counties Dairies Ltd.* v. *Skilton* [1970] 1 W.L.R. 526;
Marion White Ltd. v. *Francis* [1972] 1 W.L.R. 1423; *T. Lucas & Co. Ltd.* v. *Mitchell*
[1974] Ch. 129; *Stenhouse Australia Ltd.* v. *Phillips* [1974] A.C. 391.
[56] *Nordenfelt* v. *Maxim Nordenfelt Guns and Ammunition Co.* [1894] A.C. 535.

has rarely been used as a ground of invalidity, and it has been strongly criticised [57] because the court will pay little, if any, heed to economic conditions (*e.g.*, large-scale unemployment) in assessing the "public interest." Nevertheless, in one recent case a pension fund rule, to which an employee had agreed as a term of his employment, was held to be void on this ground.[58] The rule in question provided that pension benefits could be cancelled if a retired employee was "employed or engaged in any activity or occupation which is in competition to " that of the employers.

The doctrines of judge-made public policy against restraints of trade are far less likely to be applied to restrictions on trade during the continuance of the contract than those after the contract has come to an end.[59]

Confidential information

288   The real purpose of an express restraint of trade clause in a contract of employment is to prevent the employee from entering a rival's employment, rather than to forestall the disclosure of confidential information as such. Every contract of employment, however, contains an implied term that the employee will not disclose to another his employer's trade secrets or misuse confidential information acquired by him as a result of his employment.[60] This obligation may continue even after the period of employment has come to an end. The employer has several remedies: he may seek an injunction to restrain the employee or ex-employee from continuing to make disclosure of the trade secrets or from misusing the confidential information; he may claim an account of profits made through its use; he may seek damages for breach of contract; he may be entitled to dismiss the employee summarily.[61]

289   The employer may also have remedies against a third party to whom the employee has passed on the secrets or confidences. The third party may be restrained by injunction from using the information even though it was innocently received, without notice of the fact that it was originally given in confidence to the employee.[62] The granting of an injunction rests on the general equitable duty to be of good faith.[63] There may also be a right to damages against a third party, although the precise scope of this right to damages is controversial. It is clear that, if the third party co-operated with the employee or ex-employee, even without exerting

---

[57] Goodhart, 49 L.Q.R. 465.

[58] *Bull* v. *Pitney-Bowes Ltd.* [1967] 1 W.L.R. 273, following *Wyatt* v. *Kreglinger and Fernau* [1933] 1 K.B. 793.

[59] *Instone* v. *A. Schroeder Music Publishing Co. Ltd.* [1974] 1 All E.R. 171 (C.A.); *cf. Esso Petroleum Co. Ltd.* v. *Harper's Garage (Stourport) Ltd.* [1968] A.C. 269 at pp. 329, 333–334, where Lord Pearce warned against dangers of "litigious abuse" in such cases.

[60] *Merryweather* v. *Moore* [1892] 2 Ch. 518, in which Kekewich J. speaks of this as "arising out of the mere fact of employment." In *Bent's Brewery Co. Ltd.* v. *Hogan* [1945] 2 All E.R. 570, Lynskey J. says: "Sometimes it has been said that the obligation was the result of an implied term in the contract of service; sometimes that it was an obligation arising out of the employee's position or status as such; and sometimes that the obligation arises because of the trust or confidence which an employee owes of necessity to his employer."

[61] See below, Chap. 15. Certain workers (*e.g.* civil servants, journalists, employees of government contractors) also run the risk of criminal prosecution under the Official Secrets Act 1911, s. 2.

[62] *e.g. Hivac Ltd.* v. *Park Royal Scientific Instruments Ltd.* [1946] Ch. 169, in which the injunction was issued to restrain not the employees but the rival employers.

[63] *Fraser* v. *Evans* [1969] 1 Q.B. 349, 361.

pressure on him, in a course of conduct which he knew involved a breach on his part of his implied duty of fidelity to his employers, he will be liable in damages.[64] This liability rests on the tort of inducement of breach of contract,[65] and may even extend to situations where the third party is " reckless " as to whether or not a contractual obligation exists.[66] Moreover, there are some recent indications that the third party may be liable in damages even where the elements of the tort of inducement of breach of contract cannot be established. In *Seager* v. *Copydex*[67] (which did not involve an employment relationship) the defendants had " unconsciously " made use of information entrusted to them by the plaintiff. The Court of Appeal held that they were liable in damages, even though they had acted in good faith throughout (and so were not enjoined from using the information or made to account for their profits from it). The court treated confidential information as analogous to a property interest: the damages were assessed on the basis of the value of the information, and once they were paid the information belonged to the defendants. The implications of this decision (which has been criticised)[68] remain to be worked out by the courts, but in so far as employment law is concerned the result may be to give an employer a right to damages (a) against an employee, and (b) against a third party recipient of the information, without the need to establish an implied contractual duty between employer and employee, or a tortious inducement of breach of contract by the third party. The most controversial aspect of this possible right to damages is the degree of knowledge of the confidentiality of the information required to render the recipient liable. In *Seager* v. *Copydex*,[69] the defendants were held liable even though the court accepted that they believed that the product they were marketing was the result of their own ideas and not derived from the information previously given to them by the plaintiffs. If the information is treated as " property " then, on an analogy with the tort of conversion, it does not matter much whether the defendant knew of the confidence. The result of the action for damages (unlike an injunction) is, after all, simply to force the defendant to " buy " the information which really " belongs " to the plaintiff.

290   Whatever the precise scope or legal basis of the protection of trade secrets and confidential information, it is necessary to define the nature of the secrets and confidences which will be protected. It is usually said that an employee is free to use his " individual skill and experience " (or " know-how ") which he acquires in the course of his employment.[70] On the other hand he cannot disclose or use for his own profit secret processes,

---

[64] *Printers & Finishers Ltd.* v. *Holloway* [1965] R.P.C. 239, 252 (in which damages were refused because guilty knowledge was not proved, but an equitable injunction was granted).

[65] *Ibid.*; and *Bents Brewery Co. Ltd.* v. *Hogan·* (above, note 60).

[66] This was suggested by Lord Denning M.R. in *Emerald Construction Co. Ltd.* v. *Lowthian* [1966] 1 W.L.R. 691, in respect of this tort, in general.

[67] [1967] 1 W.L.R. 923; and *Seager* v. *Copydex (No. 2)* [1969] 1 W.L.R. 809.

[68] Gareth Jones (1970) 86 L.Q.R. 463; but *cf.* P. M. North, " Breach of Confidence: Is there a new tort? " (1972) 12 J.S.P.T.L. 149. The Committee on Privacy (Cmnd. 5012, Chap. 21) have proposed a clarification and statement in legislative form of the law relating to breach of confidence.

[69] Above, note 67.

[70] *Herbert Morris Ltd.* v. *Saxelby* [1916] 1 A.C. 688, 704.

documents, names of customers (except those accidentally acquired),[71] information about the employer's prospects or about the salaries and wages which the employer pays to other employees.[72] The information need not be in tangible form,[73] although there are judicial dicta which suggest that the employee who *memorises* information (*e.g.*, about customers' names) does not break his duty of fidelity, if he subsequently uses them for his own benefit.[74] It has been suggested,[75] we think correctly, that these dicta should be taken to refer only to such information as contributes to the employee's own " know-how."

291   The implied obligation not to disclose confidential information is subject to an exception. It is not a breach of the duty to disclose " any misconduct of such a nature that it ought in the public interest to be disclosed to others." [76] " There is no confidence," Wood V.-C. said, " as to the disclosure of iniquity." [77] The difficulty is to know what the courts will regard as an " iniquity." The commission of a crime or other unlawful act, actual or contemplated, is likely to fall within this category. But even in this case it seems that the employee must satisfy the court that there is some " public interest " justifying disclosure. So in *Weld-Blundell* v. *Stephens*,[78] Warrington L.J. took the view that an employeè could be bound not to disclose defamatory information confided to him by the employer. On the other hand, in *Initial Services Ltd.* v. *Putterill*,[79] the Court of Appeal held that a sales manager was entitled to disclose an arrangement by his former employers to maintain prices, allegedly contrary to the Restrictive Trade Practices Act 1956. The judgments in the latter case even suggest that conduct which does not amount to an unlawful act may be disclosed, provided it affects the public interest.[80] The mere fact that disclosure can be made, however, does not mean that it can be made to anyone. The person receiving the information must have a " proper interest " in it (*e.g.*, the police if a crime has been committed).[81] It is but rarely that the misdeed will warrant disclosure to the press.

Disclosure of information to trade unions

292   One of the consequences of the ordinary legal rules about confidential information is that an employee who obtains information about the profitability of his employer's enterprise, his wage and salary structure, and other information essential to effective collective bargaining is not at liberty

---

[71] *Robb* v. *Green* [1895] 2 Q.B. 1, 13.
[72] *Bent's Brewery Co. Ltd.* v. *Hogan* (above, note 60).
[73] *Printers & Finishers Ltd.* v. *Holloway* (above, note 64).
[74] *e.g.* in *Merryweather* v. *Moore* (above note 60).
[75] Goff and Jones, *Law of Restitution*, p. 457, note 67. In *Baker* v. *Gibbons* [1972] 1 W.L.R. 693, it was said that there is no general rule of law that where, during the tenure of his office, a director had learnt the name of an employee of his company that information was *ipso facto* to be regarded as confidential.
[76] *Per* Lord Denning M.R. in *Initial Services Ltd.* v. *Putterill* [1968] 1 Q.B. 396.
[77] *Gartside* v. *Outram* (1856) 3 Jur.(N.S.) 39.
[78] [1919] 1 K.B. 520, 535; affirmed [1920] A.C. 956.
[79] Above, note 76; see also *Hubbard* v. *Vosper* [1972] 2 Q.B. 84 and *Beloff* v. *Pressdram Ltd.* [1973] 1 All E.R. 241 at p. 260.
[80] Note in particular the test used by Salmon L.J. in *Initial Services Ltd.* v. *Putterill* (*supra* at p. 410) and Winn L.J. (*ibid.* at p. 411), namely, whether if there had been express agreement by the employee not to disclose the information the court would have struck down that covenant on grounds of public policy.
[81] *Ibid.* pp. 405–406, 410, 411.

to disclose this information to his trade union.[82] This is sometimes over-come by a clause in the collective agreement between the employer and union (then incorporated into the individual contract) which provides that the obligation not to divulge confidential information " shall in no way preclude the union from legitimately protecting the interests of the members." [83] This would appear to protect the individual employee from breaking his contract, and might also protect the union from tortious liability by way of the defence of justification.[84] In each case it would need to be shown that the information was necessary for " legitimate protection " of members' interests.

Inventions, patents and copyright

293   There may be, and often is in the case of research workers, an express agreement about the ownership of inventions, patents and copyright.[85] Such an agreement will be enforced unless it is void as an unreasonable restraint of trade (see above, para. 286).[86] In the absence of agreement, the position as regards copyright is governed by the Copyright Act 1956 (as regards works made after June 1, 1957). Section 4 of this Act provides, in effect, that the employer is the first owner of the copyright if the maker of the work was employed by him under a contract of service or apprentice-ship and the work was made in the course of the employment.[87] However, the author of a literary, dramatic or artistic work for a newspaper, magazine or similar periodical has copyright, except for the right of publication of the work in any periodical which is vested in the owner of the periodical who employed him.

294   Where there is no express agreement, between employer and employee, about inventions and patents then, as a general rule, the invention belongs to the employer if the employee was employed to make inventions of that sort, and it would be inconsistent with the relationship of good faith between the parties for the employee to exploit the invention for his own benefit.[88] In deciding whether the employee made the invention in connec-tion with the proper fulfilment of his contractual obligations, much attention will be paid to the employee's status. A factory hand is not normally expected to invent; a research chemist is. It does not matter that the employee was not expressly asked to make the invention, so long as it was an implicit part of his contractual duties. On the other hand, if the invention was only of incidental value to the employer's business, the inven-

---

[82] *Bent's Brewery Co. Ltd.* v. *Hogan* (above, note 60). The *employer* may, however, be under a duty to disclose information, by virtue of E.P.A., ss. 17–21, or the Industry Act 1975, Pt. IV. See Chap. 1.

[83] This example is taken from the agreement between A.C.T.T. and the British Film Producers' Association and another (December 20, 1965).

[84] It is not clear whether compliance with the terms of a collective agreement is justification for purposes of the tort of inducement of breach of contract: *Read* v. *Friendly Society of Stonemasons* [1902] 2 K.B. 88, 96; *cf. Smithies* v. *National Association of Operative Plasterers* [1909] 1 K.B. 310.

[85] *e.g. British Celanese* v. *Moncrieff* [1948] Ch. 564.

[86] *e.g. Triplex Safety Glass Co.* v. *Scorah* [1938] Ch. 211.

[87] *University of London Press Ltd.* v. *University Tutorial Press Ltd.* [1916] 2 Ch. 601. For detailed treatment see *Copinger and Skone James on Copyright* (11th ed., London 1971), Chap. 7.

[88] *British Syphon Co. Ltd.* v. *Homewood* [1956] 1 W.L.R. 1190; *Triplex Safety Glass Co.* v. *Scorah* (above, note 86).

tion may belong to the employee.[89] In that event, it does not affect his ownership of the invention and rights to the patent that the employee misappropriated the employer's time and materials in order to make it. Conversely, if the invention belongs to the employer then the employee holds the benefit in trust for him, even though the invention has not yet been patented, and even though the employee only exploits the invention after his employment has come to an end.[90]

295   Section 56 (2) of the Patents Act 1949 provides that the court or comptroller may order the apportionment of the benefit of an invention between the employer and his employee, unless satisfied that one or other is entitled to the benefit to the exclusion of the other. This section was given a narrow interpretation in *Sterling Engineering Co. Ltd.* v. *Patchett.*[91] It appears not to confer a discretion on the court or comptroller to apportion the benefit whenever it may appear equitable to do so. Since, under the general law, the invention must belong to either the employer or the employee but never to both, the section is confined to cases where there is an *express* agreement to share the invention. This means that section 56 (1) has not altered the law, because it has always been within the court's power to make an apportionment in such cases.

[The next paragraph is 301.]

---

[89] *e.g. Selz Ltd.'s Application* (1951) 72 R.P.C. 158.
[90] *Triplex Safety Glass Co.* v. *Scorah* (above, note 86).
[91] [1955] A.C. 534. For detailed treatment see T. A. Blanco White, *Patents for Inventions* (4th ed., London, 1974), paras. 9–301—9–307. The Government has announced its preparedness to introduce a statutory award scheme for employee inventors: *Patent Law Reform* (Cmnd. 6000, April 1975).

CHAPTER 10

REMUNERATION, HOURS, HOLIDAYS AND TIME OFF

1. REMUNERATION

Nature of the employer's duty

301   The employer's duty to remunerate his employee lies at the foundation of the contract between them so that a failure to pay wages over a fairly long period, either promptly or at all, entitles an employee to terminate the contract without notice.[1] For example, in *Duckworth* v. *Farnish & Co. Ltd.*,[2] an employee was " loaned " by his employer, with his consent, to another employer and was told, after a few days, that he would have to look to this new " employer " for payment. The Court of Appeal held that the failure of the original employer to provide the employee with remuneration for over one month entitled him to terminate his contract without notice. The original employer could not discharge his obligations by finding another employer who would provide him with remunerative employment. This does not mean that a failure to pay wages on a single occasion either promptly or at all can be treated as a breach entitling the employee to treat the contract as at an end. The test is whether the employer's conduct in failing to pay indicates an intention on his part to repudiate his basic obligations under the contract. In each case this will be a question of fact and degree.[3] In practice, workers' organisations usually treat failure to pay wages, even on a single occasion, as a fundamental breach of contract, entitling the worker to walk out.

Rate of remuneration

302   The rate at which the employee is to be remunerated may be expressly agreed between the parties, or (as is frequently the case) it may be specified in a collective agreement which is expressly or impliedly incorporated in the individual contract, or it may be fixed by some statutory authority (*e.g.* Wages Council, Agricultural Wages Board, or the Central Arbitration Committee).[4] In all these cases questions of construction may arise, which can be resolved only in the light of the circumstances of each case. Thus, there is no general legal rule which enables one to say whether " overtime " or " standby " payments are contractually enforceable.[5] All will depend on factors such as whether the employee was to be remunerated at a certain rate irrespective of the duties performed or hours worked, whether or not in working " overtime " he was doing something he was already contractually bound to do, and whether there was an express or implied promise to pay extra remuneration for these further duties.[6]

---

[1] *e.g. Broadhurst* v. *Buchan & Son* (1969) 4 I.T.R. 247 (Tribunal, Manchester).

[2] (1970) 5 I.T.R. 17.

[3] In *Runham* v. *Wood Bros. & Runham Ltd.* [1972] I.T.R. 277 (N.I.R.C.) the point was raised but not decided whether expressed inability to pay was a repudiation.

[4] *Cf.* Chap. 8.

[5] *e.g. Byrne* v. *Lakers (Sanitation & Heating) Ltd.* (1968) 3 I.T.R. 105.

[6] *Stilk* v. *Myrick* (1809) 2 Camp. 317.

Calculation of a " week's pay "

303   In a variety of statutory contexts it is necessary to calculate an employee's normal working hours and a "week's pay," for example in order to determine the amount of a guarantee payment,[7] or redundancy payment,[8] or remuneration during the period of notice.[9] Schedule 4 to the Employment Protection Act 1975 lays down the rules according to which such calculations are to be made. It is first necessary to determine whether there are "normal working hours." This is obviously the case if the contract of employment fixes the number or the minimum number of hours of employment in the week. The mere fact that employees may be obliged by their employers to work overtime does not mean that the employees do not have "normal working hours," [10] but the overtime will only count towards "normal working hours" in exceptional circumstances. The Court of Appeal [11] has analysed the position as follows: (a) where there is a fixed number of compulsory working hours, and thereafter overtime is voluntary on *both* sides, then, although overtime is worked regularly each week it does not count as normal working hours; (b) where there is a fixed number of compulsory working hours and in addition a fixed period of overtime is obligatory on *both* sides, so that the employer is bound to provide overtime to the employee and the employee bound to serve it, then the fixed period of overtime is added to the fixed period of compulsory working hours so that the total counts as normal working hours; and (c) where there is a fixed number of compulsory working hours and overtime is compulsory on the man if asked, but not on the employer, so that the employer is entitled to call upon the man to work overtime, but is not bound to call upon him to do so, then overtime does not come within normal working hours.

304   If there are normal working hours, then the amount of a week's pay depends upon whether or not the employee's remuneration varies with the amount of work done. If it does not, then a week's pay is the amount payable under the contract of employment on the calculation date.[12] (The calculation date is separately specified for each of the statutory rights.) If it does vary, the amount of the week's pay is the amount of remuneration for the number of normal working hours in a week calculated at the average hourly rate of remuneration payable in respect of a 12-week period.[13] This period is the one ending with the calculation date, where that day is the last day of a week, or, in any other case, ending with the last complete week before the calculation date.[14] If the employee has normal working hours which vary from week to week or over a longer period, his week's pay is taken to be the amount of remuneration for the average weekly number of normal working hours.[15] In arriving at the

---

[7] E.P.A., s. 24.   [8] R.P.A., Sched. 1.
[9] C.E.A., s. 2.
[10] *Minister of Labour* v. *Country Bake* (1968) 5 K.I.R. 332 (D.C.); *cf. Allison's Freight-liners* v. *Smylie*, 1972 S.L.T. 50 (C.S.).
[11] *Tarmac Roadstone Holdings Ltd.* v. *Peacock* [1973] I.C.R. 273 (C.A.).
[12] E.P.A., Sched. 4, para. 3 (2).
[13] *Ibid.* para. 3 (3).
[14] *Ibid.* A " week " means for an employee whose remuneration is calculated weekly by a week ending with a day other than Saturday, a week ending with that other day, and, for other employees, means a week ending with Saturday: *ibid.* para. 8 (*b*).
[15] *Ibid.* para. 4.

average hourly rate of remuneration only the hours when the employee was working and only the remuneration payable for, or apportionable to, those hours may be brought in.[16] In cases where there are no normal working hours a week's pay is the amount of the employee's average weekly remuneration over the relevant 12-week period.[17] If the employee has not been employed for long enough for a calculation to be made under any of these rules, the tribunal must determine an amount " which fairly represents a week's pay." [18] In calculating " remuneration " benefits in kind (*e.g.* free accommodation, travelling allowances) are disregarded.[19]

No remuneration fixed

305   If the contract says nothing specific about the rate of remuneration, and no term can be implied from a collective agreement or ascertained from a statutory order or award, it may still be possible for the employee to claim that he is entitled to be paid a reasonable remuneration. If it can be shown that the work was done by the employee and was accepted by the employer on the basis that some remuneration was to be paid, the law will imply a promise by the employer to pay on a *quantum meruit*, that is, to pay what the services were worth.[20] In calculating this remuneration the court will consider what has passed between the parties, by way of correspondence, etc., to indicate what may be regarded as reasonable in the circumstances. Sometimes, however, the circumstances show that the parties intended the contract to be binding only if they reached agreement on the rate of remuneration or some specified event occurred. For example, in one case [21] a managing director was promised " such remuneration as the directors may determine." The directors made no determination and Plowman J. held that the managing director was entitled to nothing by way of remuneration on the liquidation of the company. The words used indicated that he was to be at the mercy of the directors: only if they had determined to pay him, would he have got anything.

Pro rata payment

306   No action lies for remuneration until it is due. Wages or salary may be payable hourly, daily, weekly, monthly or even yearly. In each case it is necessary to consider the express or implied terms of the contract to discover the period of the employment for which the employee is entitled to be paid. Some employers follow this rule so strictly that they pay their monthly-paid employees only on the first day of the month following that in which the services were rendered.

307   A problem does arise whether an employee can recover any remuneration at all if, for any reason other than a breach of contract by his employer, he is prevented from completing a period of employment. This is illustrated by the old case of *Cutter* v. *Powell*,[22] in which a second

---

[16] *Ibid.* para. 5. *Mole Mining Ltd.* v. *H. G. Jenkins* [1972] I.C.R. 282; *Adams* v. *John Wright & Sons (Blackwall) Ltd.* [1972] I.T.R. 191 (N.I.R.C.).

[17] E.P.A., Sched. 4, para. 6.   [18] *Ibid.* para 7.

[19] *S. & U. Stores Ltd.* v. *Wilkes* [1974] I.C.R. 645.

[20] *Way* v. *Latilla* [1937] 3 All E.R. 759, 763; *Bryant* v. *Flight* (1839) 5 M. & W. 114; *Powell* v. *Braun* [1954] 1 W.L.R. 401.

[21] *Re Richmond Gate Property Co. Ltd.* [1965] 1 W.L.R. 335; and see, too, *Taylor* v. *Brewer* (1813) 1 M. & S. 290; *Roberts* v. *Smith* (1859) 28 L.J.Ex. 164.

[22] (1795) 6 T.R. 320.

mate on a voyage from Jamaica to Liverpool took a promissory note for 30 guineas from the master of the ship, payable " provided he proceeds, continues and does his duty as second mate, in the said ship from hence to the port of Liverpool." Three weeks before the end of the two-month voyage, he died. The Court of King's Bench held that his widow could not recover upon a *quantum meruit* (*i.e.*, such payment as the services deserved) for services rendered before his death. The court was influenced by the high rate of remuneration (as compared to the usual £4 per month) and the express terms of the promissory note which appeared to put the risk of non-completion of the voyage on Cutter. Had there been no express provision in the contract, *i.e.* had Cutter been hired on the usual basis of £4 per month payable monthly rather than at the (high) rate of pay of thirty guineas for the completed voyage as stipulated in the contract, Cutter's widow would have been entitled to receive payment for services rendered by Cutter before his death. The special features of the case were, however, overlooked in later cases in which a general rule was laid down that, at common law, an employee was not entitled to *pro rata payment* of remuneration in respect of an uncompleted period of service.[23] This rule was applied whether or not it was a breach of contract by the employee which had terminated the contract before the wages were due.[24] This could have harsh results, especially because of the presumption which was applied by the courts in the nineteenth century that a general hiring was intended to be for one year. So in *Lilley* v. *Elwin*,[25] an agricultural labourer on a general hiring for one year was held not to be entitled to any wages at all for that year when he was dismissed, shortly before the end of the period, because he had left the harvest field in annoyance with his employer for supplying him with " very bad small beer, not so good as water " instead of the strong beer which he (mistakenly) believed was his due in terms of the custom of the county.

308   The common law rule appears to have been remedied, at least in part, by the Apportionment Act 1870, section 2 of which provides that: " all rents, annuities, dividends, and other periodical payments in the nature of income . . . shall . . . be considered as accruing from day to day, and shall be apportioned in respect of time accordingly." Section 5 of the Act defines " annuities " as including " salaries and pensions." It is an unresolved question whether " salaries " for this purpose can be taken to includes " wages." [26] If the Act does not apply to wages it is possible for an employee to claim the equivalent of one day's wages for each completed day's work, even though he has not completed the full wage-payment period. Even if it does apply, however, it is not clear whether an employee can rely on the Act when he is discharged for misconduct. In the only judicial dictum on the subject, Lush J. suggested that an employee could not do so in these circumstances because he " forfeited

---

[23] *Boston Deep Sea Fishing & Ice Co.* v. *Ansell* (1888) 39 Ch.D. 339, 360, 364–365.

[24] *Moriarty* v. *Regent's Garage Co. Ltd.* [1921] 2 K.B. 766 (C.A.).

[25] (1848) 11 Q.B. 742. The presumption of a yearly hiring no longer applies: *Richardson* v. *Koefod* [1969] 1 W.L.R. 1812.

[26] *Moriarty* v. *Regent's Garage Co. Ltd.* [1921] 1 K.B. 433, *per* McCardie and Lush JJ. (reversed on a technical ground by C.A. which expressed no opinion on this point). *Re William Porter & Co. Ltd.* [1937] 2 All E.R. 361, 363, *per* Simonds J.

his right to salary." [27] This is misconceived, however, because the common law rule was not based on forfeiture but on non-completion of the period of service. The view expressed by Professor Glanville Williams, in his seminal article on the subject,[28] that the Act applies in all cases of part performance seems preferable to that of Lush J. It should be noted that the parties are free to contract out of the provisions of the Act, and that by section 3 no claim for the apportioned sum can be made until the entire sum would have become due. Where the contract has been frustrated (*e.g.*, the *Cutter* v. *Powell* situation) [29] the provisions of the Law Reform (Frustrated Contracts) Act 1943 will be relevant. The court may order payment of a " just " amount when the other party has obtained a " valuable benefit " (*e.g.*, services) before the frustrating event.[30]

Remuneration during absence from work

309   The right of an employee to be paid (and the rate of that payment), while he is absent due to sickness or otherwise without fault on his part, is often covered by an express term of the contract. About 73 per cent. of male workers and 67 per cent. of female workers are covered by sick-pay schemes.[31] These schemes may be set out in works rules or collective agreements. The Contracts of Employment Act 1972, s. 4 (1) (*d*) (ii), encourages this by requiring the employer to give the employee written particulars of any terms and conditions relating to " incapacity for work due to sickness or injury, including any provisions for sick pay."

310   If there is no express provision, and no collective agreement which can be incorporated into the contract, it may be possible to imply a term entitling the employee to sick pay. Two different approaches to this question can be discovered in the decided cases. In *Orman* v. *Saville Sportswear Ltd.*,[32] it was suggested by Pilcher J. that there is a presumption that the employer's obligation to pay wages continues unless and until an implied term to the contrary (*i.e.*, not to pay during sickness) can be shown. On the other hand, no such presumption was applied by the Court of Appeal in the earlier case of *Petrie* v. *MacFisheries Ltd.*,[33] when it was held that a notice placed on the wall at the place of work constituted an implied term of the contract. The notice stated that the employee would be paid, only as a matter of grace, and not as of right, at half-rates for twenty-one days of sickness a year. Nor can an employee paid by only piece-rates claim wages if, through illness, he does not work.[34] Therefore, it seems misleading to speak of a presumption. In each case the court must decide, in the light of all the circumstances, what custom or implied term governs the question of sick pay.

[27] In *Moriarty's* case (above).
[28] (1941) 57 L.Q.R. 373, 383.
[29] A seaman in Cutter's position would today be protected by regulations made by the Department of Trade under the Merchant Shipping Act 1970, s. 9 (*d*) (and note s. 7 (1) of the same Act) regulating the manner in which wages are to be paid. *Quaere* whether this entirely obviates the problems of *Cutter* v. *Powell.*
[30] See also Chap. 14.
[31] *New Earnings Survey 1970* (H.M.S.O., 1971). Tables 110–112; see too *General Household Survey* (H.M.S.O., 1973), Table 6.17 and the earlier Ministry of Labour survey, *Sick Pay Schemes* (1964).
[32] [1960] 1 W.L.R. 1055.
[33] [1940] 1 K.B. 258; *O'Grady* v. *Saper Ltd.* [1940] 2 K.B. 469.
[34] *Browning* v. *Crumlin Valley Collieries Ltd.* [1926] 1 K.B. 522.

Sickness and injury benefits

311   The fact that an employee is in receipt of social security payments for incapacity does not in itself prevent the employee from claiming his full wages while in receipt of those benefits.[35] In *Marrison* v. *Bell*,[36] the Court of Appeal held that the right to sickness benefits is in addition to, and not in substitution for, the rights of an employee under his contract of service. Conversely, the mere fact that an employee is in receipt of full wages during absence from work will not preclude him from receiving sickness or injury benefits from the state, provided he is otherwise eligible under the Social Security Act.[37] In this respect, sickness benefit differs from unemployment benefit which cannot be claimed while an employee is in receipt of wages. He will be deprived of his sickness benefit, however, for any day on which he works unless this is done under medical supervision as part of his treatment, or it is "work as a non-employed person which he has good cause for doing."[38] The latter seems to be designed to enable him to do odd jobs around his home without losing benefits. But in neither of these exceptional cases may he earn more than a specified amount and get his benefit as well. In practice, sick-pay schemes frequently take account of the entitlement to social security benefits. For example, the scheme may provide that the employee's earnings will be made up during illness by giving him the difference between his normal earnings and the social security benefits actually received (or, sometimes, those payable to a single man). The fact that some sick employees appear to be "overpaid" during illness should not cause any anxiety, provided medical certificates are insisted upon, because those who are ill are likely to incur additional expenses (*e.g.*, prescription charges, attendance at home, etc.). It should be remembered that sickness benefits are not payable for the first three days of illness,[39] and that they nearly always fall below actual net earnings.

Sick pay during period of notice

312   An employee may be incapable of work because of sickness or injury, during a period of notice to terminate his employment (indeed, the employer may actually have given him notice while he was away ill). If this occurs during the compulsory minimum period of notice laid down by the Contracts of Employment Act 1972, the employee is entitled to have his earnings made up in full during that period, in accordance with the detailed provisions of Schedule 4 to the Employment Protection Act 1975.[40]

Maternity pay

313   An employee absent from work wholly or partly because of pregnancy or confinement[41] is entitled to maternity pay.[42] This is payable for a

---

[35] This is subject to qualification in respect of entitlement to wages during the statutory minimum period of notice: Contracts of Employment Act 1972, Sched. 2. See below, Chap. 16.   [36] [1939] 2 K.B. 187, 203–204.

[37] Social Security Act 1975, Pt. II. See generally Chap. 19.

[38] National Insurance (Unemployment and Sickness Benefit) Regulations, S.I. 1967 No. 330, reg. 7 (1).

[39] See Chap. 19.   [40] C.E.A., s. 2; E.P.A., s. 85. See para. 303 above.

[41] "Confinement" means the birth of a living child or the birth of a child whether living or dead after 28 weeks of pregnancy: E.P.A., s. 52.

[42] E.P.A., s. 35 (1) (*a*), ss. 26–28. See Chap. 5 regarding continuity of employment and Chap. 18 regarding dismissal and the right to return to work.

period not exceeding, or for periods not exceeding in the aggregate, six weeks.[43] The right exists whether or not the contract of employment subsists during her period of absence [44] and it does not matter that she does not intend to return to work after her confinement.

314   The following conditions must be satisfied:

(1) *She must be an employee,*[45] and not fall in an excluded class.[46]

(2) *She must have continued to be employed until immediately before the beginning of the eleventh week before the expected week of her confinement.*[47] But she need not have been at work until then (*e.g.* she may have been away ill or on leave).

(3) *She must, at the beginning of that eleventh week, have been continuously employed for a period of not less than two years.*[48]

(4) *She must inform her employer (in writing if he so requests) at least three weeks before her absence begins* or, if that is not reasonably practicable, as soon as is reasonably practicable, that she will be (or is) absent from work wholly or partly because of pregnancy or confinement.[49]

(5) *If she has been fairly dismissed, because of pregnancy or confinement,*[50] *and not re-engaged, she remains entitled to maternity pay if, but for the dismissal, she would at the beginning of the eleventh week have been continuously employed for a period of not less than two years.* If she is unfairly dismissed [51] and not re-engaged, the amount of the maternity pay which would have been due to her, but for the dismissal, should be included in the assessment of her compensation for unfair dismissal. If she is unfairly dismissed and reinstated or re-engaged the tribunal's order should specify the amount of maternity pay due to her.[52] If the employee resigns before the eleventh week she loses her right to maternity pay. If she resigns after the eleventh week she does not.

(6) *The employee must produce, on request, for her employer's inspection a medical practitioner's or midwife's certificate stating the expected week of her confinement.* The employer need not make the payment until this certificate is received, but once it is provided she is entitled to be paid in respect of that part of the period of absence which fell before production of the certificate.[53]

---

43 *Ibid.* s. 36.
44 *Ibid.* s. 35 (2).
45 As defined in E.P.A., s. 126, which refers to T.U.L.R.A., s. 30. See Chap 3.
46 These are the wife of the employer, share fisherwomen, and those ordinarily working outside G.B.: E.P.A., s. 119 (2) (4) (5).
47 E.P.A., s. 35 (2) (*a*).
48 *Ibid.* s. 35 (2) (*b*). The Secretary of State may vary this period: s. 35 (5).
49 *Ibid.* s. 35 (2) (*c*).
50 *Ibid.* s. 35 (3).
51 See Chap. 17 for details of the circumstances when dismissal by reason of pregnancy or confinement is unfair.
52 E.P.A., s. 71 (3) (4).
53 *Ibid.* ss. 35 (4), 36 (4).

315   The amount of the statutory maternity pay is nine-tenths of a week's pay [54] for the first six weeks' absence starting on or after the eleventh week before the expected week of confinement.[55] From this amount must be deducted the full amount of the maternity allowance payable for each week under the Social Security Act 1975. Since, by April 1977 (when the maternity pay provisions described here are due to come into force), maternity allowances will be earnings-related, the effect is that employers are being required to "top-up" state benefits to a level not exceeding nine-tenths of basic wages.

316   The statutory rights do not affect rights to remuneration under the contract of employment,[56] for example by virtue of a collective agreement or company scheme which improves on the statutory scheme and is expressly or impliedly incorporated in the individual contract. But there is a mutual set-off of the contractual remuneration and maternity pay.[57]

317   One oddity in the calculation of a "week's pay" for purposes of maternity pay is that the "calculation date" is "the last day on which the employee worked under the contract of employment in force immediately before the beginning of her absence." [58] So if she accepted an offer of alternative employment from her employer at a lower salary, she is paid maternity pay calculated on that lower pay. But if she refused the offer she is paid at the rate for the old job. However, by refusing the offer (if it is adjudged suitable) she may be losing her right to complain of unfair dismissal.[59]

318   If the employer fails to pay, the employee may complain to an industrial tribunal within three months.[60] The tribunal has power to order the employer to make the payment.[61]

The Employment Protection Act sets up a Maternity Pay Fund to which all employers paying secondary class one social security contributions (whether or not they employ women) must contribute.[62] The Fund is on similar lines to the Redundancy Fund but the right to claim rebates is more extensive. Every employer liable to pay who has paid maternity pay to an employee is entitled to claim a full rebate from the Fund.[63] The Secretary of State has a discretion to pay a rebate to an employer who has paid an employee who was time-barred from presenting her claim.[64]

319   The Fund is also to be used to pay employees who have not been paid by their employers despite having taken all reasonable steps to recover the amount due,[65] or whose employer is insolvent.[66] The Secretary of State

---

[54] This is calculated in accordance with Sched. 4 to E.P.A., above, para. 304.
[55] E.P.A., ss. 37 (1), 36 (2). The periods may be varied by the Secretary of State: s. 36 (3).
[56] E.P.A., s. 37 (3).
[57] *Ibid.* s. 37 (4).
[58] *Ibid.* s. 37 (5). See above, para. 303, regarding a "week's pay."
[59] *Ibid.* s. 34 (3).
[60] *Ibid.* s. 38 (1). The three-month period is calculated from the last day on which payment was due. An extension is possible if it was not reasonably practicable to present the claim in time: see Chap. 22.
[61] E.P.A., s. 38 (3).
[62] *Ibid.* ss. 29–47.
[63] *Ibid.* s. 42 (1).
[64] *Ibid.* s. 42 (2).
[65] *Ibid.* s. 43 (1) (*a*).   [66] *Ibid.* ss. 43 (1) (*b*), 45.

may recover the amount from the defaulting employer for the benefit of the Fund.[67]

An employer refused a rebate or paid less than the amount to which he claims to be entitled may present a complaint to an industrial tribunal.[68] So can employees refused payments direct from the Fund.[69] The tribunal may make a declaration as to the amount of the payment due. An employer may also appeal against any recovery the Secretary of State determines to make.[70]

Remuneration during suspension on medical grounds

320   An employee [71] with four weeks' service [72] who is suspended from work by his employer on medical grounds in consequence of certain statutory requirements [73] or any provision of a code of practice issued under section 16 of the Health and Safety at Work, etc. Act 1974, is entitled to be paid by his employer while suspended for a period not exceeding 26 weeks.[74] The right to remuneration exists " only if, and so long as, he continues to be employed by his employer, but is not provided with work or does not perform the work he normally performed before the suspension." [75] The employee loses his right to payment during any period of suspension when he is incapable of work by reason of disease or bodily or mental impairment,[76] or if he unreasonably refuses a suitable offer of alternative work,[77] or if he does not comply with reasonable requirements laid down by his employer to ensure that his services are available.[78]

321   The amount of the payment is a week's pay calculated in accordance with Schedule 4 to the Employment Protection Act in respect of each week of suspension.[79] There is a rule of mutual set-off of contractual remuneration and any payment due under the statutory provisions.[80] A complaint that an employer has failed to make a statutory payment must be presented by the employee to an industrial tribunal within three months. The tribunal may order payment of the amount due.[81]

Remuneration during disciplinary suspension

322   This topic is dealt with in Chapter 13 in relation to work discipline.

---

[67] *Ibid.* s. 44.

[68] *Ibid.* s. 46 (1) (*a*).

[69] *Ibid.* s. 46 (1) (*b*).

[70] *Ibid.* s. 46 (4). There is a three-month time limit: s. 46. The Secretary of State may, in certain circumstances, require the employer to provide information in respect of a claim against the Fund by an employee: s. 47.

[71] Defined in T.U.L.R.A., s. 30. Certain classes of employee are excluded: E.P.A., s. 119 (2) (3) (4) (5) (7).

[72] Ending with the last complete week before the day on which suspension begins: E.P.A., s. 30 (1).

[73] These statutory requirements are listed in Sched. 2 to E.P.A.

[74] E.P.A., s. 29.

[75] *Ibid.* s. 29 (2).

[76] *Ibid.* s. 30 (2).

[77] *Ibid.* s. 30 (3) (*a*).

[78] *Ibid.* s. 30 (3) (*b*).

[79] *Ibid.* s. 31.

[80] *Ibid.* s. 31 (4).

[81] *Ibid.* s. 32. The dismissal of a replacement of a medically suspended employee is not unfair provided that s. 33 is complied with: see Chap. 17.

Guarantee payments when work is not available

323   The widespread industrial practice of laying-off employees during periods of recession, or shortage of supplies, or other occurrences affecting normal working of the business (*e.g.* the flooding of the factory) may take one of at least four different legal forms: (1) frustration of the contract; (2) dismissal of the employee; (3) dismissal followed by re-engagement when normal working is resumed; or (4) suspension of the contractual relationship until normal working can be resumed. The first situation rarely arises. It is narrowly confined to the situation in which some supervening external event disables the employer from providing work, without his fault (*e.g.* the flooded factory).[82] It seems likely that if there is any possibility of offering the employee work within a reasonable period, there will be no frustration. The mutual rights of the parties where there is frustration are discussed in Chapter 14.

324   The second situation is also rare because by its nature a lay-off is intended to be temporary and not to bring a permanent end to the relationship of employer and employee. However, we have seen (para. 273) that in certain exceptional cases the failure of an employer to provide work (*e.g.* to an actor) may constitute a repudiation and so count as a dismissal in law. This may give rise to claims in respect of unfair dismissal (see Chapter 17) or wrongful dismissal (see Chapter 15).

325   The third situation occurs quite frequently in practice. In industries like shipbuilding and construction employees are usually laid-off until the next job. If the employee has two years' continuous service, he may claim a redundancy payment on the grounds that his dismissal is attributable to the cessation or diminution of a particular kind of work (see Chapter 18). If he has six months' continuous service and is unfairly selected for redundancy he may be able to claim that he has been unfairly dismissed (see Chapter 17). If he does not claim a redundancy payment and is subsequently re-engaged, the "temporary cessation of work" attributable to the lay-off will not normally break his continuity of employment but will actually count towards his total period of continuous service (see Chapter 5). However, since the contract has been terminated he will not be entitled to any contractual remuneration.

326   It is the fourth situation, suspensory lay-off, with which we are concerned in this section. Here a distinction may be drawn between suspension from the duties of employment without loss of pay, and suspension without pay (or with some loss of pay). We have seen that, at common law, the employer is under no general obligation to provide work. Apart from a few exceptional situations (para. 272) the employer can suspend an employee without loss of pay. However, there is no general right to suspend without pay. While the contract subsists, the employee on time rates is entitled to be paid his contractual remuneration even though he is not provided with work. The same applies, in principle, to a worker on piece-rates. For example, in *Devonald* v. *Rosser & Sons*,[83] the employer shut down his tinplate factory because trade was slack and gave his piece-

---

[82] *e.g.* *Turner* v. *Goldsmith* [1891] 1 Q.B. 544 (sales representative's contract not frustrated when employer's factory burned down because his duties were not defined in such a way as to depend entirely upon the factory's output).
[83] [1906] 2 K.B. 728; *Bauman* v. *Hulton Press Ltd.* [1952] W.N. 556.

rate rollermen one month's notice. They were given no work during the period of notice and so could earn no wages. The Court of Appeal held that there was an implied term that the rollermen would be enabled to earn wages during the period of notice. The breach of this term entitled them to damages assessed on the basis of their average earnings during the previous six weeks.

327   There are two exceptions to this general right to remuneration during the subsistence of the contract. The first is where, by express or implied agreement or custom, the right to be paid is excluded. In *Devonald* v. *Rosser & Sons*,[84] an attempt to prove such a custom failed, on the ground that it would have been unreasonable for the employer to have the right to close down the works without notice at any time they were running at a loss whereas the employees would remain bound to him for the period of notice during which time they would not have been able to earn any remuneration at all. The courts tend to construe restrictions on the right to wages restrictively. For example, an express clause which provided that musicians were not to be paid when they did not play was held not to give the employer the right to lay them off without wages for as long as he liked.[85] The clause meant simply that they were not entitled to be paid for such performances as it was reasonable (in the eyes of the court) for the employer to cancel. Many manual workers are "hourly paid," even though they may be entitled to the minimum periods of up to eight weeks' notice under the Contracts of Employment Act 1972. It is often believed [86] that the hourly calculation of payment means that they are entitled to pay only for such hours as work is actually made available to them. This view, as far as is known, has never been tested (and is, in our view, questionable),[87] but it has been responsible for the development of "guaranteed week" collective agreements, which become incorporated into individual contracts.

328   The second exception is where the employer fails to provide work, during the subsistence of the contract, due to circumstances beyond his control. This seems to be the principle underlying the judicial dicta in *Devonald* v. *Rosser & Sons* that had the reason for the lack of work been a lack of materials or a power breakdown or mechanical mishap, rather than a falling off of trade, the employer would not have had to enable the piece-rate workers to earn remuneration. These dicta were acted upon in *Browning* v. *Crumlin Valley Collieries Ltd.*,[88] in which a colliery had to close down for a period, while repairs were done, because it had become unsafe due to no fault on the part of the employers. Greer J. held that "no employer would have consented" to an implied term in the contracts of employees on piece-rates that he should provide them with work to enable them to earn wages when he had no control over

---

[84] Above, note 83. For an example of a case where an agreement not to provide work existed, see *Puttick* v. *John Wright & Sons Ltd.* [1972] I.C.R. 457 (N.I.R.C.).

[85] *Minnevitch* v. *Café de Paris (Londres) Ltd.* [1936] 1 All E.R. 884.

[86] *e.g.* H. A. Clegg, *System of Industrial Relations in Great Britain* (London, 1970), p. 215.

[87] We would argue that the "custom" is an unreasonable one, because the employees would be bound for the period of notice (since 1963, at least one week) while the employer would have the power to deprive them of remuneration during that period: see *Devonald* v. *Rosser & Sons* (above).

[88] [1926] 1 K.B. 522.

the cause of the closure. The intention was that employer and employees should share the risks of untoward events, like unsafe conditions and breakage of machinery. It is not certain how far this principle goes, but presumably the courts would apply it to deprive employees of remuneration during lay-offs caused by strikes at the premises of suppliers. The real difficulty is in knowing what circumstances will be regarded as " beyond the control " of an employer. There seems no logic in suggesting that unsafe conditions are beyond an employer's control, but a general trade depression is not. Yet that is how the courts have drawn the line.

329   The lack of security of income for employees has led to three important developments: (1) " guaranteed week " collective agreements; (2) guarantee payments under the Employment Protection Act 1975; and (3) redundancy payments for employees who have no right to remuneration at all by reason of lack of work. The third topic will be discussed in Chapter 18. Here we shall first discuss the nature and effect of " guaranteed week " agreements, and, secondly, outline the provisions of the Employment Protection Act.

(1) Guaranteed week collective agreements [89]

330   There is a wide variety of collective agreements which have the effect of guaranteeing workers some of their normal wages for the first few days or weeks of lay-off. These agreements appear to have had their origin in the war-time Essential Works Orders [90] which guaranteed the employee's wage in return for his showing reasonable occupational mobility. Following the war-time example most agreements require the employee to be willing to accept an offer of suitable alternative employment. Most provide for payment of less than a full week's pay. These agreements generally take effect as express or implied terms of individual contracts of employment (see Chapter 8). To the extent that they are less favourable than the minimum standards laid down in the Employment Protection Act 1975 they are superseded by that Act.

331   The question arises not infrequently whether the employer has legal power to suspend the guaranteed week agreement. If the agreement has become incorporated in the individual employee's contract then the employer cannot lawfully suspend the agreement without the employee's consent. This consent may, of course, have been given in general terms in advance. An example is a collective agreement in the Hosiery Manufacture industry which provides that " the guaranteed week may be suspended from the end of any working week on notice in writing to this effect being given by the employer." Most agreements are not this wide but do allow suspension in the event of industrial action causing dislocation of production.[91] Many codify the common law rule (para. 328

---

[89] For a general review, see Incomes Data Studies Nos. 20 (Jan. 1972) and 22 (Feb. 1972) and for the legal implications I.D.S. Brief Nos. 56 and 57 (March 1975); Freedland, *The Contract of Employment* (Oxford, 1976), pp. 86 *et seq.*

[90] *e.g.* S.R. & O. 1942 No. 1594. Guaranteed pay provisions are also found in Wages Councils Orders made under the Wages Councils Act 1959.

[91] *e.g.* an agreement between the Engineering Employers' Federation and the Confederation of Shipbuilding and Engineering Unions which provides: " In the event of dislocation of production in a federated establishment as a result of an industrial dispute in that or any other federated establishment, the operation of the period of the guarantee

above) that no payment will be made if work is not available because of circumstances beyond the employer's control.

332   In the absence of an express power to suspend the guaranteed week agreement, it appears that the courts will be reluctant to imply such a power. In *Powell Duffryn Ltd.* v. *House* [92] (a redundancy payments case) the N.I.R.C. indicated that cogent evidence must be produced to support a contention that employees have given up their right to guaranteed pay. It is submitted that the mere fact that the employees have entered into a guaranteed week agreement, without express power to suspend, is itself cogent evidence of an intention that the employees should be paid in any event.

(2) *Guarantee payments under the Employment Protection Act* 1975 [93]

333   The inadequacy of collective bargaining in this field has led to the creation of this statutory floor of rights. It is not possible to contract-out of these rights [94] (by collective agreement or otherwise) unless there is an exemption order in force made by the Secretary of State in respect of a collective agreement [95] or wages order [96] which gives employees a *right* to guaranteed remuneration. Exemption will be granted only on the application of all the parties to the agreement and because there must be a "right" to remuneration the employer must not have power to suspend the agreement. In view of this, and the other stringent conditions to be satisfied before an exemption order will be made, it seems likely that in future collective agreements will be used simply to improve upon the minimum standards laid down in the Act.

334   An employee is entitled to be paid a "guarantee payment" for certain days when he is not provided with work. The maximum amount payable is £6 per day [97] and in any quarter [98] an employee cannot receive guarantee payments for more than five days.[99] These limits can be raised by an order made by the Secretary of State.[1]

335   In order to be eligible for a guarantee payment the employee must satisfy the following requirements:
    (a) He must be an employee,[2] and not fall within an excluded class.[3]

---

shall be automatically suspended." Under E.P.A., s. 22, the trade dispute disqualification is limited to a dispute with an associated employer; this overrides the engineering agreement.
[92] [1974] I.C.R. 123.
[93] E.P.A., ss. 22–28.
[94] *Ibid.* s. 118 (1), subject to s. 118 (2) (*a*).
[95] Defined in T.U.L.R.A., s. 29.
[96] E.P.A., s. 28.
[97] *Ibid.* s. 25 (1).
[98] The quarters begin on February 1, May 1, August 1, November 1: s. 25 (2).
[99] E.P.A., s. 25 (3) (*a*). If the average number of days which the employee normally works in a week, under his contract, is only three·or four, then only that number of days' payment need be made. S. 25 (3) gives the precise calculation: number of days normally worked under contract for 12 weeks ending with last complete week before payment claimed divided by 12, and rounded up to next whole number, *e.g.* 40 divided by 12 equals 3·3, *i.e.* four days' payment. S. 25 (3) (*c*) deals with the case where less than 12 weeks have been worked.
[1] E.P.A., s. 25 (5). There must be annual reviews: s. 86.
[2] E.P.A., s. 126, which refers to T.U.L.R.A., s. 30. See Chap. 3.
[3] These are husband or wife of employer (s. 119 (2)); registered dockworkers (s. 119 (3)); share fishermen (s. 119 (4)); those working outside G.B. (s. 119 (5) (6)); those under fixed term contracts or on specific tasks for 12 weeks or less (s. 119 (7)).

(b) He must have been continuously employed for four weeks ending with the last complete week before the day in respect of which payment is claimed.[4]

(c) He must normally be required to work, in accordance with his contract of employment, during any part of the day (known as a " workless day ") for which the payment is claimed.[5] For example, if Saturday working is not required under the contract but is voluntary no payment can be claimed for a Saturday on which no work is provided.

(d) He must not be provided with work throughout the workless day.[6]

(e) The reason for not being provided with work must be either (i) a diminution in the requirements of the employer's business for work of the kind which the employee is employed to do[7] ; or (ii) any other occurrence affecting the normal working of the employer's business in relation to work of the kind which the employee is employed to do.[8]

(f) The employee must have normal working hours on the workless day.[9]

336   There are three general *exclusions* from the right to a guarantee payment. First, if the failure to provide work occurs in consequence of a trade dispute.[10] Since this disqualification is far wider than the trade dispute disqualification in respect of unemployment benefit and supplementary benefit[11] there will be cases where the employee laid-off due to a trade dispute will be eligible for these state benefits but not for a guarantee payment. For example, the dispute may occur at a place other than his own place of employment, or be a dispute between an associated employer of his employer and its employees. A second exclusion is where the employee has unreasonably refused suitable alternative work for the workless day. It is to be noted that the work may be adjudged suitable although the employee is not contractually bound to perform it and what is reasonable for purposes of a temporary lay-off may be different from what would be reasonable for permanent work (the latter being in issue where a redundancy payment is claimed following dismissal).[12] Thirdly, the employee is not entitled to a payment if he fails to comply with reasonable requirements imposed by the employer with a view to ensuring that his services are available.[13]

337   Subject to the limits mentioned above the amount of the guarantee payment on any workless day is the sum produced by multiplying the

---

[4] E.P.A., s. 22 (3). The definition of " continuous employment " is in Sched. 1 to C.E.A., as amended by E.P.A., Sched. 16, Pt. II, paras. 12–19: see Chap. 5. Definition of " week " in s. 24 (5) will presumably be followed in this context.

[5] E.P.A., s. 22 (1). The relevant contract is that in force on the last day before short-time working began: s. 24 (4). Definition of " day " in s. 22 (2).

[6] E.P.A., s. 22 (1).

[7] *Ibid.* s. 22 (1) (*a*). In this situation there may also be an entitlement to a redundancy payment: see Chap. 18.

[8] *Ibid.* s. 22 (1) (*b*). " Occurrence " is not defined, and would presumably include any industrial action (such as a political strike) not falling within the trade dispute exclusion (below).

[9] *Ibid.* s. 24 (1).

[10] E.P.A., s. 23 (1). For definition, see T.U.L.R.A., s. 29, as applied by E.P.A., s. 126. The dispute must involve any employee of his employer or an associated employer.

[11] Social Security Act 1975, s. 10 (2); Supplementary Benefits Act 1966, s. 10, as amended by E.P.A., s. 111. These statutes allow the employee to show that he has nothing to do with the dispute. See Chap. 19.

[12] E.P.A., s. 23 (2) (*a*). *Cf.* R.P.A., s. 2 (4).

[13] E.P.A., s. 23 (1) (*b*).

number of normal working hours on that day by the so-called " guaranteed hourly rate." [14] (There can be no guarantee payment if there are no normal hours on the day in question.) The " guaranteed hourly rate " is calculated by dividing one week's pay by the number of normal hours in a week under the contract of employment in force on the workless day.[15] This should be straightforward when the hours do not vary. When the hours differ from week to week, a 12-week average is taken.[16] It may happen that the employee accepts short-time working and thereby consents to a variation of his contractual hours of work. In that event the employee's guarantee payment is protected because it is then to be calculated by reference to the last day of full-time working under the original contract.[17]

(3) *Relation between guarantee payment and contractual remuneration*

338   Rights conferred under the employee's contract (by the incorporation of a collective agreement or otherwise) are separate from the rights under the Employment Protection Act. However, the Act applies a rule of mutual set-off.[18] Any contractual remuneration paid to an employee in respect of a workless day goes towards discharging the liability of the employer to pay a guarantee payment in respect of that day. Conversely the guarantee payment paid in respect of a workless day is set off against any contractual remuneration due.

(4) *Relation between guarantee payment and social security benefits*

339   During the first three days of lay-off no unemployment benefit is payable [19] so the employee is entitled to the full guarantee payment for those days. After the first three days he may become eligible for unemployment benefit. Regulations are to be made by the Secretary of State [20] regarding the relationship of guarantee payments and social security benefits.

(5) *Remedies*

340   While failure to pay contractual remuneration is at present a matter for the ordinary courts, and social security benefits are dealt with by insurance officers and local insurance tribunals, a complaint of failure to pay the whole or part of a statutory guarantee payment may be presented to an industrial tribunal within three months of the day for which it was payable. The tribunal may order payment.[21]

The minimum amount of wages

341   There is remarkably little statutory regulation of wage rates. There is no national minimum wage, although the system of non-contributory

---

[14] *Ibid*. s. 24 (1).
[15] *Ibid*. s. 24 (2) (*a*). " Week " is defined in s. 24 (5).
[16] *Ibid*. s. 24 (2) (*b*). See s. 24 (2) (*c*) for the situation where 12 weeks have not been worked. For " week's pay," see Sched. 4 to E.P.A.: discussed above.
[17] E.P.A., ss. 24 (4), 25 (4).
[18] *Ibid*. s. 26 (2) The extent of the set-off will depend upon the form in which the contractual remuneration is expressed in the contract: s. 26 (3). Once there has been a set-off of contractual remuneration for a particular workless day, that day is not to count towards the maximum number of days under s. 25 (3).
[19] Social Security Act 1975, s. 14 (3). See Chap. 19.
[20] E.P.A., s. 112 (at the time of writing these have not been made).
[21] *Ibid*. s. 27.

family income supplements, payable through the social security system in terms of the Family Income Supplements Act 1970, is an attempt to bring the incomes of certain poorer families up to a subsistence level. This minimum standard is to be achieved by means external to the individual employment relationship.

Parliament has intervened, however, to support the voluntary system of collective bargaining by providing machinery to protect certain low-paid and non-organised workers. These statutes, in so far as they result in awards or orders incorporated into individual contracts, are discussed in Chapters 1 to 8.

Pay control

342   Several attempts have been made in recent years to impose statutory limits on pay. Statutory controls were, however, abolished in 1974,[22] while price controls continue.[23] The Remuneration, Charges and Grants Act 1975 lends statutory support to the incomes policy agreed between the TUC and the Government, from time to time.[24] The 1975 Act does not impose direct legal controls over pay. However, an employer who observes the voluntary pay limits is afforded a statutory defence against claims for breach of contract,[25] and a pay settlement in excess of the voluntary norm, as certified by the Secretary of State, may be disallowed for the purpose of price increases.[26]

Expenses incurred in employment

343   Some of the books say that an employee is entitled to be indemnified against all liabilities, losses and expenses which he incurs in consequence of obedience to orders or in the proper performance of his work.[27] The principle may, however, be somewhat narrower than this. The decided cases in which an indemnity has been granted concern employees who were acting within the scope of their authority as agents, *i.e.,* employed to bring the employer into contractual relations with others.[28] The principle of indemnity is not necessarily limited to the principal/agency relationship,[29] but it may be significant that in *Re Famatina Development Corporation Ltd.*[30] the Court of Appeal, in holding that a consulting engineer was entitled to be indemnified against claims for libel and slander unwittingly committed in the discharge of his work, was careful to say that the engineer "was more than a servant of the company and the duties imposed on him were far wider than those of consulting engineer." [31] The true principle, it

---

[22] Counter-Inflation (Abolition of Pay Board) Order (S.I. 1974 No. 1218) made under the Prices Act 1974, s. 6.

[23] Under the Counter-Inflation Act 1973 and Prices Act 1974.

[24] The policy until July 31, 1976, is set out in a White Paper, " The Attack on Inflation," Cmnd. 6151. The voluntary limits do not interfere with the application of legislation extending terms and conditions of employment and equal pay (H.C. Deb. Vol. 896, col. 804, July 24, 1975).

[25] Remuneration, Charges and Grants Act 1975, s. 1.

[26] *Ibid.* s. 3. Local authorities breaching the pay limit may have their rate support grant reduced: s. 4.

[27] Halsbury's *Laws of England* (3rd ed.), Vol. 25, para. 906; Drake, *Labour Law,* 2nd ed., p. 53.

[28] *Adamson* v. *Jarvis* (1827) 4 Bing. 66; *Betts* v. *Gibbins* (1834) 2 Ald. & E. 57.

[29] *Dugdale* v. *Lovering* (1875) L.R. 10 C.P. 196.

[30] [1914] 2 Ch. 271.

[31] *Ibid.* at p. 282.

is suggested, is that an employee is entitled to be indemnified in respect of expenses necessarily incurred in the course of his employment, if this was an express or implied term of his contract. An implied term will more readily be found in the case of an employee who is engaged to bring his employer into contractual relations with third parties than in the case of an ordinary employee. It should be remembered that the holder of an office or employment may be allowed to deduct certain expenses " wholly, exclusively and necessarily " incurred in the performance of his duties for purposes of the assessment of income tax.[32] This is narrowly construed. " The test," said Donovan L.J., " is not whether the employer imposes the expense but whether the duties do, in the sense that, irrespective of what the employer may prescribe, the duties cannot be performed without incurring the particular outlay." [33] Moreover, the expenses, to be deductible, must be necessary to the office or employment and not simply necessary to the particular employee. So the manager of an insurance company who had to maintain an office at home because defective eyesight kept him from driving to town was not entitled to deduce his special household expenses.[34]

Manner of payment

344   At common law the employer and employee are free to agree how wages are to be paid, whether in cash, or by cheque, or through a bank or post office giro account, or in kind. They can also agree on the place of payment and the periods at which payments are to be made. To this common law rule there is an important exception. The Truck Acts 1831–1940 prohibit the payment of wages otherwise than in the current coin of the realm to a " workman " to whom the Acts apply. We saw in Chapter 3 that " workman " is confined to manual workers, other than domestic or menial employees.[35] A redrafting of these statutes has long been overdue, not least because they do not cover white-collar workers who may be less well unionised, and less protected in practice than manual workers, against the abuses which the Acts were designed to prevent.

These abuses were described by the word " truck," from the French *troq* or *troquer* (to barter). In fact this word indicates only one of those abuses, namely, the " tommy shop " run by the employer or his relatives at which vouchers or credits in lieu of wages could be exchanged for goods, often of poor quality. Other evils were payments in kind, and the arbitrary imposition of fines, for example for bad workmanship or bad time-keeping. The objection to all these forms of payment was that the worker was deprived of the full value of his wages, both because of the methods of

---

[32] Income and Corporation Taxes Act 1970, s. 189; see, too, *ibid.* s. 191 (official emoluments); s. 192 (certain fees and subscriptions); ss. 195–203 (expenses of directors and certain others); s. 411 (entertainment expenses).

[33] *Blackwell* v. *Mills* (1945) 26 T.C. 468.

[34] *Roskams* v. *Bennett* (1950) T.R. 343; *Humbles* v. *Brooks* [1962] T.R. 297 (teacher's expenses in attending course relevant to subject he taught); *cf. Pook* v. *Owen* [1969] 2 W.L.R. 775 (exceptional case where doctor's expenses in travelling to hospital allowed because his duties began when summoned from home). *Owen* v. *Burden, The Times,* October 21, 1971 (surveyor's expenses in going to international Congress on own initiative not deductible); *cf. Horton* v. *Young* [1972] Ch. 157 (C.A.) (sub-contracting bricklayer's travelling expenses deductible from taxable profits under Schedule D); *Taylor* v. *Provan* [1975] A.C. 194 (travelling expenses deductible).

[35] Above, paras. 123 and 124. The Acts are enforced by officers appointed by the Secretary of State (in practice wages inspectors): Truck Act 1896, s. 10, as substituted by Truck Acts 1831 to 1896 (Enforcement) Regs. 1974 (S.I. 1974 No. 1887).

performance chosen by the employer and because of the assertion of counterclaims by the employer.

345   Section 1 of the Truck Act 1831 renders " illegal null and void " any contract for the payment of wages " otherwise than in the current coin of the realm." Section 3 obliges the employer to pay " in the current coin of this realm, and not otherwise . . . the entire amount of the wages earned or payable to the workman in respect of any labour done by him." The House of Lords held, in *Williams* v. *North's Navigation Collieries*,[36] that section 3 means that the employer must pay in current coin, not only the entire amount he actually pays, but also the entire amount he has promised to pay. In other words, section 3 defines the manner of payment (current coin) and prohibits any deductions from the promised amount. So if the employer owes the workman £20 a payment of £19 would be illegal. It would likewise be illegal to agree with a workman to pay him in kind, or to break a contract for payment in cash by paying in kind. It is a criminal offence under section 9 of the Act " to make any payment hereby declared illegal." [37]

346   The 1831 Act included banknotes in the definition of " current coin." [38] It permitted payment by cheque only if the workman consented and the cheque was payable to bearer and drawn on a bank licensed to issue notes and situated within fifteen miles of the place of payment.[39] This became obsolete in practice when, later in the century, the Bank of England became the only bank so licensed in England. Eventually, by the Payment of Wages Act 1960, a complicated scheme of exceptions to the employer's obligation to pay in current coin or notes was introduced. The Act permits payment to Truck Act workmen into a bank account, by money order or postal order or by cheque.[40] In all cases the workman must make a written request for payment by one of these methods and the employer must agree. The employer may not make such a request a condition of employment,[41] and either the employer or the workman can cancel the request, or agreement, on giving four weeks' notice in writing.[42] There is only one situation in which the workman can be compelled to accept one of these methods of payment. This is where he is absent from the proper or usual place of payment, either on duty or sick, and is entitled to wages.[43] Even in this case the workman can give written notice that he does not wish to receive payment in one of these ways.[44] A number of formalities must be complied with in respect of an authorised method of payment (*e.g.*, the cheque must be made payable to or to the order of the workman, he must be given at or before the time of payment a statement of particulars etc.).[45]

---

[36] [1906] A.C. 136.

[37] And see Truck Amendment Act 1887, s. 12 (power of employer to exempt himself from penalty on conviction of actual offender); a person " engaged in the same trade or occupation as an employer charged with an offence " may not act as a justice in hearing or determining the charge: *ibid.* s. 15.

[38] Truck Act 1831, s. 8.

[39] *Ibid.*

[40] Payment of Wages Act 1960, s. 1.

[41] *Ibid.* s. 6 (7).

[42] *Ibid.* s. 3.

[43] *Ibid.* s. 4.

[44] *Ibid.* s. 4 (5).

[45] *Ibid.* s. 2 and Sched., Pt. I.

According to an official memorandum submitted to the Donovan Commission, there is no evidence that the 1960 Act has brought about widespread changes in methods of wage payment.[46] It must be remembered that for Truck Act workmen payments in kind, of the variety which exists among some white-collar workers such as luncheon vouchers [47] or shares in the enterprise,[48] remain illegal. One other historical legacy, applicable only to manual workers, is the Payment of Wages in Public Houses Prohibition Act 1883. The fine for paying wages at or near any public-house is up to £10.[49]

Deductions from wages of Truck Act workmen

347   The Act of 1831 and the Truck Amendment Act 1887 authorise certain deductions from wages (*e.g.*, for food on premises if specially agreed; rent for a dwelling; medical attendance; education of children; provender for beasts).[50] The Truck Act 1896 (which applies to shop assistants as well as workmen) authorises deductions for fines, damaged goods and damaged materials, provided certain formalities are complied with.[51] Since the 1896 Act, deductions are an important aspect of the employer's disciplinary powers; they are dealt with below in Chapter 13. Apart from these specific statutory authorisations of deductions from the wages of Truck Act workmen, the courts have found a way around the Acts in the case of deductions made at the request of the workman for payment to a third person independent of the employer. In *Hewlett* v. *Allen* [52] the plaintiff was obliged by the works rules, which formed part of her contract, to join the works sick and accident club. Her subscriptions were deducted from her weekly wages. The House of Lords, in a decision which was subsequently described by Lord Wright as going " to the limit of what is permissible in the way of liberal construction," [53] held that a request to place money in the hands of a third person, other than the employer, was not affected by the Truck Acts. In a later case,[54] the House of Lords held that the third person must be independent of the employer. (Incidentally, it is by no means clear that this was the case in *Hewlett* v. *Allen*.) The employer cannot be both payer and payee. It is these decisions which are usually taken to authorise the check-off system, in respect of trade union subscriptions, for manual workers. However, an employer may act on a check-off arrangement with a union only so long as the arrangement can be regarded as part of the individual contract of employment.[55]

---

[46] Ministry of Labour, *Written Evidence* (H.M.S.O., 1965), p. 124.

[47] *Pratt* v. *Cook* [1940] A.C. 437 (workman allowed to recover illegal deductions for meals). This led to the passing of the Truck Act 1940 (now largely repealed), which prohibited actions for recovery of deductions from wages prior to July 10, 1940, in respect of matters set out in s. 23 of the 1831 Act. This does not apply to deductions, contrary to s. 23, *after* that date.

[48] *Kenyon* v. *Darwen Cotton Manufacturing Co.* [1936] 2 K.B. 193.

[49] s. 4. The Act applies to any workman who is a " labourer, servant in husbandry, journeyman, artificer, handicraftsman, or is otherwise engaged in manual labour . . . but does not include a domestic or menial servant."

[50] Truck Act 1831, ss. 23, 24; Truck Amendment Act 1887, ss. 3, 4, 7, 8, 9.

[51] Truck Act 1896, ss. 1, 2, 3.

[52] [1894] A.C. 383.

[53] *Penman* v. *Fife Coal Co. Ltd.* [1936] A.C. 45 (workman agreed employers should deduct rent owed by his father to employers. Held: illegal).

[54] *Ibid.*

[55] *Williams* v. *Butlers Ltd.* [1974] I.R.L.R. 253 (D.C.) and [1975] I.C.R. 208 (second hearing); and see Freedland (1975) 4 I.L.J. 241.

Deductions: other protected employees

348   Apart from the Truck Acts, there are several statutes applying to special groups of workers, limiting the parties' contractual freedom in regard to deductions. For example, the Hosiery Manufacture (Wages) Act 1874 renders " illegal, null, and void " all contracts to stop wages and all frame rents and charges between employers and " artificers " [56] in the hosiery trade, and prohibits deductions except for bad and disputed workmanship. These exceptions are discussed in Chapter 13, in connection with disciplinary action. Notwithstanding the Truck Acts, the wages of a check-weigher may be proportionately deducted from the wages of the miners who appointed him.[57] The Merchant Shipping Act 1970 contains detailed provisions about the payment of wages to merchant seamen.[58] The Act specifically restricts assignments and charges on wages and at the same time protects the " check-off " system in regard to payment of contributions to approved funds and bodies to which the seaman belongs.[59] A seaman may, by means of an allotment note issued in accordance with regulations made by the Department of Trade, allot to any person part of the wages to which he will become entitled in the course of his seafaring employment. Regulations have been made limiting the circumstances in which allotments may be made, the persons to whom and the times at which they may be made and limiting the allottable part of the wages.[60] A person named in the allotment note may (contrary to ordinary principles of privity of contract) sue in his own name for recovery of the allotted wages.[61]

Deductions: unprotected employees

349   We have seen that the Truck Acts, and other legislation limiting deductions, were designed to prevent the abuses which arose from the attempts of employers to assert set-offs and counterclaims against claims for wages due. The piecemeal development of the protective legislation since 1831 means that many categories of employees, in particular most of those in white-collar jobs, may still lawfully agree to any form of deduction from their wages. Even without agreement, the employer may set off, against a claim for wages, debts owing to him by an unprotected employee, for example for goods supplied. There are, however, certain restraints on the power to make unilateral deductions for disciplinary reasons. These are discussed in Chapter 13.

Compulsory deductions

350   There are certain deductions which an employer must make from wages, whether he and the employee wish it or not. These are statutory obligations, for example:

---

[56] " Artificers " include all workmen, labourers and other persons in any manner engaged in the performance or any employment or operation in or about hosiery manufacture. The Act was designed to reverse judicial decisions in which it had been held that the letting of frames to knitters and the deductions from their wages for the rents were not illegal: *e.g.*, *Chawner* v. *Cummings* (1846) 8 Q.B. 311.

[57] A majority must assent to the deductions. See para. 351.

[58] Merchant Shipping Act 1970, ss. 7–18.

[59] *Ibid.* s. 11 and regulations made thereunder.

[60] *Ibid.* s. 13 and regulations made thereunder.

[61] *Ibid.* s. 14.

(a) Pay As You Earn tax, applicable to persons liable to assessment under Schedule E.[62]

(b) Attachment of earnings orders, made by a court, in respect of maintenance orders, judgment debts, administration orders and legal aid contribution orders,[63] applicable to any debtor in employment.[64]

(c) Social Security contributions.[65]

Calculation of wages

351   In certain industries, in which workers were regarded as being particularly vulnerable to fraudulent miscalculation of wages, there are statutes regulating the mode of calculation. The most important example is mining, in which there have been elaborate statutory provisions since 1887 to protect those who are paid by the weight of the material gotten by them.[66] The miners may, at their own cost, and by majority vote, appoint a check-weigher to determine correctly the weight of the mineral and the deductions to be made. The owner or manager may make complaints about the conduct of the check-weigher, and apply for his removal, to a court of summary jurisdiction. The principle contained in these Acts was extended in 1919 [67] to various other industries in which employees are paid according to the weight or measure of the material produced. These industries include iron and steel manufacture, the loading and unloading of goods, chalk and limestone quarrying, and cement and lime manufacture. There is power (not yet exercised) to extend this to other industries. A provision in the Factories Act 1961 enables the inspectors appointed under the Weights and Measures Acts to check the accuracy of weights, measures and weighing and measuring instruments used in factories in ascertaining wages.[68] Another provision in the Factories Act (following the precedent of earlier legislation affecting the hosiery and silk weaving trades) requires the occupier of a textile factory, and certain other kinds of factories to which the provision has been extended by ministerial regulation, to give written particulars of wage rates and to take specified steps to enable the accuracy of automatic indicators to be checked.[69]

---

[62] Income and Corporation Taxes Act 1970, ss. 204–207.

[63] Attachment of Earnings Act 1971 and Administration of Justice Act 1970, Pt. II (both in force August 2, 1971). S. 7 (4) of the 1971 Act entitles the employer to deduct 13p towards his clerical and administrative expenses (*cf.* the Truck Acts which do not make provision for clerical etc. expenses involved in making permitted deductions).

[64] The order is directed to a person appearing to the court to have the debtor in his employment. For purposes of the Attachment of Earnings Act 1971 the relationship of employer and employee " shall be treated as subsisting between two persons if one of them, as a principal and not as a servant or agent, pays to the other any sums defined as earnings by s. 24 of the Act ": *ibid.* s. 6 (2).

[65] Social Security Act 1975, Sched. 1, and regulations made thereunder which provide for Class 1 and Class 2 contributions to be paid in like manner as income tax deductions.

[66] Stannaries Act 1887, s. 15; Coal Mines Regulation Act 1887, s. 13; Coal Mines (Weighing of Minerals) Act 1905; Coal Mines (Check Weigher) Act 1894, as amended by Mines and Quarries Act 1954, ss. 188, 189, Scheds. IV and V.

[67] Check Weighing in Various Industries Act 1919 (matters required to be submitted to arbitration under this Act must be referred to a single arbitrator appointed, in default of agreement, by a county court judge).

[68] Factories Act 1961, s. 144.

[69] *Ibid.* s. 135. This is now enforced by officers appointed by the Secretary of State (in practice wages inspectors): s. 135A inserted by S.I. 1974 No. 1776.

Itemised pay statements

352 The Employment Protection Act 1975 confers on every employee [70] the right to be given, every time payment of wages or salary is made, a written pay statement.[71] This must itemise: (1) the gross amount of wages or salary; (2) variable and fixed deductions; (3) net amount of wages or salary payable; (4) where different parts of the net amount are paid in different ways, the amount and method of each part-payment. Fixed deductions need not be itemised every time provided the aggregate amount of these deductions is given each time and the employee has been given a written statement of fixed deductions containing specified particulars.[72]

An industrial tribunal may be asked to determine what particulars ought to have been included in the pay statement and it may order the employer to pay the employee a sum not exceeding in the aggregate any unnotified deductions made from pay during the 13 weeks preceding the date of application to the tribunal.[73]

Recovery of wages

353 At the beginning of this chapter we noticed that failure to pay wages may, in certain circumstances, entitle the employee to terminate the contract. More usually, he will simply wish to institute an ordinary civil action for recovery of the debt owing to him. In this connection it should be observed that the mere fact that the employee agreed to a deduction which was described as "illegal, null, and void" under the protective legislation will not deprive him of a claim for restitution. The general rule against recovery of moneys paid in terms of an illegal transaction does not apply where the illegality results from a statute designed to protect the plaintiff.[74] Certain statutes provide particular remedies for the recovery of wages which have not been paid to an employee in breach of the statutory obligations.[75] Where, under his contract, an employee authorises deductions (*e.g.* of pension fund contributions) and the employer makes the deductions but fails to pay them to the third party, the employee may bring an action to recover those contributions.[76]

Employee's rights in insolvency

354 Under legislation, unpaid wages or salary owed by an insolvent employer are treated as preferential debts.[77] The priority extends only to "wages"

---

[70] Defined in T.U.L.R.A., s. 30, as applied by E.P.A., s. 126: see Chap. 3. The following employees are excluded: husband or wife of employer (s. 119 (2)); share fishermen (s. 119 (4)); employees normally working less than 16 hours weekly (s. 119 (8)); merchant seamen (s. 119 (12)).

[71] E.P.A., s. 81. This replaces the now superfluous provisions of the Payment of Wages Act 1960, s. 2 (4)–(8): E.P.A., Sched. 18.   [72] E.P.A., s. 82.

[73] *Ibid.* s. 84. The application must be made within three months of the ending of the employment.

[74] See Goff and Jones, *Law of Restitution* (London, 1966), p. 292.

[75] Truck Act 1831, s. 4; Truck Act 1896, s. 5 (proceedings are barred six months after date of payment for claims under this section, but apparently not under the 1831 and 1887 Acts); Wages Councils Act 1959, s. 12; Agricultural Wages Act 1948, s. 4; Merchant Shipping Act 1970, ss. 7–18.

[76] *The Halcyon Skies* [1976] 1 All E.R. 856 (Admiralty). If the employer's contributions are unpaid the employee has an action for damages: *ibid.* at p. 863.

[77] Bankruptcy Act 1914, s. 33 (covering clerks, servants, labourers and workmen, all of whom were put on the same footing by the Companies Act 1947, s. 115); Companies Act 1948, s. 319; Bankruptcy (Scotland) Act 1913, s. 118.

accruing during the four months before the date of the receiving order (appointment of a provisional liquidator or, if none appointed, date of winding-up order in case of compulsory winding up of a company) [78] and is limited to an amount of £200. For this purpose " wages " includes remuneration in respect of holidays, ordinary absence from work through sickness or other good cause, and accrued holiday remuneration,[79] as well as ordinary wages or salary whether or not wholly or partly earned by way of commission.[80] It also now includes, by virtue of the Employment Protection Act 1975,[81] any amount owed by an employer in respect of a guarantee payment, remuneration during suspension on medical grounds, payment for time off and remuneration due under a protective award.

355   The Employment Protection Act 1975 gives an employee [82] an important new right to recover certain amounts owing to him by an insolvent [83] employer from the Redundancy Fund. The employee may apply in writing at any time to the Secretary of State for payment of the following: (1) up to 8 weeks' arrears of pay (including the new statutory payments mentioned above); (2) pay for the minimum period of notice required under the Contracts of Employment Act 1972; (3) up to 6 weeks' holiday pay to which he became entitled in the 12 months before insolvency; (4) any basic award of compensation for unfair dismissal; and (5) reimbursement of premiums or fees paid for apprenticeship or articles of clerkship.[84] Where any of these amounts is calculated by time the maximum payable out of the Fund is £80 a week in respect of any one debt. It will be noted that while the maximum arrears of pay treated as a preferential debt claimable from the employer is £200, the maximum arrears of pay recoverable from the Fund is £640 (8 weeks × £80). In addition to claims by employees, certain others " competent to act " (usually trustees of a pension fund) may apply to the Secretary of State for payment from the Redundancy Fund of the unpaid contributions owing by an insolvent employer to an occupational pensions scheme.[85]

356   Where the Secretary of State makes a payment from the Fund he is in effect subrogated to the rights and remedies of the employee against the insolvent employer.[86] In other words, the Secretary of State will take over the employee's preferential claim for arrears of wages up to £200 but will be an ordinary unsecured creditor as to the excess paid to the employee from the Fund. The employee will be an unsecured creditor for any balance (*i.e.* over the statutory limit) not recovered from the Fund. The Secretary of State has power to obtain information from persons dealing with the insolvent's debts.[87]

---

[78] Companies Act 1948, s. 319 (8) (*d*). Where this does not apply the relevant date is the date of the passing of the winding-up resolution.

[79] Companies Act 1947, s. 91 (4) (5) (6) (*a*) (*b*).

[80] Bankruptcy (Amendment) Act 1926, s. 2.

[81] E.P.A., s. 63.

[82] Defined in T.U.L.R.A., s. 30, as applied by E.P.A., s. 126: see Chap. 3. Excluded are husband or wife of the employer (s. 119 (2)); registered dockworkers (s. 119 (3)); share fishermen (s. 119 (4)); those ordinarily working outside G.B. (s. 119 (5)); merchant seamen (s. 119 (12)).

[83] Defined in E.P.A., s. 69 (1).

[84] E.P.A., s. 64.

[85] *Ibid. s.* 65.

[86] *Ibid.* s. 67.

[87] *Ibid.* s. 68.

357 Complaints that the Secretary of State has failed to make payment, or that the amount is less than should have been paid, may be presented to an industrial tribunal within three months of the Secretary of State's decision.[88] The tribunal has power to make a declaration as to the amount it considers to be due.

Reform of the law

358 To an outside observer it must seem incredible that the law relating to one of the most central areas of the employment relationship, the payment of wages, is in such a problematical, patchwork and confused state. This is partly due to the fact that employers and workers have not been much concerned with the law in the past, and most of the problems have not been canvassed in litigation. It is also due to Parliament's pre-occupation with specific abuses rather than with the formulation of a general floor of rights for all workers. Perhaps, above all else, it is a reflection of the widely varied, sometimes chaotic, systems of wage payment which exist in British industry. The result of all these factors has been to prevent the development of a rational and clear body of law covering all workers. So the proposals made by the Karmel Committee in 1961 have been indefinitely shelved.[89] That committee recommended the repeal of the Truck Acts, the enactment of new legislation to cover all employees, the removal of legal obstacles to "fringe" benefits, and statutory restrictions on the right to make deductions, subject to a right of appeal to local tribunals.

2. HOURS OF WORK

Collective agreements

359 The United Kingdom has not accepted the obligation in the European Social Charter " to provide for reasonable daily and weekly working hours, the working week to be progressively reduced to the extent that the increase of productivity and other relevant factors permit." [90] And there is no general statute providing for a maximum number of working hours. This question, including the amount of overtime and night-shift work, is largely governed by collective agreements. These may be expressly or impliedly incorporated into the individual contract. Proof of this is facilitated by section 4 (1) (c) of the Contracts of Employment Act 1972, which requires employers to give written particulars to each employee of any terms and conditions relating to hours of work (including any terms and conditions relating to normal working hours). The forty-hour, five-day, week has

---

[88] *Ibid.* s. 66. The time limit may be extended if it was not " reasonably practicable " to present the complaint within the three-month period.

[89] Report of the Committee on the Truck Acts, Ministry of Labour, 1961. Discussed by O. Aiken (1962) 25 M.L.R. 220 and M. A. Hickling, *ibid.* p. 512.

[90] Art. 2 (1). See generally Chap. 20. Moreover the U.K. Government has not accepted I.L.O. Recommendation No. 116, concerning reduction of hours of work, which requires progressive reduction towards a forty-hour week: see Cmnd. 1993, 1963. The reason given is that the Recommendation is " not consistent with the methods by which conditions of employment are normally determined in the U.K."

been achieved in some industries, although even in those there may be a considerable amount of overtime working.[91]

Statutory restrictions: women and young persons

360   In the nineteenth century, legislation was found by the trade unions to be an effective way of limiting working hours. Through the activities of social reformers, legislation was enacted, from 1802 onwards, limiting the working hours of children, and later those of young persons and women. These groups were selected because their plight disturbed the public conscience and, as the Hammonds declared, " the man who [like Lord Shaftesbury] could once rouse their conscience could convince statesmen that a remedy must be tried even though he could not convince them that that remedy was wise." [92] This movement, restrained by restrictive and hostile judicial interpretations of the statutes,[93] has left us with a number of Acts, revised during this century, applicable only to children, young persons and women, and confined to particular kinds of employment. Some of those relating to children below school-leaving age have been mentioned in paragraph 185.

361   The hours of work of young persons and women are affected by a variety of statutes. In particular, Part VI of the Factories Act 1961 provides that the total hours worked by women over eighteen in a factory may not exceed nine a day or forty-eight in any week; they may not begin earlier than 7 a.m. nor end later than 8 p.m., and periods of continuous employment are limited. To these and other rules there are many complicated exceptions. The Secretary of State, and in some cases, the Health and Safety Executive, have the power to make exemption orders from these provisions, and they frequently do so. However, the mere fact that an employer has introduced equal pay for women is not of itself regarded as a sufficient reason for exemption, unless the women concerned agree with the employer's request to the Secretary of State.[94] To a very large extent the provisions relating to women in factories also apply to young persons, *i.e.*, those who are over compulsory school-leaving age but have not attained the age of eighteen. Some sections of the Factories Act apply particularly to young persons : for example, total weekly hours for those under sixteen must not exceed forty-four, and their overtime working is prohibited; for those over sixteen, overtime must not go beyond fifty hours a year, and then only by ministerial order; and there are special restrictions on shift work and continuous employment of male young persons over sixteen. The Employment of Women, Young Persons and Children

---

[91] A detailed discussion of the problems raised in this paragraph will be found in National Board for Prices and Incomes, Report No. 161 (Hours of Work, Overtime and Shift Working), Cmnd. 4554, 1970. See too I.D.S. Study No. 84, *Flexible Working Hours* (1974).

[92] J. L. and Barbara Hammond, *Lord Shaftesbury* (London, 1923), p. 69.

[93] *Ibid.* p. 135, quoting the Attorney-General's report to Lord Shaftesbury that Parke J. had said that as the Ten Hours Act of 1844 was " a law to restrain the exercise of capital and property, it must be construed stringently."

[94] The Equal Opportunities Commission, in consultation with the Health and Safety Commission, must keep these and other discriminatory health and safety provisions under review: S.D.A., s. 55. See Chap. 11. A Working Party of the National Joint Advisory Council was divided on the need for statutory control of women's hours of work: *Hours of Employment of Women and Young Persons employed in Factories. A Report* (H.M.S.O., 1969).

Act 1920 and the Hours of Employment (Conventions) Act 1936, giving effect to ILO Conventions, ban the employment of children in industrial undertakings and severely restrict the employment of women and young persons in those undertakings at night (*i.e.*, between 10 p.m. and 5 a.m.). The meal times and hours of employment of young shop assistants are also specially restricted.[95] The employment below ground in mines and quarries of children, and in mines of women and some young persons, is totally prohibited, and there are restrictions on their hours of employment above ground.[96]

The Young Persons (Employment) Acts 1938 and 1964 regulate the hours and holidays of young persons in a number of specified occupations, including goods delivery, errands, hotels, public places, lifts, cinemas and laundries.

Statutory restrictions covering adult males

362   Despite several attempts, since Cobbett's Bills of 1853 and 1855, to restrict the hours of working men by statute, it is exceptional to find legislation which applies to them. A miner may spend no more than seven hours a day underground, with certain exceptions, as a result of Acts passed in 1908, 1919 and 1954.[97] The Baking Industry (Hours of Work) Act 1954 limits the hours of night work in bakeries, the Hours of Employment (Conventions) Act 1936 restricts those of sheet glass workers, and the Shops Act 1950 and Shops (Early Closing Days) Act 1965 limit those of shop assistants. Part VI of the Transport Act 1968 limits the hours of work of drivers of public service vehicles, large motor-vehicles, heavy and light locomotives and goods vehicles to eleven hours a day (or exceptionally fourteen), with a maximum of sixty hours per week. There are provisions for rest periods and for limits on periods of continuous driving.[98]

Enforcement of the statutory restrictions

363   Each of the restrictions carries with it a criminal offence usually leading, on conviction, to a fine. Enforcement is in the hands of the relevant inspectorate, *i.e.*, of factories, or mines, or shops, or bakeries.[99]

3. HOLIDAYS

364   The European Social Charter requires states to provide for public holidays with pay and a minimum of two weeks' annual holiday with pay for all workers. In the United Kingdom there is no general statutory guarantee of these rights. Indeed, the only statute which directly regulates holidays is the Factories Act 1961,[1] which provides that, subject to certain

---

[95] Shops Act 1950, which defines " young person " in very much the same way as the Factories Act.

[96] Mines and Quarries Act 1954, ss. 124, 125, 126, 127, 128, Sched. IV.

[97] Coal Mines Regulation Act 1908, s. 1; as amended by Coal Mines Act 1919, s. 1; and Mines and Quarries Act 1954, s. 189, Sched. V.

[98] These provisions are extended to drivers of foreign goods vehicles and foreign public service vehicles by the Road Traffic (Foreign Vehicles) Act 1972, s. 1 and Sched. 2.

[99] These are, in fact, officers appointed under the Wages Councils Act and furnished with a certificate of appointment under the Baking Industry (Hours of Work) Act 1954.

[1] s. 94; and note *ibid.* s. 109 (Jewish sabbath).

exceptions, a factory occupier must allow the whole of Christmas Day, Good Friday and every bank holiday [2] to every woman and young person employed in the factory. On giving three weeks' notice the occupier may substitute some other weekday for each of these holidays. There is indirect statutory regulation by Wages Councils and the Agricultural Wages Board, which have power to fix holidays and holiday pay for workers whose wages they regulate.[3]

365   Apart from these provisions, the right to holidays, including bank holidays, depends entirely upon the terms of the contract. Proof of these terms is facilitated by section 4 (1) (*d*) of the Contracts of Employment Act 1972, which requires the employer to inform the employee of any terms and conditions relating to " entitlement to holidays, including public holidays, and holiday pay, the particulars given being sufficient to enable the employee's entitlement, including any entitlement to accrued holiday pay on the termination of employment, to be precisely calculated." These matters will often be dealt with in collective agreements. Where they are not, the employee will have to prove an express or implied term or some custom entitling him to holidays and holiday pay. He may have particular difficulty in proving a contractual right to accrued holiday pay on failure to take a holiday at the stipulated time,[4] or on termination of employment before his holiday is due.[5]

4. TIME OFF WORK

366   The Employment Protection Act 1975 gives employees [6] the right to take time off during working hours [7] in four situations.

---

[2] Current bank holidays are New Year's day, Easter Monday, Spring Holiday, Late Summer Holiday, Boxing Day. A private member's Bill to extend these holidays as a right to all employees was not given a second reading in 1969.

[3] Holidays with Pay Act 1938, as amended; Agricultural Wages Act 1948, s. 3; Wages Councils Act 1959, s. 11. The U.K. Government is not to ratify the revised I.L.O. Convention (No. 132) which calls for a minimum three weeks' annual holiday, with normal average earnings, for all workers. The reasons given are similar to those regarding reduction of working hours (above footnote 90): see Cmnd. 4706, 1971.

[4] *e.g. Hurt* v. *Sheffield Corporation* (1916) 85 L.J.K.B. 1684 (an employee who failed to take his holiday during the stipulated period was held to have lost his right to accrued holiday pay).

[5] Note that under the Contracts of Employment Act, Sched. 2, para. 2 (1) (*c*), an employee absent from work, in accordance with the terms of his employment relating to holidays, during the statutory minimum period of notice, is entitled to payment for his normal working hours. This does not protect the employee who cannot establish a contractual entitlement to leave during the period of notice. For current practice, see I.D.S. Study No. 109, *Holidays 1975* (November 1975).

[6] Defined in T.U.L.R.A., s. 30, as applied by E.P.A., s. 126: see Chap. 3. Excluded from all these rights are share fishermen (s. 119 (4)); and those ordinarily working outside G.B. (s. 119 (5) (6)). Those normally working less than 16 hours weekly, with some exceptions for those working more than eight hours, are excluded from the rights for union officials, union members and public duties (s. 119 (8)–(11)). Merchant seamen are excluded from the rights in respect of public duties and work-seeking (s. 119 (12)). The husband or wife of the employer is excluded from all the rights except those of union officials (s. 119 (2)).

[7] Defined in s. 62 (*b*) as any time when, in accordance with his contract of employment, he is required to be at work.

(1) Union officials

367   An employee who is an official [8] of an independent trade union [9] recognised by the employer for purposes of collective bargaining [10] is entitled to reasonable time off *with pay*.[11] The time off need not be used for collective bargaining as such. It may be for any official duties concerned with industrial relations with his employer or an associated employer or for industrial relations training relevant to his official duties and approved by his union or the T.U.C. The thorny problems surrounding the precise purposes and amount of time off and the conditions to be attached are to be described in a Code of Practice to be issued by the A.C.A.S. The code must include guidance as to the circumstances in which time off is permissible for duties in connection with industrial action. Ultimately it will be for the industrial tribunals, and not the A.C.A.S., to determine whether the time taken off is reasonable although the Code of Practice will be taken into account.[12]

(2) Union members

368   Members of an independent trade union [13] recognised by the employer are entitled to reasonable time off for activities of their union (this is not limited to matters connected with their employer's business) and in order to represent the union.[14] However, any activities which themselves consist of industrial action [15] whether or not in contemplation or furtherance of a trade dispute are excluded. This does not exclude activities *connected with* industrial action, on which the A.C.A.S. is to give guidance. This will be part of the Code of Practice to be issued by the A.C.A.S. giving guidance as to how, when and where time off is to be taken. Once again, it is ultimately an industrial tribunal which must decide, in the light of this guidance, what is reasonable.[16] The time off for union members under these provisions is *without pay*.

(3) Public duties

369   An employee is entitled to reasonable time off for public duties (for example as justice of the peace, member of a tribunal, or member of a local authority or health or water authority or of the governing body of an educational establishment).[17] This is limited to attendance at meetings and for executive functions.[18] No Code of Practice is to be issued giving guidance as to what time off is to be considered reasonable but an indus-

---

8 Defined in T.U.L.R.A., s. 30 (1).
9 Defined in T.U.L.R.A., s. 30, and see E.P.A., s. 8.
10 E.P.A., s. 62 (*a*), equates an operative A.C.A.S. recommendation with actual recognition.
11 Calculated on the criteria set out in E.P.A., s. 57 (4), which differs from the normal method of calculating pay under E.P.A., Sched. 4. The criteria depend upon fairness, comparability and reasonableness and so the pay may include overtime and need not be contractual. There is a mutual set-off of statutory and contractual remuneration: s. 57 (7).
12 E.P.A., s. 57. Unlike s. 58 (below) this section does not expressly exclude activities which themselves consist of industrial action.
13 Defined in T.U.L.R.A., s. 30, and see E.P.A., ss. 8 and 62 (*a*).
14 E.P.A., s. 58.
15 *Ibid*. s. 58 (2). " Industrial action " is not defined. For " trade dispute," see T.U.L.R.A., s. 28.
16 E.P.A., s. 58 (3).
17 *Ibid*. s. 59.
18 *Ibid*. s. 59 (3) (*a*) (*b*).

trial tribunal is required to have regard to the time required to perform the duties of the office, how much time has already been permitted by the employer to the employee in his capacity as a union official or union member, and the effect on the employer's business.[19] This is time off *without pay.*

(4) Workseeking by redundant employees

370   An employee who has been given notice of dismissal by reason of redundancy has the right to reasonable time off during the notice period to look for new employment or to make arrangements for training for future employment.[20] The employee must have been continuously employed for two years or more.[21] The amount of reasonable time off is not statutorily defined. However, an employee who complains that his employer has unreasonably refused time off is limited to claiming a maximum of two-fifths of a week's pay.[22] The time off is with pay at the appropriate " hourly rate." [23] Any contractual remuneration paid to an employee in respect of time off will be set off against the statutory payment and vice versa.[24]

(5) Remedies

371   In each of these four rights the employee's remedy is by way of complaint to an industrial tribunal, which must be presented within three months of the failure to give time off, which may be extended if it was not reasonably practicable to present the complaint within that period.[25] In the first three situations—union officials and members and public duties —the tribunal may make a declaration and such award of compensation as it considers just and equitable having regard to the employer's default and to any loss sustained by the employee which is attributable to the matters complained of.[26] It appears that this does not permit the tribunal to award general damages, for example for injury to feelings, humiliation, inconvenience, etc., since some actual loss must be proved by the employee. A union official may be awarded the remuneration due to him in addition to any other compensation.[27] A redundant employee denied time off may seek a declaration and an award of the amount due to him.[28]

[The next paragraph is 381.]

---

[19] *Ibid.* s. 59 (4). Certain Crown employees whose terms of employment restrict participation in political or other activities are not entitled to time off for public duties: s. 121 (8).
[20] *Ibid.* s. 61.
[21] See Chap. 5. This does not mean, however, that the employee must be eligible for a redundancy payment in every other respect (*e.g.* he may work for less than 21 hours per week, or may have refused a suitable offer of alternative employment).
[22] E.P.A., s. 61 (11).
[23] *Ibid.* s. 61 (4).
[24] *Ibid.* s. 61 (13).
[25] *Ibid.* s. 60 (1) and s. 61 (8).
[26] *Ibid.* s. 60 (2).
[27] *Ibid.* s. 60 (3).
[28] *Ibid.* s. 61 (10).

CHAPTER 11

UNFAIR DISCRIMINATION

381 AT common law an employer is at liberty to treat workers unequally either by the bestowal of favours or by the imposition of burdens. This conflicts with the ILO Convention Concerning Discrimination in Respect of Employment and Occupation 1958 (No. 111), which requires those ratifying the Convention to take measures against " any distinction, exclusion or preference made on the basis of race, colour, sex, religion, political opinion, national extraction or social origin, which has the effect of nullifying or impairing equality of opportunity or treatment in employment or occupation." The UN International Covenant on Social and Cultural Rights calls for action against an even greater number of pretexts for discrimination, including " language, political *or other* opinion, property, birth or other status." The United Kingdom Government has not yet ratified the ILO Convention (No. 111), although it has signed the International Covenant, and has ratified the European Social Charter and the European Convention for the Protection of Human Rights and Fundamental Freedoms which enumerate a number of human rights secured without discrimination on grounds similar to those in the International Covenant.[1] Moreover, within the EEC the social action programme and the aim of avoiding competitive advantages for member states which have not eliminated sex discrimination has led to various measures towards the achievement of equal pay and equal opportunity.

382   In recent years legislation has been enacted in Great Britain which goes some way towards meeting these international and European standards: the Race Relations Act 1968, which prohibits discrimination on racial grounds; the Equal Pay Act 1970, which requires equal terms of employment between men and women workers; and the Sex Discrimination Act 1975, which prohibits discrimination on grounds of sex or marital status in the employment field which falls outside the scope of the Equal Pay Act. The model of the Sex Discrimination Act has been used to frame a new Race Relations Bill which is expected to be enacted in the course of 1976. In addition to these measures the law against unfair dismissal (first introduced in 1971) may be invoked against discriminatory dismissals. Consideration of the scope of unfair dismissal law, and its relationship with these other measures, is postponed to Chapter 17. In this chapter we shall examine first the concept of discrimination; secondly, the grounds of unlawful discrimination; thirdly, the areas of employment discrimination prohibited by statute; and fourthly, the methods of enforcement. Since the Sex Discrimination Act 1975 and the Race Relations Bill 1976 are couched in similar terms, it will be convenient to expound the general principles of these measures together.[2] We shall then examine the Equal Pay Act 1970 and the provisions of article 119 of the Treaty of Rome.

---

[1] See below, Chap. 20, regarding the effect of international standards.
[2] The account which follows is based on the provisions of the Race Relations Bill (H.C. Bill 68, February 17, 1976).

152

383   Before doing so, it should be noted that there are various ways in which other general statutes may be utilised against discrimination in respect of terms and conditions of employment. In particular, Schedule 11 to the Employment Protection Act 1975 enables representative trade unions and employers' associations to report a claim to the A.C.A.S. that an employer is not observing " recognised terms and conditions." If the A.C.A.S. fails to settle the matter, it must refer it to the Central Arbitration Committee which may make an award, which becomes a term in the contract of employment of each worker, compelling the employer to observe the " recognised " terms. From the point of view of the discriminated worker, however, this procedure suffers from the disadvantage that complaints can be initiated only by a representative union. Another group of statutory duties which are relevant are those requiring an occupier of premises to provide " sufficient and suitable " facilities for sanitation, washing, etc.[3] The various enforcement agencies might utilise their powers to enforce these duties so as to prevent an occupier from providing unequal facilities for different groups of employed persons (*e.g.* ethnic minorities, women).

The concept of discrimination

384   The Sex Discrimination Act 1975 and the Race Relations Bill 1976 recognise three forms of discrimination: (1) direct discrimination; (2) indirect discrimination; and (3) discrimination by victimisation.

(1) *Direct discrimination*

385   This is " less favourable " treatment, on grounds of sex[4] or marital status[5] or racial grounds.[6] A single act of discrimination is sufficient. The act must have been committed with a discriminatory motive, although motive may be inferred from conduct (*e.g.* an employer who on a series of occasions engages men only from a pool of applicants of both sexes). The act must be directed against an individual and sex, marital status or race must be shown to be the reason for the discrimination. For example, an employer whose business involves heavy manual labour is not required to provide less physically demanding work for his employees so that women will have greater opportunities to work for him; but he must, of course, treat every job applicant on his or her merits and not simply stereotype all women as being incapable of doing heavy work.

(2) *Indirect discrimination*

386   The Sex Discrimination Act and the Race Relations Bill 1976 recognise that women, married persons and blacks suffer from a legacy of past discrimination which in many cases prevents direct comparison with men, single persons and whites respectively.[7] For this reason the statutes seek

---

[3] *e.g.* Factories Act 1961, s. 7; Offices, Shops and Railway Premises Act 1963, s. 9.
[4] S.D.A., s. 1 (1) (*a*).
[5] S.D.A., s. 3 (1) (*a*).
[6] R.R.B., cl. 1 (1) (*a*). For the meaning of " racial grounds," see below, para. 393. Separate but equal treatment is not permissible: cl. 1 (2) which repeats Race Relations Act 1968, s. 1 (2).
[7] *Racial Discrimination*, Cmnd. 6234 (1975), para. 55. The White Paper, *Equality for Women*, Cmnd. 5724 (1974) proposed not to deal with indirect discrimination but the subsequent Bill included provision for this.

to cover conduct which may be said to have a discriminatory effect on an underprivileged group, although the discriminator has no intention to discriminate. The concept of indirect or effects discrimination in the British legislation bears a close family resemblance and may owe its origin to the interpretation by the United States Supreme Court of Title VII of the U.S. Civil Rights Act 1964.[8] Although the U.S. legislation has a different background and a unique method of enforcement, some comparison with the judicial interpretations in the U.S.A. seem appropriate.[9]

387   In order to establish indirect discrimination under the British legislation, the complainant must establish three matters:

(a) The respondent applied a " requirement or condition " which he applies or would apply equally to members of the other sex, or to single persons, or to persons of another racial group as the case may be.[10] In the U.S.A. the case law has arisen in the context of employment testing, but the British legislation does not seem to be confined to employment tests, or entrance or promotion requirements.

(b) The proportion of the complainant's sex, or of married persons, or the complainant's racial group is considerably smaller than the proportion of persons of the other sex, or of single persons, or of persons not of that racial group, as the case may be, who can comply with it.[11] In the U.S.A. apparently neutral selection tests which purport to measure general intelligence or comprehension have been shown to result in the selection of employees in a racial pattern significantly different from that of the pool of applicants. This has been held to constitute prima facie evidence of discrimination.[12] Under the British legislation it would appear that if an employer requires applicants to pass an educational test for a job or promotion this would be discriminatory if it were proved that the test operates to disqualify, say, black applicants at a substantially higher rate that white applicants, and the employer is unable to show that the test is significantly related to job performance.[13] Another example of a discriminatory requirement would be a prohibition on the wearing of turbans or saris, unless the employer could show this to be justifiable, *e.g.* on safety grounds. A craft or apprenticeship requirement imposed by a trade union might be discriminatory if the proportion of, say, women able to fulfil that requirement is significantly less than the proportion of men able to do so, unless the union could show that the requirement was job-related, and not simply a relic of a bygone age.

388   Difficult questions are bound to arise as to admissibility of statistical evidence to prove disparate effects, and, if admissible, the weight to be attached to such evidence. Since the industrial tribunals (which are entrusted with jurisdiction in employment cases) are entitled to act on any evidence which is logically probative there is no reason why they should not admit

---

[8] *e.g. Griggs* v. *Duke Power Co.,* 401 U.S. 424; 28 L.Ed. 2d 158 (1971); *McDonnell Douglas Corp.* v. *Green,* 411 U.S. 792; 36 L.Ed. 2d 668; *Albermarle Paper Co.* v. *Moody,* 45 L.Ed. 280 (1975).

[9] In *Post Office* v. *Crouch* [1973] I.C.R. 366 at 379, 385, 395 (C.A.) the legitimacy of comparisons with similarly worded American law was recognised.

[10] S.D.A., ss. 1 (1) (*b*), 3 (1) (*b*); R.R.B., cl. 1 (1) (*b*).

[11] S.D.A., ss. 1 (1) (*b*) (i); s. 3 (1) (*b*) (i); R.R.B., cl. 1 (1) (*b*) (i).

[12] See cases above, note 8.

[13] The example is used in Cmnd. 6234, para. 55 (above, note 7).

statistical evidence which is properly produced by either party. The first real problem is to decide the groups from which the proportion of men and women, married and single persons, or persons of different racial groups, as the case may be, are to be drawn for the purposes of comparison. In one case it may be the populations of these categories in the country as a whole, in another it may be these categories in a particular locality, or these categories among employees in a particular undertaking.

389 A second problem is what is meant by " considerably smaller." A very small percentage difference is plainly insufficient. We would suggest that what is necessary is a difference between the categories sufficiently large for it to be a logical inference that there is indirect bias. Thirdly, how are the disparities to be proved? In the U.S.A. the mere demonstration of a significant percentage difference has been held to constitute a prima facie case of indirect discrimination, which can be rebutted by evidence that the requirement is job-related.[14] It is suggested that the British Act invites a similar approach.

390 (c) The requirement or condition is to the complainant's detriment because he or she cannot comply with it.[15] The purpose of this seems to be to restrict complaints to those who have actually been affected by indirect discrimination. A woman who can comply with a height requirement cannot complain simply because the proportion of women generally who can comply with that requirement is smaller than the proportion of men. However, it should be noted that the Equal Opportunities Commission, or Commission for Racial Equality, as the case may be, may issue a non-discrimination notice where a requirement or condition results in an act of indirect discrimination " or which would be likely to result in such an act of discrimination if the persons to whom it is applied were not all of one sex [or the same racial group]." [16]

391 It is then for the respondent to prove that the requirement or condition is " justifiable " irrespective of the sex of the person to whom it is applied or irrespective of marital status or irrespective of colour, race, nationality or ethnic or national origins, as the case may be. In the U.S.A., the employer must establish job-relatedness. The British legislation deliberately uses the wider notion of " justifiability " but it is suggested that the prima facie test will be whether the requirement or condition fits the employee for the particular job. In the absence of clear criteria of job performance it is likely to be difficult to establish the justifiability of a requirement or condition for holding that job. However, even if the respondent fails to prove " justifiability," no compensation can be awarded if he proves that he did not intend to treat the complainant less favourably.[17]

(3) *Discrimination by way of victimisation*

392 Persons who bring proceedings, give evidence or information, allege a contravention, or otherwise act under the Equal Pay Act, Sex Discrimination Act or Race Relations Bill are protected from victimisation, unless

---

[14] For a review of the U.S. law and a proposal for more refined statistical techniques, see Note (1975) 89 Harv. L.R. 387.
[15] S.D.A., s. 1 (1) (*b*) (iii); s. 3 (1) (*b*) (iii); R.R.B., cl. 1 (1) (*b*) (iii).
[16] S.D.A., s. 37 (1), and s. 67 (1) (*b*); R.R.B., cll. 28 and 57 (1) (*b*).
[17] S.D.A., s. 66 (3); R.R.B., cl. 56 (3).

the allegation is false and not made in good faith.[18] The criterion for protection is that the person victimised must have been treated less favourably by the discriminator than in those circumstances he treats or would treat other persons.

Grounds of unlawful discrimination

393   In order to fall within the scope of the legislation the discrimination must be on one of the following grounds.

(1) Racial grounds

These are defined as " colour, race, nationality or ethnic or national origin." A " racial group " means a group defined by one of these criteria.[19] Discrimination on grounds of religion is not covered (although separate legislation for Northern Ireland which was enacted in 1976 makes employment discrimination on grounds of religious belief or political opinion unlawful in that country).[20] The omission of religion has not proved to be a serious loophole in Great Britain as regards recent immigrants because discrimination against, say, a Sikh is unlikely to be on grounds of his beliefs. In practice, when an employer refuses a Sikh employment, allegedly on grounds of the turban and beard which are symbols of his faith, investigation may reveal that the employer's real motives were objection to the Sikh's ethnic or national origins. In any event, as we have seen, dress and similar requirements may now constitute indirect discrimination, unless for reasons such as hygiene or safety these requirements can be shown to be justifiable. Nationality was not included in the Race Relations Act 1968.[21] The effect of its inclusion in the 1976 legislation will be to render unlawful those few remaining trade union rules and collective agreements which discriminate against foreigners on grounds of citizenship.[22] However, the legislation does not affect the legality of acts of discrimination done under statutory authority, for example against non-patrial U.K. citizens and aliens.[23] Moreover, discrimination on grounds of nationality or ordinary residence or the length of time for which a person has been resident in the U.K. is permitted if the act is done (a) in pursuance of arrangements made by or with the approval of a Minister of the Crown or (b) in order to comply with a condition imposed by a Minister of the Crown.[24] Acts done to safeguard national security[25] and discrimination under Civil Service rules which restrict Crown employment on grounds of birth, nationality, descent or residence, are not unlawful.[26]

---

[18] S.D.A., s. 4; R.R.B., cl. 2. A vexatious or frivolous party may also be penalised by an award of costs in industrial tribunal proceedings: see Chap. 22.

[19] R.R.B., cl. 3 (1).

[20] Fair Employment (Northern Ireland) Act 1976, which establishes an Agency with duties of promoting equality of opportunity in employment in Northern Ireland between people of different religious beliefs, and of working for the elimination of discrimination made unlawful by the Act.

[21] *Ealing London Borough Council* v. *Race Relations Board* [1972] A.C. 342 (H.L.).

[22] Described in Hepple, *Race, Jobs and the Law in Britain* (2nd ed., Penguin, 1970), pp. 51–54. Discrimination against nationals of the EEC is unlawful by virtue of Article 48 of the Treaty of Rome and the implementing Reg. 1612/68 (*O.J.* 1968 L257/2). The regulation is directly applicable. See further Chap. 20, below.

[23] R.R.B., cl. 41 (1) (a) (b) (c).

[24] R.R.B., cl. 41 (2).

[25] R.R.B., cl. 42. A certificate by a Minister is conclusive evidence on this point, cl. 68.

[26] R.R.B., cl. 73 (5).

(2) *Sex*

394   The Sex Discrimination Act applies equally to discrimination against men or women of any age.[27] However, in making comparisons no account is to be taken of special treatment afforded to women in connection with pregnancy or childbirth.[28] Like must be compared with like. For example, the treatment of a married woman must be compared with the treatment of a married man, and vice versa, and not with the treatment of a single man or woman, as the case may be.[29]

(3) *Marital status*

395   The Sex Discrimination Act applies, but only in the employment field, to discrimination against married persons. It is not unlawful to discriminate against a single person on grounds of his or her status. Nice questions may arise whether some forms of discrimination against single persons are indirect *sex* discrimination. For example, a requirement or condition that job applicants must not be responsible for the care of pre-school age children may adversely affect more single women than single men or married women than married men. Unless the requirement can be shown to be justifiable irrespective of sex, it would be unlawful in those circumstances.[30]

396   In all these situations a very important qualification is that the comparison of the cases of persons of different sexes, or of married and single persons, or of persons of a particular racial group and those not of that group, as the case may be, "must be such that the relevant circumstances in the one case are the same, or not materially different, in the others."[31]

Areas of unlawful discrimination

397   The Sex Discrimination Act 1975 and the Race Relations Bill 1976 make it unlawful for a person, in relation to employment by him[32] at an establishment in Great Britain,[33] to discriminate on any of the above grounds against applicants in selection arrangements and job offers, and against those employed in access to promotion, training, and any other benefits, facilities or services.[34] The legislation also covers discriminatory dismissals, but since the burden of proof is on the complainant in proceedings under this legislation, complainants are more likely to succeed under the unfair dismissals provisions of the Trade Unon and Labour Relations Act 1974, which effectively places the burden of proof on the employer.[35]

---

[27] S.D.A., s. 2.
[28] S.D.A., s. 2 (2).
[29] S.D.A., s. 1 (2).
[30] S.D.A., s. 1 (1) (*b*).
[31] S.D.A., s. 5 (3); R.R.B., cl. 3 (4).
[32] The legislation places the primary liability on the employer (S.D.A., s. 6; R.R.B., cl. 4). However, S.D.A. s. 41, and R.R.B., cl. 32, provide that " anything done by a person in the course of his employment " is to be treated as done by his employer as well as by him, whether or not it was done with the employer's knowledge or approval. The employer may safeguard himself by taking such steps as are reasonably practicable to prevent the employee from doing that act or doing in the course of his employment acts of that description. Among such steps, it is suggested, would be clear written guidelines to employees as to how they should proceed to avoid both direct and indirect discrimination.
[33] Defined in S.D.A., s. 10; R.R.B., cl. 8.
[34] S.D.A., s. 6 (2); R.R.B., cl. 4 (2).
[35] See Chap. 17.

The anti-discrimination legislation applies to discrimination against contract-workers, that is those not employed by the principal himself but by another who supplies them under a contract made with the principal.[36]

398   The legislation also renders unlawful discrimination on the above grounds by partnerships of six or more partners,[37] by organisations of workers or of employers and by professional and trade associations,[38] as well as by bodies which can confer an authorisation or qualification needed for or facilitating engagement in a particular trade or profession.[39] Discrimination by vocational training bodies,[40] employment agencies [41] and the Manpower Services Commission [42] is also made unlawful.

399   It is unlawful to publish or cause to be published an advertisement which indicates or might reasonably be understood as indicating an intention to do an act which is or might be unlawful under the Sex Discrimination Act or Race Relations Bill.[43] This does not apply if the intended act would in fact be lawful. The use of a sexual connotation (such as " waiter," " salesgirl," " postman " or " stewardess ") is taken to indicate an intention to discriminate unless the advertisement contains an indication to the contrary.[44] The publisher is not subject to any liability if he proves that he acted reasonably in reliance on a statement by the person causing it to be published to the effect that publication would not be unlawful.[45]

The legislation also makes it unlawful to instruct [46] or pressurise another [47] to discriminate or knowingly to aid [48] an unlawful act.

Exceptions

400   All exceptions to anti-discrimination legislation tend to weaken the basic principle of equal opportunity. There are now relatively few exceptions to the legislation (unlike the position under the Race Relations Act 1968) but some of these are important.

401   In the case of all types of unlawful discrimination employment for the purposes of a private household is excluded.[49] In respect of discrimination on grounds of sex or marital status discrimination by small employers (where the number of employees of the employer and any associated employer do not exceed five) is excluded [50]; and the legislation does not apply to provisions in relation to death or retirement (although from April 1, 1978, there must be equal access to occupational pension schemes).[51]

---

[36] S.D.A., s. 9; R.R.B., cl. 7.
[37] S.D.A., s. 11; R.R.B., cl. 10.
[38] S.D.A., s. 12, R.R.B., cl. 11. S.D.A., Sched. 4, para. 2, grants a two-year exemption to teachers' organisations.
[39] S.D.A., s. 13; R.R.B., cl. 12.
[40] S.D.A., s. 14; R.R.B., cl. 13.
[41] S.D.A., s. 15; R.R.B., cl. 14.
[42] S.D.A., s. 16; R.R.B., cl. 15.
[43] S.D.A., s. 38; R.R.B., cl. 29. Only the E.O C. or C.R.E. may bring proceedings.
[44] S.D.A., s. 38 (3). See too exception for employment outside G.B. where only nationality specified: R.R.B., cl. 29 (3).
[45] S.D.A., s. 38 (4); R.R.B., cl. 29 (4). There is a penalty for making a false statement.
[46] S.D.A., s. 39; R.R.B., cl. 30.
[47] S.D.A., s. 40; R.R.B., cl. 31.
[48] S.D.A., s. 42; R.R.B., cl. 33.
[49] S.D.A., s. 6 (3) (*a*); R.R.B., cl. 4 (3).
[50] S.D.A., s. 6 (3) (*b*).
[51] S.D.A., s. 6 (4). But see para. 413.

402   There are a number of circumstances listed in section 7 of the Sex Discrimination Act where being a man or woman, as the case may be, is a " genuine occupational qualification." In these circumstances discrimination is lawful. These include the case of models and actors, toilet attendants, hospital and prison staff, personal welfare counsellors and jobs to be performed outside the U.K. in a country whose laws or customs preclude a member of that sex from performing the duties.[52] The Act does not apply to employment as a midwife [53] or as a minister of religion.[54] The office of police constable is excluded in respect of discrimination on grounds of height, uniform, equipment, pensions and the special treatment given to women in pregnancy or childbirth.[55] Prison officers are excluded in respect of discrimination on ground of height.[56] The Race Relations Bill 1976 has a much narrower list of genuine occupational qualifications. It includes actors, models, personal welfare counsellors, and jobs involving " working in a place where food or drink is (for payment or not) provided to and consumed by members of the public or a section of the public in a special ambience for which, in that job, a person of that racial group is required for reasons of authenticity " (the Chinese waiter in a Chinese restaurant!).[57]

403   Nothing in the legislation requires " reverse " discrimination in favour of women or blacks. Indeed, the definition of discrimination means that in general " reverse " discrimination would be unlawful. There are, however, certain exceptional situations in which special treatment may be given to members of a particular sex or racial group. The Sex Discrimination Act allows discriminatory training for members of one sex by certain training bodies,[58] by employers,[59] and by trade unions and similar organisations.[60] This is permitted where during the preceding 12 months there were no persons of the sex in question doing the job or the number of such persons was comparatively small. Training bodies may also offer discriminatory training to fit those who have been discharging domestic or family responsibilities for employment.[61] Trade unions and similar bodies may reserve seats on elective bodies for members of one sex.[62] The Act also retains the special protection given to women employees under the Factories Act and associated legislation relating to hours of work and safety,[63] and (in modified form) the prohibition on underground work by women.[64] However, the Equal Opportunities Commission in consultation

---

[52] These are given as examples. The wording of s. 7 should be consulted.
[53] S.D.A., s. 20; the Midwives Act 1951 has been amended to allow men to be midwives (although such men can be discriminated against in their employment).
[54] S.D.A., s. 19.
[55] Ibid. s. 17.
[56] Ibid. s. 18.
[57] R.R.B., cl. 5.
[58] S.D.A., s. 47. The bodies are industrial training boards, the Manpower Services Commission, Employment Services Agency and Training Services Agency (s. 14 (2) (a) (b)) and others may be designated (s. 47 (4) (b)).
[59] S.D.A., s. 48 (1).
[60] S.D.A., s. 48 (2) (3). These bodies are defined in s. 12.
[61] S.D.A., s. 47 (3).
[62] Ibid. s. 49.
[63] Ibid. s. 51. See Chap. 10.
[64] Ibid. s. 21 (1). The Mines and Quarries Act 1954, s. 124 (1), has been modified so as to prohibit only those women who would spend " a significant proportion of time " underground.

with the Health and Safety Commission must keep this legislation under review.[65]

404   The Race Relations Bill 1976 also permits (but, like the Sex Discrimination Act, does not require) reverse discrimination in providing for the special needs of particular racial groups in regard to education, training and welfare.[66] Discriminatory education and training is also allowed for persons not ordinarily resident in Great Britain who intend to leave at the end of the period of education or training.[67] Trade unions and similar organisations may give discriminatory training for posts in the organisation or to encourage persons of a particular racial group to join the organisation.[68]

405   A general exception under both the Sex Discrimination Act and Race Relations Bill is created for charities. The former does not render unlawful anything done under a provision contained in a charitable instrument for conferring benefits on persons of one sex only,[69] and the latter (while removing restrictions based on colour) permits benefits to be conferred on members of a particular racial group in a charitable instrument.[70] This may occasionally be relevant in cases of employment, *e.g.* by an independent school or college.

Enforcement

406   Two principal methods of enforcement are utilised in the anti-discrimination legislation. The first is the method of individual civil action before industrial tribunals (in cases outside the employment field, county courts). The second method is strategic enforcement in the public interest by the Equal Opportunities Commissions (E.O.C.) and the Commission for Racial Equality (C.R.E.), which are to deal with discriminatory practices by industries, firms and institutions and are to encourage positive action to secure equal opportunity. The first method on its own was regarded as inadequate because " it would depend too heavily on the initiative of individuals in presenting and pursuing complaints and would therefore tend to be random in its operation and impact." [71] On the other hand, the model of the Race Relations Board (which under the 1968 legislation alone had the power to investigate complaints and, where conciliation failed, to bring civil proceedings) was rejected because the investigation of all individual complaints by a public agency was regarded as " vast, costly and wasteful " [72] and as creating " resentment and hostility " among those it was designed to assist.[73]

(1) *Complaints by individuals*

407   A complaint in respect of an act of unlawful discrimination may be presented to an industrial tribunal.[74] (It has been suggested by the Govern-

---

[65] S.D.A., s. 55.
[66] R.R.B., cll. 35, 37, 38.
[67] R.R.B., cl. 36.
[68] *Ibid.* cl. 38 (3) (4) (5). The bodies are defined in cl. 11.
[69] S.D.A., s. 43. S. 78 enables trustees of an educational charity to obtain removal of such a restriction.
[70] R.R.B., cl. 34.
[71] *Equality for Women* (Cmnd. 5724, 1974), para. 28.
[72] *Ibid.*; and *Racial Discrimination* (Cmnd. 6234, 1975), para. 41.
[73] *Racial Discrimination*, paras. 40, 41.   [74] S.D.A., s. 63; R.R.B., cl. 53.

ment that it would be desirable to include more members of racial minorities and more women on the panels of members of these tribunals.[75]) The complaint must be presented within three months of the act complained of being done, but this period may be extended if the tribunal considers it just and equitable to do so.[76] The E.O.C. or C.R.E. (as appropriate) may, in their discretion, assist individuals for example by giving advice, procuring settlements, arranging for legal advice or assistance or arranging representation. In deciding whether or not to help, the Commissions must consider whether the case raises a question of principle, or is complex, and must have regard to the applicant's position and any other special consideration.[77]

408   In employment cases, a copy of every complaint is to be sent to the A.C.A.S. which may attempt conciliation.[78] Where appropriate conciliation officers must " have regard to the desirability of encouraging the use of other procedures available for the settlement of grievances." [79] This is a marked change from the procedure under the Race Relations Act 1968, which required complaints to go through voluntary industrial machinery approved for this purpose by the Secretary of State.

409   The most serious difficulty facing complainants is that of proving unlawful discrimination. The Race Relations Board has reported that " many complainants can initially prove no more than a suspicion that others would have been treated differently or more favourably." [80] Individuals may find it difficult to present evidence comparing their treatment with that of others. Despite this difficulty neither the Sex Discrimination Act nor the Race Relations Bill reverse the normal burden of proof.[81] The burden of proving that discrimination has taken place, whether direct or indirect, rests on the complainant. The only concession made by the legislation is to enable the complainant to obtain information in order to decide whether to institute proceedings, and if he or she does so, to formulate and present his or her case in the most effective manner.[82] The complainant may submit questions to the respondent on a prescribed form.[83] The respondent need not reply but a failure to do so, or an evasive or equivocal reply, entitles the tribunal to draw an inference that unlawful discrimination has occurred.[84]

410   The remedies which the tribunal may grant are far less effective than those available under corresponding legislation in the U.S.A. The tribunal may (a) make an order declaring the rights of the parties; (b) award com-

---

[75] *Equality for Women*, para. 83; *Racial Discrimination*, para. 83.
[76] S.D.A., s. 76; R.R.B., cl. 67.
[77] S.D.A., s. 75; R.R.B., cl. 65.
[78] S.D.A., s. 64; R.R.B., cl. 54. See Chap. 22 below.
[79] S.D.A., s. 64 (3); R.R.B., cl. 54 (3).
[80] Report of the Race Relations Board for 1974, App. IX, p. 46, and Report for 1973, p. 51.
[81] *Cf.* T.U.L.R.A., Sched. 1, para. 6, which casts the burden of proof on the employer in cases of unfair dismissal: see Chap. 17. In cases of indirect discrimination, the burden of proof is on the respondent to show that a particular requirement or condition is justifiable, and to prove that he had no intention to discriminate if he wishes to avoid liability to pay compensation: above, para. 391.
[82] S.D.A., s. 74; R.R.B., cl. 64.
[83] Sex Discrimination (Questions and Replies) Order 1975 (S.I. 1975 No. 2048). It is expected that a similar Order will be made when the Race Relations Bill is enacted.
[84] S.D.A., s. 74 (2); R.R.B., cl. 64 (2).

pensation; and (c) recommend that the respondent take within a specified period action appearing to the tribunal to be practicable for the purpose of obviating or reducing the adverse effect on the complainant of the act of discrimination to which the complaint relates.[85] There is no power to order reinstatement or re-engagement, although these remedies are available under the Trade Union and Labour Relations Act in cases of unfair dismissal. The amount of compensation awarded may not exceed the maximum compensatory award for the time being prescribed for cases of unfair dismissal under the Trade Union and Labour Relations Act (at present £5,200).[86] At the same time, the anti-discrimination legislation says that the compensation shall be of an amount "corresponding to any damages" that could have been awarded by a county court in respect of an act of discrimination otherwise than in the employment field. It seems that this does not mean that the maximum amount of the award is limited to the maximum award possible under the county court's jurisdiction (£1,000) but that, like the county court, the tribunal must award damages "in like manner as any other claim in tort."[87] Unlike statutory compensation (e.g. for unfair dismissal) tort damages may include recompense for losses which have no financial equivalent such as injury to feelings, loss of happiness, inconvenience and loss of reputation. For the avoidance of doubt the legislation specifically declares that compensation for injury to feelings may be awarded.[88] On the basis of comparable awards in tort cases it seems unlikely that tribunals will award more than £200 under this head. In addition, the compensation will include recompense for loss of existing assets and loss of future advantages, profits and earnings. In view of the equation with claims in tort, it would seem that the complainant's damages may be reduced to such extent as the tribunal considers just and equitable in the case of contributory fault on the part of the complainant, under the provisions of the Law Reform (Contributory Negligence) Act 1945.[89] The amount of compensation awarded may be increased if, without reasonable justification, the respondent refuses to comply with a recommendation (but not so as to exceed the overall limit of £5,200).[90]

(2) *Enforcement by the Commissions*

411   The Equal Opportunities Commission (E.O.C.) and Commission for Racial Equality (C.R.E.) are similarly composed and have similar functions, but each operates in its own field.[91] Each Commission has a chairman and up to 14 members. The main functions of each Commission are: (a) to

---

[85] S.D.A., s. 65; R.R.B., cl. 55.

[86] S.D.A., s. 65 (2); R.R.B., cl. 55 (2).

[87] S.D.A., s. 66 (1); R.R.B., cl. 56 (1). In Scotland the equation is with "reparation for breach of statutory duty."

[88] S.D.A., s. 66 (4); R.R.B., cl. 56 (4).

[89] Unlike T.U.L.R.A., Sched. 1, para. 19 (below Chap. 17), the S.D.A. and R.R.B. contain no specific provision on contributory fault.

[90] S.D.A., s. 65 (3); R.R.B., cl. 55 (3).

[91] The House of Commons Select Committee on Race Relations and Immigration (H.C. 448–I), para. 62, has recommended co-operation between the Commissions and, no doubt, common policies will be involved with a view to the eventual unification of law enforcement.

conduct investigations and to take action to remove unlawful practices [92]; (b) where investigation discloses an unlawful practice, the Commission may serve a non-discrimination notice requiring the recipient to cease the practice or otherwise comply with the law,[93] subject to a right of appeal to an industrial tribunal [94]; (c) if, within five years of a non-discrimination notice becoming final or of a finding by a court or tribunal of unlawful discrimination, it appears to the Commission that the respondent is likely again to act unlawfully, it may apply to a county court for an injunction, after the facts have been ascertained by an industrial tribunal [95]; (d) to institute proceedings relating to discriminatory advertisements [96]; (e) to institute proceedings in respect of instructions to discriminate or pressure to discriminate [97]; (f) to assist individual complainants [98]; (g) to conduct inquiries into areas not specifically covered by the legislation [99]; (h) to monitor the legislation and to promote research and education.[1]

Equal Pay Act 1970

412   The aim of this Act is according to its long title " to prevent discrimination, as regards terms and conditions of employment, between men and women." It was amended in certain respects by the Sex Discrimination Act 1975. The Act is, in part, a response to the claim for equal pay made by the TUC since 1888 and, in part, the result of international pressure on successive United Kingdom Governments to ratify the ILO Convention of 1951 on Equal Pay (No. 100).[2]

413   The short title of the Act is misleading because it aims to achieve equal treatment not only in respect of pay, but also in other terms and conditions of employment, such as holidays, hours, provision of clothing, and sick-pay. However, certain terms are expressly excluded from the scope of the Act:

(a) terms and conditions " affected by compliance with the law regulating the employment of women "[3] (*e.g.* Part VI of the Factories Act 1961, the Employment of Women, Young Persons and Children Act 1920 and the Hours of Employment (Conventions) Act 1936) [4];

(b) " any special treatment accorded to women in connection with pregnancy or childbirth "[5];

---

[92] S.D.A., s. 57; R.R.B., cl. 47. There are powers to obtain information, to summon witnesses etc.: S.D.A., s. 58; R.R.B., cl. 48. This will now make it necessary for employers to keep records of the sex and racial composition of the workforce (*cf.* Report of the Race Relations Board for 1974, paras. 45–50 for the arguments for and against record-keeping in the race relations field).

[93] S.D.A., s. 67; R.R.B., cl. 57. The notice may require the respondent to make known to those likely to be affected (*e.g.* job-seekers) the changes being made, and to report to the Commission on progress. The rules of procedure are set out in Industrial Tribunals (Non-Discrimination Notices Appeals) Regs. 1975 (S.I. 1975 No. 2098).

[94] S.D.A., s. 68; R.R.B., cl. 58.

[95] S.D.A., ss. 71–73; R.R.B., cll. 61–63.

[96] S.D.A., ss. 38, 67, 72; R.R.B., cll. 29, 57, 62.

[97] S.D.A., ss. 39, 40, 57, 72; R.R.B., cll. 30, 31, 57, 62.

[98] S.D.A., s. 74; R.R.B., cl. 64.

[99] S.D.A., s. 53; R.R.B., cl. 43.

[1] S.D.A., s. 54; R.R.B., cl. 54.

[2] The Convention was ratified by the U.K. Government in June 1971.

[3] *Ibid.* s. 6 (1) (*a*).

[4] Above, paras. 360, 361.

[5] Equal Pay Act 1970, s. 6 (1) (*b*).

(c) " terms and conditions related to death or retirement, or to any provision made in connection with death or retirement," [6] but equal access must be afforded to occupational pension schemes (from April 1, 1978).[7]

414   Another important limitation is that the principle of equal treatment applies to men and women only " when employed." [8] " Employed " means " employed under a contract of service or of apprenticeship or a contract personally to execute any work or labour." [9] While this is wide enough to cover self-employed contractors (who do the work in person),[10] and has been expressly extended to those in Crown employment,[11] it means that the Act covers only contractually binding terms and conditions.

Although the Act will usually be invoked on behalf of women, its provisions apply equally to men, so that references to a " woman " in the Act (and in this discussion) include references to a " man." [12] It covers persons of all ages.[13]

415   The Act adopts three main devices for preventing discrimination. The first is the amendment of collective agreements,[14] employers' pay structures,[15] wages regulation orders [16] and agricultural wages orders,[17] which contain any provision " applying specifically to men only or to women only." These may be referred by the parties [18] or by the Secretary of State [19] to the Central Arbitration Committee. The Committee must first amend the agreement to extend to both men and women any provision applying to men only or to women only.[20] For example, if a collective agreement lays down a rate for skilled men of £80 and for skilled women of £70, the Committee must extend the men's rate to women and the women's rate to men. The Committee must then eliminate the resulting duplication by striking out the lower rate. The final result would be a single rate of £80 for skilled workers, irrespective of sex. However, an agreement cannot be extended to women (or men) not already covered by it. For example, if the agreement lays down a skilled men's rate of £80, an unskilled men's rate of £70, but no semi-skilled men's rate, and a women's rate for all categories of £60, the Committee must amend the agreement so that skilled workers are paid £80 and unskilled workers £70, irrespective of sex. However, a rate " applying specifically to women only " continues to be required because there is no category of semi-skilled

---

[6] *Ibid.* s. 6 (1A). " Retirement " includes retirement, whether voluntary or not, on grounds of age, length of service or incapacity.

[7] *Ibid.* s. 6 (1A) (*a*), and the Social Security Pensions Act 1975, Part IV. " Equal access " relates only to age and length of service necessary to become a member and whether membership is voluntary or not. See generally Reid (1976) 5 I.L.J. 54.

[8] *Ibid.* s. 1 (2).

[9] *Ibid.* s. 1 (6) (*a*).

[10] Above, Chap. 3.

[11] Equal Pay Act, s. 1 (8).

[12] Equal Pay Act 1970, s. 1 (13).

[13] *Ibid.* s. 11 (2).

[14] *Ibid.* s. 3 (as defined in s. 3 (5)).

[15] *Ibid.* s. 3 (6).

[16] *Ibid.* s. 4.

[17] *Ibid.* s. 5.

[18] *i.e.* any party to a collective agreement, the employer in respect of his pay structure.

[19] Either on his own initiative or at the request of a member of a wages council or a body nominating members of an Agricultural Wages Board.

[20] Equal Pay Act 1970, s. 3 (4) (*a*) (*b*).

men in the agreement. In this case, the Committee must amend the women's rate to the lowest rate in the agreement applicable to men, *i.e.* £70.[21] The Committee may specify a date before or after its decision on which the amendments are to become effective, provided these are not earlier than the date of the reference.[22]

416   The second device is contained in section 1 (2) (*a*). A woman has a right to equal treatment when employed on work of "the same or a broadly similar" nature to that of men in the same employment. In comparing her work to theirs "regard shall be had to the frequency or otherwise" with which any differences between her work and theirs occur in practice, as well as the nature and extent of the differences.[23] For example, if men employed on heavy machine work are occasionally employed to "fill in" for women on light machine work, but are paid their usual heavy-machine rates while doing so, the frequency with which the heavy machine operators do the light work will be a relevant factor in determining whether the women's work is "the same or broadly similar" to that of the men. The consequences of employing men on "women's" work, or women on "men's" work, may lead some employers to maintain a strict segregation although this may now lead to contravention of the Sex Discrimination Act (*above*). For it is only if there are men doing "the same or broadly similar work" that women will be able to establish a claim to equal treatment.

417   The concept of "equal pay for work of equal value," put in the words of section 1 (5) of the Act, is the third device relied on to prevent discrimination. A woman must receive the same pay and conditions as men if her job and theirs have been given an equal value under a job evaluation exercise.[24] There is no obligation to undertake such an exercise, and only if the employer in fact bases the terms and conditions of employment of men on that exercise is he obliged to apply it to women.[25] A "job evaluation" is defined as a study undertaken with a view to evaluating jobs to be done by all or any employees in an undertaking or group of undertakings. The evaluation must have been made "in terms of the demand made on the worker under various headings (for instance, effort, skill, decision)." [26] The exercise is conclusive, except where an equal value would have been given "but for a system setting different values for men and women on the same demand under any heading." For example, if two jobs make the same demand in terms of effort, skill, etc., but they have been rated differently simply because one is carried on by men and the other by women, the results of the exercise must be adjusted so as to set equal values for the two jobs.[27]

418   A question which is crucial in regard to both concepts is the *area of comparison* which a woman may draw with men's jobs. She may only compare her job with those of men "in the same employment." This means that the comparison is limited to men:

---

21 *Ibid.*
22 *Ibid.* s. 3 (3).
23 *Ibid.* s. 1 (4).
24 Equal Pay Act, s. 1 (2) (*b*) and s. 1 (5).
25 *Ibid.*
26 *Ibid.*
27 *Ibid.*

(a) employed by her employer or any associated employer (two employers may be treated as associated if one is a company of which the other (directly or indirectly) has control or if both are companies of which a third person (directly or indirectly) has control) [28]; and

(b) employed " at the same establishment or at establishments in Great Britain which include that one and at which common terms and conditions of employment are observed either generally or for employees of the relevant classes." [29]

The operation of this comparison may be shown by an example. Suppose an employer has three establishments, A, B and C. The same job is carried out in all three establishments by men and women. The men at A and B are paid at the same rate but the women at A, B and C and the men at C are paid at a lower rate. The women at A and B are entitled to be paid the same as the men at these establishments; but neither the women at C nor the men at C are entitled to be paid the same as the men and women at A and B, because common terms are not observed at all three establishments. The term " establishment " may give rise to difficulties of interpretation: the question is one of fact and degree.[30]

419   The individual woman may enforce her right to equal treatment through a statutory term of her contract of employment (known as the " equality clause ").[31] Any claim in respect of the operation of this clause may be referred to an industrial tribunal either by the woman herself, or by the employer, or by the Secretary of State, but by the latter only if it is " not reasonable " to expect the parties to take steps to determine the questions.[32] An ordinary civil court in which proceedings are pending in respect of the operation of an equal pay clause may refer the matter to an industrial tribunal.[33] The claim will be one either for arrears of remuneration or for damages for breach of the equal pay clause, but in either case she is not entitled to be awarded any payment in respect of a time earlier than two years before the date on which the proceedings were instituted.[34] The burden rests on the employer, in any proceedings, to show that the advantage enjoyed by men, in comparison with the women, is genuinely due to a material difference (other than the difference of sex) between her case and his.[35]

Relationship between Equal Pay Act and Sex Discrimination Act

420   There is no overlap between these two Acts. The complainant's case will fall either under the Equal Pay Act or the Sex Discrimination Act but never under both. (In some situations of discrimination neither Act may apply.) For enforcement purposes, however, the complainant need not

---

[28] *Ibid.* ss. 1 (2), 1 (6) (*c*).
[29] *Ibid.*
[30] For the meaning of " establishment," see S.D.A., s. 10. *Cf.* the meaning given to " establishment " in the Selective Employment Tax Act 1966, s. 10 (2), and *Secretary of State for Employment* v. *Hellam* (1970) 5 I.T.R. 108. See Chap. 1.
[31] Equal Pay Act 1970, ss. 1 (1), 2 (1) (1A).
[32] *Ibid.* s. 2 (2).
[33] *Ibid.* s. 2 (3).
[34] *Ibid.* s. 2 (5). Moreover, she must have been employed in that employment within the six months preceding the date of the reference: s. 2 (4).
[35] *Ibid.* s. 1 (3).

specify precisely which of the two Acts is relevant; this is a matter for the tribunal to decide when all the facts are known.

421 Broadly speaking, the distinction between the two Acts has been summarised as follows[36]:

" (a) If the less favourable treatment relates to the payment of money which is regulated by a contract of employment, only the Equal Pay Act can apply.

(b) If the employee is treated less favourably than an employee of the other sex who is doing the same or broadly similar work, or whose work has been given an equal value under job evaluation, and the less favourable treatment relates to some matter which is regulated by the contract of employment of either of them, only the Equal Pay Act can apply.

(c) If the less favourable treatment relates to a matter which is not included in a contract (either expressly or by virtue of the Equal Pay Act), only the Sex Discrimination Act can apply.

(d) If the less favourable treatment relates to a matter (other than the payment of money) in a contract, and the comparision is with workers who are *not* doing the same or broadly similar work, or work which has been given an equal value under job evaluation, only the Sex Discrimination Act can apply.

(e) If the complaint relates to a matter (other than the payment of money) which is regulated by an employee's contract of employment, but is based on an allegation that an employee of the other sex *would* be treated more favourably in similar circumstances (*i.e.* it does not relate to the *actual* treatment of an existing employee of the other sex), only the Sex Discrimination Act can apply."

Article 119 of the Treaty of Rome

422 As a member of the EEC, the United Kingdom is obliged to apply the principle of " equal pay for equal work." This is the concept utilised in article 119 of the Treaty of Rome and it has been interpreted as being confined to the situation where men and women are engaged on identical work.[37] Moreover, the European Court of Justice has given a restrictive interpretation to the concept of " pay," so as to exclude a retirement pension which is instituted within the framework of a social security scheme financed by workers' and employers' contributions and state grants.[38] However, pensions directly paid by the employer and occupational pensions independent of the state system of management and financing and having their origin in collective agreements appear to be capable of constituting " pay " for purposes of article 119.[39] This qualification may

---

[36] This is the summary which appears in the Home Office guide to the Sex Discrimination Act, pp. 12–13. See S.D.A., ss. 6 (5) (6) (7), 8 (3)–(5).

[37] *Defrenne* v. *Sabena Belgian Airlines, The Times,* April 20, 1976 (E.C.J.); *Perego* v. *Marzotto* [1965] C.M.L.R. 139 (Monza, Italy). EEC Council Dir. 75–117, O.J. L45/19 (February 19, 1975) purports to extend the principle to equal pay for work to which an equal value has been attributed under a non-discriminatory job evaluation. Although there is, as yet, no authoritative ruling it would appear that, to this extent, the Directive is *ultra vires* the Treaty.

[38] *Defrenne* v. *Belgium* [1974] C.M.L.R. 494; see too *Sabbatini* v. *European Parliament and Chollet* v. *EEC Commission* [1972] C.M.L.R. 945.

[39] [1974] C.M.L.R. at p. 508.

be difficult to apply in the U.K. context because it has been suggested that once an occupational pension scheme is extended to workers not represented in the bargaining process it becomes compulsory and so falls outside the concept of "pay."

423   Despite these limits and ambiguities, article 119 may be of some importance as providing a residual basis for a remedy before the English (or Scottish) courts. This is because the European Court has decided that article 119 is directly enforceable by individuals before national courts of Member States.[40] However, article 119 may not be invoked to claim back payment for periods before the date of the E.C.J.'s ruling, in April 1976, that the article is directly enforceable, apart from proceedings instituted before that date.

[The next paragraph is 431.]

---

[40] *Defrenne* v. *Sabena Belgian Airlines, The Times,* April 20, 1976.

CHAPTER 12

APPRENTICESHIP AND TRAINING

431   APPRENTICESHIP was first noticed in an Act of Parliament in 1383, although the guilds of masters and apprentices had made their own rules, for hundreds of years before then. Parliamentary intervention was aimed, at first, towards preventing abuses by the guilds of their exclusive privileges to practise particular crafts, and, later, towards propping up a decaying system. The Apprentices Act 1814 (parts of which are still in force) swept away the old system of compulsory apprenticeship and it signified the demise of the old forms of guild, or domestic, apprenticeship. Instead of living without wages under strict personal control of the master, the apprentice lived at home, was sometimes paid in lieu of board and lodging, and had his obligations defined by contract. Apprenticeship became the usual method of recruiting and training skilled workers in the engineering, shipbuilding, construction and other industries during Britain's industrial revolution. Towards the end of the nineteenth century employers became less willing than before to spend time and money on training, so the trade unions intervened through their own rules and collective agreements to place restrictions on the number of apprentices and the conditions of their employment. These craft restrictions are still important in several industries.

432   The decline of apprenticeship, as a method of training, and changed social and economic conditions, give a curious ring to many of the common law rules which still regulate the relationship between employer and apprentice.[1] The contract is defined as one in which the employer agrees to instruct and teach the apprentice his trade, profession or business and to maintain him during the existence of that relationship, and the apprentice, in turn, agrees to serve the employer and to learn from him. The agreement need not be under seal, but if it is not in writing, signed by both parties, the apprentice cannot claim the advantages of apprenticeship. These benefits include the employer's obligation to instruct and his limited rights of dismissal (the latter are dealt with briefly in Chapter 16). Special rules apply to apprentices who are minors: the contract must be for the minor's benefit, and, conversely, he may not repudiate it unless it is beneficial for him to do so. He is also entitled to repudiate within a reasonable time after reaching the age of majority. There is no implied promise to pay wages, and it is therefore usual to have an express stipulation to this effect. The apprentice is not free to leave his employer during indenture unless the employer's conduct indicates that he is no longer ready and willing to teach him.

433   These common law rules live uneasily by the side of recent general

---

[1] See Fridman, *Modern Law of Employment*, p. 973, for a detailed account. Some professions and trades have their own statutory provisions: *e.g.*, merchant shipping, solicitors, etc. On the decline of apprenticeship see *The Work of the Youth Employment Service 1968–71* (H.M.S.O., 1971). According to the same Report, the Industrial Training Act has not led to a significant increase in the numbers of young people granted day release for purposes of further education.

statutory provisions about training and retraining. These cannot be adequately dealt with in a book of the present kind. But attention is drawn to certain statutes. First, the Employment and Training Act 1973 [2] creates three bodies: the Manpower Services Commission (M.S.C.) which is responsible for making " such arrangements as it considers appropriate for the purpose of assisting persons to select, train for, obtain and retain employment suitable for their ages and capacities and to obtain suitable employees " [3]; the Employment Services Agency (E.S.A.) and the Training Services Agency (T.S.A.) both of which perform such of the M.S.C.'s functions as the M.S.C. directs them to exercise. The M.S.C. is responsible for many different schemes and services including the public employment service,[4] professional and executive recruitment, occupational guidance, training opportunities and government training centres. The M.S.C. is a semi-autonomous body, composed of employers', employees', local authority and educational organisations' representatives. The Department of Employment retains overall general responsibility for manpower policy and the Secretary of State has residual power to issue directives to the M.S.C. Secondly, the Industrial Training Act 1964 (modified in important respects by the Employment and Training Act 1973) establishes a system for the making of grants for training in certain industries. Orders are made, after consultation, authorising the imposition of a levy on employers engaged in a particular industry. Industrial training boards (I.T.B.s) decide whether an employer belongs to the industry covered by the order, and may grant exemption certificates to employers who already have satisfactory training arrangements. Decisions whether to issue exemption certificates are based on criteria published after approval by the M.S.C. and the Secretary of State. Any employer dissatisfied with an I.T.B.'s decision to refuse or revoke a certificate or with the conditions attached to it, may apply to the I.T.B. to reconsider it. If the employer remains dissatisfied he may refer the matter to a body of Referees set up by the Secretary of State.[5] Those employers who are not exempted must pay the levy (the upper limit of which is 1 per cent. of payroll unless the Secretary of State otherwise determines). The levies collected are then disbursed in the form of grants to employers who carry out training which meets the I.T.B.'s requirements. There is an appeal to an industrial tribunal against a levy, and from the tribunal to the High Court, on questions of law.

Thirdly, attention must be drawn to the provisions of the Disabled Persons (Employment) Acts 1944 and 1958 which enable the Department of Employment to run industrial rehabilitation centres for the disabled.

[The next paragraph is 441.]

---

[2] For the background to this legislation, see *People and Jobs* (D.E., 1971); *Training for the Future* (D.E., 1972); *Into Action: Plan for a Modern Employment Service* (D.E., 1972), and *Employment and Training: Government Proposals*, Cmnd. 5250 (1973).

[3] s. 2 (1).

[4] It must be noticed, in passing, that private employment agencies and employment businesses (whether profit-making or not) are required to operate under licence, and must comply with regulations made by the Secretary of State: Employment Agencies Act 1973.

[5] Industrial Training Act 1964, s. 4 (B) (4).

Part Three

DISCIPLINE AND LOSS OF EMPLOYMENT

CHAPTER 13

DISCIPLINARY ACTION

Law of work discipline

441   It is one of the odd consequences of the Employment Protection Act 1975 that it not only establishes new legal minimum standards for employees but it also " revives," in the disciplinary area, legal standards which have been almost universally ignored in practice for the last half-century. There is a substantial body of law relating to the exercise of the employer's disciplinary powers, especially the Truck Act 1896, which has been treated as being of no practical importance. However, the new obligation established by the amendment by the Employment Protection Act of the provisions of the Contracts of Employment Act 1972 as to the contents of the written statement [1] to be issued to employees by employers, requiring employers to tell employees what are the disciplinary rules that apply to them, now means that wherever misconduct is raised as an issue in proceedings before an Industrial Tribunal, the tribunal is likely to inquire of the employer, " Where is the written copy of the disciplinary rules which the Contracts of Employment Act requires you to have issued to the employee? " If the employer has not issued or has not got written disciplinary rules this must weigh in the balance against the employer. If the employer has prepared and issued written copies of the disciplinary rules, if the rules themselves and the sanctions involved in them, fail to comply with the law on disciplinary rules, that too must weigh very heavily against the employer and, in the discretion of the tribunal, may even cause the employer to lose a case before the tribunal that he might otherwise have won.

442   The law of work discipline has five aspects. There are first of all the sanctions imposed, external to the employment relationship, by the law of social security [2] upon employees seeking some social security benefit in cases where they have been guilty of conduct which social security law seeks to deter or penalise. Secondly, there may be civil or criminal remedies available to the employer in the courts and tribunals as a means of disciplining the work force. Such remedies may arise out of the contract of employment itself, as in the case of a claim for damages against an employee who acts in breach of his contract.[3] Such remedies can also be provided by statute, as with the now repealed Industrial Relations Act 1971, which provided for a remedy against a trade union which had failed to take steps against such of its members as had acted in the workplace in a manner which was inconsistent with a legally enforceable collective agreement to which the employer was a party.[4] A very interesting example of statutory back up for workplace discipline is section 11 of the Explosive Substances Act 1875. This requires employers in premises where

---

[1] See for the contents of the written statement Chap. 7 above.
[2] See Chap. 19.
[3] *Cf. National Coal Board* v. *Galley* [1958] 1 W.L.R. 16.
[4] s. 36 (2) and (3). Now repealed by the Trade Union and Labour Relations Act 1974, s. 1.

certain explosive substances are used or manufactured to make rules, with the approval of the Secretary of State, to secure compliance with the Act and to ensure the safety and " proper discipline " of the workforce. Breach of these disciplinary rules is a criminal offence punishable by a £20 fine.[5] Another example may be found in the Conspiracy and Protection of Property Act 1875 which makes it a criminal offence in certain circumstances to hide a fellow worker's tools.[6] Thirdly, there may be rules made by the workers themselves, *e.g.,* an agreement to pay wages earned by working more than an agreed maximum number of hours on overtime into a common kitty. Fourthly, rules of occupational pension funds may penalise workers who act in prescribed ways. Lastly, there are the disciplinary rules imposed by employers inside the employment relationship.

Although dismissal is the ultimate and most dramatic disciplinary sanction which may be imposed by an employer, it is by no means the commonest or most important sanction. The disciplinary sanctions which are imposed in practice are almost infinite in their variety and include such things as fines, suspension with or without pay, sending piece-workers home, withholding of bonuses, forfeiture of wages,[7] deprivation of pension rights, withholding of long-service awards, or other fringe benefits, denial of promotion, demotion, transfer, etc., etc. In the past such sanctions were often imposed without any regard being had to their legality. The change of atmosphere engendered by a number of factors including initially the Industrial Relations Act 1971, and later the Employment Protection Act 1975, and the consequent infusion of greater legalism into the employment relationship, has made some employers more aware of the restrictions of the law and some employees more willing to challenge any unlawful act on the part of an employer. It becomes of critical importance to understand that the legality of disciplinary action taken by an employer is ultimately dependent upon the terms of the individual contracts of employment to which he is a party. The legality of such disciplinary action may be further limited in certain cases by statutory rules. In the public sector disciplinary rules may be wholly or partly based upon statutory provisions, or upon the royal prerogative.[8] We are here, however, concerned primarily with disciplinary rules which rest upon the contract of employment, and are not derived from statute or prerogative. In such cases the position may be summarised as follows :

(i) any sanction prohibited by the contract of employment cannot be imposed without a breach of contract on the employer's part;

(ii) any sanction which does not derogate from the employee's contractual rights may lawfully be imposed by an employer without rendering him liable for breach of contract;

(iii) any sanction which involves a derogation from the employee's contractual rights, which is not expressly or impliedly authorised

---

[5] Criminal Justice Act 1967, ss. 92, 106 (2), Sched. 3, Part II.

[6] s. 7 (3). See *Fowler* v. *Kibble* [1922] 1 Ch. 487.

[7] We are referring here only to forfeiture of wages *without* termination of the contract of employment. Forfeiture of wages accompanying dismissal is dealt with separately, below, Chap. 16.

[8] These disciplinary rules are fully discussed in B. A. Hepple and P. O'Higgins, *Public Employee Trade Unionism in the U.K.: The Legal Framework* (Ann Arbor, 1971) pp. 175–181.

by the contract itself, involves the employer in liability for breach of contract;

(iv) any sanction expressly or impliedly authorised by the contract of employment is prima facie lawful; and

(v) the above principles are subject to any restriction or exceptions imposed by statute or common law.

443 Principle (i) requires no illustration. An example of the operation of principle (ii) is the withholding of a bonus as a punishment for an employee who had taken part in strike activity, in a situation where despite a practice for 50 years of paying a bonus, entitlement to such bonus had never become an express or implied term of the employee's contract.[9] Similarly, since the employee normally is entitled only to be paid, and not also to be provided with work,[10] it is lawful for an employer to suspend any worker, provided he pays him the contractual wages.[11-12]

Suspension without pay

444 Suspension of an employee without pay involves a derogation from the employee's contractual right to be paid and therefore is a breach of contract unless authorised by the contract itself.[13] This illustrates principle (iii). If the contract itself provides for a particular procedure to be followed in order to suspend the employee, suspension other than in compliance with such procedure is a breach of contract and the employee will be entitled to recover accrued salary during the period of the suspension.[14] Such withholding of pay is not, however, a violation of the truck legislation,[15] in the case of an employee to whom such legislation applies,[16] provided it is authorised by the contract of employment of the worker concerned.

Statutory restrictions

445 The Truck Act 1896[17] imposes important restrictions on the disciplinary rules which may be agreed between employer and employee. This act applies only to shop assistants[18] and persons who are workmen for the purposes of truck legislation. In those cases where it applies, truck legislation would prevent deductions being made by employers from the wages of their employees; and also would prevent cash payments being made by employees to their employers. Contracts providing for such deductions or payments would be void. However, the Truck Act 1896 made provision for two exceptions, provided certain conditions were fulfilled. The exceptions were in respect of deductions for defective

---

[9] *Grieve* v. *Imperial Tobacco Co.*, *The Guardian*, April 30, 1963; K. W. Wedderburn, *Cases and Materials on Labour Law* (Cambridge, 1967), p. 118.

[10] *Turner* v. *Sawdon* [1901] 2 K.B. 653. See Chap. 9.

[11-12] But see now *suggestions* to the contrary in *Langston* v. *A.U.E.W.* [1974] I.C.R. 180, at 190 F–G, 192 F, and 193 G (*per* Lord Denning M.R. and Stephenson L.J.).

[13] *Hanley* v. *Pease* [1915] 1 K.B. 698; *Marshall* v. *English Electric Co. Ltd.* [1945] 61 T.L.R. 379.

[14] *Gorse* v. *Durham C.C.* [1971] 1 W.L.R. 775.

[15] *Bird* v. *British Celanese Ltd.* [1945] K.B. 336.

[16] See above, Chap. 3.

[17] See also above, Chap. 10.

[18] " Shop assistant " is not defined, and has been held to include a dairy roundsman whose employers owned no shop. See *Airedale Dairy Co.* v. *Bishop* (1913) 48 L.J.News. 188.

workmanship and fines. In the case of deductions for bad workmanship the Act of 1896 provides that no employer

> "shall make any contract with any workman for any deduction from any sum contracted to be paid by the employer to the workman, or for any payment to the employer by the workman for or in respect of bad or negligent work or injury to the materials or other property of the employer, unless—
>
> (a) the terms of the contract are contained in a notice kept constantly affixed at such place or places open to the workmen and in such a position that it may be easily seen, read, and copied by any person whom it affects; or the contract is in writing, signed by the workman; and
>
> (b) the deduction or payment to be made under the contract does not exceed the actual or estimated damage or loss occasioned to the employer by the act or omission of the workman, or of some person over whom he has control or for whom he has by the contract agreed to be responsible; and
>
> (c) the amount of the deduction or payment is fair and reasonable, having regard to all the circumstances of the case." [19]

446   Any deduction or payment made must be in accordance with the contract (which in turn must comply with the above conditions) and the employer must supply to the worker "particulars in writing showing the acts or omissions in respect of which the deduction or payment is made and the amount thereof . . . on each occasion when a deduction or payment is made." [20] It is a criminal offence for an employer to make any deduction or to receive any payment in respect of bad workmanship where the provisions of the Act are not complied with. [21]

A possible way round the prohibition of the Truck Act 1896 in respect of penalising workers for bad workmanship has been approved by the Court of Appeal, who have held in a case in 1934 that, where wages are paid on a piece-rate basis, if provision is made for differential rates to be paid for well and badly finished pieces then, since an allowance is made for bad workmanship in calculating the total wages due, there is therefore no *deduction* from the total wages due in respect of bad workmanship. There being no deduction there is no violation of the Truck Acts. [22]

Fines

447   The Truck Act 1896 makes similar provision in relation to any contract authorising the employer to deduct or levy fines upon his employees. For such a contract to be lawful it must comply with condition (a) (para. 445, above); and

> "(b) the contract [must have] specified the acts or omissions in respect

---

[19] Truck Act 1896, s. 2 (1).
[20] *Ibid.* s. 2 (2).
[21] *Ibid.* s. 4.
[22] *Sagar* v. *Ridehalgh* [1931] 1 Ch. 310. But see *Pritchard* v. *Clay (Wellington) Ltd.* [1926] 1 K.B. 238, where a different view was taken.

of which the fine may be imposed, and the amount of the fine or the particulars from which that amount may be ascertained [23];

(c) the fine imposed under the contract is in respect of some act or omission which causes or is likely to cause damage or loss to the employer, or interruption or hindrance to his business;

(d) the amount of the fine is fair and reasonable having regard to all the circumstances of the case." [24]

The Act further provides that the employer shall not make any deduction or receive payment of any fine except one which is made in accordance with a contract fulfilling the conditions enumerated above. For a deduction or fine lawfully to be made or paid, the employee must be given a written statement of the same kind as a deduction in respect of bad workmanship. [25]

448   In order to be within the prohibition of the 1896 Act there must either be a deduction from wages due or a separate payment made by way of a fine. Where an employee, who was to be paid 8s. for a working week of fifty-five and a half hours plus a bonus of 2s. for full attendance during the week, missed half a day, the withholding in accordance with the works rules of the bonus was not unlawful. It was not a deduction from wages due; until there had been a full attendance the bonus did not become payable as part of the wages; nor was there a payment by the worker of 2s. to the employer. [26]

Hosiery

449   In the hosiery industry a special Act applies forbidding " any deduction or stoppage of any description whatever [from wages], save and except for bad and disputed workmanship." [27] It was held, before the passing of the Truck Act 1896, that this did not render unlawful the making of a reasonable deduction from wages by way of fine for non-attendance at work in accordance with the works rules. [28] The Truck Act 1896 applies even in the hosiery industry and therefore fines and deductions for bad workmanship must comply with the provisions of that Act. [29]

Register of fines

450   Every employer operating a contract in accordance with the provisions of the Truck Act 1896 must furnish copies of such contract on

---

[23] This might imply that the disciplinary rules in respect of which fines may lawfully be imposed must be specified with some particularity. Notwithstanding this a works rule that a worker should observe " good order and decorum " has been held to be valid in a case where a worker who had danced in a factory workroom during a meal break and raised dust was held to have been lawfully fined in accordance with this provision. See *Squire* v. *Bayer & Co.* [1901] 2 K.B. 299.

[24] Truck Act 1896, s. 1 (1).

[25] *Ibid.* s. 1 (1).

[26] *Deane* v. *Wilson* [1906] 2 I.R. 405.

[27] The Hosiery Manufacture (Wages) Act 1874.

[28] *Willis* v. *Thorp* (1875) L.R. 10 Q.B. 383.

[29] Note, however, that the Secretary of State may exempt certain employees from the operation of the Truck Act 1896. See s. 9. Two Orders have been made under this section: S.R. & O. 1897 No. 299 (cotton weaving in Lancashire, Cheshire, Derbyshire and East Riding of Yorkshire), and S.R. & O. 1897 No. 629 (iron ore mines and limestone quarries in certain parts of Lancashire and Cumberland, and iron-stone mines in the North Riding of Yorkshire).

demand to the wages inspectorate [30]; must make a copy available free on request to the employee party to it [31]; and in case of fines or deductions by way of fines a register must be kept in which must be entered:

> "every deduction or payment for or in respect of any fine purporting to be made under any such contract, specifying the amount and the nature of the act or omission in respect of which the fine was imposed, and this register shall be at all times open to inspection by one of Her Majesty's [wages inspectors]." [32]

Forfeiture of wages

451　　Forfeiture of wages while the employment relationship continues [33] is governed by the provisions of the Truck Act 1896 in the case of persons to whom that Act applies. Forfeiture of wages can only lawfully occur if there is a provision in a contract providing for it. The above provision will override any inconsistent contractual provision.

Incorporation of collective agreements

452　　The Trade Union and Labour Relations Act 1974 introduced a novel kind of statutory restriction on the exercise of disciplinary powers by employers, which will apply to any situation where disciplinary rules are agreed to as part of a collective agreement, which in turn is incorporated expressly or impliedly into the contracts of employment of the workers concerned. Section 18 of that Act provides, in part:

> "(4) Notwithstanding anything in subsections (2) and (3) [34] above, any terms of a collective agreement (whether made before or after the commencement of this section) which prohibit or restrict the right of workers to engage in a strike or other industrial action, or have the effect of prohibiting or restricting that right, shall not form part of any contract between any worker and the person for whom he works unless the collective agreement—
>
> (a) is in writing; and
>
> (b) contains a provision expressly stating that those terms shall or may be incorporated in such a contract; and
>
> (c) is reasonably accessible at his place of work to the worker to whom it applies and is available for him to consult during working hours; and
>
> (d) is one where each trade union which is a party to the agreement is an independent trade union;
>
> and unless the contract with that worker expressly or impliedly incorporates those terms in the contract.

---

[30] s. 6 (1). Enforcement of the Act used to be the responsibility of the factory inspectorate. With the reorganisation of that body under the Health and Safety at Work etc. Act 1974 factory inspectors ceased to have this role. Acting under reg. 2 of the Truck Acts 1831 to 1896 (Enforcement) Regs. (S.I. 1974 No. 1887), the Secretary of State for Employment has transferred the responsibility to the Wages Inspectorate.

[31] s. 6 (2).

[32] Truck Act 1896, s. 6 (3).

[33] Forfeiture of wages in cases of termination of the contract is dealt with below, Chap. 16.

[34] Subss. (2) and (3) relate to the legal enforceability of collective agreements between the parties. See Chap. 8, above.

(5) Subsection (4) above shall have effect notwithstanding any provision to the contrary in any agreement (including a collective agreement or a contract with any worker)."

The result of this appears to be that if there are provisions embodied in a collective agreement requiring flexibility, *i.e.*, that workers traditionally employed to do one kind of work may be required by employers to do other kinds of work, and if workers pursued a policy of non-co-operation, refused to operate the flexibility agreement to put pressure on the employer, this being a form of industrial action [35] would not be a breach of their contracts of employment. The employer could not lawfully take any form of disciplinary action against them, unless the provision of the collective agreement had been incorporated in accordance with the provisions of section 18 (4). The presence of an express term in their contracts of employment would be irrelevant unless the other conditions had been fulfilled. At the present time this is rarely the case. Very few collective agreements contain the express statement that they are intended to be incorporated in the contracts of employment of the workers concerned. An interesting consequence of this provision is that workers are entitled to time off during working hours to consult collective agreements restricting their freedom to take industrial action, and where such agreements are kept only in the manager's office are to be allowed to leave their work place for the purpose of consulting them. If the employer refuses to allow this he could not lawfully invoke the provisions of the collective agreement to justify disciplinary measures against the workers.

Common law restrictions

453   There are a number of common law restrictions on the disciplinary powers of an employer. First of all any provisions in a contract of employment which have the effect of placing the worker in the position of a serf are void.[36] The law will not permit servile incidents to be attached to a contract of employment.[37] " Hence a distinction must be drawn between contracts which limit the freedom of the employee to do as he wishes, in the light of the reasonable interests and the necessary protection of his employer, and contracts of employment which would tend to reduce too greatly the freedom of an employee to live and work." [38]

Penalties

454   Secondly, the common law will invalidate any provision in a contract providing for payment, whether referred to as a fine or not, by one party to another of any sum of money, or deduction or forfeiture of wages, as a sanction for a breach by the other side, unless the amount concerned can be regarded as a genuine pre-estimate of the damage likely to result from the breach by the offending party.[39] In any case the amount of the penalty must be specified in the contract or readily ascertainable in accordance with its terms. Where the amount of the sum to be paid or forfeited is

---

[35] For a discussion of what is meant by " industrial action " see Chaps. 1 and 17.
[36] *Davies* v. *Davies* (1887) 36 Ch.D. 359.
[37] *Horwood* v. *Millar's Timber and Trading Co. Ltd.* [1917] 1 K.B. 305.
[38] G. H. L. Fridman, *Modern Law of Employment* (London, 1963), p. 48.
[39] *Dunlop Pneumatic Tyre Co. Ltd.* v. *New Garage and Motor Co. Ltd.* [1915] A.C. 79.

such that it is fixed simply as a means of *deterring* the potential offender it is void. The distinction is between a genuine pre-estimate of liquidated damages or a penalty. If the latter, it is void.

Lock-outs

455 Unless there is a term in the contract permitting a lock-out, or lawful notice to terminate the contract is given, there being no implied right on the part of an employer to lock out his employees for disciplinary or other reasons, any such lock-out is a breach of contract on the employer's part.[40]

Strikes

456 Disciplinary action of various sorts may be taken in respect of strike action by employees.[41] Where the legality of such disciplinary action is contingent upon the strike concerned involving a breach of contract, it is important to note the different forms that strike notice [42] takes. A strike not preceded by the giving of strike notice is very likely to involve a breach of contract by the individual striker.[43]

Strike notice

457 In order to understand the significance of strike notice two points should be made: (1) The legality of disciplinary action taken by an employer in respect of a threat of strike action (and indeed in respect of participation in a strike) often depends upon whether there has been an anticipatory breach [43] (*i.e.*, a statement of intention to break the contract), and whether in respect of participation in a strike there has been a breach or a termination.[44] (2) The forms which strike notices actually take vary enormously, but they can be summarised in this way. A notice of intention to strike can take one of the following main forms:

(a) (i) An explicit statement of an intention " to break the contract " of employment, or

(ii) a more equivocal statement amounting to the same thing in law, *i.e.*, a statement of an intention " to withdraw labour " from the employer.

(b) A statement of an intention " to suspend the contract of employment."

(c) A statement of an intention " to terminate the contract."

(d) A statement of intention " to strike."

458 Considering the different forms that strike notice may take we find as follows:

(1) Strike notice in the form of (a) (i). This is clearly such that the

---

[40] *Jas. Cummings* v. *C. Connell & Co. Ltd.*, 1969 S.L.T. 25; *cf. E. & J. Davis Transport Ltd.* v. *Chattaway* [1972] I.C.R. 267, 271 (N.I.R.C.) where it was said that a strike or a lock-out are not of themselves tantamount to a repudiation.

[41] On the legality of working to rule, see Chap. 9 above.

[42] As to the form of strike notice, see *Horizon Holidays* v. *A.S.T.M.S.* [1973] I.R.L.R. 22 (N.I.R.C.).

[43] Participation in a strike intended to disrupt the employer's business is usually construed as a breach by the employee: *Stratford* v. *Lindley* [1965] A.C. 269, 335; *Seaboard World Airlines Inc.* v. *T.G.W.U.* [1973] I.C.R. 458, 460; *Sanders* v. *Ernest Neale Ltd.* [1974] I.C.R. 565, 568. See *Simmons* v. *Hoover Ltd., The Times*, July 20, 1976 (E.A.T.).

[44] This would mean that the employee had, by repudiating the contract, in effect dismissed himself: see *Chappell* v. *Times Newspapers Ltd.* [1975] I.C.R. 145 at p. 158 (Megarry J.), *cf.* p. 175 (Lord Denning M.R.). See, too, Chap. 2 above.

employer is normally entitled to regard it as an anticipatory breach or repudiation in advance of the contract.

459 (2) Strike notice taking the form of (a) (ii) is at common law repudiation of the contract.

460 (3) At common law a notice to strike may exceptionally [45] have the effect of suspending the contract if there is a term in the contract giving employers the right to suspend. In the case of contracts which provide for the incorporation of certain procedure agreements, the effect of such incorporation may be to confer a right to suspend. Thus if the agreement provides that there shall be no strike action until procedure is exhausted, such a provision incorporated in an individual contract *might* be interpreted as giving a right for a worker to take part in strike action without breaking it, *i.e.*, by suspending it, after procedure is exhausted. Where there is a contractual right to suspend, then the contract is suspended.

461 (4) With a nice disregard of legal technicalities most strike notices take form (d) expressing an intention " to strike." Only in this case is there really something to construe because notice " to strike " is ambiguous and may mean either notice to break, to terminate or to suspend. In the case of the incorporation of a procedure agreement of the kind discussed in (3) above, such notice is notice to suspend. At common law notice " to strike " could in differing circumstances be a notice to break or a notice to terminate.

The Code

462 The Code of Industrial Relations Practice imposes an obligation on the employer to keep employees fully informed of their rights and obligations, including in particular details of the circumstances which may lead to suspension or dismissal.[46] Under the Code management must ensure that fair and effective (and agreed) procedures exist for dealing with disciplinary matters. Except in very small enterprises there should be a disciplinary procedure.[47] In addition to specifying who may take disciplinary action, the written procedure should give the employee an opportunity of stating his case either in person or by a representative. There should be a right of appeal, and a provision for arbitration if the parties wish. The Code also says:

" Where there has been misconduct, the disciplinary action to be taken will depend, on the circumstances, including the nature of the misconduct. But normally the procedure should operate as follows:

---

[45] In *Morgan* v. *Fry* [1968] 2 Q.B. 710 at p. 730, Lord Denning M.R. expressed the opinion that strike notice of a length equal to the period necessary to terminate the contract, even in the absence of express contractual provision for suspension, operated as suspension of the contract. This view is inconsistent with high authority and must now be regarded as wrong. See *Bowes* v. *Press* [1894] 1 Q.B. 202; *Parkin* v. *South Hetton Coal Co.* (1907) 97 L.T. 98; Wedderburn, *Cases and Materials on Labour Law* (Cambridge, 1967), pp. 525–526; *ibid.*, *The Worker and the Law* (2nd ed., Penguin, 1971), pp. 109–111, and P. O'Higgins, " Notice to Strike " [1968] C.L.J. 223; K. Foster, " Strike Notice: section 147 " (1973) 2 I.L.J. 28, and P. O'Higgins, " Strike Notices: Another Approach," *ibid.*, 152. See now *Simmons* v. *Hoover Ltd. The Times*, July 20, 1976, where the E.A.T. declined to follow *Morgan* v. *Fry*. See also *Cummings* v. *C. Connell & Co. Ltd.*, 1969 S.L.T. 25; [1969] A.S.C.L. 502 (Notice of lock-out).
[46] Code, paras. 62 (ii) and 131 (ii).
[47] Code, para. 130.

   (i) the first step should be an oral warning [48] or, in the case of more
       serious misconduct, a written warning setting out the circumstances;
  (ii) no employee should be dismissed for a first breach of discipline
       except in the case of gross misconduct;
 (iii) action on any further misconduct, for example, final warning,
       suspension without pay or dismissal, should be recorded in writing;
  (iv) details of any disciplinary action should be given in writing to the
       employee and, if he so wishes, to his employee representative;
   (v) no disciplinary action should be taken against a shop steward until
       the circumstances of the case have been discussed with a full-time
       official of the union concerned." [49]

Although the Code may give the impression that an employer may
unilaterally prescribe for the definition of disciplinary offences and the
sanctions to be imposed in respect of them, this would be unlawful. As
we have seen, the disciplinary powers of the employer rest primarily upon
the terms, express or implied, of the contract of employment of the
employee concerned.

Warnings

463   A warning should be explicit.[50] It should indicate clearly at least four
things: (1) what standards of performance or conduct are expected of the
employee, (2) the ways in which he falls short of the expected standards,
(3) what he must do to rectify the situation, and (4) what sanction will
be imposed if he fails within a reasonable period of time to rectify the
situation.[51]

464   The Advisory Conciliation and Arbitration Service published for discussion a *Draft Code of Practice on Disciplinary Practice and Procedures*
in May 1976. This makes it very likely that there will be in operation some-
time in 1977 a new A.C.A.S. Code on disciplinary rules and procedures.

[The next paragraph is 471.]

---

[48] Because of difficulties of proof it may be desirable to have a written record of an
oral warning. Some employers give employees written confirmation of terms of an *oral*
warning.
[49] Code, para. 133.
[50] J. E. McGlyne, *Unfair Dismissal Cases* (London, 1976), pp. 157 *et seq.*
[51] See Chap. 17 for the implications of warnings in claims for unfair dismissal.

CHAPTER 14

TERMINATION—GENERAL

Introduction

471   The contract of employment may come to an end in a wide variety of ways. Briefly the principal modes of termination are as follows:

    (i) by operation of law, which includes death, dissolution of a partnership, appointment of a receiver, the making of a winding-up order, and frustration;

    (ii) by agreement between the parties;

    (iii) by an act of either side terminating the contract without notice [1];

    (iv) by an act of either side terminating the contract with notice. [2]

472   It should be carefully noted that although the term "dismissal" is normally used to describe a positive act by an employer bringing the contract to an end under (iii) and (iv) above for statutory purposes, *i.e.* in claims for redundancy compensation under the R.P.A. [3] and claims for unfair dismissal under T.U.L.R.A., [4] the term "dismissal" is so defined as to include some forms of termination which fall under (i) and (ii) above.

1. TERMINATION BY OPERATION OF LAW

Death

473   The death of either party to the contract will terminate it. [5]

Dissolution of partnership

474   The modern view appears to be that where the employer is a partnership its dissolution [6] by the retirement or death of an existing partner will terminate the contracts of employment of its employees, at least in the absence of an express or implied contractual provision. The issue may also be affected by the extent to which the personality or identity [7] of the individual partners is an essential element in the employment relationship.

---

  [1] See below, Chap. 15.

  [2] See below, Chap. 16.

  [3] See below, Chap. 18.

  [4] See below, Chap. 17.

  [5] *Farrow* v. *Wilson* (1889) L.R. 4 C.P. 744. Where the employer or employee dies *after* a dismissal there are special statutory provisions permitting a claim for unfair dismissal (E.P.A., Sched. 12) and redundancy compensation (R.P.A., Sched. 4, Pt. II, as amended by E.P.A., Sched. 16, Pt. I).

  [6] Such dissolution may amount to a wrongful dismissal. See *Brace* v. *Calder* [1895] 2 Q.B. 253. For differing views as to the effects of dissolution of a partnership, see Freedland, *The Contract of Employment*, pp. 345–348, Rideout, *Labour Law* (2nd ed.), pp. 157–158, and Grunfeld, *Law of Redundancy*, pp. 50–52.

  [7] *Cf. Phillips* v. *Alhambra Palace Co.* [1901] 1 Q.B. 59.

183

Winding up

475   An order for compulsory winding up will operate to terminate the contracts of employment of the employees of the company concerned.[8]

Appointment of a receiver

476   The effect of the appointment of a receiver and manager of a company upon the contracts of employment of employees of the company depends upon the type of receiver appointed. If the receiver is appointed by the court this automatically terminates the contracts of the employees.[9] The same appears to apply where the receiver is appointed by and acts on behalf of the debenture holders. But there appears " to be no very good reason in principle why an appointment out of court of a receiver who is the agent of the company should determine contracts of employment " [10] of the employees of the company. In *Griffiths* v. *Secretary of State for Social Services* [11] Lawson J. held that the appointment out of court by debenture holders of a receiver and manager of a company to act as agent of the company does not terminate the contracts of employment of the company *unless* (a) the appointment was accompanied by a˙ sale of the business of the company so that there is no longer any business for which employees can work; or (b) simultaneously with, or very soon after the appointment, the receiver entered into a new agreement with a particular employee which was inconsistent with the continuance of his previous contract of employment, or (c) the continuation of the particular employee's employment was inconsistent with the role and functions of the receiver.

Frustration

477   Some of the above principles can be explained on the ground that the contract of employment is one (however artificial this may appear when most employers are companies) in which the personal relationship between the parties is of the essence, *e.g.,* the death of an employee or the winding up of a company. Again some may be explained in terms of the doctrine of frustration, *e.g.,* death of either party. By frustration is meant that there has been such a change of circumstances that the performance of the contract has become unlawful (as by the passing of a statute after the contract was made), or that events make it physically impossible for the contract to be performed (as where the illness of the employee lasts or is likely to last for a prolonged period), or that, although performance is not physically impossible, there has been such a change as to destroy the whole object of the contract; to make performance no longer viable in commercial terms.

---

[8] *Re General Rolling Stock Co.* (1866) L.R. 1 Eq. 346; *Nokes* v. *Doncaster Amalgamated Collieries Ltd.* [1940] A.C. 1014, *per* Lord Atkin at p. 1020. The employees may be able to sue for damages. See *Oriental Bank Corp. (McDowall's Case)* (1886) 32 Ch.D. 366. A voluntary winding up, *e.g.* for purposes of reorganisation, may not automatically terminate the contracts of employment of employees. See *Midland Counties District Bank Ltd.* v. *Attwood* [1905] 1 Ch. 357. For a discussion of the somewhat conflicting judicial decisions in this area, see Freedland, *op. cit.,* pp. 333–337.

[9] *Re Foster Clark Ltd.'s Indenture Trusts* [1966] 1 W.L.R. 125.

[10] *Ibid.* at p. 132, *per* Plowman J.

[11] [1974] Q.B. 468.

Illustrations

478   Although it is not easy to determine in some instances whether there has been such a change in circumstances as to frustrate the contract, where an Act of Parliament has made the performance of a particular kind of agreement unlawful, there is no problem. In the case of illness or incapacity of an employee the problem is more difficult. Illness or incapacity which is permanent will frustrate the contract, and so will illness which is of so prolonged a nature as to prevent the employer from getting substantially what he has bargained for. Where a member of a " pop-group," who contracted to play the drums under a five-year contract which required him to play seven nights weekly, often twice a night, had a collapse as a result of which he was able only to play for three or four nights, this was held to have frustrated the contract, there being no reasonable likelihood that he would be able to perform seven nights a week in the near future.[12] This may be contrasted with the case of a works manager employed under a five-year contract, who became ill after two years' employment. There was a likelihood of his recovering. It was held that the employer could not regard the contract as being frustrated as the circumstances were not such as to make it foreseeable that the employer would not obtain substantial performance of his contract by the manager.[13] The cases involving sickness involve some nice distinctions. In one case a singer had contracted to attend rehearsals and to perform in public at various places. She missed the rehearsals owing to illness but was able to attend the scheduled performances. The contract was held not to be frustrated.[14] In another contrasting case illness prevented a singer from attending both the rehearsals and the first four performances of an opera for which she had been hired. In this case it was held that the contract had been frustrated.[15] Because of the difficulty of drawing the line in particular cases, many employers follow the practice of dismissing with notice employees whose illness or incapacity prevents them temporarily from performing the work for which they are hired.[16] However, if a frustrating event has occurred, the contract terminates automatically and there is no need in fact for the employer to have given notice.[17] In other words, unbeknown to the employee, and even perhaps to the employer, the contract may have come to an end.[18]

In *Marshall* v. *Harland & Wolff Ltd.*[19] Sir John Donaldson outlined the factors to be taken account of in deciding whether the illness of the employee was of such a character as to frustrate the contract:

" (a) *The terms of the contract, including the provisions as to sickness pay.*—The whole basis of weekly employment may be destroyed more

---

[12] *Condor* v. *Barron Knights Ltd.* [1966] 1 W.L.R. 87.
[13] *Storey* v. *Fulham Steel Works Co.* (1907) 24 T.L.R. 89.
[14] *Bettini* v. *Gye* (1876) 1 Q.B.D. 183.
[15] *Poussard* v. *Spiers* (1876) 1 Q.B.D. 410.
[16] Such dismissal might now constitute an unfair dismissal, depending upon the circumstances. See Chap. 17, below.
[17] *Pritchard* v. *Dinorwic Slate Quarries Ltd.* [1971] I.T.R. 102, at p. 104. But *cf. Thomas* v. *John Archer & Co. Ltd.* (1971) 6 I.T.R. 146. The suggestion that some positive act by the employer may be required indicating that the contract is at an end is wrong. See *Marshall* v. *Harland & Wolff Ltd.* [1972] 1 W.L.R. 899, discussed in *Tan* v. *Berry Bros. & Rudd Ltd.* [1974] I.C.R. 586, at pp. 589–590.
[18] *Cf. Jones* v. *Wagon Repairs Ltd.* [1968] I.T.R. 361.
[19] [1972] 1 W.L.R. 899 at pp. 902–904.

quickly than that of monthly employment and that in turn more quickly than annual employment. When the contract provides for sick pay, it is plain that the contract cannot be frustrated so long as the employee returns to work, or appears likely to return to work, within the period during which such sick pay is payable. But the converse is not necessarily true, for the right to sick pay may expire before the incapacity has gone on, or appears likely to go on, for so long as to make a return to work impossible or radically different from the obligations undertaken under the contract of employment.

(b) *How long the employment was likely to last in the absence of sickness.*—The relationship is less likely to survive if the employment was inherently temporary in its nature or for the duration of a particular job, than if it was expected to be long term or even lifelong.

(c) *The nature of the employment.*—Where the employee is one of many in the same category, the relationship is more likely to survive the period of incapacity than if he occupies a key post which must be filled on a permanent basis if his absence is prolonged.

(d) *The nature of the illness or injury and how long it has already continued and the prospects of recovery.*—The greater the degree of incapacity and the longer the period over which it has persisted and is likely to persist, the more likely it is that the relationship has been destroyed.[20]

(e) *The period of past employment.*—A relationship which is of long standing is not so easily destroyed as one which has but a short history. This is good sense and, we think, no less good law, even if it involves some implied and scarcely detectable change in the contract of employment year by year as the duration of the relationship lengthens. The legal basis is that over a long period of service the parties must be assumed to have contemplated a longer period or periods of sickness than over a shorter period.

These factors are interrelated and cumulative, but are not necessarily exhaustive of those which have to be taken into account. The question is and remains: was the employee's incapacity, looked at before the purported dismissal, of such a nature, or did it appear likely to continue for such a period, that further performance of his obligations in the future would either be impossible or would be a thing radically different from that undertaken by him and accepted by the employer under the agreed terms of his employment? Any other factors which bear on this issue must also be considered." [21]

479   Events, other than sickness, which make the employee unavailable for the performance of work will also frustrate the contract. Thus the call-up of a comedian in 1940 for the Army had the effect of frustrating a contract under which he had given the exclusive management of his performances to a manager for a period of ten years. The comedian was demobbed in 1946, when the manager attempted to hold the comedian to his contract. It was held that there had been such a change in circum-

---

[20] *Cf. Hebden* v. *Forsey & Son* [1973] I.C.R. 607.

[21] For example, where an employee who is away sick fails to keep his employer fully informed as to his progress, this may amount to an implied determination of the contract by the employee: *Harrison* v. *George Wimpey & Co. Ltd.* [1972] I.T.R. 188 (N.I.R.C.).

stances and for such a duration that the original contract had been frustrated.[22]

Subject to the proviso that neither side can invoke any frustrating event brought about by his own act (*i.e.*, self-induced frustration) as a ground of treating the contract as being at an end, the effect of frustration is to bring the contract to an end automatically, neither side of course being liable to pay damages to the other. All contractual obligations are ended and originally payment could not be required for services already performed under a frustrated contract.[23] Now under the Law Reform (Frustrated Contracts) Act 1943 it may be possible for an employee to recover, in respect of services performed before the frustrating event occurred, a sum " not exceeding the value of any benefit " his services may have conferred on his employer. Thus, where a seaman died before he completed a voyage in respect of which he was entitled to a lump sum payment,[24] his widow could have probably recovered under the 1943 Act in respect of the benefit her husband's employer received in virtue of having the benefit of the seaman's services for a part of the voyage.[25]

2. TERMINATION BY AGREEMENT

480   In the absence of any other factor bringing the contract to an end the parties may put an end to the contract by mutual agreement. Sometimes this agreement to the termination of the contract may exist from the moment of the initial agreement to enter into the employment relationship. It may be agreed for example that the contract is to last only for the duration of a particular job. When the job is completed the contract automatically comes to an end.

Contracts of limited duration

481   There may be an agreement that the contract is to last only for a certain period of time. Contracts of this kind may include an agreement which provides that the contract is not to last in any event for longer than a certain period of time, but that one or both parties have the right to terminate it before then in certain circumstances, as for example if notice of a particular length of time is given. Other contracts which are agreed to last only for a certain period of time may not contain a provision permitting termination by either side before the expiry of that period of time. Whether there is any difference in the legal significance of the two kinds of contracts, both of which have occurred in practice for many years, is a matter of considerable importance. Both the R.P.A. and T.U.L.R.A.

---

[22] *Morgan* v. *Manser* [1948] 1 K.B. 184. The internment of one of the parties as an enemy alien will have the same effect. See *Unger* v. *Preston Corporation* [1942] 1 All E.R. 200. In *Hare* v. *Murphy Bros.* [1974] I.C.R. 603 (C.A.) a 12-month prison sentence imposed by a court frustrated the contract of employment (*per* Lord Denning M.R.) or terminated it by making it impossible for the employee to perform his part of the contract (*per* Stephenson and Lawton L.JJ.).

[23] In certain cases the Apportionment Act 1870 might have been invoked. Under this Act, assuming that it applied to wages in addition to salary which it specifically covers, in any case where wages were to be paid periodically as opposed to a fixed single payment when the task was completed, wages would be regarded as accruing from day to day, and would be recoverable up to the day on which frustration occurred. See Chap. 10.

[24] The Apportionment Act 1870 could not apply here.

[25] *Cf. Cutter* v. *Powell* (1795) 6 T.R. 320.

use the term " fixed term " contracts for two purposes. Both Acts permit employees who are parties to contracts of employment for a fixed term of two years or more to waive their rights to claim for unfair dismissal or redundancy compensation.[26] Both Acts also define " dismissal "—in the absence of a dismissal no employee can bring a claim under the Acts [27] —so as to include the expiry of the contract of employment of an employee employed under a contract of employment for a " fixed term of two years or more."

482   In *B.B.C.* v. *Ioannou* [28] the Court of Appeal had to consider the meaning of a " fixed term for two years or more " for the purpose of the waiver provisions of the two Acts. Lord Denning M.R. said:

> " In my opinion a ' fixed term ' is one which cannot be unfixed by notice. To be a ' fixed term,' the parties must be bound for the term stated in the agreement: and unable to determine it by notice on either side. . . . [d]etermination by notice is destructive of any ' fixed term.' " [29]

483   No cases were referred to in the judgments in this case and none were cited in argument. Is the decision a correct one? This has to be considered against the background of the purpose of the two Acts which in the case of the R.P.A., is *inter alia,* to compensate workers for loss of employment where the reason for this is redundancy, and in the case of T.U.L.R.A. that employment should validly come to an end only where the reason for the end of employment is one which, when submitted to independent examination by an industrial tribunal, makes sense as a justifiable reason for termination. It would be inconsistent with the deliberate intention of the Acts if employers were able to insist on employing people only on terms which expressly or impliedly precluded the right of the employee on termination to submit that termination to the scrutiny of an industrial tribunal. Both Acts are protective legislation. However they do permit contracting out where the employee is employed under a contract of employment for a fixed term of two years or more. In such circumstances the employee may give up his rights to compensation in respect of the expiry of the fixed term if he, being " an employee under a contract of employment " [30] agrees in writing to do so. No case has yet decided *when* such waiver may occur. If the Acts were to be interpreted from the point of view that the employee could waive his rights only when he was in a position to bargain a price for such waiver, then the phrase " under a contract of employment " would mean that the employee would have had to have commenced employment before he could agree to surrender his rights. The effect of the *Ioannou* case is that the employee can only waive his rights in respect of the expiry if there is no provision in the contract permitting either side to terminate it before the end of the prescribed period. The decision has the effect of limiting the scope of the contracting out provisions. One can justify it in its application to the waiver provisions

---

[26] R.P.A., s. 15 (2), and T.U.L.R.A., Sched. 1, para. 12 (b).
[27] R.P.A., s. 6, provides an apparent exception.
[28] [1975] I.C.R. 267.
[29] *Ibid.* at pp. 271–272.
[30] This is the phrase used in R.P.A., s. 15 (2); T.U.L.R.A., Sched. 1, para. 12 (b), uses the term " employee," which would appear to have the same implications.

of the two Acts, as giving a beneficial interpretation to protective legislation, so as to permit contracting out in situations clearly within the intention of Parliament.

484　It must be insisted that the *Ioannou* case was solely concerned with the definition of " fixed term " for the purposes of the waiver provisions. It is when one considers the question whether the same approach should apply to the provisions of the Acts defining " dismissal " that one runs into difficulties. The two Acts [31] define " dismissal " as including the expiry of a contract of employment for a fixed term. If the same interpretation were applied to the concept of a fixed term here, there would immediately be established an enormous loophole in the legislation. It would mean that any employer who employed his workers on terms that the contract should not last in any event for longer than a year or ten years, but was terminable with notice before then, but could be renewed, whenever such a contract expired there would in law be no dismissal, and hence no claim for redundancy compensation or unfair dismissal would lie. It would in effect be a contracting out of the provisions of the Acts in circumstances where the employee offered employment only on these terms would not be in a position to bargain over the price in exchange for which he would be willing to waive his statutory rights.

485　The policy of the legislation can only be maintained by confining the *Ioannou* decision to the waiver provisions and regarding fixed term contracts for the purpose of the definition of dismissal as including both types of contract of agreed finite duration, those where there is no provision for earlier termination by notice as well as those where there is such provision.

486　There remains the problem of contracts which the parties have agreed are not to last indefinitely but where the limited duration of the contract is not fixed in terms of a specific period of time, but is fixed by the duration of a particular job. At least for purposes of the definition of dismissal it is suggested that such contracts should also be regarded as contracts for a fixed term, otherwise there would be no claim for redundancy compensation or unfair dismissal, in case of the ending of such employment.[32]

3. DEFINITION OF DISMISSAL

487　Both the R.P.A. and T.U.L.R.A. now define " dismissal " in practically identical terms :

" . . . an employee shall be treated as dismissed if, but only if—
　(a) the contract under which he is employed by the employer is terminated by the employer, whether it is so terminated by notice or without notice, or
　(b) where under that contract he is employed for a fixed term, that term expires without being renewed under the same contract, or
　(c) the employee terminates that contract, with or without notice,

---

[31] R.P.A., s. 3 (1) (*b*), and T.U.L.R.A., Sched. 1, para. 5 (2) (*b*).
[32] See too, C.E.A., s. 9 (2A) (no minimum notice for jobs of 12 or less weeks).

in circumstances such that he is entitled to terminate it without notice by reason of the employer's conduct." [33]

488   The only difference so far as the above quotation is concerned between the two Acts is that the R.P.A. expressly provides that (c) does not apply where the employee is entitled to terminate his contract " by reason of a lock-out by his employer." [34]

489   We shall discuss (a) in the above statutory definition later in Chapters 15 and 16. It is to be noted that in some of the cases we have considered above of termination by operation of law, in paras. 473 to 475, where dissolution of a partnership, a winding-up order or the appointment of a receiver does not, because of the particular facts of the case, terminate by operation of law the contracts of employment of the employees, there may nonetheless be a dismissal entitling the employees to bring their claim for redundancy compensation or for unfair dismissal on the grounds that they have been dismissed within (c) of the statutory definition above.

490   Ordinarily however termination of the contract of employment by operation of law will not entitle the employee to bring a claim for unfair dismissal. In case of claims for redundancy compensation the position is different because the R.P.A.[35] provides:

" Where in accordance with any enactment or rule of law
(i) any act on the part of an employer, or
(ii) any event affecting an employer (including, in the case of an individual, his death),
operates so as to terminate a contract under which an employee is employed by him, that act or event shall for the purposes of this Act be treated as a termination of the contract by the employer, if apart from this subsection it would not constitute a termination of the contract by him. . . . "

491   A number of comments need to be made on the concept of dismissal as outlined above. First of all, a notice to dismiss by an employer must be such as to evince an intention that the contract shall be ended as at an ascertainable date. A mere warning of impending redundancy at some time in the future is not a notice of dismissal; if an employee acts on such warning by leaving and seeking alternative employment, since he has not been dismissed by his employer, he is not entitled to redundancy compensation.[36] Secondly, if the employee leaves as a result of an agreement with his employer, this is consensual termination, and not dismissal, which is essentially a unilateral act by the employer.[37] Thirdly, a distinction is drawn by the Acts between " certain acts of the employer which are so far outside the terms of the contract that they can be construed as dismissal by him. Others merely entitle the employee to terminate the contract, . . . Unfortunately, it is virtually impossible to distinguish between the two categories of acts." [38] In *Marriott* v. *Oxford & District Co-operative Society Ltd. (No. 2)* [39] the claimant was employed as a foreman. A

---

[33] R.P.A., s. 3 (1), and T.U.L.R.A., Sched. 1, para. 5 (2).   [34] R.P.A., s. 10 (4).
[35] R.P.A., s. 22 (1) as amended by E.P.A., Sched. 16, Pt. I, para. 10.
[36] *Morton Sundour Fabrics* v. *Shaw* [1967] I.T.R. 84.
[37] *Steadman* v. *Halsales Ltd.* [1967] I.T.R. 77.
[38] O. Aiken and J. Reid, *Labour Law 1: Employment, etc.* (Penguin, 1971), p. 170.
[39] [1969] 3 All E.R. 1126. See too, Chap. 5.

letter from his employer informing him that as from a certain date he would no longer be employed as a foreman and would be demoted to supervisor, and that his wages would be reduced by £1 a week, was held to amount to a termination of the contract by the employer. Fourthly, the same case emphasised that, if the employee had agreed with his employer to vary the terms of his contract, including the reduction in wages and demotion, that this would not be a dismissal.

492   One cannot pretend that (b), providing that the expiry of a fixed term contract is to be regarded as a dismissal, is very happily expressed. There is some uncertainty as to the significance of the phrase " without being renewed under the same contract." It is to be noted that no claim for unfair dismissal can be brought in respect of the expiry of a fixed term contract entered into before February 28, 1972, unless it is a contract of apprenticeship. No claim can be brought for redundancy compensation in respect of the expiry of a fixed term contract entered into before December 6, 1965.

493   The provision in (c) covers the case of " constructive dismissal " so-called. (This is discussed in para. 514, below.)

494   The provisions, both of the T.U.L.R.A. and R.P.A., permit an employee under notice of dismissal to give notice to the employer so as to be able to leave earlier, without thereby losing any claim he may have to claim for unfair dismissal or for redundancy compensation. The provisions of the two Acts are different. Under the T.U.L.R.A. an employee can give notice in any form, in writing or orally, at any time, and when it expires can leave the employment and still claim for unfair dismissal.[40] In the case of the R.P.A.[41] the employee must give his notice *in writing* during the " obligatory period of notice " if his right to redundancy compensation is not to be lost. This means that he must give notice *either* after the employer has given him the minimum period of notice required by law (by statute or otherwise), *or*, where the employer has given him a longer period of notice than the necessary minimum then the employee must give in his notice during the period which being equal to the necessary minimum period, expires at the time when the employer's notice expires.

This means, for example, in the case of an employee who has been employed for four years the minimum period of notice the employer is required to give under the Contracts of Employment Act 1972, s. 1 (1), is four weeks. Assuming the contract of the worker concerned does not provide for a longer period of notice, this is the *minimum period required by law*. If the employer gives the worker four weeks' notice, the employee's rights are not prejudiced in respect of a claim for redundancy compensation if he himself gives his employer written notice during this period, even if the employee's notice expires before the employer's. If the employer, however, in this case gives six weeks' notice (*i.e.* two weeks longer than the minimum period required by law) then the employee forfeits his right to bring a claim for a redundancy payment if he himself gives notice during the first two weeks of the notice given by his employer. If he delays and gives notice in writing during the last four weeks of his employer's notice,

---

[40] T.U.L.R.A., Sched. 1, Pt. II, para. 5 (3) as amended.
[41] R.P.A., s. 4.

then his rights are not prejudiced in respect of any claim for redundancy compensation.

4. EFFECTIVE DATE OF TERMINATION/RELEVANT DATE

495   Under both the R.P.A. and T.U.L.R.A. it is necessary to establish the date on which the dismissal is to be regarded as having taken effect, principally for the purposes of determining whether the employee is qualified to bring a claim by having the appropriate required period of continuous employment and also of assessing the amount of redundancy compensation or of the basic award in case of unfair dismissal, where the quantum of any award made is also dependent upon length of continuous employment of the employee. Somewhat confusingly the R.P.A. uses the term " relevant date," whereas the T.U.L.R.A. uses the term " effective date of termination." The definition of " relevant date " and " effective date of termination " is practically the same. We summarise the position below (using the term " relevant date " to include " effective date of termination ") :

496   (a) Where a contract of employment is terminated by notice, whether given by the employer or the employee, the relevant date means the date on which the notice expires.[42]

(b) Where a contract of employment is terminated without notice, relevant date means the date on which the termination takes effect.[43]

(c) Where the employee is employed under a contract for a fixed term, relevant date means the date on which the term expires.[44]

(d) Where the notice required to be given by an employer to terminate a contract of employment by section 1 (1) of the Contracts of Employment Act 1972 as regards statutory minimum periods of notice,[45] would, if duly given when notice of termination was given by the employer, or (where no notice was given) when the contract of employment was terminated by the employer, expire on a date later than the relevant date as defined in (a) and (b) above, then that later date is to be treated as the relevant date.[46]

497   Where the employer gives notice of his intention that the contract will be terminated forthwith then the effective date of termination (or relevant date) will be the date of the receipt of the employer's notice of termination. This was decided in the case of *British Building and Engineering Appliances Ltd.* v. *Dedman*[47] by the Court of Appeal. This in effect affirms a dictum by Lord Denning M.R. in *Hill* v. *C. A. Parsons Ltd.*[48] :

> " Suppose, however, that the master insists on the employment terminating on the named day? What is the consequence in law? *In the ordinary course of things,* the relationship of master and servant thereupon comes to an end, for it is inconsistent with the confidential

---

[42] R.P.A., s. 3 (9) (*a*), and T.U.L.R.A., Sched. 1, para. 5 (5) (*a*).
[43] R.P.A., s. 3 (9) (*b*), and T.U.L.R.A., Sched. 1, para. 5 (5) (*b*).
[44] R.P.A., s. 3 (9) (*c*), and T.U.L.R.A., Sched. 1, para. 5 (5) (*c*).
[45] For periods of notice, see Chap. 16.
[46] R.P.A., s. 3 (10), and T.U.L.R.A., Sched. 1, para. 5 (6).
[47] [1974] I.C.R. 53.
[48] [1972] Ch. 305, at 314.

nature of the relationship that it should continue contrary to the will of one of the parties thereto."

In *Lees* v. *Arthur Greaves* (*Lees*) *Ltd.*[49] the Court rejected a very narrow distinction which could operate to the employee's disadvantage. An employer gave six months' notice of termination, but before the period of notice had fully run the employee agreed to finish work immediately. It was held that this did not amount to a dismissal and therefore the employee could bring no claim for unfair dismissal. This decision was overruled by the Court of Appeal, which held that the proper inference was that the employee had reluctantly agreed not to work out his notice. In so doing the Court approved a dictum by Sir John Donaldson:

> " We would further suggest that it would be a very rare case, indeed, in which it could properly be found that the employer and employee had got together and, notwithstanding that there was a current notice of termination of the employment, agreed mutually to terminate the contract, particularly when one realises the financial consequences to the employee involved in such an agreement.[50]

In such a case the effective date of termination (or relevant date) is the date of expiry of the original notice.

[The next paragraph is 501.]

---

[49] [1974] I.C.R. 501.
[50] *McAlwane* v. *Boughton Estates Ltd.* [1973] I.C.R. 470, 473.

CHAPTER 15

TERMINATION WITHOUT NOTICE

General principles

501   At common law either side may terminate the contract of employment by giving notice of the required length to terminate the contract.[1] Termination without notice, and in the case of the employer this would be summary dismissal, ordinarily is a breach of contract unless there are grounds which the law regards as sufficient to justify termination without notice. There still remains some uncertainty as to what these grounds are in the case of summary dismissal by an employer.[2] As McCardie J. said some years ago, " the principles [governing summary dismissal] are but rarely revealed." [3] Few areas of the law reflect so much changing attitudes to proper standards of behaviour by employees. Although there are statements suggesting that the law governing summary dismissal is simply an application of the ordinary principles of the law of contract to the employment area,[4] this is historically unsound.[5] It is not possible to squeeze the old cases into the modern law of contract. However, on the other hand, modern courts tend to arrive at decisions which, theoretically at any rate, can be fitted into a framework of the general law of contract, although it remains noteworthy that in many cases the judges are unable to arrive at a common statement of the legal principles underlying their judgments.[6] The common law makes a distinction between terms of a contract which are conditions, *i.e.*, important terms, and warranties which are secondary or subsidiary terms. Breach of a condition ordinarily gives the injured party a choice of either claiming damages or of rescinding the contract (summary dismissal in the case of a contract of employment); breach of

---

[1] See Chap. 16, below, for discussion of notice.
[2] Summary termination by the employee is discussed below.
[3] *Re Rubel Bronze & Metal Co. Ltd.* [1918] 1 K.B. 315.
[4] *Ibid.* at p. 321. See also footnote 10 below.
[5] This is because of two factors. Early decisions on dismissals commonly arose not out of litigation between masters and servants but out of litigation to determine whether a particular community was legally obliged to provide aid for a destitute person on the ground that he had acquired a settlement in the community concerned in virtue of having been employed there for the appropriate period. The object of these decisions was to do justice between two communities one of which would be liable to support a pauper; they were not concerned to do justice between master and servant. For example, the case of *R.* v. *Brampton* (*Inhabitants*) (1777) Cald.Mag.Cas. 11, which decided that a maidservant was properly dismissed on being found to be pregnant, was concerned with just such a question, whether the maidservant had acquired a settlement. Yet it has been solemnly cited in a modern work, as still establishing a principle relevant to the modern law of summary dismissal. See F. R. Batt, *Law of Master and Servant* (5th ed. by G. J. Webber, London, 1967), p. 89. A second factor is that any breach of a contract by a servant was a criminal offence until 1867. See above, Chap. 2.
[6] *e.g. Sinclair* v. *Neighbour* [1967] 2 Q.B. 279. *Per* Sellers L.J.: " The whole question is whether that conduct [of the employee] was of such a type that it was inconsistent, in a grave way—incompatible—with the employment in which he had been engaged as a manager " (at p. 287); *per* Davies L.J.: ". . . it was conduct of such a grave and weighty character as to amount to a breach of the confidential relationship between master and servant, such as would render the servant unfit for continuance in the master's employment . . ." (at p. 289); and *per* Sachs L.J.: " It is well-established law that a servant can be instantly dismissed when his conduct is such that it not only amounts to ' a wrongful act inconsistent with his duty towards his master ' but is also inconsistent with the ' continuance of confidence between them ' " (at p. 289).

warranty gives rise only to a claim for damages. The distinction between a warranty and a condition is often difficult to determine, and is usually dependent upon the importance attached by the parties themselves to the particular obligation. On the other hand, the social attitudes of the judges may determine in fact whether the court will regard breach of a particular obligation as breach of a condition, therefore justifying summary dismissal, or merely a warranty, breach of which sounds in damages only.[7] In recent times the courts have said, as a matter of general contract law, that there are certain terms which are neither conditions nor warranties, and that a party's right to treat the contract as at an end will depend not on the nature of the term, as a condition or warranty, but on the consequences (actual or foreseeable) of the particular breach. We shall see (below) that this general principle has not yet been fully assimilated into the law relating to summary dismissal.

502   For most practical purposes the employer's right of summary dismissal [8] arises from the terms, express or implied, of the contract of employment. The parties are free to limit the employer's right of summary dismissal or to extend it by the incorporation of the works rules, which may make dismissable acts which otherwise might not give rise to a right of summary dismissal.[9]

Conduct justifying summary dismissal

503   There is little doubt that few other areas of case-law have so directly reflected the judges' views as to what was fit and proper behaviour on the part of " servants " in their dealings with their " masters." Furthermore, whatever was the situation in the past, nowadays most people are employed by corporations, be they commercial companies, or public bodies. The typical employer is I.C.I. rather than plain Mr. Jones. Because of this it is increasingly less relevant to refer to the old cases on dismissal. Recently in *Wilson* v. *Racher*,[9a] Edmund Davies L.J. said:

" Reported decisions provide useful, but only general guides, each case turning upon its own facts. Many of the decisions which are customarily cited date from the last century and may be wholly out of accord with current social conditions. What would today be regarded as almost an attitude of Czar-serf, which is to be found in some of the older cases where a dismissed employee failed to recover damages, would, I venture to think, be decided differently

---

[7] An example may be *Pepper* v. *Webb* [1969] 1 W.L.R. 514. *Cf. Wilson* v. *Racher* [1974] I.C.R. 428.

[8] Sometimes the term " summary dismissal " is used where an employer is notifying the employee of the fact that the contract has been terminated by frustration. Clearly where the contract has been frustrated no notice need be given to terminate it. See *Condor* v. *Barron Knights Ltd.* [1966] 1 W.L.R. 87, and Chap. 14.

[9] Difficulties may sometimes arise where the works rules introduce a subjective element, *e.g.*, where a person is dismissable if he does not carry out his duties to the satisfaction of management. *Cf.* Chap. 17. In *Diggle* v. *Ogston Motor Co.* (1915) 84 L.J.K.B. 2165, employment was made subject to " your carrying out your duties to the satisfaction of the directors." It was held that a court could inquire into the question whether a reasonable board of directors could honestly have come to the conclusion that they were not satisfied with the employee's work. If the answer to that was " yes," then the court could not inquire further into the correctness of the directors' decision that they were not satisfied with the employee's work.

[9a] [1974] I.C.R. 428, at p. 430.

today. We have by now come to realise that a contract of service imposes upon the parties a duty of mutual respect."

Perhaps some help may be derived in understanding the degree of misconduct necessary to establish a right to dismiss summarily from the following series of principles:

(1) The modern test is basically whether the conduct complained of by the employee is a breach of an important term of the contract of employment.[10]

(2) It is primarily the conduct of the parties, the words they have used in the contract (or in the works rules where such are embodied in the contract) which are the best guide to the identification of the important terms which will give rise to a right of summary dismissal if they are broken.

(3) Certain terms, particularly certain implied terms, will be regarded by the judges as always prima facie being important, e.g., the obligation not to steal one's employer's property; the obligation not to deal with his property dishonestly, not to damage it deliberately; the obligation to obey reasonable and lawful orders, etc.

(4) Breach of an important term nowadays will not necessarily give rise to a right of summary dismissal if it occurs in such circumstances that the employee has a reasonable excuse or justification for his conduct.[11]

(5) Single acts of misconduct are somewhat less likely to give rise to a right of summary dismissal than is a persistent pattern of misconduct[12]; in the case of a single act of misconduct a record of unsatisfactory behaviour may tip the balance and lead the judge to the view that there are grounds for summary dismissal.[13]

(6) What is to be regarded as an important term will also depend upon the nature of the business or industry and the position of the employee.[14]

(7) Misconduct inside the workplace is likelier to give rise to breach of an obligation entitling the employer summarily to dismiss than misconduct outside the workplace or outside working hours; but dependent upon the terms of the contract, and sometimes on the position of the employee,

---

[10] Lord Evershed M.R. in *Laws* v. *London Chronicle Ltd.* [1959] 1 W.L.R. 698 at p. 701: "... since a contract of service is but an example of contracts in general, so that the general law of contract will be applicable, it follows that the question must be—if summary dismissal is claimed to be justifiable—whether the conduct complained of is such as to show the servant to have disregarded the essential conditions of the contract of service."

[11] *e.g. Laws* v. *London Chronicle Ltd.* [1959] 1 W.L.R. 698. Here the employee obeyed her immediate departmental head instead of the managing director of the company employing her. There were conflicting orders, only one of which she could obey. Here her disobedience of the managing director's order occurred in such circumstances that her disobedience was excusable; it was not such as could properly be regarded as entitling the company summarily to dismiss her.

[12] Lord Maugham, in *Jupiter General Insurance Co. Ltd.* v. *Shroff* [1937] 3 All E.R. 67, said at p. 73: "... it can be in exceptional circumstances only that an employer is acting properly in dismissing an employee on his committing a single act of negligence."

[13] In *Pepper* v. *Webb* [1969] 1 W.L.R. 514 Harman L.J. clearly considered it relevant in upholding the summary dismissal of a gardener for disobedience of an order (and for " insolence ") that he " had been acting in a very unsatisfactory way " for some time.

[14] Lord Maugham in *Jupiter General Insurance Co. Ltd.* v. *Shroff* [1937] 3 All E.R. 67 at p. 73: " It must be remembered that the test to be applied must vary with the nature of the business and the position held by the employee ..."

misconduct outside the workplace or working hours may exceptionally give rise to a right of summary dismissal.[15]

(8) Decisions of the courts in other cases are of little relevance in deciding in a particular case whether there is a right of summary dismissal [16]; misconduct serious enough to justify summary dismissal needs to be examined in the light of all the surrounding circumstances.[17]

(9) Whether misconduct is sufficient to justify summary dismissal is not dependent upon proof that such misconduct has had in fact serious consequences; the test is the nature of the misconduct itself [18]; and

(10) At the end of the day in any particular case it is usually only possible to guess the answer to the question, "Does this misconduct justify in law summary dismissal?" The more serious the misconduct the likelier it is that a court will regard it as justifying summary dismissal; the more trivial the less likely is a court to uphold a right of summary dismissal.

Giving a reason for dismissal

504 At common law an employer is not required to give any reason for a dismissal. An employee feeling aggrieved may bring an action for wrongful dismissal to which the employer may then plead the reason for dismissal and, if that is shown to be a sufficient reason for a summary dismissal, the employer has a complete defence. The rules regarding the giving of a reason for dismissal are still more antique than what has been said so far would suggest. In 1818 a corporation decided to dismiss its clerk and passed a resolution to call a meeting to elect his successor. The clerk whose duty it was to keep the minute book entered a protest of his own in the book at what he regarded as an injustice. On the question of whether the clerk had been properly dismissed it was held that all that was necessary was that there should be an adequate ground for the dismissal, which the protest entered by the clerk in the minute book was. It was immaterial that this was not the reason for the original decision to dismiss. Lord Denman C.J. said:

> "Now it is not necessary that a master, having a good ground of dismissal, should either state it to the servant, or act upon it. It is enough if it exist, and if there be improper conduct in fact. Suppose a servant had heard that his master intended to dismiss him without notice, and were to insult him in consequence: it is clear that the insult would justify the master in dismissing the servant; and yet, if he intended to dismiss him independently of the insult, the motive for the dismissal would be different from such ground of justification." [19]

---

15 *Per* Lord Esher M.R. in *Pearce* v. *Foster* (1886) 17 Q.B.D. 536, at pp. 539–540: " But if the servant is guilty of such a crime outside his service as to make it unsafe for a master to keep him in his employ, then the servant may be dismissed by his master; and if the servant's conduct is so grossly immoral that all reasonable men would say he cannot be trusted, the master may dismiss him." Typically the language used here is so woolly as not to be capable of any very certain interpretation. See also *Tomlinson* v. *London, Midland & Scottish Ry.* [1944] 1 All E.R. 537.

16 Lord Maugham, *loc. cit.*, " decisions in other cases are of little value."

17 *Laws* v. *London Chronicle Ltd.* [1959] 1 W.L.R. 698.

18 *Savage* v. *British India Steam Navigation Co.* (1930) 46 T.L.R. 294.

19 *Ridgway* v. *Hungerford Market Co.* (1835) Ad. & El. 171 at p. 172.

505   In other words, if an employer decides to dismiss an employee for a reason which would not justify summary dismissal, the reaction of the employee to intimation of such impending dismissal can provide a complete defence to an employer sued for a wrongful dismissal. It is important to emphasise that this extraordinary rule is inconsistent with the ordinary rules of contract. Yet despite this fact the rule has been further developed. In *Boston Deep Sea Fishing* v. *Ansell* [20] it was decided that, if an employer dismissed an employee in circumstances which would constitute a wrongful dismissal, it would still be a complete defence to the employer sued for such wrongful dismissal to establish that, unknown to the employer at the date of the dismissal, there had been in existence a reason which, had the employer known of it, would have justified the employee's summary dismissal. [21]

506   Although the common law rule continues to apply to any employee who does not, at the effective date of termination, [22] have 26 weeks' continuous employment with an employer, any employee who does have this length of service is, as a result of the Employment Protection Act 1975, [23] entitled to be provided by his employer within 14 days of his so requesting " a written statement giving the particulars of the reasons for his dismissal." Any employee may lodge a complaint with an industrial tribunal, providing it is presented during the period within which an industrial tribunal is willing to entertain a claim for unfair dismissal [24]—this will usually be within three months of the effective date of termination—that his employer has " unreasonably refused " to give such statement or that the particulars of the reasons given are inadequate or untrue. Clearly the employer may escape liability if he can show that the refusal [25] was not unreasonable.

What is meant by the particulars being adequate? Probably this means that sufficient details must be given to enable the employee to decide what kind of claim to bring, *e.g.* for redundancy compensation as opposed to unfair dismissal; to enable the employee to assess whether it is worthwhile bringing a claim, and if a claim is brought sufficient details should be given to enable the employee to know the kind of evidence the employee would need to assemble to rebut the evidence the employer is likely to bring to justify the particular dismissal.

507   The sanction for a refusal to give a written statement, or for giving

---

[20] (1888) 39 Ch.D. 339.

[21] These rules were approved by the Court of Appeal in *Cyril Leonard & Co.* v. *Simo Securities Trust Ltd.* [1972] 1 W.L.R. 80 at pp. 82, 86.

[22] For meaning of effective date of termination, see Chap. 14.

[23] E.P.A., s. 70.

[24] For a discussion of the period within which claims for unfair dismissal may be entertained, see Chap. 22.

[25] Because of the problems created by the often unhappy draftsmanship of the E.P.A., one has to ask whether the use of the word " refused " as opposed to " failed " in the Act is significant. There could be situations where although there had been no refusal there might be a failure to *provide* the written statement to the employee. It is of course open to the courts to decide that refusal and failure to provide are to be regarded as synonymous in the context of the Act. One may also ask whether a delay in providing the statement beyond the 14 days from the request is a refusal to provide the statement.

a written statement whose particulars are untrue [26] or inadequate is that the industrial tribunal to whom a complaint is made must—in the absence of the employer showing that his refusal was not unreasonable the tribunal has no discretion—award to the complainant employee a sum equal to two weeks' pay. This is not compensation. It is a penalty awarded against an employer who breaks the law. Further the tribunal has a discretion to make a declaration as to what it finds were the employer's reasons for the dismissal. Although the Act does not say so one must assume that where the tribunal makes such a declaration it will be binding on the employer in any subsequent claim brought against him by the employee for a remedy arising out of the dismissal. It seems also to be unlikely that if the employer does issue a written statement on request that he will be able to give another reason for the dismissal in subsequent litigation. It is likely that he will be bound by his first statement of reasons for the dismissal.

Some employers do now automatically give written statements to employees, who are dismissed, of the reasons for their dismissal. If such statements contain particulars which are inadequate or untrue the employee *cannot* bring a claim in respect of such statements before an industrial tribunal. The tribunal may only hear complaints in respect to statements issued in response to an employee's request. Where an employer, in the absence of a request, does issue a written statement of his reasons, the employee could bring a claim if he first asks the employer for the statement to which the employee is entitled under the E.P.A. If the employer then adopts the voluntary statement and expressly or by implication repeats it *in response to the employee's request,* then the employee may bring a claim.

Waiver

508   If either party to the contract of employment is aware of a breach by the other side of such seriousness as to justify repudiation (*i.e.*, summary dismissal or summary termination by the employee), but does not within a reasonable period invoke that reason and exercise the right to end the contract, he will be taken to have waived his right to end the contract and this right will be lost, leaving only the remedy open to him of seeking damages.[27] What constitutes a reasonable period will depend upon all the facts of the case.

Effect of summary dismissal on contract

509   If the dismissal is lawful, because there is a reason which constitutes a breach of a condition by the employee, the contract is terminated by the giving of notice of summary dismissal. Even if the summary dismissal is not justified, and is therefore in law a wrongful dismissal,[28] as a general rule the employee has not got the option of continuing with the contract and claiming damages if he wishes; he must accept the fact that the contract is ended, and has only the remedy of damages.[29] It is controversial

---

[26] It seems that the Employment Appeal Tribunal is likely to lay down that particulars of reasons given are untrue, so as to entitle an employee to two weeks' wages, if they are untrue only *in some substantial or significant respect.* Mere errors of minor detail will probably be ignored.   [27] *Beattie* v. *Parmenter* (1889) 5 T.L.R. 396.

[28] As to the important question as to the date on which dismissal, in particular wrongful dismissal, takes effect, see Chap. 14 above.

[29] *Denmark Productions Ltd.* v. *Boscobel Productions Ltd.* [1969] 1 Q.B. 699.

whether this is a strict legal rule or simply a practical result of the fact that an employee who is refused access to his work cannot claim contractual remuneration for services he does not render, nor (save, apparently, in exceptional circumstances) [30] will specific performance of the contract be granted. It has been judicially doubted whether the contract terminates as a matter of law,[31] and, in *Hill* v. *C. A. Parsons & Co. Ltd.*,[32] the Court of Appeal held that in " special circumstances " a contract of employment could be treated as subsisting despite a wrongful termination. The circumstances were not defined, and the reason for the decision in that case was clearly a desire to keep the employee in his job until the remedies for unfair dismissal under the Industrial Relations Act were brought into operation and became available to him. Lord Denning M.R., without defining other circumstances in which the contract might stay alive, simply gave as an illustration the case of an employee under a fixed-term contract with " fringe benefits." In such a case, the Master of the Rolls thought, the employer could not terminate the relationship before the expiry of the term so as to frustrate the employee's claim to a pension. Traditionally, this would be thought of as a case in which the contract would end and damages would be an adequate remedy; it remains to be seen how far the courts will assimilate the rules relating to the repudiation of employment contracts with the general principles of contract law.[33]

Procedure for dismissal

510   The common law [34] does not require the employer to follow any particular procedure in summarily dismissing an employee. Not only is there no general requirement that the employee be given a chance to be heard in his own defence, or that the rules of natural justice be complied with,[35] but it has been expressly ruled recently that the absence of any previous warning by an employer cannot be a ground for refusing to recognise a summary dismissal as lawful.[36] To the general rule that an employer is not obliged to follow a proper procedure in dismissing an employee there are the following exceptions:

(1) The contract itself may make provision for a procedure to be followed in the case of dismissal, and this will happen frequently where a collective agreement laying down the steps to be followed by management in a

---

[30] As held in *Hill* v. *C. A. Parsons & Co. Ltd.* [1971] 1 Ch. 305; above, Chap. 2.

[31] *Decro-Wall International S. A.* v. *Practitioners in Marketing Ltd.* [1971] 1 W.L.R. 361, 369–370 (Salmon L.J.), 375 (Sachs L.J.), 381 (Buckley L.J.). But *cf. Denmark Productions Ltd.* v. *Boscobel Productions Ltd.* [1969] 1 Q.B. 699; M. R. Freedland (1969) 32 M.L.R. 314; *Sanders* v. *E. Neale Ltd.* [1974] I.C.R. 565.

[32] [1971] 1 Ch. 305; above, Chap. 2. But in *G.K.N. (Cwmbran) Ltd.* v. *Lloyd* [1972] I.C.R. 214, 221 (N.I.R.C.) it was said that, " it will be rare indeed for an unjustifiable dismissal to be ineffective to terminate the contract."

[33] It is uncertain how far the general law recognises a principle that contracts requiring co-operation cannot continue contrary to the will of one party: see *Decro-Wall* case (above, note 31).

[34] See, however, Chap. 17 regarding unfair dismissal.

[35] The rules of natural justice cover three principles: (1) No one must be condemned without being told of the charge against him and without being given an opportunity to state his side of the case; (2) nobody should be judge in his own cause, *i.e.*, the person deciding on the guilt of another should not also be the person who acts as his accuser; and (3) any hearing or trial must be conducted honestly. These are not rigid rules of law but where a court decides these principles are applicable the court may, if practicable, seek to uphold them.

[36] *Pepper* v. *Webb* [1969] 1 W.L.R. 514.

dismissal has been incorporated into the contracts of employment of the workers concerned.[37]

(2) The employee may be dismissed in such circumstances that because his rights as a member of a trade union as well as an employee of the union may be affected by the dismissal the rules of natural justice will be applied by the courts.[38]

(3) If the person dismissed is what is known as an office-holder (*i.e.*, he holds a job involving the exercise of some public function, *e.g.*, a police constable,[39]) the rules of natural justice must be complied with.[40]

(4) If a statute regulates the appointment and dismissal of the employee the requirements of the statute must be complied with [41]; where a hearing is provided for, the hearing must comply with the rules of natural justice. The presence of a statute may lead to the implication of the right to a hearing [42] (and hence to the application of the rules of natural justice), but the courts will not always draw such an implication.[43] Where the line is drawn is not easy to determine, but the test, has been said by the House of Lords to be whether the relationship is simply an ordinary contract of employment or is of a sufficiently public character [44] or involves a special statutory status.[45]

Remedies for failure to comply with procedure [46]

511   Where the circumstances are such that there is requirement that a procedure be followed non-compliance may have the following consequences:

(1) Where the procedure is laid down by the contract itself, this will give rise only to a claim for damages [47]; the contract will be effectively terminated.[48]

(2) In the second case referred to in paragraph 510, above, the person concerned is entitled to damages for breach of contract.[49]

(3) In the third case failure to comply with the rules of natural justice means that the dismissal is ineffective to terminate the employment relationship, and the person concerned is entitled to a declaration to that

---

[37] In *Tomlinson* v. *L.M. & S.R.* [1944] 1 All E.R. 537, a collective agreement between the employer and a trade union which provided for a hearing in certain cases before dismissal was incorporated into the individual contracts of employment. See also Chap. 8. *Cf. Rodwell* v. *Thomas* [1944] K.B. 596.

[38] *Cf. Taylor* v. *National Union of Seamen* [1967] 1 W.L.R. 532. See also Chap. 1.

[39] The category of office-holder is far from clear. For a curious Irish case in which it was held that a technical director of a company was entitled to a hearing before dismissal because he held a job which " resembled that of the holder of an office," see *Glover* v. *B.L.N. Ltd.* [1968] *Irish Jurist* 322–323. See also *Leary* v. *N.U.V.B.* [1970] 3 W.L.R. 434 and Chap. 3.

[40] *Cf. Ridge* v. *Baldwin* [1964] A.C. 40 (esp. *per* Lord Reid at p. 65).

[41] *Cf. Vine* v. *National Dock Labour Board* [1957] A.C. 488.

[42] *Malloch* v. *Aberdeen Corporation* [1971] 1 W.L.R. 1578.

[43] See *Barber* v. *Manchester Regional Hospital Board* [1958] 1 W.L.R. 181.

[44] *Malloch* v. *Aberdeen Corpn.* [1971] 1 W.L.R. 1578, at p. 1596 (*per* Lord Wilberforce).

[45] *Ibid.* p. 1582 (*per* Lord Reid) and p. 1599 (*per* Lord Simon).

[46] Non-compliance with any relevant procedure may also be relevant in the context of an unfair dismissal; see Chap. 17, below.

[47] As to the law governing compensation for wrongful dismissal, see Chap. 16, below.

[48] *Vine* v. *National Dock Labour Board* [1957] A.C. 488 at p. 493, *per* Lord Keith: " ... if the master wrongfully dismisses the servant either summarily or by giving insufficient notice, the employment is effectively terminated."

[49] *Taylor* v. *National Union of Seamen* [1967] 1 W.L.R. 532.

effect, as well as to damages[50]; an injunction may also be available, and in the case of a statutory authority a prerogative order may be available.

(4) Where there is a statute regulating dismissal, a procedure for dismissal that does not accord with the statute is ineffective to terminate the employment relationship[51] and the person concerned is entitled to damages.[52] In addition he may be entitled to the other remedies mentioned in (3) above.[53]

References

512   Just as at common law the employer need not give a reason for a dismissal, there is no obligation on an employer to provide a former employee with any reference or testimonial. If such reference is provided the employer giving it may be liable, if it is false, for a number of possible legal wrongs: (1) defamation, (2) deceit or (3) negligent mis-statement under the principle in *Hedley Byrne* v. *Heller*.[54] *Deceit* requires the making of a deliberately false statement with the intention that it should be acted upon. A person who has suffered a loss in consequence of his having acted in reliance on the false statement may recover damages. *Defamation* consists in making a false statement which damages the reputation of another. There is a defence of *qualified privilege* which will exist where a person, such as an employer, makes a statement relating to a former employee acting under some social, moral or legal duty to another, say, another prospective employer, who has an interest to receive it. Where there is *qualified privilege* there is no liability unless it can be shown that the statement was inspired by *malice, e.g.*, was made knowing it to be false deliberately with a view to injure the former employee. Under *Hedley Byrne* v. *Heller* it has been established that a person making a merely negligently false statement can be made liable for financial loss caused by it. The relationship between the person making the statement and the person acting upon it must be such that the law will impose a duty upon the former to exercise reasonable care not to injure the latter. It is highly probable, but not yet certain, that such a relationship exists between a former employer and a prospective future employer of a common employee. There remains a further odd hurdle before liability can be established in the case of deceit. The Statute of Frauds Amendment Act 1828, s. 6, provides, in effect, that before any action can be brought on any alleged false statement as to the character of a former employee the statement must be made in writing signed by the person making the statement.[55] The Servants Characters Act 1792 makes it a criminal offence to give a false written testimonial of a " servant."

---

[50] *Ridge* v. *Baldwin* [1964] A.C. 40.

[51] *Palmer* v. *Inverness Hospitals Committee*, 1963 S.C. 311.

[52] *Vine* v. *National Dock Labour Board* [1957] A.C. 488.

[53] *Malloch* v. *Aberdeen Corporation* [1971] 1 W.L.R. 1578. But *cf. Hannam* v. *Bradford Corporation* [1970] 1 W.L.R. 937 (on difficulty of establishing a contractual right to damages; but note suggestion that had the teacher been in time he might have got mandamus).

[54] [1964] A.C. 465.

[55] The Act does not apparently apply to negligent misrepresentations. *W. B. Anderson and Sons* v. *Rhodes (Liverpool)* [1967] 2 All E.R. 850.

Rehabilitation of offenders

13   Where an employer is asked for a reference with respect to an employee, whose conviction of a criminal offence has become spent in accordance with the provisions of the Rehabilitation of Offenders Act 1974, the following provisions of that Act apply:

> "Section 4 (4) . . . where a question seeking information with respect to a person's previous convictions, offences, conduct or circumstances is put to him or to any other person otherwise than in proceedings before a judicial authority—
>
> (a) the question shall be treated as not relating to spent convictions or to any circumstances ancillary to spent convictions, and the answer thereto may be framed accordingly; and
>
> (b) the person questioned shall not be subjected to any liability or otherwise prejudiced in law by reason of any failure to acknowledge or disclose a spent conviction or any circumstances ancillary to a spent conviction in his answer to the question."

This appears not only to impose an obligation on an employer responding to an inquiry *not* to refer to any spent conviction, *or any circumstances ancillary to it,* in his reference but gives him a defence against any claim, such as a claim in deceit, which might be brought by a person relying upon the reference.

Summary termination by employee

514   The employee is entitled to terminate the contract without notice if his employer breaks an important term of the contract of employment. In general the principles to determine whether there has been such a breach by the employer as would justify summary termination by the employee are the same as in the case of summary dismissal by the employer.[56]

Wrongful dismissal and unfair dismissal

515   In most instances claims for compensation for dismissal will be brought in the form of claims for an unfair dismissal. However, in cases where the limit on the amount of compensation for unfair dismissal is such that the loss suffered by the dismissed employee is much greater than the statutory limit, or where the dismissed employee belongs to one of the excluded classes and is therefore unable to bring a claim for unfair dismissal, wrongful dismissal claims are still likely to be brought.

[The next paragraph is 521.]

---

[56] See above, Chap. 14, regarding the importance of this in the statutory definition of " dismissal."

CHAPTER 16

TERMINATION BY NOTICE

Common law

521   Subject to certain exceptions either of the parties to a contract of employment is ordinarily entitled to terminate the contract at any time by giving notice to terminate to the other. This right to terminate the contract with notice is quite separate from the right to terminate the contract summarily in case of breach by the other side.[1] The exceptions to the right to terminate the contract by giving a reasonable period of notice are first of all contracts which are for a fixed duration. Where the parties have agreed in advance that the contract is to last for a fixed period, there is no notice which can terminate it before that period comes to an end.[2] Secondly, the parties may limit the right of either side to terminate the contract except for specified reasons. Thus in *McClelland* v. *Northern Ireland General Health Services Board*,[3] a clerk had a contract which was stated to be permanent and pensionable, but which went on further to state that it was terminable only on a number of specified grounds. The House of Lords held that this meant that the contract could be terminated only for these reasons and for no others.

Length of notice

522   The length of notice required on either side to terminate the contract may be agreed upon expressly in the contract itself. It may be fixed as a result of a term implied in the contract, or it may be fixed by a custom[4] applicable to the particular industry or occupation. In the absence of any such term or any such custom, the period of notice required by law is a *reasonable period of notice*.[5] What length this is depends upon all the circumstances of the relationship. It is not necessarily the same as the interval between pay-days. In the case of a short-service employee paid weekly it may be a convenient starting point to regard a week as the likely reasonable period, but the connection between the reasonable period of notice and the frequency of payment is not a necessary one.[6] Factors such as length of service, seniority, rate and periodicity of pay are amongst those to be taken into account, as well as the convenience of the employer,[7] in assessing what is a reasonable period of notice. Two authoritative

---

[1] See Chap. 15, above. Once notice to terminate the contract has been given by either side, it cannot be unilaterally withdrawn. See *Riordan* v. *War Office* [1959] 1 W.L.R. 1046; *Harris & Russell Ltd.* v. *Slingsby* [1973] I.T.R. 433.

[2] The right to terminate on grounds of a breach of an important term of the contract by the other side is not affected by the fact that it is a fixed term contract.

[3] [1957] 1 W.L.R. 594.

[4] It has been held, in *Davson* v. *France* (1959) 109 L.J. 526 that there is a custom that in the absence of any agreement to the contrary musicians hired otherwise than for the day or for a fixed term are entitled to fourteen days' notice. In the case of domestic servants either party may terminate the contract at the end of the first month by notice given at or before the end of the first fortnight. See *George* v. *Davies* [1911] 2 K.B. 445.

[5] There used to be a presumption that if there was a hiring for an employee for an indefinite period (known as a general hiring) it was a hiring for a year. It now appears that this presumption no longer exists. See *Richardson* v. *Koefod* [1969] 1 W.L.R. 1812.

[6] *Levy* v. *Electrical Wonder Co.* (1893) 9 T.L.R. 495.

[7] *Adams* v. *Union Cinemas Ltd.* [1939] 3 All E.R. 136 at p. 142, *per* du Parcq L.J.

statements on the question are worth referring to. In a Canadian case recently it was said:

> " The question, what is reasonable notice, depends upon the capacity in which the employee is engaged, the general standing in the community of the class of persons, having regard to their profession to which the employee belongs, the probable facility or difficulty the employee would have in procuring other employment in the case of dismissal, having regard to the demand for persons of that profession, and the general character of the services which the engagement contemplates." [8]

This has been echoed in cases in this country.

> " The defendant . . . claims damages for wrongful dismissal, alleging that nothing less than three months' notice was a reasonable notice, having regard to the position which the defendant held after he ceased to be manager, which was I think a position of considerable responsibility requiring specialised knowledge, and to the fact that it would not so far as I know have been easy for him to find a similar post, I am of opinion that the defendant's contention is correct . . ." [9]

523   It is worth noticing that the length of the period of reasonable notice is only ascertainable as of the date of the dismissal because, amongst the factors to be taken into account, are matters which must necessarily vary during the life of the contract, and are therefore only properly ascertainable at the date of dismissal, *e.g.*, length of service of the employee concerned and the difficulty the dismissed employee may experience in obtaining alternative employment. The reasonable period of notice to be given by an employer to terminate a contract of employment is identical with the period of reasonable notice to be given by an employee to terminate his contract, as their obligations are in principle mutual. In the absence of agreement the period is identical regardless of which party gives it.

Statutory minimum period of notice

524   What we have said about the length of notice is now subject to the fixing of minimum periods of notice by statute. The Contracts of Employment Act 1972,[10] provides for the following minimum periods of notice to be given:

> " The notice required to be given by an employer to terminate the contract of employment of a person who has been continuously employed [11] for four weeks or more—
>
>   (a) shall be not less than one week's notice if his period of continuous employment is less than two years; and
>
>   (b) shall be not less than one week's notice for each year of con-

---

[8] *Warren* v. *Super Drug Markets Ltd.* (1965) 54 D.L.R. (2d) 183, approving this statement made by Berk J. in *Speakman* v. *Calgary City* (1908) 9 W.L.R. 264 at p. 265. See [1966] A.S.C.L. 608.

[9] *Strange* v. *Mann* [1965] 1 W.L.R. 629 at p. 642, *per* Stamp J.

[10] s. 1 (1), as amended by E.P.A., Sched. 16, Part II, paras. 1–2.

[11] For the discussion of the concept of " continuous employment," see above, Chap. 5.

tinuous employment if his period of continuous employment is two years or more but less than twelve years; and

(c) shall be not less than twelve weeks' notice if his period of continuous employment is twelve years or more."

Regardless of increasing length of employment the minimum period of notice to be given to terminate his contract by any employee who has been continuously employed for four weeks or more shall be not less than one week.[12]

525   The Contracts of Employment Act then goes on to provide in effect that provision in a contract of employment for any period of notice shorter than the statutory minimum is to be ineffective to oust the statutory minimum.[13] It then goes on to say that this " shall not be taken to prevent either party from waiving his right to notice on any occasion, or from accepting a payment in lieu of notice." [14] Clearly this means that, if someone is willing to waive his statutory right " to notice," he is free to do so.[15] But the provision relating to accepting a payment in lieu of notice gives rise to difficulties. In practice it would appear that the giving of wages in lieu of notice would operate to terminate the contract (a) where the contract itself provided that it was terminable by the giving of notice or wages in lieu, and (b) where wages were given and accepted in lieu. It would appear also that in the past the employee may have had no option but to accept the wages,[16] and if they were refused the contract would still be—albeit perhaps wrongfully—terminated. The language used by the 1972 Act, that it does not prevent an employee " from accepting a payment in lieu of notice," gives rise to the clear implication that the employee now has the right to refuse to accept wages in lieu of notice.[17] This may well have practical importance in cases of alleged victimisation for trade union activity when trade union officials often advise workers not to accept payment in lieu of notice, as it is more difficult to secure reinstatement of a worker once he has left the firm.[18]

Wages during notice

526   In the case of any person given notice to terminate his contract, provided such notice is not required by his contract of employment to be at least one week longer than the applicable statutory minimum period [19] he is guaranteed a minimum income, details of which are prescribed by Schedule 5 to the Employment Protection Act 1975.

The Act contains a provision [20] that, in the case of an employee to whom the provisions relating to the guaranteed minimum income apply, if such

---

[12] Contracts of Employment Act 1972, s. 1 (2). For excepted categories of employees, see s. 9, as amended.

[13] s. 1 (3); see also s. 1 (4).

[14] Ibid.

[15] See below as to the difficulties of interpretation to which this gives rise.

[16] Konski v. Peet [1915] 1 Ch. 530.

[17] This is because s. 1 (3) preserves the right of accepting wages in lieu. It says nothing about the right to give wages in lieu.

[18] A number of industrial tribunals have acted on this view of the law. See Freedland, The Contract of Employment, p. 186. As regards the date of termination see Chap. 14 above.

[19] Contracts of Employment Act 1972, s. 2 (3).

[20] E.P.A., Sched. 5, para. 4.

person being incapable of work through illness or injury during that period has received both sickness benefit (or industrial injury benefit) under the National Insurance scheme [21] and also sick pay under an arrangement with the employer, and *if in determining the amount of the employer's sick pay the amount of benefit under the Social Security Act 1975 has been taken into account,* either by way of deduction or by way of calculation, such amount of social security benefit is to be regarded as having been paid by the employer towards fulfilment of the employer's obligation to pay the minimum guaranteed wage. To illustrate this, an employee paid £50 a week will be entitled for the minimum statutory period of notice to receive this £50 a week even if he is ill. If under the terms of his contract when sick he is entitled to be paid £38 a week instead of his normal wage, an amount arrived at by deducting the amount the worker receives by way of sickness benefit under the Social Security Act, say £12 in the case of a single man, then the employer does not have to pay an extra £12, being the amount to bring the wage up to the statutory guaranteed minimum; he need pay only £38 because he will be credited with the £12 a week paid by the state Social Security scheme by way of sickness benefit.

Remedies for wrongful termination

527   The basic remedy for wrongful termination of the contract of employment is damages. Specific performance is not available,[22] and only exceptionally, where a declaration is made that the wrongful termination has not been effective to terminate the contract, will the employee still have a valid contract of employment in existence.[23]

Wrongful termination by employer: measure of damages

528   The ordinary rule applies as regards the amount of compensation to which a wrongfully dismissed employee is entitled, namely, he is entitled to such money to cover his loss as arises naturally in the ordinary course of things from the breach and also for any loss which it was reasonably foreseeable by the parties as being likely to arise from the breach. This is normally loss of wages in the case of a contract of employment.[24] Damages are not recoverable for hurt feelings, for the manner in which the dismissal took place, or for the fact that dismissal made it difficult for the employee to obtain alternative employment.[25] Only exceptionally,

---

[21] See Chap. 19, below.
[22] See Chap. 2 above.
[23] See Chap. 15 above.
[24] *Cf. Manubens* v. *Leon* [1919] 1 K.B. 208 (hairdresser's assistant entitled to wages and commission for the reasonable period of notice together with sum representing lost tips because the employer " knew and contemplated when the contract was entered into that, if it should be broken by the plaintiff being summarily dismissed, the plaintiff would sustain a loss in respect of tips which he would otherwise have received," *per* Lush J. at p. 211). But *cf. Lavarack* v. *Woods* [1967] 1 Q.B. 278 (employee dismissed wrongfully despite five-year contract under which he was entitled to £4,000 p.a. plus such bonus " as directors shall from time to time determine." Dismissed in the third year of five-year contract; after dismissal company replaced bonus with higher fixed salary. *Held*, he was entitled only to basic salary for unexpired period of his contract and bonus up to date of its abolition; bonus was something to which he was not contractually entitled, therefore not entitled to higher salary which replaced it.
[25] *Addis* v. *Gramophone Co.* [1909] A.C. 488. See also *Cox* v. *Phillips Industries* [1975] I.R.L.R. 344, where an employee received damages for depression, anxiety and illness caused by employer's breach of contract.

as for example in the case of actors, where it was reasonably foreseeable that performance of the contract would have provided an opportunity for the actor to enhance his reputation by appearing before the public in a prominent role, can damages be recovered for loss of reputation, or more precisely for loss of an opportunity which the parties had contemplated should be provided by the proper performance of the contract of enhancing the actor's reputation.[26]

Deductions from damages awarded to an employee

529   A dismissed employee is under a legal duty to mitigate his loss. He must take active steps to seek alternative employment. If he does not do so he will have deducted from the damages given him any sum which he might reasonably have earned had he performed his obligation of mitigating his loss. This principle may be a source of difficulty in the case of alleged victimisation of a worker who is advised by his union, as part of their effort to secure his reinstatement, not to seek alternative employment. If he does mitigate his loss, any wages he earns during the period, of what would have been a proper period of notice, will be deducted from the amount of compensation his employer will have to pay him. Damages do not take the form of a windfall. They exist to compensate people only for the actual loss they have suffered. Apart from this there will be deducted from the damages payable by the employer certain sums of money which the unemployed worker may have received. First of all, there will be deducted from the damages in respect of any amount of loss of wages or salary under £5,000, whatever would have been the income tax which the employee would have had to pay on it had he received that sum as earnings.[27] In the case of any amount in excess of £5,000, since the law now provides that this is to be taxed in the hands of the recipient, this is paid without deduction.[28] The effect is that if an employee is entitled notionally to £7,000 in respect of loss of earnings, he receives £2,000 being the excess over £5,000, gross because he will have to pay tax on it when he gets it himself; but he will receive the £5,000 less such tax he would have had to pay on it had it been income. Secondly, there will be deducted any sum which the employee may have received by way of unemployment benefit.[29] Thirdly there will be deducted whatever contributions would have been deducted from the wages by way of National Insurance contributions had the money concerned been paid as wages.[30] Fourthly, it is uncertain whether a redundancy payment made is to be deducted.[31] It has been suggested that because of its discretionary character supplementary benefit paid to an out-of-work employee should not be deducted.[32]

---

[26] *Clayton* v. *Oliver* [1930] A.C. 209.

[27] *British Transport Commission* v. *Gourley* [1956] A.C. 185.

[28] *Parsons* v. *B.N.M. Laboratories* [1964] 1 Q.B. 95 applying the Finance Act 1963, now Income and Corporation Taxes Act 1970, ss. 187, 188.

[29] *Ibid.*

[30] *Cooper* v. *Firth Brown Ltd.* [1963] 1 W.L.R. 418.

[31] *Stocks* v. *Magna Merchants Ltd.* [1973] I.C.R. 530 (Q.B.D.), Arnold J. said it should. This was strongly disapproved in *Yorks. Engineering* v. *Burnham* [1974] I.C.R. 77 (N.I.R.C.) and *Basnett* v. *J. & A. Jackson Ltd.* [1976] I.C.R. 63 (Q.B.D.).

[32] *Foxley* v. *Olton* [1965] 2 Q.B. 306. To the same effect *Ruffley* v. *Frisby Jarvis & Co. Ltd.* (Q.B.D., unreported, May 18, 1972), referred to in Kemp & Kemp, *The Quantum of Damages*, Vol. 1 (4th ed.), p. 163 and see *Basnett* v. *Jackson Ltd.* (above).

Payments under private insurance schemes are not deductible.[33] The validity
of the decisions regarding deductions enumerated above has been thrown
into some uncertainty as a result of the decision of the House of Lords in
Parry v. *Cleaver*.[34]

Damages under Contracts of Employment Act

30   The Contracts of Employment Act 1972 provides that in case of
wrongful dismissal by the employer the rights to a guaranteed minimum
in income for the period of notice given by section 2 and Schedule 2 [35]
" shall be taken into account in assessing his liability for breach of
contract." [36]

Damages for wrongful termination by employee

31   The principle here is essentially the same as those outlined in paragraph 528, above. The employer is entitled to recover in damages the
loss which flows naturally, or was reasonably foreseeable as arising, from
the employee's breach. Where the employee is a productive worker the
value of the lost production (less of course the amount spent by the
employer in obtaining it) is easy enough to assess. Where the worker is
non-productive it may not be so easy to establish loss. The likeliest it is to be
is the extra cost of providing a replacement if such was necessary. Where
a number of workers break their contracts simultaneously, the accumulated
lost production can be recovered against any or all of them only if there
is proof of a common agreement, or conspiracy amongst them; otherwise
each may be sued only in respect of the loss for which he is personally
responsible.[37]

Forfeiture of wages

32   Where an employee is justifiably summarily dismissed or himself
terminates the contract of employment, he is entitled only to be paid such
wages as were accrued due at the date of termination.[38] Thus, an employee
paid weekly on Friday but dismissed properly or resigning on Wednesday
would at common law not be entitled to be paid any wages for the
incomplete week's work. The Apportionment Act 1870, if it applies to
wages as it does to salaries,[39] may have the effect that wages accrue from
day to day whatever be the provisions regarding periodicity of payment,
so that the employee would be entitled to be paid for the completed days'
service during the broken week.

Summary dismissal of apprentices

3   A contract of apprenticeship is more than a contract of employment;
it is also an educational contract and hence there are special rules
governing its termination by an employer. The presence of a reason which

---

[33] *Bradburn* v. *Great Western Ry.* (1874) L.R. 10 Exch. 1.
[34] [1970] A.C. 1. See also P. S. Atiyah, " Collateral Benefits again," (1969) 32 M.L.R.
397.
[35] As substituted by E.P.A., Sched. 5. See above.
[36] s. 3.
[37] *National Coal Board* v. *Galley* [1958] 1 W.L.R. 16.
[38] *George* v. *Davies* [1911] 2 K.B. 445.
[39] See above, Chap. 10.

would justify summary dismissal in the case of an ordinary worker is insufficient to justify the dismissal of an apprentice.[40] In the absence of an express term permitting dismissal summarily for misconduct, the employer's only remedy is to sue the apprentice for breach of contract.[41] However, the employer may terminate the contract if the apprentice's conduct made it impossible for the employer to perform his part of the contract.[42] Ordinarily damages for wrongful dismissal are fairly restricted,[43] but in the case of apprentices these rules have been relaxed, so that a wrongfully dismissed apprentice can claim not only in respect of loss of earnings but also a sum in respect of the value of his loss of future prospects as a qualified person, assuming he had completed his apprenticeship.[44]

[The next paragraph is 541.]

---

[40] *Newell* v. *Gillingham Corporation* [1941] 1 All E.R. 552.
[41] *Walter* v. *Everard* [1891] 2 Q.B. 369.
[42] *Learoyd* v. *Brook* [1891] 1 Q.B. 431.
[43] See above.
[44] *Dunk* v. *George Waller & Son Ltd.* [1970] 2 Q.B. 163. One of the main problems in relation to dismissal of apprentices is in respect of firms in process of liquidation. In such cases the apprentices concerned *may* be entitled to redundancy compensation. See Chap. 18.

CHAPTER 17

UNFAIR DISMISSAL

541   THE concept of unfair dismissal, which was first introduced into English and Scots law by the Industrial Relations Act 1971, and is now embodied in the First Schedule to the Trade Union and Labour Relations Act 1974 as amended by the Employment Protection Act 1975, is a further step along the path, already signposted by the Contracts of Employment Act 1963 (now 1972) and the Redundancy Payments Act 1965, towards recognition of a person's property interest in his or her job. Already recognised to some extent by the law of many advanced industrial countries, this concept restricts the hitherto largely unlimited authority of an employer to dismiss his employees for whatever reason he thinks fit. The immediate germ of the new concept, so far as the United Kingdom is concerned, was Recommendation 119 of the International Labour Organisation, approved by the International Labour Conference at Geneva in 1963, including the British delegation to the Conference which voted for it.[1] As British legislation does not yet go quite as far as the Recommendation in the protection of workers against unfair dismissal, those parts of the Recommendation not yet implemented in British law are relevant, as they indicate the possible, if not probable, content which future amendments of the concept of unfair dismissal in British law are likely to take.

ILO Recommendation 119

542   The basic principle is that termination of employment shall not take place unless there is a valid reason for termination connected with the capacity or conduct of the worker or based on the operational requirements of the enterprise. Certain reasons are always to be invalid reasons for termination: participation in union activities or membership; the taking in good faith of legal proceedings against an employer alleging a breach of some legal obligation; race; colour; sex; marital status; religion; political opinion; national extraction or social origin. Workers who feel aggrieved by an unjustifiable dismissal are to be entitled to a right of appeal. Workers given notice should be given time off from work to look for alternative employment. A dismissed worker should be entitled to receive a certificate from his employer specifying the dates of his employment and the nature of the work done, without containing anything unfavourable to the worker concerned. Dismissal for serious misconduct should take place only where the employer could not reasonably be expected to take any other course. Proper rules should be laid down for the selection of workers to be dismissed where economic necessity requires a reduction in the labour force. Reinstatement of workers unfairly dismissed appears to be the Recommendation's preferred solution where an invalid dismissal occurs. In the absence of reinstatement adequate compensation is to be paid.

---

[1] See International Labour Conference, 47th Session, Geneva, 1963. Report of the Delegates of Her Majesty's Government (Cmnd. 2159, 1963). This Report includes the full text of Recommendation 119.

Unfair dismissal under the Trade Union and Labour Relations Act 1974 [2]

543   Every employee,[3] subject to the exceptions mentioned below, has the right not to be unfairly dismissed by his employer.[4] In a leading case, Phillips J. (now President of E.A.T.) pointed out that " the expression ' unfair dismissal ' is in no sense a common-sense expression capable of being understood by the man in the street, which at first sight one would think it is. In fact, under the Act, it is narrowly and to some extent arbitrarily defined. And so the concept of unfair dismissal is not really a common-sense concept; it is a form of words which could be translated as being equivalent to dismissal ' contrary to the statute ' and to which the label ' unfair dismissal ' has been given." [5] In the same case, Phillips J. mentioned the four principal matters involved in an inquiry into an alleged unfair dismissal.[6]

544   (1) *Was there a dismissal and, if so, when and what was its nature?* The burden of proving that there was a dismissal (and the effective date of termination) is on the employee.[7] (This matter is discussed in Chapter 14, above.)

545   (2) *What was the reason for the dismissal?* The burden of proving the reason (or, if there was more than one, the principal reason) for the dismissal, is on the employer.[8] The reason must be one which falls within a number of specified categories,[9] such as capability or qualifications, conduct, redundancy, statutory requirements, or " some other substantial reason of a kind such as to justify the dismissal of an employee holding the position which the employee held." [10] In contrast to I.L.O. Recommendation 119 the Act provides for only four reasons which must make a dismissal an unfair dismissal subject to certain exceptions. These are trade union membership, trade union activity, refusal to belong to a non-independent trade union,[11] and pregnancy.[12] All the other reasons are ones which *can* justify dismissal not which do justify dismissal because the employer must also satisfy the tribunal that he acted reasonably in treating it as a sufficient reason for dismissal (see below).[13]

In proving his reason the employer must show " a set of facts known to the employer, or it may be beliefs held by him, which cause him to dismiss the employee." [14] It is not necessary for the reason to be correctly *labelled* at the time of the dismissal. For example, the employer may euphemistically describe the reason as " redundancy," and even offer a redundancy payment, when the real reason is the employee's incapability.[15]

---

[2] Sched. 1, Pt. II, as amended by E.P.A., Sched. 16, Pt. III.
[3] See Chap. 3.
[4] Sched. 1, para. 4.
[5] *W. Devis & Sons, Ltd.* v. *Atkins* [1976] I.T.R. 15 at p. 22 (Q.B.D.).
[6] *Ibid.* at p. 22.
[7] Sched. 1, para. 5.
[8] Para. 6 (1) (*a*).
[9] Para. 6 (1) (*b*).
[10] Para. 6 (2) read with para. 6 (1) (*b*).
[11] Para. 6 (4).
[12] E.P.A., s. 34.
[13] T.U.L.R.A., Sched. 1, para. 6 (8), see below, and *Mercia Rubber Mouldings Ltd.* v. *Lingwood* [1974] I.C.R. 256 (N.I.R.C.).
[14] *Per* Cairns L.J. in *Abernethy* v. *Mott, Hay and Anderson* [1974] I.T.R. 251 at p. 255 (C.A.).
[15] As in *Abernethy* case, above.

In proceedings for unfair dismissal the employer can only rely on the reason *in fact* for which he dismissed the employee and not the *label* which he attached to those facts. The facts may, of course, include honestly held beliefs but Lord Denning M.R. has stressed that in order to rely on a set of facts the employer must show that those facts were sufficiently known or made known to the employee.[16] The employee may on request, within 14 days of the dismissal, obtain a written statement giving the particulars of the reasons for his dismissal, and this statement is admissible in evidence in the unfair dismissal proceedings.[17] It is submitted that, as a general rule, the employer will be estopped in those proceedings from denying the accuracy of the particulars given in the statement.

546 In establishing the reason, or principal reason, evidence of what happened subsequent to the dismissal is not relevant or admissible.[18] This is because the wording of the Act requires the tribunal to have regard to the reasonableness of the behaviour of the employer at and leading up to the time of the dismissal.[19] There may, however, be exceptional circumstances when evidence of subsequent events might be admissible to prove the accuracy or otherwise of evidence given in relation to a date before the dismissal. An example (suggested by Phillips J.)[20] would be where the employer gives evidence to show that on a number of occasions the employee was drunk in the course of his duties. If, before the tribunal, it should be in issue as to whether such evidence was accurate, then evidence of later drunkenness would be admissible to establish the accuracy of the evidence of earlier drunkenness, but not as evidence of the later drunkenness in order to constitute a subsequent reason.

547 It must also be noted that it is not relevant to the question of unfair dismissal, whether or not the dismissal was wrongful at common law. The statutory right to complain of unfair dismissal is entirely distinct from the common law. This means that an otherwise fair dismissal is not *ipso facto* rendered unfair by an employer's failure to give any or sufficient notice.[21] If the employee's complaint is that the dismissal was wrongful at common law, but not otherwise " unfair," he must bring his action in the ordinary courts, until such time as the Lord Chancellor exercises his power under section 109 of the Employment Protection Act 1975 to confer jurisdiction on the tribunals, in respect of such claims.

548 (3) *What were the circumstances?* The tribunal is obliged to look not simply at the particular event which gave rise to the dismissal but, as a matter of common sense, to why the employee was dismissed.[22]

549 (4) *Did the employer act reasonably?* Unless the dismissal was for a reason which was automatically unfair (below).

" the determination of the question whether the dismissal was fair or

---

[16] *Ibid.*
[17] E.P.A., s. 70. See above, Chap. 15.
[18] *W. Devis & Sons Ltd.* v. *Atkins* [1976] I.T.R. 15; *cf.* the opposite rule applied to wrongful dismissal at common law, above, Chap. 15.
[19] *Ibid.* at p. 23.
[20] *Ibid.* at p. 24.
[21] *Treganowan* v. *Robert Knee & Co. Ltd.* [1975] I.T.R. 121 (Q.B.D.).
[22] *Turner* v. *Wadham Stringer Commercials (Portsmouth) Ltd.* [1974] I.C.R. 277 at p. 281 (N.I.R.C.).

unfair, having regard to the reason shown by the employer, shall depend upon whether the employer can satisfy the tribunal that in the circumstances (having regard to equity and the substantial merits of the case) he acted reasonably in treating it as a sufficient reason for dismissing the employee." [23]

This requires the tribunal to adopt a broad approach of "commonsense and common fairness eschewing all legal and other technicality, by reference to the circumstances known to the employer at the date of dismissal." [24] The industrial tribunal, considering a case of alleged unfair dismissal, has been likened to an "industrial jury," but it needs to be stressed (in the words of Phillips J.) that "the function of the tribunal is . . . to decide not what they would have done had they been the management; they have to decide . . . whether or not the dismissal was fair or unfair, which depends on whether the employer acted reasonably in treating it as a sufficient reason for dismissing the employee . . . [P]rovided the employers have applied their minds to the problem and acted from genuine motives, they cannot really be faulted, or be said to have acted unreasonably. . . ." [25] Although these words were used in the context of selection for redundancy, it is submitted that they are of general guidance.

550   Essentially questions of "reasonableness" depend on the facts of particular cases. It is therefore in our view erroneous to regard the decisions of tribunals on particular facts as precedents. Some useful guidance can be obtained from the Code of Practice, but although this is an important factor, its significance varies according to the circumstances of each case. [26] Another significant factor may be the recommendation of a domestic appeals body which has fully considered the material facts. [27]

551   The wording of paragraph 6 (8) (quoted above) requires the tribunal to have regard to the "substantial merits" of the case. For this reason it is erroneous to draw a line between the "substantive" and the "procedural" aspects of reasonableness. In the early days of the new law, the National Industrial Relations Court suggested that an employee must always be given the opportunity to explain his conduct if his conduct is the reason for his dismissal, [28] but it is now clear that this is not a rigid rule. If it is clear that there is no point in giving him a hearing, for example, because he states in terms that his conduct of non-co-operativeness is the result of his considered view and not merely a passing emotion, then a hearing may be dispensed with. [29] (See, too, below, in relation to warnings in cases of misconduct or incapability.) Similarly where, despite "procedural" unfairness, the employee would have been dismissed in any event because he had no explanation or otherwise had suffered no loss because the sole

---

[23] T.U.L.R.A., Sched. 1, para. 6 (8).

[24] *Earl* v. *Slater & Wheeler (Airlyne) Ltd.* [1973] I.T.R. 33 at p. 37 (N.I.R.C.) and see above.

[25] *Grundy (Teddington) Ltd.* v. *Willis* [1976] I.T.R. 26 (Q.B.D.); *Ferodo Ltd.* v. *Barnes, The Times,* July 3, 1976 (E.A.T.).

[26] *Lewis Shops Group* v. *Wiggins* [1974] I.T.R. 55 (N.I.R.C.); E.P.A., s. 6.

[27] *James* v. *Waltham Holy Cross U.D.C.* [1973] I.T.R. 467 at p. 472 (N.I.R.C.).

[28] *Earl* v. *Slater & Wheeler (Airlyne) Ltd.,* above.

[29] *James* v. *Waltham Holy Cross U.D.C.,* above; *A. J. Dunning & Sons (Shopfitters) Ltd.* v. *Jacomb* [1973] I.T.R. 453 at p. 456 (N.I.R.C.) *cf. Budgen & Co.* v. *Thomas* [1976] I.C.R. 344 (E.A.T.).

cause of dismissal was his own misconduct, the proper decision of the tribunal would appear to be that the employee was not unfairly dismissed.[30]

552 We shall now consider each of the specified categories of potentially fair dismissal, in the light of these general considerations, and then turn to the automatically unfair grounds of dismissal.

Capability or qualifications

553 The employer may show a reason which "related to the capability or qualifications of the employee for performing work of the kind which he was employed by the employer to do." [31] "Capability" means "capability assessed by reference to skill aptitude, health or any other physical or mental quality." [32] "Qualifications" means "any degree, diploma or other academic technical or professional qualification relevant to the position which the employee held." [33] For example, a failure to pass aptitude tests may relate both to "capability" and "qualifications." [34] The most usual example of "capability" is the question of ill-health. The proper test of reasonableness in such cases is to consider all the relevant factors; it is not necessary to apply the test whether the contract has been frustrated before finding that a dismissal on grounds of ill-health is reasonable.[35] One of the relevant factors may be whether the employers have a suitable alternative job available for an employee who is too ill to perform his regular job, but they are under no general obligation to create a special job for him suited to his handicap.[36] Where the reason relates to the unsatisfactory work performance of the employee then, as a general rule, it will be considered unreasonable to dismiss the employee without giving him a clear warning and an opportunity to improve.[37] However, if it can be shown that the employee was incapable of improving,[38] or held a senior position in which he should have known what was expected of him, no warning may be considered necessary.[39]

Conduct

554 The employer may show a reason "related to the conduct of the employee." [40] For off-duty conduct to qualify under this head it would seem that it must in some way be linked with the general relationship between the employer and employee.[41] A common example of misconduct is disobedience to orders, but disobedience will not be unreasonable if the

---

[30] *Per* Phillips J. in *W. Devis & Sons.* v. *Atkins*, above, at p. 25, a distinct change from the approach in *Earl* v. *Slater & Wheeler (Airlyne) Ltd.*, above.

[31] Para. 6 (2) (*a*).

[32] Para. 6 (9) (*a*).

[33] Para. 6 (9) (*b*).

[34] *Blackman* v. *Post Office* [1974] I.C.R. 151 (N.I.R.C.).

[35] *Tan* v. *Berry Bros. & Rudd* [1974] I.C.R. 586 (N.I.R.C.).

[36] *Merseyside & N.W. Electricity Board* v. *Taylor* [1975] I.C.R. 185 (Q.B.D.).

[37] *O'Hara* v. *Fram Gerrard Ltd.* [1973] I.R.L.R. 94 (N.I.R.C.); *Judge International* v. *Moss* [1973] I.R.L.R. 208 (N.I.R.C.); *Lewis Shops Group* v. *Wiggins* [1974] I.T.R. 55 (N.I.R.C.).

[38] *A. J. Dunning & Sons (Shopfitters) Ltd.* v. *Jacomb*, above.

[39] *Titpools* v. *T. W. Curtis* [1973] I.R.L.R. 276 (N.I.R.C.); *Winterhalter Gastronom Ltd.* v. *Webb* [1973] I.C.R. 245 (N.I.R.C.).

[40] Para. 6 (2) (*b*).

[41] *Tomlinson* v. *L.M. & S. Ry.* [1944] 1 All E.R. 537 at p. 540; *Singh* v. *London County Bus Services Ltd.* [1976] I.R.L.R. 176 (E.A.T.).

order was unlawful or required dishonesty on the employee's part.[42] In most cases, it would be unreasonable for an employer to dismiss on grounds of misconduct without giving the employee an opportunity to explain, even if the misconduct appears to the employer to be gross.[43] Moreover, the provisions of the Code of Practice relating to warnings are important factors when considering the reasonableness of disciplinary action.[44] The appeal courts have, however, regarded the question whether a warning is necessary as being ultimately one of fact for the tribunal to decide. In cases of non-co-operation by a senior employee, however, a warning may be considered as unnecessary [45]; and it is sometimes sufficient to issue a general warning (*e.g.*, about drunkenness).[46]

Redundancy

555   The employer may show that the employee was redundant.[47] This must be construed by reference to the facts specified in section 1 (2) (*a*) and (*b*) of the Redundancy Payments Act 1965,[48] which is discussed in Chapter 18, below. Where redundancy is established there are two situations in which the dismissal will be *automatically unfair*. In both these situations it is for the employee to show " that the circumstances constituting the redundancy applied equally to one or more other employees in the same undertaking who held positions similar to that held by him and who have not been dismissed by the employer." [49] The employee must then show one of the following:

" (a) that the reason (or if more than one, the principal reason) for which he was selected for dismissal was an inadmissible reason [that is a reason relating to trade union membership or activities, see below]; or

(b) that he was selected for dismissal in contravention of a customary arrangement or agreed procedure relating to redundancy and that there were no special reasons justifying a departure from that arrangement or procedure in his case."

It is essential for the tribunal to investigate whether there is an agreed procedure,[50] but such an agreement must be reasonably construed.[51] A " customary arrangement " is something so well known, certain and clear as to be " implied procedure " as opposed to " agreed procedure " not merely a normal custom in the industry.[52] It is, accordingly, not possible for an employee to rely on a general " custom " such as " last in, first out." He must establish that his custom is well known, certain and clear in the undertaking in which he worked.

---

[42] *Morrish* v. *Henleys (Folkestone) Ltd.* [1973] I.C.R. 482 (N.I.R.C.).
[43] *Clarkson International Tools Ltd.* v. *Short* [1973] I.C.R. 191 (N.I.R.C.) and see above.
[44] See above, Chap 13.
[45] *Farnborough* v. *Governors of Edinburgh College of Art* [1974] I.R.L.R. 245 (N.I.R.C.); *Atkin* v. *Enfield Group Hospital Management Committee* (1975) 119 S.J. 575.
[46] *Connelly* v. *Liverpool Corpn.* [1974] I.T.R. 51 (N.I.R.C.); and see *Dalton* v. *Burton's Gold Medal Biscuits* [1974] I.R.L.R. 45 (N.I.R.C.).
[47] Para. 6 (2) (*c*).
[48] Para. 6 (9) (*c*).
[49] Para. 6 (7).
[50] *Gibb* v. *Lanarkshire Bolt Ltd.* [1973] I.T.R. 53 (N.I.R.C.).
[51] *Gargrave* v. *Hotel & Catering I.T.B.* [1974] I.R.L.R. 85 (N.I.R.C.).
[52] *Bessenden Properties Ltd.* v. *Corness* [1974] I.T.R. 128 (N.I.R.C.).

556   In cases of redundancy not covered by these two automatically unfair selective dismissals, the normal tests of reasonableness will be applied. Among the circumstances which may render selection for dismissal on grounds of redundancy unfair are: failure to consult an employee or his union before selection [53]; failure to give reasons for his selection for redundancy [54]; and failure to find the employee suitable alternative employment in the undertaking, or if need be, with an associated employer.[55] If the selection is found to be unfair it is possible for the employee to be awarded both a redundancy payment and compensation for unfair dismissal, but an adjustment in the amount of the basic award will be made.[56]

Statutory requirement

557   The employer may show " that the employee could not continue to work in the position which he held without contravention (either on his part or that of his employer) of a duty or restriction imposed by or under any enactment." [57] Examples might be a driving disqualification imposed by a court under statutory powers, or absence of a work permit for a non-patrial employee.[58]

Other substantial reasons

558   The employer may show " some other substantial reason of a kind such as to justify the dismissal of an employee holding the position which the employee held." [59] It has been held that these words are not to be read *ejusdem generis* (*i.e.,* as limited by the meaning of the class of words preceding them) with the reasons so far considered.[60] Among reasons which have been found to fall within this category are: unreasonable refusal to agree to a change in terms of employment [61]; the temporary nature of the employment [62]; and an irreconcilable conflict of personalities principally caused by the dismissed employee.[63] Moreover, statute has introduced two reasons which are to be treated as " substantial reasons " which can justify dismissal. These are the dismissal of a replacement in cases of medical suspension of a permanent employee provided the replacement was warned of the temporary nature of the job at the time of engagement [64]; and dismissal of a replacement for a pregnant employee absent from work provided the temporary employee is warned at the time of engagement.[65]

---

[53] *Clarkson International Tools Ltd.* v. *Short,* above; and see now the special protection under E.P.A., Part IV, below Chap. 18.

[54] *Rigby* v. *British Steel Corpn.* [1973] I.T.R. 191 (N.I.R.C.).

[55] *Vokes Ltd.* v. *Bear* [1974] I.T.R. 85 (N.I.R.C.); *cf. Rowbotham* v. *Arthur Lees & Sons Ltd.* [1975] I.C.R. 109 (Q.B.D.); *Modern Injection Moulds Ltd.* v. *Price* [1976] I.C.R. 370 (E.A.T.).

[56] *Midland Foot Comfort Centre* v. *Moppett* [1973] I.C.R. 219 (N.I.R.C.).

[57] Para. 6 (2) (*d*).

[58] See Chap. 5 above.

[59] Para. 6 (1) (*b*).

[60] *R.S. Components Ltd.* v. *Irwin* [1973] I.C.R. 535 (N.I.R.C.).

[61] *Ibid.*

[62] *Dean* v. *Polytechnic of North London* [1973] I.T.R. 526 (N.I.R.C.).

[63] *Treganowan* v. *Robert Knee & Co. Ltd.* [1975] I.T.R. 121 (N.I.R.C.).

[64] E.P.A., s. 33.

[65] E.P.A.. s. 51.

National security

559   If in any claim for compensation for an unfair dismissal it is shown that the dismissal was taken "for the purpose of safeguarding national security," the tribunal must dismiss the complaint.[66] Any certificate purporting to be signed by or on behalf of a Minister certifying that the dismissal was for the purpose of safeguarding national security is to be conclusive evidence of that fact.[67] The scope of this provision is not confined to claims by civil servants alleging unfair dismissal, but applies to any employment.[68] The commonest case where it may be used in private employment is in relation to the dismissal of employees of a contractor working on government contracts, under the terms of which the contractor must dismiss such employees as the Crown requires him to dismiss.

Automatically unfair reasons

560   Certain reasons for dismissal can never be fair, and to these reasons the test of "reasonableness" in paragraph 6 (8) (above) is inapplicable. These are (1) dismissal of an employee with a spent conviction; (2) dismissal of an employee because she is pregnant or for any other reason connected with her pregnancy or refusal of her right to return to work after confinement; and (3) an "inadmissible reason" which is the term used to describe three separate matters related to trade union membership or activities.

Employees with spent convictions

561   The Rehabilitation of Offenders Act 1974, s. 4 (3) provides that a spent conviction or a failure to disclose a spent conviction shall not be a proper ground for dismissing a person from an office, profession, occupation or employment (if covered by the Act and regulations made thereunder).[69] The Act does not specify any particular sanction, but it would seem to follow that a dismissal in these circumstances would automatically be unfair, under the provisions of the Trade Union and Labour Relations Act.

Pregnancy and confinement

562   An employee is to be treated as unfairly dismissed if the reason or principal reason for her dismissal is that she is pregnant or is "any other reason connected with her pregnancy." [70] The latter phrase is wide enough to cover matters occurring after as well as before confinement (e.g., miscarriage, post-natal illness). It is not, in terms, limited to medical reasons and so absences from work for social and family reasons connected with pregnancy appear to be included.[71]

563   The employer may, however, show that the dismissal was fair, for one of the following reasons:

"(a) that at the effective date of termination she is or will have become,

---

66 T.U.L.R.A., Sched. 1, para. 18.
67 *Ibid.*
68 Civil servants are intended to receive the benefit of protection against unfair dismissal. See *ibid.* para. 33 (1).
69 See Chap. 6 above.
70 E.P.A., s. 34 (1).
71 *Ibid.*

because of her pregnancy, incapable of adequately doing the work she is employed to do;

(b) that because of her pregnancy she cannot or will not be able to continue after that date to work without a contravention (either by her or her employer) of a duty or restriction imposed by or under any enactment." [72]

The word " incapable " is not defined. Apparently,[73] it must be construed by reference to the definition in the Trade Union and Labour Relations Act 1974, Sched. 1, para. 6 (9) (a) (above). In any event, the employer must act reasonably in the circumstances in treating it as a sufficient reason for dismissing her.[74] In either of these two situations the employer must make an offer of a new contract of employment if there is a suitable alternative vacancy.[75] Failure to do so, irrespective of whether the employee asked for such an alternative job, will render the dismissal automatically unfair. The burden of proving the offer and that there was no suitable vacancy is on the employer.[76] In effect this means that the employer will have to produce evidence of the vacancies which were available at the time.

564 The new contract must take effect immediately on the ending of the old one,[77] and the work to be done must be suitable to the employee and appropriate for her to do in the circumstances.[78] The provisions of the new contract must not be substantially less favourable than those of the old one.[79] But it is to be noted that the Act does not say that the woman must accept such an offer. Curiously, however, if the employer does dismiss for one of the two reasons above, the woman has no right to anticipate the date of termination.[80] A woman is, therefore, in danger of losing her right to claim that she was dismissed if, having been dismissed because her pregnancy has rendered her incapable but having been offered no suitable alternative job, she has taken up light work elsewhere before the notice of dismissal has expired. The purpose, if any, behind this may be to give the employer more time to find a replacement.

565 If the woman is fairly dismissed (for one of the above two reasons) she retains her right to maternity pay. If unfairly dismissed for pregnancy, she may include her loss of maternity pay in her claim for compensation (see below).

566 A second situation in which a reason relating to pregnancy or confinement may be automatically unfair arises out of the right of a woman to return to work after confinement. An employee who has been absent wholly or partly because of pregnancy or confinement is entitled to return to work with her original employer or his successor.[81] She can do so at any time before the end of the period of 29 weeks beginning with the week in

---

[72] *Ibid.*
[73] E.P.A., s. 126 (3).
[74] T.U.L.R.A., para. 6 (8), as adapted by E.P.A., Sched. 3, para. 2 (1).
[75] E.P.A., s. 34 (2).
[76] s. 34 (4).
[77] s. 34 (3) (a).
[78] s. 34 (3) (b).
[79] s. 34 (3) (a).
[80] s. 34 (5) modifying para. 5 (3) of T.U.L.R.A., Sched. 1.
[81] s. 35 (1).

which the date of confinement falls.[82] She is entitled to return to the job [83] in which she was employed under her original contract of employment and on terms and conditions not less favourable than would have been applicable to her had she not been absent.[84]

567	It appears that she can claim either her old job or an identical one. The employer does not have the right to offer alternative employment unless it is not practicable by reason of redundancy for the employer to permit her to return to the old job.[85] In the event of redundancy, the woman is entitled to a suitable available vacancy with her employer or his successor or an associated company under a new contract of employment which satisfies certain conditions, in particular the work must be suitable and the terms must be not less favourable than would have applied to her had she returned to her original job.[86] Failure to make such an offer is treated as an automatically unfair dismissal.[87] If there is redundancy and no vacancy exists the employee may claim a redundancy payment.[88] The employee denied her right to return is treated as having been continuously employed [89] until her notified day of return (see below), but if the employer can show that the reason for the failure to permit her return is redundancy and that the woman would have been made redundant during her absence on a day between the eleventh week and the notified day of her return then her entitlement to redundancy payment (which depends on two years' continuous service) and, if eligible for a payment, the amount of that payment will be calculated only up to that earlier day.[90]

568	In order to claim this right to return to work the employee must satisfy the same six conditions which have to be met for entitlement to maternity pay. (These are set out in Chapter 10, above.) *In addition,* she must inform the employer (in writing if so requested) before or as soon as reasonably practicable after her dismissal (on grounds that she is incapable of working or would be in breach of statute), that she intends to return to work for him,[91] and she must give at least one week's notice of her intention to return to work on a particular day (" the notified day of return ").[92] The employee can postpone this day of return, but on *one* occasion only, for up to four weeks from the notified day, even if this means extending the 29-week period. She may do this for medical reasons only.[93] The employer can put off the day of return on more than one occasion, for up to four weeks in all, but he must state his reasons.[94] If she has notified a day of return but there is an interruption of work (whether due to industrial action or some other reason) which makes it unreasonable for her to return on the

---

[82] s. 48 (1).
[83] s. 48 (2) (a).
[84] ss. 48 (1) and 48 (2) (b).
[85] s. 48 (4).
[86] s. 48 (5) and see s. 34 (3) (b) (c).
[87] Sched. 3, para. 2 (2).
[88] s. 50 and Sched. 3.
[89] C.E.A., Sched. 1, paras. 5 (1) and 5A, as amended by E.P.A., Sched. 16. Pt. II, paras. 15–17. See Chap. 5.
[90] Sched. 3, para. 6.
[91] s. 35 (3).
[92] s. 49 (1).
[93] s. 49 (3).
[94] s. 49 (2).

notified day she may go back as soon as reasonably practicable thereafter.[95] If she has not notified a day of return and work is interrupted she may return within 14 days of the end of the interruption, even if this is outside the 29-week period.[96]

Inadmissible reasons

569   Paragraph 6 (4) of the Schedule to the 1974 Act lists the following three reasons which render a dismissal automatically unfair. These are styled, by the Act, " inadmissible reasons." The reasons are that the employee:

" (a) was, or proposed, to become a member of an independent trade union [97];

(b) had taken, or proposed to take, part at any appropriate time in the activities of an independent trade union; or

(c) had refused, or proposed to refuse, to become or remain a member of a trade union which was not an independent trade union."

In regard to trade union activities it is to be noted that these must be at an " appropriate time " a term now defined in the Employment Protection Act.[98] In effect this definition envisages that an employee may participate outside working hours off the employer's premises, or on the premises, while there with the express or implied permission of the employer (*e.g.,* before starting, during breaks, etc.), but while not actually at work. The right to participate during working hours depends on the employer's consent, but this may be loosely gathered from " arrangements "—a nod from the employer over a period of time may, it seems, suffice. There is, however, no definition of what constitutes " activities " of a trade union. Presumably they must be lawful ones (*e.g.,* not threats of violence to employees to join); more precise guidance is to be issued by A.C.A.S.[99] The mere fact that the employer disapproves of the way in which the activities are conducted does not justify dismissal.[99a]

Union membership agreements

570   There is an exception to these rights in respect of trade union membership and activities where there is a union membership agreement. Since there are many misconceptions about the provisions of the Trade Union and Labour Relations Act (as amended in 1976) on this point it is worth pointing out that nothing in the law requires an employer to *agree* to a union membership agreement. It might, however, be said that this has become a quasi-mandatory bargaining subject, because an independent trade union (whether or not already recognised) may refer an employer's refusal to negotiate such an agreement to A.C.A.S. under the Employment Protection Act's recognition procedures (see Chapter 1, above). The legal relevance of a union membership agreement arises, however, only on dismissal of those who refuse to join a union specified in such an agreement.

---

[95] s. 49 (5).
[96] s. 49 (6).
[97] T.U.L.R.A., s. 30 (1). See Chap. 1.
[98] Def. in E.P.A., s. 53 (2), as applied by E.P.A., Sched. 16, Pt. III, para. 11, in similar terms to Industrial Relations Act 1971, s. 5 (5), on which see *Post Office* v. *Crouch* [1974] 1 W.L.R. 89 (H.L.) and see Chap. 1 above.
[99] E.P.A., s. 6 (2) (*b*) (ii).
[99a] *Lyon & Scherk* v. *St. James Press Ltd.*, E.A.T., May 25, 1976.

571   Paragraph 6 (5) of the Schedule to the 1974 Act (as amended) provides that a dismissal is fair if—

" (a) it is the practice, in accordance with a union membership agreement, for all the employees of that employer or all employees of the same class as the dismissed employee to belong to a specified independent trade union, or to one of a number of specified independent trade unions; and

(b) the reason for the dismissal was that the employee was not a member of the specified union or one of the specified unions, or had refused or proposed to refuse to become or remain a member of that union or one of those unions;

unless the employee genuinely objects on grounds of religious belief [1] to being a member of any trade union whatsoever . . ."

572   The definition of " union membership agreement " in section 30 (1) of the 1974 Act, as amended in 1976, does not require a contractually binding agreement. An " arrangement " is sufficient. This must be made between one or more independent trade unions and one or more employers or employers' associations. It must relate to employees of an identifiable class, and it must have the effect " *in practice* of requiring the employees for the time being of that class to which it relates (*whether or not there is a condition to that effect in their contract of employment*) to be or become a member of the union or one of the unions which is or are parties to the agreement or arrangement or of another *specified* independent trade union." The words which we have italicised are important. They indicate that the employer must show a *practice*. Until such a practice is established over time, therefore, it might be unfair to dismiss an existing employee who refuses to join a specified union. Moreover, although a dismissal in breach of a term of an employment contract regarding union membership or activity is not unfair, the employer will need to give employees with such terms in their contracts lawful notice to terminate their contracts and an offer to re-engage on new terms, otherwise remedies may be available in the ordinary courts to restrain the employer from acting on the wrongful dismissal.[2] Finally, it is to be noted that the choice of union is left to the parties to the agreement; but some union must be *specified* in the agreement. Because of the fears that these provisions, applied to the mass media, might endanger the freedom of journalists and editors, section 1A of the Trade Union and Labour Relations Act 1974 (as inserted by the 1976 Act) requires a Charter on freedom of the Press to be drawn up providing practical guidance on various matters including the application of union membership agreements to journalists. When brought into operation the Charter will be admissible and relevant in legal proceedings.

Excluded categories

573   The provisions of the Trade Union and Labour Relations Act 1974

---

[1] Even under the 1971 Act " grounds of conscience " was narrowly construed so as to be limited to " religious belief ": see *Hynds* v. *Spillers-French Baking Ltd.* [1974] I.T.R. 261 at p. 265 (N.I.R.C.).

[2] As in *Hill* v. *C. A. Parsons & Co. Ltd.* [1972] 1 Ch. 305 (C.A.). See Chap. 2 above.

regarding unfair dismissal have no application to employees in any of the following categories:

(a) Employees who have not been continuously employed for 26 weeks or more at the effective date of termination.[3] This does not apply if the dismissal was for an inadmissible reason.[4] In cases of dismissal by reason of a medical suspension requirement or recommendation the period is four weeks.[5] The 26-week qualifying period appears to apply to dismissal on grounds of pregnancy, although there is no such qualifying period in respect of a refusal to allow a return to work after confinement.[6]

(b) Any employee who, on or before the effective date of termination, has attained the age of 65 in the case of a man or 60 in the case of a woman.[7]

(c) Any employee under the age of 65 in the case of a man and 60 in the case of a woman who has attained the normal retiring age appropriate for persons holding his particular job.[8]

(d) Persons employed by their husbands or wives.[9]

(e) Registered dockworkers as defined by any scheme in force under the Dock Workers (Regulations of Employment) Act 1946, unless the person concerned is wholly or mainly engaged in work which is not dock work.[10]

(f) Mate or crew member of a fishing vessel not remunerated otherwise than by a share in the profits or gross earnings of the vessel.[11]

(g) Persons employed under contracts which involve them ordinarily working outside Great Britain.[12]

(h) Persons employed on board ships registered in the United Kingdom whose employment is wholly outside Great Britain or who are not ordinarily resident in Great Britain.[13]

The Secretary of State may add to, or vary the above provisions relating to excluded categories of persons, or exempt them from the operation of any of the provisions enumerated above.[14] Persons falling within categories (a), (b) and (c) above are however protected against unfair dismissal if the

---

[3] Para. 10 (a). See Coulson v. City of London Polytechnic [1976] I.T.R. 121 (E.A.T.) for method of calculation.

[4] Para. 11.

[5] E.P.A., s. 29 (4).

[6] E.P.A., Sched. 3, para. 2 (5).

[7] Para. 10 (b). Cf. Ord v. Maidstone and District Hospital Management Committee [1974] I.C.R. 369.

[8] Para. 10 (b). This means that, if an employer fixes a retiring age for a particular job, which is below the age qualifying for a retirement pension under social security law, any employee above that age but below the age qualifying for a social security retirement pension is unable to bring a claim for compensation in respect of an unfair dismissal.

[9] Para. 9 (1) (b), as amended by E.P.A., Sched. 16, Pt. III, para. 14 (1) (c).

[10] Para. 9 (1) (c).

[11] Para. 9 (1) (d).

[12] Para. 9 (2). This applies even if he also works in Great Britain: Portec (U.K.) Ltd. v. Mogenson, L.S. Gaz., May 26, 1976 (E.A.T.). The disqualification refers to the place and not the kind of work: Roux International Ltd. v. Licudi [1975] I.T.R. 162; cf. Maulik v. Air India [1974] I.T.R. 257. See Chap. 21, below.

[13] Para. 9 (3). The Act has, however, been extended to certain employments in territorial waters and designated areas of the Continental Shelf.

[14] Para. 11 (2).

reason for their dismissal (or if more than one reason, the principal reason) was an inadmissible reason.[15]

   (i) Persons employed under fixed term contracts for two years or more (other than contracts of apprenticeship) made before February 28, 1972.[16]

   (j) Persons employed under fixed term contracts for two years or more who have agreed in writing to waive their right not to be unfairly dismissed.[17]

   (k) Persons who do not present a complaint of unfair dismissal within three months of the effective date of termination or within such further period as the tribunal considers reasonable in a case where it is satisfied that it was not reasonably practicable for the complaint to be presented before the end of three months.[18] However, where the dismissal is with notice, the complaint may be presented after the notice is given notwithstanding that this is before the effective date of termination.[19]

   (l) Persons who claim to have been unfairly dismissed but were, at the date of dismissal involved in industrial action, subject to certain exceptions.[20] This is separately considered in the next paragraph.

Dismissal in connection with industrial action

574   Paragraph 7 of Schedule 1 to the 1974 Act (as inserted by the Employment Protection Act 1975) provides that an industrial tribunal shall not determine whether a dismissal was fair or unfair where at the date of the dismissal—

   " (a) the employer was conducting or instituting a lock-out; or

   (b) the employee was taking part in a strike or other industrial action."
The words " lock-out," " strike " and " other industrial action " are not defined in the statute. There must obviously be an element of concerted action, but " other industrial action " is wide enough to cover action short of a withdrawal of labour.[21] The policy of paragraph 7, like its differently worded predecessors, seems to be " to give a measure of protection to an employer if his business is faced with ruin by a strike. It enables him in those circumstances, if he cannot carry on the business without a labour force to dismiss the labour force on strike; to take on another labour force without the stigma of its being an unfair dismissal." [22] However, the " date of dismissal " in paragraph 7 has been construed as meaning " at the time " of the dismissal, so that if on any given date the employer is told the strike is over he is not free during the rest of the calendar day to dismiss those who had taken part.[23]

---

15 Para. 11 (1).
16 Para. 12 (a).
17 Para. 12 (b). Apart from these provisions and the approval procedures (para. 590) contracting out is prohibited: para. 32. See Chap. 14.
18 Para. 21 (4). See Chap. 14 regarding effective date of termination.
19 Para. 21 (4A) as inserted by E.P.A., Sched. 16, Pt. III, para. 19.
20 Para. 7, inserted by E.P.A., Sched. 16, Pt. III, para. 13, in place of T.U.L.R.A., Sched. 1, paras. 7 and 8.
21 See *Thompson* v. *Eaton Ltd.* [1976] I.C.R. 336 (E.A.T.), and the discussion in Chap. 1 above. A strike engineered by the employer would probably fall outside para. 7: *ibid.* at p. 342.
22 *Health* v. *J. Longman* (*Meat Salesmen*) *Ltd.* [1973] I.C.R. 407 at p. 410.
23 *Ibid.*

575   There are two exceptions to the general rule that the tribunal has no jurisdiction in the case of the dismissal of those on strike or locked-out. The tribunal must determine the case, on the ordinary principles applicable to unfair dismissal, in either of the following situations [24] :

(a) where it is shown that one or more " relevant employees " of the same employer have not been dismissed.

" Relevant employees " in the case of a lock-out are those directly interested in the trade dispute in contemplation or furtherance of which the lock-out occurred. In relation to a strike or other industrial action they are the employees who participated. This has the curious result that in a strike *all* the employees are relevant; but there can only be relevant employees in a lock-out if there is a " trade dispute." [25]

(b) where it is shown that one or more such relevant employees have been offered re-engagement, but that the employee concerned has not been offered re-engagement.

The effect of this is to make selective dismissals during industrial action, whatever the criterion of selection, subject to the legislation.

Remedies for unfair dismissal

576   The three remedies available under the Employment Protection Act are: (1) reinstatement, (2) re-engagement, (3) compensation. (1) and (2) are the primary remedies.

(1) *Meaning of reinstatement* [26]

577   This requires the employer to treat the employee in all respects as if he had not been dismissed. Thus his pay, pension, seniority rights, etc. must be restored to him, and he will benefit from any improvement in terms and conditions which came into operation whilst he was dismissed. Also any pay arrears and other lost benefits must be granted to him.

(2) *Meaning of re-engagement* [27]

578   This differs from reinstatement in that the employee may be re-engaged in a different job from that which he formerly held, provided that the new job is comparable to the old or is otherwise suitable employment. The terms and conditions of the new job may therefore differ from the old. Also the re-engagement need not be by the same employer; it may instead be with a successor of the employer or an associated employer. The tribunal has a discretion as to how much it should award for the loss of benefits between the date of dismissal and re-engagement. However, except in those cases where the employee caused or contributed to his own dismissal, the tribunal *must* order re-engagement on terms which are, as far as is reasonably practicable, as favourable as would apply under an order for reinstatement.

---

[24] Para. 7 (3); and see *Stock* v. *Frank Jones (Tipton) Ltd.* [1976] I.T.R. 63 (Q.B.D.).
[25] Para. 7 (5) (b), and note the meaning of dismissal in para. 7 (5) (a). See Chap. 1.
[26] E.P.A., s. 71 (3).
[27] s. 71 (5).

(3) *When reinstatement or re-engagement ordered* [28]

579   Once a complaint of unfair dismissal is held to be well-founded, the tribunal must first consider whether to grant reinstatement, and only if this is not suitable should it go on to consider re-engagement. In both cases the tribunal must exercise its discretion after considering the complainant's wishes, whether he caused or contributed to the dismissal; and whether it is *practicable* for the employer to comply with the order.[29] The mere fact that the employer has engaged a permanent replacement does not automatically indicate that re-engagement or reinstatement is impracticable.[30]

(4) *Breach of an order of reinstatement or re-engagement*

580   If the employee is reinstated or re-engaged but the terms of the order are not fully complied with, the tribunal must award compensation having regard to the loss sustained [31] (s. 72 (1)) with a maximum of £5,200.[32]

     If, however, the order is not implemented at all then (unless the employer shows it was not practicable to comply) [33] the tribunal must award [34]:

(a) a basic and compensatory award under sections 73–76 of the Employment Protection Act (see below); and

(b) an *additional* award of compensation which will be either: (i) between 13–26 weeks' pay, or (ii) between 26–52 weeks' pay in the case of a "discriminatory" dismissal (sex, race, trade union activity).[35]

Compensation

581   If orders for reinstatement or re-engagement are not made the tribunal must award compensation under two heads [36]: (1) a basic award and (2) a compensatory award.

(1) *The basic award* [37]

582   The irreducible minimum is *two weeks' pay* [38] (£80 maximum weekly pay limit). Subject to this minimum and to a maximum of £2,400 (*i.e.*, a maximum weekly pay limit of £80 × 20 × 1½), the basic award is calculated in the same way as the amount of redundancy payment under the Redundancy Payments Act 1965 [39]

—for each year of continuous employment
from 18–22—half week's pay;
—for each year of continuous employment
from 22–41—one week's pay;

---

[28] s. 71. An explanation must be given to the complainant.
[29] ss. 71 (6) (7).
[30] s. 71 (8).
[31] s. 72 (1).
[32] T.U.L.R.A., Sched. 1, para. 20.
[33] E.P.A., s. 72 (2) (*b*) and s. 72 (4).
[34] s. 72 (2).
[35] s. 72 (3). The maximum weekly pay under (b) is £80.
[36] ss. 72 (5), 73.
[37] ss. 74–75.
[38] s. 74 (2).
[39] See Chap. 18,

—for each year of continuous employment
from 41–65—one and a half weeks' pay.

Deductions must be made for (a) the employee's contribution to dismissal [40] (see below); and (b) the amount of any redundancy payment made in pursuance of the Redundancy Payments Act or otherwise.[41] Failure to mitigate loss is ignored in respect of this basic award.

(2) *The compensatory award* [42]

583   This is " such amount as the tribunal considers just and equitable in all the circumstances having regard to the loss sustained by the complainant in consequence of the dismissal in so far as that loss is attributable to action taken by the employer." [43] This amount will be calculated according to the principles laid down in the case law under the unfair dismissal provisions of the Industrial Relations Act 1971 and the Act of 1974 since the wording of section 76 (1) of the Employment Protection Act is essentially the same as the relevant provisions of those earlier Acts.

The leading case is *Norton Tool Co. Ltd.* v. *Tewson*.[44] The common law rules on wrongful dismissal are irrelevant.[45] The tribunal must specify the particular heads under which compensation has been assessed and the amount falling under each.[46]

584   The main heads are:

(a) *Expenses* [47]
    E.g. incurred in seeking new employment, but not expenses in presenting a case to a tribunal.[48]
(b) *Benefits lost up to date of hearing*
    (i) If dismissed without notice or wages in lieu of notice the net wages payable in respect of the period of notice to which he was entitled will be awarded. No deduction is made for anything earned elsewhere in this period.[49] (ii) From the end of notice period to the date of hearing, *net* wages (*i.e.* net of tax, national insurance, etc.) will be awarded, *LESS* (1) unemployment benefit and possibly other social security payments; (2) wages from any new employment. (iii) Benefits in kind, *e.g.* free house, car allowance.
(c) *Estimated future loss of benefits*
    (i) Net average wages for such number of weeks as tribunal considers just and equitable (the *usual* maximum two years from date of dismissal) in light of local employment conditions.[49a] (ii)

---

40 s. 75 (7) and see below.
41 s. 75 (8).
42 s. 76.
43 s. 76 (1).
44 [1973] I.T.R. 23 (N.I.R.C.).   45 *Ibid.*
46 *Donnelly* v. *Feniger & Blackburn* [1973] I.T.R. 134 (N.I.R.C.); *Blackwell* v. *G.E.C. Elliott Process Automation Ltd.* [1976] I.T.R. 103 (E.A.T.).
47 E.P.A., s. 76 (2) (*a*).
48 *Nohar* v. *Granitstone Ltd.* [1974] I.T.R. 155 at p. 156 (N.I.R.C.).
49 *Everwear Ltd.* v. *Isaac* [1974] I.T.R. 334 (N.I.R.C.); *Vaughan* v. *Weighpack Ltd.* [1974] I.T.R. 226 (N.I.R.C.).
49a In view of the provisions of the Social Security (Unemployment, Sickness and Invalidity Benefit) Amendment Regs. 1976 S.I. 1976 No. 328 as amended by S.I. 1976 No. 677, no deduction should be made under this head for unemployment benefit or supplementary benefit which the applicant is likely to draw after the hearing.

Risk of financial loss by manner of dismissal making him less acceptable to potential employers and exceptionally liable to selection for dismissal.[50] (iii) Loss of protection against unfair dismissal and loss of right to longer notice. (In view of the reduction of the qualifying period to 26 weeks and longer periods of notice this is not likely to exceed one-quarter of a week's pay.)

It is to be noted that under section 76 (3) of the 1975 Act loss of any entitlement to or potential entitlement to, or expectation of, a redundancy payment, whether in pursuance of the Redundancy Payments Act or otherwise will *not* be awarded, except to the extent that the payment would have exceeded the basic award, apart from any reduction of the basic award under section 75 (7) or (8).

(iv) Other benefits reasonably expected, *e.g.* wage increases or promotion (may be included in estimate (i) above and should not be double-counted).

(d) *Loss of pension rights*

The tribunal may allow for the return of the employee's contributions and treat the employer's contributions as addition to salary[51]; or it may allow for loss of benefit of the employer's contributions during service and the time allowed for finding new employment and also allowing for the possibility that the employee might have left before retiring age and might have a pension in his new employment.[52]

Deduction must be made for:

585

(1) The employee's failure to mitigate his loss (either generally,[53] or by preventing compliance with reinstatement or re-engagement order).[54]

(2) The employee's contribution to his dismissal.[55] This involves some element of blameworthiness.[56] Presumably all the circumstances are still relevant, but one should compare the present wording with " the matters to which the complaint relates " in para. 19 (3) of Schedule 1 to the 1974 Act as interpreted in *Maris* v. *Rotherham C.B.C.*[57] Only in exceptional circumstances can contributions anywhere near 100 per cent. be justified.[58]

(3) The amount by which any redundancy payment (under R.P.A. or otherwise) exceeds amount of basic award.[59]

---

[50] *Norton Tool Co. Ltd.* v. *Tewson*, above; " cogent evidence " is required: *ibid.; cf.* common law award for distress in *Cox* v. *Phillips Industries Ltd.* [1975] I.R.L.R. 344. Benefits may be assessed beyond retiring age: *Barrel Plating & Phosphating Co. Ltd.* v. *Dank*, E.A.T., June 14, 1976.

[51] *S.C.W.S. Ltd.* v. *Lloyd* [1973] I.T.R. 178 (N.I.R.C.).

[52] *Gill* v. *Harold Andrews Sheepbridge Ltd.* [1974] I.T.R. 219 (N.I.R.C.); *John Millar & Sons Ltd.* v. *Quinn* [1974] I.T.R. 277 (N.I.R.C.). See D. Jackson (1975) 4 I.L.J. 24.

[53] E.P.A., s. 76 (4).

[54] E.P.A., s. 72 (6); *cf.* s. 71 (9) (*b*).

[55] s. 76 (6).

[56] *Morrish* v. *Henlys (Folkestone) Ltd.* [1973] I.T.R. 167 (N.I.R.C.).

[57] [1974] I.T.R. 288 (N.I.R.C.).

[58] *Cooper* v. *British Steel Corpn.* [1975] I.T.R. 137 (Q.B.D.); *Kemp* v. *Shipton Automation Ltd., The Times*, July 21, 1976 (E.A.T.) (maximum should be about 80 per cent.).

[59] s. 76 (7).

(3) *Summary*

586   Maximum award:

(1)	Basic award	£2,400 (£80 weekly limit)
(2)	Compensatory award	£5,200 (no weekly limit)
(3)	Additional award for failure to reinstate or re-engage	£4,160 (52 × £80 limit)

£11,760

Interim relief for those claiming anti-union discrimination [60]

587   A special procedure is available for those who claim they have been dismissed for wishing to join an independent trade union or take part in its activities. The procedure enables the tribunal to order either that the individual be reinstated or, if both he and the employer agree, re-engaged in another job or, if the employer refuses to do either, suspended on full pay (" an order for the continuation of the contract of employment ") [61] until final determination of the complaint. The claim must be presented to the tribunal before the end of a period of seven days immediately following the effective date of termination.[62] A duly authorised official of an independent trade union must certify that there are reasonable grounds for supposing that the reason for the dismissal was the employee's desire to join an independent trade union, etc.[63] In addition, the tribunal must find that it is *likely* that the employee will succeed at the final hearing.[64]

Industrial pressure in connection with dismissals

588   In determining whether a dismissal was fair or unfair no account is to taken of any pressure put upon the employer, to dismiss or discriminate against any employee, by strike or other industrial action.[65]

Approved dismissal procedures

589   In certain exceptional circumstances the rights and procedures established by the Act in relation to protection against unfair dismissal may be replaced by the provisions of a procedure agreement relating to dismissal.[66] A joint application must first of all be made to the Secretary of State by *all* the parties to the agreement concerned. The Secretary may then make an order authorising the substitution of the provisions of the agreement for those of the Act, if satisfied that the following conditions are fulfilled:

590   (a) That every trade union which is a party to the procedure agreement is an independent trade union.

---

[60] ss. 78–80.
[61] s. 78 (9).
[62] s. 78 (2).
[63] s. 78 (2) (*b*).
[64] s. 78 (5).
[65] Para. 15.
[66] T.U.L.R.A., Sched. 1, paras. 13 and 14. This does not apply to dismissal for pregnancy: E.P.A., s. 34 (7).

591   (b) That the procedure agreement provides for procedures to be followed in cases where an employee claims that he has been, or is in course being *unfairly* (italics added) dismissed.

It might appear that a dismissal procedure to be approved by the Secretary may be either (1) a procedure which culminates in a decision to dismiss, which includes a provision for the employee to object on the ground that his dismissal in the circumstances would constitute an unfair dismissal, and (2) a dismissal procedure which provides for an appeal by the employee against a decision to dismiss him which has actually been taken. It is however clear from (d) below that only the second kind of procedure is likely to qualify to be recognised by the Secretary as an approved dismissal procedure. Furthermore, the dismissal procedure must define the reasons which will constitute a valid or fair dismissal in a similar way to the Act. The definition of what constitutes an unfair dismissal for the purposes of the voluntary procedure may be wider than the corresponding statutory provision, but they must not be narrower, *i.e.* the provisions must be as beneficial as those of the Act (see para. 593 below).

592   (c) That those procedures are available without discrimination to all employees falling within any description to which the procedure agreement applies.

It is possible that (c) may require something in the nature of a duty of fair representation if the procedure is to be approved. The crux of the matter is whether the court will permit employees covered by an approved dismissal procedure to be defined by reference *inter alia* to membership of a particular union or unions. If the court does so, then there will be discrimination between unionist and non-unionist, but such discrimination will be justified on the grounds that union membership may be made part of the description of the workers to whom the dismissal procedure is to be available. The court may take the alternative view that the description of employees must be confined to such factors as job classification, seniority, etc., so that a procedure agreement could be restricted, say, to all employees falling within the description of " manual workers " or " supervisory staff," but within that description the procedure must be equally accessible to unionist and non-unionist alike. If such was the view of the court then, if the procedure concerned involved the participation of a union or its officials, the procedure could only be approved if the union concerned in effect was under a duty of fair representation in relation to the grievances of non-unionists who complained of unfair dismissals.

593   (d) That the remedies provided by the procedure agreement in respect of unfair dismissal are on the whole as beneficial as (but not necessarily identical with) those provided in respect of unfair dismissal by this Act.

As we have seen the Act makes provision for an independent body, an industrial tribunal, to be able to recommend, reinstatement or re-engagement of dismissed employees, and to award compensation to such employees up to a maximum of £5,200. Few if any voluntary dismissals procedures make provisions of this kind and therefore few, if any, would at present qualify to be approved by the Secretary.

594   (e) That the procedures provided by the procedure agreement include a right to arbitration or adjudication by an independent referee, or by a tribunal or other independent body, in cases where (by reason of an equality of votes or for any other reason) a decision cannot otherwise be reached.

A procedure agreement which at its final stage leaves the ultimate decision to a body composed of management representatives, or to a body composed of equal numbers of management and trade union representatives might not be considered appropriate for approval by the court as it might be held to lack the right of access to an independent decision-maker.

595   (f) That the provisions of the procedure agreement are such that it can be determined with reasonable certainty whether a particular employee is one to whom the procedure agreement applies or not.

In other words, the description of the employees covered by the procedure agreement must be sufficiently precise.

Revocation of designated dismissal procedures

596   Any of the parties to a designated procedure agreement may apply to the Secretary of State for Employment for the revocation of his order approving a procedure.[67] The Secretary must revoke his order if all the parties to the procedure agreement wish for such revocation, or if the conditions for the recognition by the Secretary of an approved procedure agreement enumerated above cease to be fulfilled. If the Secretary makes an order for the revocation of an approved dismissal procedure, he may also make such transitional provisions as appear to him to be appropriate in the circumstances.

Relationship with other claims arising out of a dismissal

597   There are three other main grounds upon which compensation may be awarded arising out of a dismissal: (i) proceedings for a wrongful dismissal at common law (discussed above, Chapter 16); (ii) proceedings under the Redundancy Payments Act 1965 (discussed below, Chapter 18) and (iii) proceedings under the Sex Discrimination Act 1975 and Race Relations Bill 1976 (discussed above). The Trade Union and Labour Relations Act contains no specific provisions dealing with the relationship of a claim for damages for wrongful dismissal and a claim for compensation for an unfair dismissal. In principle the two claims are cumulative in the sense that a prior claim for damages for wrongful dismissal will not debar a subsequent claim for an unfair dismissal. But, if damages are awarded in respect of the first claim, these will probably be taken into account by a tribunal assessing compensation for an unfair dismissal, because it is required to make an award of such amount as is just and equitable in all the circumstances.[68] This problem will be overcome when the Lord Chancellor confers jurisdiction on the tribunals in respect of claims for breach of contract.[69]

---

[67] Para. 14.
[68] See above.
[69] Under E.P.A., s. 109.

Redundancy

598   The deductibility of a redundancy payment from an award of compensation for unfair dismissal is discussed above, under Compensation.

Sex Discrimination Act 1975

599   Where a complaint of dismissal on grounds of sex or marital status is made, the applicant is more likely to succeed under the provisions of the Trade Union and Labour Relations Act than the Sex Discrimination Act, because the former places the burden of proof squarely on the employer (see Chapter 11). However, if it is found that compensation falls to be awarded under both Acts in respect of any "loss or other matter" there must not be a double award in respect of that "loss or other matter." [70] The limit under both Acts is the maximum for the time being imposed in respect of claims for unfair dismissal (at present £5,200).[71] Similar provisions are made in respect of complaints of racial discrimination under the Race Relations Bill 1976.

[The next paragraph is 601.]

---

[70] E.P.A., s. 77 (1).
[71] s. 77 (2).

CHAPTER 18

REDUNDANCY: COMPENSATION AND CONSULTATION [1]

General principles

601   As Professor Wedderburn has said of the Redundancy Payments Act 1965, the "rationale of the curious Act of 1965 is still shrouded in mystery." [2] Neither the decisions of the courts and tribunals interpreting its provisions nor the words of the Act itself reveal any consistent underlying objectives. Amongst the main principles, which have from time to time been singled out as being advanced by the Act, are three which all too often are mutually conflicting; none of which is carried to its logical conclusion. They are the desirability of labour mobility [3]; the need to make provision for the hardships faced by workers who are made redundant, and the need to provide financially for them to have an opportunity of retraining and resettlement in another job in another place, and the desirability of recognising that a worker has a greater stake in his job than a mere contractual claim to a couple of weeks' wages; that he has a proprietary interest in his job. The Act gives to *employees* [4] who are dismissed, laid off or placed on short time by reason of redundancy a right to receive compensation which is to be assessed according to the length of continuous employment with the particular employer. [5]

Dismissal

602   Subject to the special rules applying in case of lay-off or short time, discussed later in this chapter, unless the employee has been dismissed [6] there is no right to receive redundancy compensation.

Redundancy

603   Having established that he has been dismissed the employee is entitled to the benefit of section 9 (2) (*b*) which provides that, in proceedings before an industrial tribunal in which the employee is claiming redundancy compensation: "the employee who has been dismissed by his employer shall, unless the contrary is proved, be presumed to have been so dismissed by reason of redundancy." Notice that this does not say "unless the

---

[1] There is an excellent detailed account of the operation of the Redundancy Payments Act to be found in Grunfeld, *The Law of Redundancy* (London, 1971). For a sharper critique which in a short space illuminates the Act's many failings, see Wedderburn, *The Worker and the Law* (2nd ed., Penguin, 1971), pp. 125–137. For a critique of the various supposed objectives of the Act, see R. H. Fryer, "The Myths of the Redundancy Payments Act" (1973) 2 I.L.J. 1 *et seq.*

[2] Wedderburn, *op. cit.* pp. 125–126. *Cf.* S. R. Parker, C. G. Thomas, N. D. Ellis and W. E. J. McCarthy, *Effects of the Redundancy Payments Act* (H.M.S.O., 1971), p. 3.

[3] *Cf.* Drake, "Labour Mobility and the Law" (1969) 5 Bulletin Ind. Law Soc. 2–22.

[4] Redundancy Payments Act 1965, s. 25, defines "employee" as any person who works under (or has worked under) a contract of service or contract of apprenticeship with an employer, but excluding not only those who have been continuously employed for less than two years by the particular employer, but also a wide group of other employees. See Chap. 3, above.

[5] Redundancy Payments Act 1965, s. 1 (1).

[6] For what is meant by a dismissal, see Chap. 14. For the right of an employee under notice of dismissal for redundancy to time off to look for work, etc., see Chap. 10.

contrary is proved *by the employer.*"[7] The reason for this is that the presumption may be rebutted either (1) by evidence given by the employee himself, (2) by evidence on the part of the employer, or (3) by evidence on behalf of the Department of Employment.[8] The Department of Employment is frequently a participant in the proceedings.[9] This is because a finding by the tribunal that the employee was dismissed by reason of redundancy obliges the employer to pay compensation to the employee and also obliges the Department to grant a rebate to the employer in respect of that payment.[10] The proceedings are therefore three-cornered when the Department is represented, and the tribunal is deciding simultaneously two interdependent questions, namely, must the employer pay compensation, and secondly must the Department grant the employer a rebate.[11] In some cases, where an employer was unwilling to rebut the presumption in favour of the employee's claim, the tribunal in the light of evidence by the Department has ruled that the employee was not entitled to a redundancy payment. Ordinarily it is for the employer to show that the reason for dismissal was other than for redundancy. The Act provides that

" an employee who is dismissed shall be taken to be dismissed by reason of redundancy if the dismissal is attributable wholly or mainly to [12]—

(a) the fact that his employer has ceased, or intends to cease to carry on the business for the purposes of which the employee was employed by him or has ceased, or intends to cease, to carry on that business in the place where the employee was so employed, or

(b) the fact that the requirements of that business for employees to carry out work of a particular kind, or for employees to carry out work of a particular kind in the place where he was so employed, have ceased or diminished or are expected to cease or diminish." [13]

604   It is not necessary that the sole reason for dismissal be redundancy; it must however at least be the main reason. The definition of redundancy

---

[7] The conventional view is to read the Act as though it did in fact contain the italicised words. See Grunfeld, *op. cit.*, p. 72, and Aiken and Reid, *op. cit.*, p. 173.

[8] Even if the tribunal is not completely convinced by the employer's reasons for the dismissal they can still, taking the evidence as a whole, decide on the balance of probability that the dismissal was not due to redundancy. See *Parkes* v. *B. & M. (Bodyworks) Ltd.* [1972] I.T.R. 48 (N.I.R.C.).

[9] Industrial Tribunals (Labour Relations) Regulations 1974 (S.I. 1974 No. 1386).

[10] Redundancy Payments Act 1965, s. 30. The amount of the rebate is now governed by the Redundancy Rebates Act 1969. It should be noted, however, that if the employer waives his right to resist a claim for a redundancy payment which is made out of time, his waiver does not prevent the Secretary of State from refusing a rebate on the grounds that the claim being out of time under s. 21 of the Act, the payment was not one to which the employee was entitled. See *Secretary of State for Employment* v. *Atkins Auto Laundries* [1972] 1 W.L.R. 507.

[11] If the Secretary of State pays a rebate under a mistaken belief that employees were dismissed by reason of redundancy, he may bring a High Court action for repayment of the money paid to the employers: *Secretary of State for Employment* v. *Wellworthy Ltd. (No. 2)* [1976] I.C.R. 13 (Q.B.D.).

[12] Where redundancy and another cause combine to cause dismissal, the onus is on the employer to show that a cause other than redundancy was the main cause. See *Mac Fisheries Ltd.* v. *Willgloss* [1972] I.T.R. 57 (N.I.R.C.).

[13] Redundancy Payments Act 1965, s. 1 (2).

has given rise to problems. The cessation of a business has caused little difficulty.[14] Cessation of business in the place where the employee is employed has given rise to the need to define the employee's workplace, and in particular to inquire whether the employer has the right to shift workers around from one factory or town to another; if the contract gives such a right, then both places are the employee's workplace, and therefore the closing down of one of two factories is not a cessation of business " in the place where " the employee was employed.[15] If the contract did not provide for this kind of mobility, the refusal of workers to move would be justified and any dismissal would be by reason of redundancy.[16] The concept of work of a particular kind has also given rise to problems. A distinction has been drawn in the cases between redundancy and the need of an employee to adapt to new methods and techniques with developing technology. Dismissal of an employee for his failure to adapt himself to such changes is not a dismissal for redundancy.[17] On the other hand, by giving a broad application to the notion of work of a particular kind, where there is no change in the name of the work, the courts seem reluctant to take the view that the demand for work of a particular kind has ceased or diminished.[18]

605   A problem which has led to a somewhat unsatisfactory interpretation of the Act, although it remains open to the House of Lords to adopt a different view, is whether if there are objective factors indicating that a redundancy situation may exist, what is the effect of the employer dismissing the employee from another motive. In *Hindle* v. *Percival Boats Ltd.*[19] it was suggested that the answer is that, provided that the employer honestly believes that his dismissal of the employee is justified by another reason however mistaken in fact it may be, the dismissal will be attributable to the employer's belief and not to redundancy. In other words, in a redundancy-type situation, where despite the presumption of redundancy being in the employee's favour, if the employer honestly, but mistakenly, believes the employee to be a thief or a trade unionist or a Conservative and regards that as a sufficient reason to dismiss the employee, such employee is not eligible for redundancy payment. It has been held, however, that an employee who is believed to have created a redundancy situation by his own conduct (*e.g.* by joining a strike which leads to closure) may succeed in a claim for redundancy payment.[20]

Misconduct and redundancy

606   If a person is dismissed because of misconduct no entitlement to redundancy payment can arise because entitlement is dependent upon the

---

14 Grunfeld, *op. cit.* p. 76.
15 *Cf. O'Brien* v. *Associated Fire Alarms Ltd.* [1968] I.T.R. 322, and *Parry* v. *Holst & Co: Ltd.* [1968] I.T.R. 317. See also Chap. 9 and other cases there cited.
16 *O'Brien* v. *Associated Fire Alarms Ltd., supra.*
17 *North Riding Garages Ltd.* v. *Butterwick* [1967] 2 Q.B. 56.
18 *Vaux and Associated Breweries Ltd.* v. *Ward* [1968] I.T.R. 385. Take-over of a pub leading to dismissal of staid quiet middle-aged barmaid in order to replace her with a young blonde of the " Bunny " type to attract a new kind of client not a dismissal for redundancy. Both were barmaids, doing barmaid's work. See also *Bromby & Hoare Ltd.* v. *Evans* [1972] I.C.R. 113 (N.I.R.C.).
19 [1969] I.T.R. 86, 92, 97, 98 (C.A.).
20 *Sanders* v. *Ernest A. Neale Ltd.* [1974] I.T.R. 395 (N.I.R.C.).

dismissal being " attributable wholly or mainly " to redundancy. The Act itself, however, contains a provision [21] relating to misconduct, a provision which Professor Grunfeld describes as " the most difficult provision in the Redundancy Payments Act with which to match a real dismissal from employment situation," [22] one which still awaits " an authoritative interpretation or statutory amendment." [23] This provision states:

> " Except as provided by section 10 of this Act,[24] an employee shall not be entitled to a redundancy payment by reason of dismissal where his employer, being entitled to terminate his contract of employment without notice by reason of his employee's misconduct, terminates it either—
>
> (a) without notice, or
>
> (b) by giving shorter notice than that which, in the absence of such conduct, the employer would be required to give to terminate the contract, or
>
> (c) by giving notice (not being such shorter notice as is mentioned in paragraph (b) of this subsection) which includes, or is accompanied by, a statement in writing that the employer would,
>
> by reason of the employee's conduct, be entitled to terminate the contract without notice." [25]

607   This provision can be interpreted on one of two assumptions. First of all that it is dealing with a situation where notice of dismissal has already been given which is wholly or mainly attributable to redundancy. Secondly, it can be regarded as applying to a situation where the dismissal takes place because of the employee's misconduct. The latter assumption is otiose because clearly there would be no entitlement to redundancy compensation on those facts. The interpretation we prefer is based upon the assumption that this provision is designed to take away from a dismissed employee a right to redundancy compensation which would already by the Act's terms have been vested in him because of the notice to dismiss him being attributable wholly or mainly to redundancy.[26] Let us illustrate the problems which arise in such a situation. The XYZ Co. decide for reasons of a decline in demand for their products to reduce their labour force of twenty by fifty per cent. Notice is given to ten employees, including John. In what circumstances could misconduct by John now be relevant? (a) He could first of all have committed an act of misconduct prior to his dismissal for redundancy which if the XYZ Co. had been aware of it would have justified them in dismissing John summarily; XYZ Co. learn of this act of misconduct before their notice of dismissal for redundancy runs out. (b) XYZ Co. may discover this act of misconduct by John only after their notice of dismissal for redundancy

---

[21] Redundancy Payments Act 1965, s. 2 (2).
[22] Grunfeld, *op. cit.* p. 121.
[23] Grunfeld, *op. cit.* p. 124. See *Sanders* v. *Ernest A. Neale Ltd.*, above; *Lane Fox & Co. Ltd.* v. *Binns* [1972] I.T.R. 125.
[24] See below.
[25] Redundancy Payments Act 1965, s. 2 (2).
[26] For alternative interpretations, see Grunfeld, *op. cit.* pp. 121–124; Wedderburn, *The Worker and the Law*, p. 131, and Aiken and Reid, *op. cit.* pp. 176–178.

has run out, and before they have made him a redundancy payment under the provisions of the Act. (c) John may be guilty of an act of misconduct during the currency of the notice of dismissal for redundancy; and (d) John commits an act of misconduct before receiving any notice of dismissal, but XYZ Co. use John's misconduct as a reason for selecting him as one of their ten employees to be made redundanct. Let us consider each of these examples in turn.

608   (a) If XYZ Co. do nothing, John's dismissal remains wholly or mainly attributable to redundancy and he is entitled to a redundancy compensation. But under section 2 (2) XYZ Co. may now do one of three things which will operate to deprive John of redundancy compensation. (1) They may lawfully dismiss him summarily—lawfully because section 2 (2) applies only where the misconduct is sufficient to justify summary dismissal. (2) They may now give him notice of dismissal shorter than that which they would at common law be required to give to terminate the contract. For example, if being careful employers XYZ Co. had given John six weeks' notice of dismissal for redundancy when under his contract he was in fact only entitled to receive two weeks' notice to terminate his contract, they can now give him one week's notice on grounds of his misconduct, which one week's notice may terminate before their more generous notice of six weeks runs out. (3) XYZ Co. may terminate John's contract during the currency of the six weeks' period of notice by giving him two weeks' notice. In this latter case, if this dismissal for misconduct is to operate to deprive John of his entitlement to redundancy payment, the XYZ Co. must give him a statement in writing indicating that they would have been entitled to terminate his contract by reason of misconduct *without any notice* whatever.

609   (b) Here XYZ Co. must pay redundancy compensation because the dismissal was wholly or mainly attributable to redundancy. One industrial tribunal has given the odd interpretation that provided when dismissing John for redundancy XYZ dismissed him summarily and unlawfully, or dismissed him with insufficient notice lawfully to terminate the contract, they can still plead his misconduct as a ground for refusing a redundancy payment.[27] This is to place too high a premium upon the right of employers to behave unlawfully in the hope that a subsequent discovery of John's misconduct will legitimise their unlawful act. The validity of this approach is dependent upon the proper interpretation of the phrase used in section 2 (2), " where his employer, being entitled to terminate his contract of employment without notice by reason of the employee's misconduct," and whether it implies that the employer must be aware of the misconduct at the time of dismissal, or whether it is irrelevant that at the time of the summary dismissal or dismissal with inadequate notice the employer is unaware of the misconduct. Common sense and indeed the terms of the Act [28] itself dictate that an interpretation of the Act which encourages

---

27 *X* v. *Y. Ltd.* [1969] I.T.R. 204.

28 It is suggested that the reason for the need to give a written statement in s. 2 (2) (*c*), whereas there is no such need in the cases in paras. (*a*) and (*b*), is that summary dismissal during the currency of a notice of dismissal for redundancy (or giving an unlawfully short period of notice during that same period) puts the employee on notice that the employer takes the view he has been guilty of misconduct; only such a view, if true, would justify doing what the employer has done. But if during a generous period of notice for redundancy

employers dismissing for reasons of redundancy to give not less than the legal minimum period of notice required lawfully to terminate contracts of employment is the one to be preferred.

610   (c) Here, if the employer does nothing, John remains entitled to redundancy compensation, because the Act clearly requires that the employer's termination must take place after he has become entitled to dismiss the employee summarily.[29] But the employer may if he wishes rely upon the misconduct to terminate John's contract in such a manner as to deprive John of his entitlement to redundancy compensation.

611   (d) Here again John remains entitled to redundancy compensation, as we are inclined to take the view that the dismissal is wholly or mainly attributable to redundancy. Let us put it like this: if the employer would not ordinarily have relied upon John's misconduct to dismiss him, his reliance upon it as a ground for selecting him as one of the ten workers inevitably to be made redundant does not mean that John's dismissal is wholly or mainly attributable to *misconduct*, any more than any other criterion used to select men to be made redundant means they are not wholly or mainly dismissed for redundancy. Thus if an employer chooses to dismiss the ten oldest men, or the ten most active members of their trade union, or the ten most abstemious men, or the ten most alcoholic, the ground for their selection (redundancy of ten out of twenty of XYZ's employees being inevitable) does not mean that the dismissal of the particular ten men chosen on any of the above grounds is wholly or mainly due to their age, their trade union membership, their abstemiousness, or their alcoholism. The dismissal remains attributable to redundancy if no one would have been dismissed except for the decline in demand for work of a particular kind. However, in John's case, if the employer either would have dismissed John independently for redundancy or wishes to take advantage of John's misconduct in order to reduce his liability to pay redundancy payment to ten men to making such payments to nine, he can invoke the provisions of the Act to this effect by dismissing John with no notice, too little notice or the lawfully required minimum (but in this latter case giving John a written statement alleging his misconduct as a ground for dimissal).

612   Where the employer, reying on the employee's misconduct to deprive him of redundancy compensation, does not comply with the obligation to give the employee a written statement, the sanction for non-compliance, in cases where the employee would otherwise be entitled to redundancy payment, dismissal being wholly or mainly attributable to redundancy, is that the employer remains liable to pay a redundancy payment.[30]

---

the issue of a further notice of dismissal giving only the legally required minimum notice is something which the employer remains legally free to do for any reason under the sun, including regretting being over-generous where generosity costs the employer money; therefore the act of the employer being ambiguous, there is a statutory requirement that in case of what might appear only to be the revocation of a generous act the employer must draw the employee's attention specifically to his reason.

[29] s. 2 (2), " where his employer, being entitled to terminate his contract of employment without notice by reason of the employee's conduct, terminates it . . ."

[30] Any suggestion to the contrary that can be read into the decision of an industrial tribunal in *Essen* v. *Vanden Plas (England) 1923 Ltd.* [1966] I.T.R. 186 is in our opinion wrong.

Section 10 of the Act provides that, except where an employee has been lawfully dismissed by an employer during the currency of a notice for dismissal by reason of redundancy on the ground that the employee is taking part in a strike,[31] the fact that an employee is dismissed for misconduct during the currency of a notice of redundancy dismissal will not prevent the industrial tribunal from awarding such part, none or all, of the redundancy payment, as the industrial tribunal thinks just and equitable in the circumstances.

Offer of re-engagement or of alternative employment

613 Section 2 (3) of the Act provides that an employee dismissed for redundancy shall be disqualified from receiving a redundancy payment if he unreasonably refuses an offer from his employer to renew the contract on the same terms as before, such renewal to take effect either immediately or after an interval of not more than four weeks following on the termination of the notice of dismissal already given. Section 2 (3) also deals with an offer of alternative employment, *i.e.* employment the terms of which differ wholly or in part from the terms of the previous employment. Such an offer must be to re-engage immediately or after an interval of not more than four weeks. An employee loses his right to redundancy compensation if the offer constitutes " an offer of suitable employment in relation to the employee " and he has unreasonably refused it. Although the concepts of *suitability* of employment and *reasonableness* of refusal are separable, they are frequently dealt with together. Decisions on these two related questions tend very much to be dependent upon the tribunal's views of all the circumstances involved in each case, this being so, often " a list of opposite results can be given in cases which differ little," [32] and decisions are really applicable only to their own special facts.[33] Section 3 provides that if the employee accepts renewal of his contract, or re-engagement, he is to be treated as not having been " dismissed."

Trial periods

614 The E.P.A. has amended the R.P.A.[34] so as to allow an employee to try the new job before deciding whether or not finally to accept it, without running the risk of losing his entitlement to claim for redundancy compensation. There is an automatic trial period, beginning with the day on which the employee begins work under the contract as renewed or the new contract. The trial period lasts for four weeks, or for such longer period as is agreed between the employer and the employee, or his representative, in writing. The agreement must be made before the employee starts work under the contract as renewed or under the new contract. It must specify the date on which the trial period ends and state the

---

31 Redundancy Payments Act 1965, s. 40, provides that if an employee under notice of dismissal for redundancy strikes, the employer can serve on him a written notice requiring him to continue at work after the employer's own notice for as many days as were lost due to the worker concerned striking. See *Simmonds* v. *Hoover Ltd., The Times,* July 20, 1976 (E.A.T.).
32 Wedderburn, *The Worker and the Law,* p. 133. See also Chap. 12 of Wedderburn and Davies, *Employment Grievances and Disputes Procedures in Britain* (Berkeley, 1969).
33 In so far as principles can be disentangled, they are well set out in Grunfeld, *Law of Redundancy,* Chap. 5.
34 See R.P.A., s. 3, as amended E.P.A., Sched. 16, Part I, para. 3.

terms and conditions of employment which are to apply after the end of the trial period. Provided the employee does not remain on beyond the end of the trial period he may still bring a claim for redundancy compensation.[35]

Change of employers

615   Sometimes the offer of further employment can be made by a different person. First of all an offer of re-engagement or of suitable alternative employment can be made by an associated employer.[36] Section 48 (4) provides

> " For the purposes of this section [any two employers are to be treated as associated if one is a company of which the other (directly or indirectly) has control, or if both are companies of which a third person (directly or indirectly) has control . . ." [37]].

Secondly, section 13 makes a similar provision with respect to the sale of a business by the original employer as a going concern.[38] Thirdly, in the case of the death of an individual employer an offer of further employment by the personal representatives has a similar effect.[39] This applies where the death of the former employer has operated to terminate the contract, *i.e.,* has operated as a dismissal under section 22 (1).[40]

Contracting out of the Act

616   The Act permits employers and employees to remove themselves from the ambit of the Act in two cases. First of all there is the case of fixed term contracts. Where there is a fixed term contract for two years or more the employee concerned will not be entitled to a redundancy payment in respect of the expiry of such term without its being renewed, " if before the term so expires he has agreed in writing to exclude any right to a redundancy payment in that event." [41]

The Act provides that such agreement may

> " be contained either in the contract itself or in a separate agreement.[42]

> (4) Where an agreement under subsection (2) of this section is made during the currency of a fixed term, and that term is renewed, the agreement under that subsection shall not be construed as applying to the term as renewed, but without prejudice to the making of a further agreement under that subsection in relation to the term as renewed." [43]

Because an increasing number of persons appear to be employed under fixed term contracts it is important to establish in what circumstances employees may lawfully surrender their rights under this Act. This is

---

[35] R.P.A., s. 3 (5)–(8) as amended.
[36] R.P.A., s. 48 (1) as amended by E.P.A., Sched. 16, Pt. I, para. 18.
[37] This overcomes difficulties created by the former limitation to " associated companies."
[38] *Cf. Woodhouse* v. *Peter Brotherhood Ltd.* [1972] 2 Q.B. 520.
[39] Sched. 4, Part II, of the Act (as amended by E.P.A.). In the case of domestic servants the offer of alternative employment must come not from the personal representative but from the person upon whom the management of the household has devolved. *Quaere* what is the definition of a domestic servant? *Cf.* Chap. 3 above.
[40] See Chap. 14 above. See Chap. 5 as regards continuity / of employment in such cases.
[41] Redundancy Payments Act 1965, s. 15 (2). See also Chap. 14.
[42] *Ibid.* s. 15 (3).
[43] *Ibid.* s. 15 (4).

particularly important because there are express safeguards written into the procedure for substituting the provisions of collective agreements for those of the Act which are apparently aimed at ensuring that an employee "contracted out" as the result of collective bargaining is at least as well off as he would be under the Act.[44] The Act applies to fixed term contracts and therefore we are here dealing with the surrender by an employee of his statutory rights, which makes sense if at least he is left in such a bargaining situation that, in exchange for a surrender of his rights, he may bargain for something in lieu of those rights.

617   We may ask first of all who may surrender statutory rights under section 15. At first sight it would appear in the words of section 15 that it is only "an employee under a contract of employment for a fixed term of two years or more." [45] When may he surrender his rights? It would appear only where there is a provision in his current contract of employment providing for such surrender, or if subsequent to the making of his current contract of employment he has made a separate agreement providing for surrender. Is it lawful for an employer to say to an employee already employed under a fixed term contract for two years or more: "I will renew this current contract for a further two years provided you agree to surrender your rights to a redundancy payment in respect of the contract as renewed"? It would appear probable that the provision in section 15 (4), providing that an agreement to surrender rights "made during the currency of a fixed term . . . shall not be construed as applying to the term as renewed," is intended to make any such offer followed by the employee's acceptance of it ineffective to deprive the employee of his statutory rights.

Collective bargains

618   The second case of exemption from its provisions occurs under section 11 of the Redundancy Payments Act 1965 which permits the Minister by order to exempt certain employees from the protection of the Act where he thinks fit, in the case of a *joint* application of the parties to any agreement making provision for voluntary payments to employees on termination of the contracts. The Act does not specify that the Minister should be satisfied that the provisions of the collective agreement shall be as beneficial to the workers as the statutory scheme, but one must suppose that the Minister will not ordinarily make an exemption order unless this is so. The Minister in any case will not make such an order unless the agreement provides for access to an industrial tribunal for the settlement of disputes arising out of the collective agreement.

Lay-off and short time

619   Where the contract of employment of the worker concerned permits the employer to lay him off or put him on short time, the Redundancy Payments Act provides a complicated machinery whereby such worker if "dismissed," for the purposes of the Act, may claim redundancy compensation. Where such entitlement is dependent upon having been laid off or

---

[44] See below.
[45] The reason for the two years is that no one who has not been employed for at least two years continuously with a particular employer is entitled to any redundancy compensation. See Redundancy Payments Act 1965, ss. 1 (1) and 8 (1).

placed on short time for a particular period, the Act (s. 7 (3)) provides
somewhat startlingly that

> "No account shall be taken of any week for which the employee is
> laid off or kept on short time where the lay-off or short-time is wholly
> or mainly attributable to a strike or lock-out, whether the strike or
> lock-out is in the trade or industry in which the employee is employed
> *or not* and whether it is in Great Britain *or elsewhere* " (italics added).

Calculation of compensation

620   Compensation is based primarily upon the dismissed employee's length
of continuous employment. Schedule 1 to the Redundancy Payments Act
provides that for each year of employment between the ages of eighteen
and twenty-one the employee is to receive half a week's pay; for each
year of completed employment between twenty-two and forty, one week's
pay, and for each year of employment between the ages of forty-one and
sixty-four, one and a half week's pay. Employees nearing the age of sixty,
in the case of a woman, and sixty-five, in the case of a man, are subject
to a scaling down: for every month by which the employee is over
fifty-nine, in the case of a woman, and over sixty-four, in the case of a
man, the total amount payable is reduced by one-twelfth. Wages over £80
per week,[46] and employment for longer than twenty years, are ignored.
What is a week's pay in each case is calculated in accordance with the
provisions of the Employment Protection Act, Sched. 4.[47]

The Code

621   The Code of Industrial Relations Practice provides that employers in
consultation with their employees (or their representatives) should

> " (i) give as much warning as practicable to the employees concerned
>   and to the Department of Employment;
> (ii) consider introducing schemes for voluntary redundancy, retirement,
>   transfer to other establishments within the undertaking and a
>   phased rundown of employment;
> (iii) establish which employees are to be made redundant and the order
>   of discharge;
> (iv) offer help to employees in finding other work in co-operation,
>   where appropriate, with the Department of Employment and allow
>   them reasonable time off for the purpose;
> (v) decide how and when to make the facts public, ensuring that
>   no announcement is made before their employees and their
>   representatives, and trade unions have been informed." [48]

Consultation

622   A novel provision introduced into British law by the E.P.A.,[49] in
order to give effect to obligations arising from Britain's membership of the

---

[46] Calculation of Redundancy Payments Order 1974 (S.I. 1974 No. 1327).
[47] See Chap. 10 above.
[48] Code 46.
[49] E.P.A., Part IV.

European Economic Community,[50] is that which requires an employer contemplating dismissal of one or more workers for redundancy to consult recognised trade unions and also to give notice to the Department of Employment. The obligation is to consult officials of the union or unions which are authorised to carry on bargaining with the employer. The obligation is not to consult trade unions whose members are to be dismissed for redundancy; the obligation is to consult a union or unions recognised by the employer for bargaining purposes in respect of the grade or category of workers from whose ranks the employer intends to select people for dismissal. If the employer is planning to dismiss a single non-unionist as redundant he will still have to consult any union recognised by him in respect of the group of workers to which the non-unionist belongs. The obligation is to consult at "*the earliest opportunity*" and in any case not less than 90 days before the first dismissal when the employer is planning to dismiss 100 or more employees over a 90-day period, or not less than 60 days before the first dismissal where the employer is planning to dismiss 10 or more employees over a 30-day period. There is no minimum period laid down where the employer plans to dismiss less than 10 employees. Consultation here has a specific statutory meaning—the Act explicity states that it is not to be construed as conferring any other rights on the unions concerned in addition to those specified by the Act—and covers three things :

(i) The employer must give to the official of the recognised union the following information—

    (a) the reasons for the proposed dismissals (N.B. redundancy is not a reason; it is a collective noun for a variety of reasons; the employer must spell out why dismissal is necessary, why there is less demand for work to be done, etc.);

    (b) the number and class of workers proposed to be dismissed;

    (c) the total number of employees belonging to the grade or class of employees from whose ranks the employer proposes to dismiss people as redundant;

    (d) the method to be used in selecting the people to be dismissed for redundancy; and

    (e) the method of dismissal, with due regard to any agreed procedure, *e.g.*, are they all to be dismissed at one moment or are the dismissals to be spread over a period of time.

(ii) The employer must consider any representations made to him by the trade union representatives about the proposed redundancies.

(iii) In so far as the employer chooses not to act upon any of the representations made to him on behalf of the union he must state his reasons for not doing so.

Protective awards

623   If the employer fails to fulfil any of the above requirements the union concerned (not, be it noted, an individual employee) may complain to an

---

[50] For a discussion of the rules of European law to which Part IV purports to give effect and the extent to which it falls short of the requirements of European law, see the discussion in Chap. 20 below.

industrial tribunal and ask for a protective award to be made. The award will be made unless the employer can show that it was not reasonably practicable for him to have done more than he has done by way of consultation. The effect of the award is that the employees are to be kept on the pay-roll for the period of the award. In other words in addition to any other claim the employees may have for wages already due, for unfair dismissal, for redundancy compensation, the employees concerned will be entitled to the wages they should have been paid for this period. The length of the award is within the discretion of the tribunal, subject to certain limitations. Where 100 or more employees are involved, then it can be for up to 100 days; where ten or more it can be for up to 60 days, and where less than ten workers are involved it can be for a period up to twenty-eight days.[51]

Notification to the Department of Employment

624   The employer must also notify the Department of Employment of the impending redundancies, at least 90 days before the first dismissal where 100 or more are to be dismissed over a 90-day period, or at least 60 days before the first dismissal where 10 or more are to be dismissed over a 30-day period. There is no duty under E.P.A. to notify the Department where less that 10 are involved. The employer must not only give advance notice to the Department but he must also state the date on which he began consultation with any recognised trade union. He must also provide the Department with such further information as it may require. The sanction for failure to give such notice is *either* a fine of up to £400 *or* loss of up to 10 per cent. of any redundancy rebate to which the employer might otherwise be entitled. It is to be noted that this is one of the very rare occasions where an individual, not himself in law the employer, but a director or manager, can also incur personal liability. If the failure to notify the Department is due to the fault or neglect of such person he may be prosecuted and be fined personally.[52]

[The next paragraph is 631.]

---

[51] This is a very general description of the complex provisions of E.P.A., ss. 100–104. An employee may complain to a tribunal that he has not been paid the amount due.
[52] E.P.A., ss. 102, 104, 105.

UNEMPLOYMENT—SOCIAL SECURITY BENEFITS

General principles

631   As we have seen, the law of work discipline has five main aspects, one of which is social security law.[2] In order to understand the rules of British social security law [3] their historical origin in the Poor Law system, under which poverty and need carried with them the stigma of second-class citizenship, should not be lost sight of. Modern social security rules attempt to fulfil at least five differing, and sometimes conflicting, objectives:

(i) To provide for the financial requirements of those in need, who have suffered a loss of income by reason of some event, often catastrophic such as injury to the breadwinner or loss of employment by the bread-winner;

(ii) To discipline the work force and to ensure that pressure be exerted upon workers to behave in the workplace in a way of which the prevailing establishment approves; and

(iii) To provide an incentive for workers to remain at work, or if temporarily absent from work, due to illness or unemployment or any other cause, to return to work without undue delay;

(iv) To discourage workers from taking strike action and, where they have gone on strike or have been locked-out, to encourage an early settlement of the dispute and a return to work, and

(v) To express moral disapproval of certain forms of behaviour by workers.

Contributions

632   For the purposes of the Social Security Act 1975 contributions paid are divided into four classes:

(a) Class 1 contributions paid in respect of employed earners, *i.e.*, persons who are gainfully employed in Great Britain [4] under a contract of service [5] or in an office with emoluments chargeable to income tax under Schedule E [6];

(b) Class 2 contributions payable by self-employed earners, *i.e.* persons

---

[1] As modern British social security law is one of the most complicated branches of the law it must be stressed that this chapter seeks primarily to expound the main principles only and is therefore, while not we hope being inaccurate, somewhat oversimplified.

[2] See above, Chap. 13.

[3] For our purposes social security law can be defined as the body of rules comprised in the following principal statutes (and statutory regulations made thereunder):
(a) Social Security Act 1975; (b) the Supplementary Benefit Act 1966 and Social Security Act 1971; (c) Family Allowances Act 1965; (d) Family Income Supplements Act, and (e) Redundancy Payments Act 1965. We have considered (e) above, Chap. 18, and as we are primarily concerned with incidents arising out of the contract of employment we are not directly concerned with (c) and (d). It should be noted that the Supplementary Benefit Act 1966 may also be referred to as the Ministry of Social Security Act 1966.

[4] Northern Ireland has its own practically identical system.

[5] This includes apprentices. For discussion of definition of the contract of service (*i.e.* employment), see above, Chap. 3.

[6] The result of this is to confer entitlement to benefits, in particular unemployment benefit, on office-holders, who might not otherwise be regarded as employees.

gainfully employed in Great Britain otherwise than in an employed earner's employment ;

(c) Class 3 payable voluntarily by self-employed or employed earners or others to secure entitlement to benefit for which they may not otherwise qualify, and

(d) Class 4 contributions payable in respect of profits or gains of a trade, profession or vocation by self-employed earners.

633   Particular benefits are payable only if the contribution conditions appropriate to them have been met, being contributions of the relevant class. In particular unemployment benefit is payable only in respect of Class 1 contributions; whereas sickness benefit is payable in respect of Class 1 or Class 2 contributions. There are no contribution conditions for the benefits payable in respect of industrial accidents, scheduled industrial diseases or deaths caused thereby (*i.e.* injury benefit, disablement benefit, and industrial death benefit) or for redundancy compensation or for supplementary benefits. It is important to notice that the benefits payable in respect of industrial accidents and scheduled industrial diseases, and redundancy compensation, are payable only to persons who are employed earners and to certain dependants.

A general principle underlying the provision of benefits under the Social Security Act is that only one payment is made for one contingency. For example, if a worker suffers a serious accident at work causing him to be off work for a period, he cannot receive sickness benefit as well as industrial injury benefit. However, as the rates of benefits provided under the Act are low, benefits may not in fact be sufficient for the basic needs of those in receipt of them, and also because some benefits such as unemployment benefit are payable only for limited periods, there is a system of supplementary benefits payable to those not adequately, or no longer, covered by benefits provided under the Social Security Act. Thus a worker may receive both supplementary as well as unemployment benefit.

Conditions for payment of benefits

634   The conditions which must be fulfilled in order to qualify for benefits may be summarised as follows :

(a) The claimant must establish that he belongs to the class of persons to whom the particular benefit is payable, *e.g.*, in case of unemployment benefit, the claimant must belong to the class of employed earners (as opposed to self-employed and non-employed).

635   (b) Where there is a condition of contributions having been paid the claimant must have paid a sufficient number of contributions.[7] There are basically two conditions: (i) in any one tax year Class 1 contributions equivalent to contributions on earnings of at least 25 times the weekly lower earnings rate (this is the rate below which employees are not liable to pay contributions), and (ii) in order to get full benefit the employee must have paid or been credited with at least 50 Class 1 contributions

---

[7] Because the Social Security Act 1975 has only come into force in April 1975 there are transitional provisions providing for benefit entitlement to be earned partly under the rules applicable under the National Insurance Act 1965. See also Hepple and O'Higgins, *Individual Employment Law* (1971) where the old rules of entitlement are summarily explained.

in the relevant contribution period. If less than 50 but at least 26 contributions have been paid or credited in the period, benefit is payable at a reduced rate. Unemployment benefit is normally payable for 312 [8] days, after which the claimant cannot get benefit until he has requalified by being back at work for an employer for at least 21 hours a week for 13 weeks. In addition to the basic benefits workers may be entitled to a further earnings-related supplement.[9] This earnings-related supplement is payable only for 156 days. Sickness benefit is payable for 168 days and is then replaced by invalidity benefit if incapacity for work continues.

636 (c) The claimant is the victim of the contingency to provide for which the particular benefit is provided, *e.g.*, industrial injuries benefit is payable in respect of an employee who is off work because of an accident, causing personal injury, which accident arose out of and in the course of his employment. If he is off work as a result of any other kind of accident he is only entitled to sickness benefit; if he is off work for reasons other than accident, disease or sickness, he may qualify for unemployment benefit. In the case of supplementary benefit the claimant must be suffering from need which is not otherwise catered for by other means, including his own financial resources.[10]

637 It is important to emphasise that unemployment benefit is payable only in respect of " any day of unemployment which forms part of a period of unemployment." [11] There is, however, no definition of what is meant by a " day of unemployment." Provisions of regulations made under the Act make it clear that having some employment is not incompatible with being unemployed.[12] The Commissioner has said

> " that a person shall not be prevented from being regarded as unemployed merely by the fact that he is following an occupation, if he can satisfy four conditions thereto, namely, (1) that the earnings do not exceed [75 p.] a day; (2) that notwithstanding the occupation, he is available for full-time employment in some employed contributor's employment; (3) that the said occupation is consistent with that full-time employment; and (4) that the said occupation, if followed under a contract of service, is not the claimant's usual main occupation." [13]

By " occupation " is meant gainful occupation.[14] The doing of unpaid work is not incompatible therefore with being unemployed. Where no work is done and no remuneration received the claimant is prima facie unemployed.[15] Where a person attends for work but performs no work and receives only part-wages,[16] or in the case of a casual dockworker

---

[8] 312 days means in effect 52 weeks because benefit is on a six-day week basis (Sundays ordinarily being the excluded day).

[9] Social Security Act 1975, s. 14 (7) and Sched. 6, Part I, para. 3, describes the limits to the amount of earnings related supplements.

[10] The level of supplementary benefit is assessed as the amount by which a claimant's " resources are insufficient to meet his requirements " (Supplementary Benefit Act 1966, s. 4 (1)).

[11] Social Security Act 1975, s. 14 (1) (*a*).

[12] National Insurance (Unemployment and Sickness) Regulations 1967, reg. 7 (1) (*i*).

[13] R (U) 16/64.

[14] R (U) 34/53.

[15] R (U) 20/51.

[16] R (U) 35/51.

attending at docks where there is no work for him, but in consequence is paid £1 " disappointment money " under a collective agreement, such person is not unemployed.[17] On the other hand, " when, however, weekly payments are made to ex-employees entirely as an act of grace on the part of the employer with the intention of assisting the recipients whilst out of work, the relationship of employer and employee no longer subsists and the recipients are properly regarded as unemployed." [18]

The presence of a contract of employment does not therefore conclusively establish that a person is not unemployed. A person attending a training course, paid only travelling expenses and a subsistence allowance, has been held to be unemployed during the period of training.[19]

The award of benefit subject to further conditions

638 (d) The claimant must have fulfilled any conditions as to waiting days. In the case of sickness, unemployment benefit and injury benefit, no benefit is payable at all in respect of the first three days' absence from work.[20] In the case of the earnings-related supplement, this is. not paid in respect of the first twelve days' absence from work.[21] Under the Supplementary Benefits Scheme there is no such restriction, although, except in the case of extreme urgency, there may be an administrative delay in making payment.

639 (e) Benefit may be subject to certain restrictions so far as the amount is concerned. Where earnings-related supplement is paid, the total amount of benefit including allowances for dependants can never exceed 85 per cent. of the recipient's reckonable weekly earnings.[22] The comparable rule, the " wage-stop," in relation to the amount of supplementary benefit that may be received has now been abolished.[23] The *raison d'être* of these kinds of rules is to encourage people receiving benefit, by reason of their being worse off when out of work than they would be if still at work, to return to work as soon as possible.

640 (f) In the case of unemployment no benefit is payable in respect of any day unless the claimant is capable of work [24] and available for employment.[25] In the case of sickness and injury benefit the claimant must be incapable of work by reason of some specific disease, or bodily or mental disablement.[26]

Disqualification for benefit

641 We have already mentioned certain grounds for disqualification such

---

[17] R (U) 11/64.
[18] R (U) 13/58.
[19] R (U) 3/67. Such a person may be disqualified on other grounds, such as non-availability.
[20] Social Security Act 1975, s. 14 (3). This abolishes a reform first introduced by the National Insurance Act 1946, s. 11.
[21] Social Security Act 1975, s. 14 (7).
[22] Social Security Act 1975, Sched. 6, Part I, para. 3 (1).
[23] Child Benefit Act 1975, s. 19.
[24] Social Security Act 1975, s. 17 (1) (a) (i).
[25] *Ibid.* and reg. 7 (1) (a) of National Insurance (Unemployment and Sickness) Benefit Regulations 1967 (S.I. 1967 No. 330).
[26] Social Security Act 1975, s. 17 (1) (a) (ii).

as not fulfilling the contribution conditions or having received the particular benefit for the prescribed maximum period.[27]

The two major grounds of disqualification which require some detailed attention are trade disputes and misconduct by the employee.[28]

Misconduct: injury benefit

642   Where an insured person suffers a personal injury by accident arising out of and in the course of his employment he is entitled to benefit.[29] The fact that the accident occurred while the worker was acting in contravention of any statutory or other regulation applicable to his work, or in breach of orders given by his employer, or in the absence of orders given by his employer, will not deprive the injured worker of benefit, provided the act done by the worker was not done purely for his own benefit, but he was merely doing the kind of thing he was normally employed to do.[30] Where however the accident was caused by another person's misconduct, skylarking or negligence, or by the behaviour of any living creature, the injured worker will still be entitled to industrial injury benefit, unless he directly or indirectly induced or contributed to the happening of the accident by his conduct outside the employment or by any act not incidental to that employment.[31]

Generally, entitlement to industrial injury benefit under the Social Security Act is dependent upon the accident having *arisen out of and in the course of the employed earner's employment.* To arise in the course of employment the accident must have occurred (subject to certain special statutory provisions) in the normal workplace and during normal working hours (leniently interpreted to include such things as packing-up time, etc.). The course of employment in other words describes the working area of the insured person spatially and temporally. If the insured person leaves this working area, then he is no longer covered by the Act, although he may be entitled to sickness benefit. Where the accident occurs in the course of employment, this gives rise to a presumption that the accident also *arose out of the employment.*[32]

643   However, a worker may notionally cease to be in the course of his employment while yet remaining within the workplace, if what he is doing has ceased to be incidental to the work he is employed to do. In *R. v. Industrial Injuries Commissioner, ex p. Amalgamated Engineering Union*[33] a worker, who was permitted to smoke during a tea-break in a special smoking-booth, found the booth occupied and waited outside it rolling a cigarette. He overstayed the tea-break by five minutes and was injured while still waiting to enter the smoking-booth. The court had to decide whether the accident had occurred while in the course of his employment, and decided that the worker had stepped outside, notionally, the course of his employment. One judge said:

---

[27] See above.
[28] There are other grounds: see Social Security Act 1975, s. 82.
[29] *Ibid.* s. 50.
[30] *Ibid.* s. 52.
[31] *Ibid.* s. 55.
[32] *Ibid.* s. 50 (3).
[33] [1966] 2 Q.B. 31.

" What is the position when a man overstays his tea-break or his meal-break? I do not think that the mere fact of overstaying his time takes him out of the course of his employment: certainly not when it is done without thinking. Even if it is done negligently or disobediently, it does not automatically take him outside the course of his employment. It is only taken out of the course of employment when the circumstances show that he is doing something of a kind different from anything he was employed to do." [34]

Although the court indicated that it was a matter of degree, they were prepared to regard the delay of five minutes as sufficient to take the worker outside the course of his employment. The effect of this kind of misconduct is to prevent the worker from being entitled to industrial injury benefit. He may however still be able to claim sickness benefit, or failing that he may get supplementary benefit.

Misconduct: sickness benefit

644   A person shall be disqualified for receiving sickness benefit and invalidity benefit for such period not exceeding six weeks as may be determined in the manner provided by the Determination of Claims and Questions Regulations if—

" (a) He has become incapable of work through his own misconduct, except that this disqualification shall not apply where the incapacity is due to venereal disease or, in the case of a woman who is not a wife, or, being a wife, is separated from her husband, to pregnancy; or

(b) He fails without good cause to comply with a notice in writing given by the Minister requiring him to attend for and to submit himself to medical or other examination on a date not earlier than the third day after the day on which the notice was sent and at a time and place specified in that notice; or

(c) he fails without good cause to attend for, or to submit himself to, medical or other treatment: provided that this disqualification shall not apply to any failure to attend for or to submit to vaccination or inoculation of any kind or to a surgical operation, unless the failure is a failure to attend for or to submit to a surgical operation of a minor character, and is considered by the determining authority to be unreasonable; or

(d) he fails without good cause to observe any of the following rules of behaviour, namely: —

    (i) to refrain from behaviour calculated to retard his recovery, and to answer any reasonable enquiries (not being enquiries relating to medical examination, treatment or advice) by the Minister or his officers directed to ascertain whether he is doing so;

    (ii) not to be absent from his place of residence without leaving word where he may be found;

    (iii) to do no work for which remuneration is, or would

---

[34] *Ibid.* at p. 103, *per* Lord Denning M.R.

ordinarily be, payable unless it is work which is described in regulation 7 (1) (h) of these regulations." [35]

We have been able to trace only a single decision of the National Insurance Commissioner on the interpretation of the provision relating to misconduct,[36] but it does not help on the interpretation to be given to the word " misconduct " in this context. This does not mean that insurance officers, who make the initial determination in all claims to benefit under the National Insurance Acts, are not applying this provision, nor does it necessarily mean that local appeal tribunals to which claimants may go if their claims are refused by an insurance officer are not interpreting it. We do, however, lack any authoritative interpretation by the National Insurance Commissioners, who are the final appellate tribunal for questions under the Social Security Acts. One may guess that it would be given a fairly reasonable interpretation by the National Insurance Commissioners. It might certainly include deliberate acts and gross carelessness, but probably not that degree of carelessness which people in a highly industrialised society, through ignorance, exhaustion, etc., are likely to be unable to avoid being guilty of on some occasion. It is nonetheless significant that the National Insurance Commissioners have not ruled on the interpretation of misconduct. This does suggest that misconduct may not be commonly invoked as a ground of disqualification for sickness benefit. The effect of such misconduct will be to disqualify the insured person from receiving sickness benefit for a maximum period of six weeks. In case of alcoholism the National Insurance Commissioners have indicated that this will operate as a ground of disqualification if it was not involuntary.[37] If it was due to a psychological illness, then no disqualification.

Misconduct: unemployment benefit

645 The Social Security Act 1975, s. 20 (1) provides:

" A person shall be disqualified for receiving unemployment benefit for such period not exceeding six weeks as may be determined . . . if—

(a) he has lost his employment as an employed earner through his misconduct, or has voluntarily left such employment without just cause . . . "

Misconduct in this context means " simply such misconduct as would lead a reasonable employer to terminate a claimant's employment." [38] It involves some degree of blameworthiness, but not necessarily a breach of any duty owed by the worker to his employer. Thus an act by a bus driver while on holiday, leading to a conviction for a driving offence for an act of carelessness in his own car, might be misconduct for the purpose of disqualifying him for unemployment benefit if his employer, hearing of the conviction, dismissed him. On the other hand, when a bus driver, while off duty in his own car, committed a traffic offence which led to

---

[35] National Insurance (Unemployment and Sickness Benefit) Regulations 1967, reg. 11 (1).
[36] R (S) 2/53.
[37] R (S) 2/53.
[38] R (U) 24/55.

the suspension of his licence, this was clearly a breach of his general duty to his employer not so to use his spare time as to disable himself from performing his duties, and this was clearly misconduct.[39] Breach of works rules, for example, dismissal of a Post Office official who broke a Post Office rule forbidding staff to bet by post, will usually be misconduct.[40] Bringing unfounded charges against a superior employee recklessly or knowing them to be false may be misconduct.[41] Similarly a worker who leaves work without just cause commits an offence, the sanction for which is withholding of unemployment benefit for a period not exceeding six weeks. What constitutes *just cause* is not easy to determine, as can be seen from the following extract from a decision of the National Insurance Commissioners:

> " The basic purpose of unemployment benefit is to provide against the misfortune of unemployment happening against a person's will. Section 13 (2) [42] however clearly recognises that it may be payable in certain cases where the claimant leaves voluntarily, if he does not do so without just cause. It is not sufficient for him to prove that he acted reasonably, in the sense of acting reasonably in his own interests. The interests of the National Insurance Fund and other contributors have to be taken into account as well. ' The notion of " just cause " involves a compromise between the rights of the individual and the interests of the rest of the community. So long as he does not break his contract with his employer, the individual is free to leave his employment when he likes. But if he wishes to claim unemployment benefit he must not leave his employment without due regard to the interests of the rest of the community . . . ' (Decision C.U. 164/50 (not reported).) This has been expressed in different ways in many decisions; see Decisions R (U) 14/55, paragraph 5 and R (U) 23/59, paragraph 12. The difficulty however lies in making a comparison between such very different elements. In deciding the question of just cause it is essential to remember throughout that the question is the one arising on the very words of the statute, and it is not permissible to substitute any other test. Further, ' It is not practicable to lay down any hard-and-fast rule to guide the Statutory Authorities as to the precise circumstances in which just cause or no just cause for leaving is shown. Each case must depend upon its own particular circumstances ' (Decision R (U) 14/52, paragraph 5). Nor should the various elements in the case be considered in watertight compartments. It is necessary to look at the whole circumstances at the relevant time in order to determine whether in a fair sense it can be said that he did not leave without just cause. It may however be helpful to draw attention to certain types of case which occur frequently, in order to give guidance as to the way in which the Commissioner has regarded these problems." [43]

---

[39] R (U) 7/57.
[40] R (U) 24/56.
[41] R (U) 24/55.
[42] *i.e.* s. 13 (2) of the National Insurance Act 1946, now s. 20 (1) (*a*) of the Social Security Act 1975.
[43] R (U) 20/64.

646 It is of interest to notice that in decisions on the question both of what is misconduct and whether the worker left his job without just cause, social security law acts in a way to encourage compliance with standards established by collective bargaining. Thus, where there is a procedure established for the settlement of grievances or where there is a trade union, if a worker dissatisfied with his conditions leaves his job without having resorted to the grievance procedure or sought the assistance of his trade union he will usually be regarded as having left his job without just cause. Similarly, a worker who is dismissed for having acted in a manner inconsistent with some collective agreement will normally be regarded as having lost his job due to his misconduct.

Effect of misconduct, etc.

647 The words of section 22 (2) of the National Insurance Act 1965 are quite clear that a person who leaves his job without just cause or who loses his job through his misconduct shall be disqualified from receiving unemployment benefit " for such period not exceeding six weeks " as may be determined by the National Insurance authorities. This would appear to give a discretion to fine the worker, as it were, up to a maximum of six weeks' benefit. This is not, however, the interpretation placed upon it by the National Insurance Commissioners in the past. They now take a common sense view that there is to be no automatic imposition of the maximum period of disqualification. The old view was that the standard penalty should in all cases be disqualification for six weeks, but exceptionally it could be reduced.[44]

Effect of misconduct on supplementary benefit [45]

648 Any person who is disqualified from receiving unemployment benefit under the Social Security Act 1975, s. 20 (1) (a) (i.e., disqualification by reference to conduct resulting in unemployment or conducive to its continuance),[46] is also subject to a 40 per cent. deduction from the amount of supplementary benefit receivable by him.[47] This 40 per cent. deduction relates to the amount of supplementary benefit payable in respect of the claimant and his wife and does not extend to benefit payable in respect of children or to rent allowance. It is moreover subject to a maximum of the allowance payable to a single householder.

Trade disputes: unemployment benefit

649 The Social Security Act 1975, s. 19 provides :

> " A person who has lost employment as an employed earner by reason of a stoppage of work which was due to a trade dispute at his place of employment shall be disqualified for receiving unemployment benefit so long as the stoppage of work continues, except in a

---

[44] Contrast R (U) 17/54 with R (U) 8/74.

[45] Supplementary Benefit Act 1966 which is the basic Act governing supplementary benefits provides in s. 40 (1), as amended, that it " may be cited as the Ministry of Social Security Act 1966 or as the Supplementary Benefit Act 1966."

[46] See above, paras. 645–647.

[47] Social Security Act 1971, s. 1 (2). This applies only where the person concerned has been given supplementary benefit conditional on his being registered for employment in accordance with the Supplementary Benefit Act 1966, s. 11.

case where, during the stoppage of work, he has become bona fide employed elsewhere in the occupation which he usually follows or has become regularly engaged in some other occupation; but this sub-section does not apply in the case of a person who proves—(a) that he is not participating in or directly interested in the trade dispute which caused the stoppage of work; . . .

" (2) . . . (b) ' trade dispute ' means any dispute between employers and employees or between employees and employees which is con-nected with the employment or non-employment or the terms of employment or the conditions of employment of any persons, whether employees in the employment of the employer with whom the dispute arises or not." [48]

650   The most important aspect of this disqualification is that it is not simply a disqualification of strikers (indeed, it applies equally to locked-out workers) but applies also to people who have nothing whatever to do with the initiation or continuation of the trade dispute, indeed it may apply to people who vehemently oppose the trade dispute and consequent stoppage. Its effect in many cases is to embitter relations between different groups of workers and to build up a pressure for a return to work. The way the Commissioners see the objective of this provision is naïvely narrow, although their interpretation of the provisions is often extra-ordinarily wide.[49] " The manifest object of the subsection (*i.e.*, s. 19) is to prevent the insurance fund from being used for financing employees during strikes or lock-outs." [50]

Place of employment

651   The subsection provides that the disqualification shall apply only to those who are out of work if the trade dispute takes place at their place of employment. Place of employment is defined as follows:

" The expression ' place of employment ' in relation to any person, means the factory, workshop, farm or other premises or place at which he was employed, so, however, that, where separate branches of work which are commonly carried on as separate businesses in separate premises or at separate places are in any case carried on in separate departments on the same premises or at the same place, each of those departments shall for the purposes of this paragraph be deemed to be a separate factory or workshop or farm or separate premises or a separate place, as the case may be."

Stoppage

652   The duration of a stoppage sometimes gives rise to difficulty in drawing the line. Normally a stoppage comes to an end when work has com-menced again and is being carried on in the normal way, without let or hindrance. After a trade dispute which occurred in a ship repairing yard was settled by agreement, it was held that where the workers' return to

---

[48] It is noteworthy that this definition, similar to that in the now repealed Trade Disputes Act 1906, s. 5, is different from the definition of " trade dispute " in T.U.L.R.A., s. 29 (1).
[49] See below.
[50] R (U) 17/52.

work was gradual owing to lack of work the stoppage had lasted until a substantial number of them were back at work.[51]

Twelve-day rule

653   By a piece of the purest judicial legislation the National Insurance Commissioners have given a special application in the case of casual workers to the concept of being out of work by reason of a stoppage due to a trade dispute. The principle runs as follows: "an employee whose employment is indefinitely suspended within twelve working days of a stoppage of work at the premises at which the employee habitually seeks work must prima facie be presumed to have lost employment by reason of the stoppage." [52]

A claimant who left work voluntarily without giving reasons four days before a strike was presumed under this rule to have left work because he anticipated the stoppage, and had therefore lost his employment as a result of the stoppage.[53]

Persons exempted from disqualification

654   The following persons prima facie covered by the disqualification may escape from such disqualification: (i) anyone who since the stoppage of work has bona fide obtained a new job, which job he has lost thereby becoming unemployed for a reason other than the original stoppage; or (ii) persons who can show that they:

(a) *are not participating in the trade dispute*

Participating is given a wide connotation. If an employee would prefer to work but does not like to pass the pickets or obeys a request not to work he is participating in the trade dispute. If he tries to go to work but is prevented by the pickets using force against him he is still regarded as participating in the dispute, as the main dispute is regarded as being extended to include the dispute between him and the pickets.[54] and

(b) *Are not directly interested in the trade dispute*

655   This provision has been interpreted as though the word *directly* was omitted. In one case a worker was held to have a direct interest in a dispute as to whether his company's superannuation scheme should be made voluntary. He intended to contribute to the scheme whether it was voluntary or not. He was *directly* interested. "The imposition of an additional obligation to pay money would clearly, in my opinion, constitute a matter of 'interest' to those upon whom the obligation was imposed; and equally, as it seems to me, the removal of an obligation to pay money must constitute a matter of 'interest' to those relieved of the obligation." [55]

Trade disputes and supplementary benefit

656   The disqualification in respect of involvement in trade disputes in the

---

[51] R (U) 25/57.
[52] R (U) 20/57.
[53] R (U) 25/57.
[54] R (U) 2/53.
[55] R (U) 17/61.

Supplementary Benefit Act 1966 [56] " corresponds closely " [57] to the disqualification from unemployment benefit under the Social Security Act 1975.[58] However, this does not of course prevent a disqualified worker's dependants receiving supplementary benefit. In assessing the amount of supplementary benefit payable in respect of a disqualified worker's dependants, account must be taken of any amount in excess of £1 received by the worker by way of income tax refunds,[59] strike pay from his union, and various other types of income.[60] This will not infrequently have the effect of bringing the total income of disqualified workers and their families well below the poverty line. Nor will it prevent the worker concerned from receiving supplementary benefit if it is urgently required.[61] In this case " any benefit that is paid is limited to what is strictly necessary to meet urgent requirements." [62]

Single workers

657   The Supplementary Benefits Commission has made it clear in a pamphlet that it will only rarely give single workers assistance on grounds of urgency. The Commission has stated as follows [63]

" The law specifically excludes anyone who is involved in a trade dispute from receiving any supplementary benefit for his own requirements. It follows that a single man or woman cannot normally get help. The Supplementary Benefits Commission may only exercise their discretion to help a single striker if they are satisfied that he is in ' urgent need ' and, in deciding whether there is urgent need, they will take account both of personal circumstances at the time and of all income received since the beginning of the dispute.

As to income, the Commission will expect a single striker to make the total amount he gets from any of the following sources last at the rate of not more than £6·50 [64] a week during the dispute—

final wages before the dispute;
any subsequent wages in hand;
any other income, including PAYE refunds or strike pay.

He cannot expect to get any help if he spends his money without regard to this advice.

As to personal circumstances, the Commission will not regard a single striker as in urgent need if he has parents or relatives to whom he could reasonably look for temporary help. He will not be regarded as in urgent need unless:

he is in lodgings (except lodgings with relatives) or a hostel, and the Commission are satisfied that he must have help to avoid being turned out; *or*

---

[56] s. 10.
[57] *Supplementary Benefits Handbook* (4th ed., H.M.S.O., 1974), para. 167.
[58] See above.
[59] In accordance with Income and Corporation Taxes Act 1970, s. 204 (" Pay as you earn ").
[60] Social Security Act 1971, s. 1 (4).
[61] Supplementary Benefit Act 1966, s. 12.
[62] *Supplementary Benefits Handbook*, para. 168.
[63] *Supplementary Benefits and Trade Disputes* (H.M.S.O.).
[64] Figures relate to November 1974.

he lives by himself in privately owned accommodation and there is nobody to whom he can turn for help; *or*

he is living with parents or other relatives, and they are themselves receiving supplementary benefit, or the Commission are satisfied that they cannot help the striker temporarily, *e.g.* because their own income is very near the supplementary benefit level.

If the striker proves he is in 'urgent need,' it will be for the Commission to decide in the light of his circumstances how much benefit he needs. The maximum they will normally allow would be the amount necessary to bring any other income and resources he has up to £5." [64]

Few topics seem to arouse more ire than the issue of payment of any form of social security benefit to workers disqualified under the trade dispute disqualification. It must be insisted that the disqualification is not of *strikers*; it is of any one out of work due to a stoppage caused by a trade dispute at their place of work, which may be a lock-out, in which they are either participating or directly interested. This latter category catches a lot of people who are in no way engaged in industrial action; many of them who will not even belong to the unions involved in the action.

Unemployment benefit: short time and lay-off [65]

658   Where an employee is laid off in accordance with a term in his contract, with the practical effect that his contract is suspended, the employee may be qualified to receive unemployment benefit. He will not be entitled to receive unemployment benefit until the period of suspension has lasted for more than twelve days; he can then receive unemployment benefit in respect of the whole period of suspension. [66] No earnings related supplement is payable in respect of the first six days of suspension. In respect of short time the position is somewhat complicated. Unemployment benefit is not paid in respect of an isolated day's unemployment. Benefit is only payable if two or more days of unemployment occur within a period of six consecutive days (not normally counting Sundays)—this is known as the " 2-in-6 " rule. The effect of this is that in the case of a worker normally working a five-day week, if in one week he does not work on Friday and then the next week on Monday, then the Mondays and Fridays can be linked under the " 2-in-6 " rule and be classed as a period of unemployment in respect of which benefit may be payable. [67] Whether benefit is in fact paid will depend also on whether there is some form of guaranteed week agreement in operation.

" Broadly speaking for the purposes of the unemployment regulations they fall into two main categories. The first category is known as the 'wages' type of agreement which guarantees the worker a

---

[65] See, generally, A. I. Ogus (1975) 4 I.L.J. 12 and H. Calvert (1974) 27 C.L.P. 146.
[66] Except, of course, for first three days.
[67] Saturday does not count as a day of unemployment in the case of a five-day week worker unless he is also unemployed on the other five days. A short-time worker who normally works a five-day week, on the other hand, who did not work every Friday would not qualify under the " 2-in-6 " rule because no two Fridays could be linked together to form two days in six consecutive working days. If he normally worked a six-day week he could invoke the " 2-in-6 " rule.

257

minimum wage. Workers covered by this type of agreement *cannot* get unemployment benefit when on short time because the guaranteed wage is assumed to be a payment made in respect of the whole week, and the workers concerned are not therefore deemed to be 'unemployed' on their idle days. The second type of agreement is known as the 'employment' type of agreement which may guarantee employment for a specified number of days in the week; many workers covered by this type of agreement have been able to claim benefit while on short time because their wages have not been held to be payments in respect of the whole week, though the right to benefit is not by any means granted automatically; it depends on the exact wording of the agreement which might debar the right to benefit on some other ground." [68]

[The next paragraph is 661.]

---

[68] Labour Research Department, *A Guide to Unemployment Benefit* (London, 1958), pp. 14–15. See also R (U) 21/56.

Part Four

INTERNATIONAL ASPECTS

CHAPTER 20

INTERNATIONAL LABOUR STANDARDS

General

661 It is no longer possible to give either a complete, or even illuminating, picture of any branch of British labour law without giving some consideration to international labour standards. There are at least three reasons for this. First of all, many statutory provisions in British law today have been adopted, not always explicitly,[1] for the purpose of giving effect to standards embodied in international instruments to which Britain is a party.[2] The latest example of this is the Employment Protection Act 1975, many of whose most important provisions are based in part at least upon international labour standards agreed to by British Governments in the past.[3] Secondly, Britain has agreed to accept a number of labour standards embodied in international treaties which have not yet been adopted in British law or practice. Some consideration of these international treaties and other international instruments enables us to gain an insight into the direction in which British law may move at some time in the future. This is also true of some international treaties to which Britain is not a party (because her current standards in certain areas lag behind the standards already achieved in some advanced industrial countries[4]). Thirdly, some international treaties to which the United Kingdom is a party have their own machinery for enforcement, sometimes accessible even to an individual, with the result that sometimes, after an individual worker has attempted unsuccessfully to enlist the aid of an English court in protecting him in the exercise of some right, he may be able to invoke a remedy available to him on the international plane. It is important not to exaggerate the significance of the machinery available for the protection of employees' rights on the international plane. It is an equal error to ignore altogether the availability of such machinery in certain limited cases. There are five main areas which it is relevant for us to consider in this context.[5] They are: (1) the European Convention on Human Rights and Fundamental Freedoms; (2) the European Social Charter; (3) a number of documents drawn up under the auspices of the United Nations; (4) the Conventions and Recommendations of the International Labour Organisation, and (5) the Rome Treaty establishing the European Economic Community.[6]

---

[1] e.g. the Employment of Women, Young Persons, and Children Act 1920; the Hours of Employment (Conventions) Act 1936; T.U.L.R.A. 1974, Sched. 1, Pt. II (concept of unfair dismissal, see para. 542, above) and Equal Pay Act 1970 (see para. 412, above).

[2] See Johnston, " The Influence of International Labour Standards on Legislation and Practice in the U.K." (1968) 97 Int.Lab.Rev., pp. 465–488.

[3] e.g. the provisions on maternity pay, dismissal of pregnant women, and the right to return to work are based on the European Social Charter, Art. 8; the provisions on anti-union discrimination are based on the International Labour Convention No. 98 (the Right to Organise and Bargain Collectively Convention); the improved provisions on unfair dismissal are based on the International Labour Recommendation 119 of 1963, and the improved periods of notice are due to the European Social Charter, Art. 4 (4).

[4] e.g. ILO Convention, No. 102: Social Security (Minimum Standards), 1952.

[5] We are attempting only to give a very superficial overall view of relevant international labour standards; we make no attempt to be comprehensive.

[6] The texts of most of the international agreements referred to in this chapter can be found in Brownlie, Basic Documents on Human Rights (Oxford, 1971).

European Convention on Human Rights and Fundamental Freedoms

662 This Convention ratified by the United Kingdom is primarily concerned with the protection of political, as opposed to social, rights, being based on the Universal Declaration of Human Rights approved by the General Assembly of the United Nations, December 1948. However, some provisions are of relevance to us. Article 4 (2) outlaws the performance of "forced or compulsory labour." Article 8 guarantees that "Everyone has the right to respect for his private and family life, his home and his correspondence." Article 10 guarantees the right to freedom of expression. Article 11 says "Everyone has the right to freedom of peaceful assembly and to freedom of association with others, including the right to form and join trade unions for the protection of his interests." Certain searches of employees by employers might conflict with Article 8. English law on picketing almost certainly conflicts with the combined effect of Articles 10 and 11.

663 Any individual in this country who feels a right, given him by the European Convention, has been denied him must first of all utilise such machinery as English law has established in an effort to obtain a remedy. If English law fails to give him adequate protection he can petition the European Commission on Human Rights at Strasbourg. The Commission, which is not a court, must seek to obtain a friendly settlement of the complaint. If the Commission fails, then the complaint can be referred to the European Court of Human Rights, which has power to make a decision binding upon the United Kingdom. Alternatively, another state which is also a party to the Convention can complain to the European Court that Britain is not complying with its obligations under the Convention.

664 Although no British trade unions or workers have yet attempted to invoke the provisions of the Convention in the field of labour relations, three complaints have been unsuccessfully made to the Commission alleging violations of Article 11 by Sweden and Belgium. In *National Union of Belgian Police* v. *Belgium*[7] a police trade union alleged that the Belgian Government was violating Article 11 by refusing to consult over terms and conditions of employment with that particular trade union. The Belgian Government consulted other trade unions, which in its opinion were the most representative trade unions. In *Schmidt*[8] *and Dahlstrom* v. *Sweden*[9] the complainants were officials of two public service trade unions which had given strike notice to the Swedish Government who retaliated by locking employees out. Eventually a settlement was reached by negotiation with the largest trade unions, excluding the two trade unions to which the complainants belonged. A new scale of wages was agreed to, with retroactive effect, but the Government refused to pay the new scale retroactively to trade union officials who were members of trade unions who had taken industrial action, including the two complainants, although neither of them had personally gone on strike. The complainants alleged that this was a violation of their industrial rights and was discrimination against them on the ground of their trade union membership. In *Swedish Engine Drivers*

---

[7] Case No. 4462/70.
[8] Professor Folke Schmidt is the leading academic labour lawyer in Sweden.
[9] Case No. 5589/72.

Union v. *Sweden* [10] the complainant was a small trade union which was refused the right to bargain over its members' terms and conditions of employment because of an official policy of only entering into general agreements with the major Swedish trade union federations. The Commission in rejecting the complaints, in so far as Article 11 was involved did so by adopting a very narrow view of the rights conferred, and in so far as Article 14, which guarantees a right not to be discriminated against was invoked, the Commission felt that the discriminatory refusal to deal with small trade unions was based upon fair and reasonable considerations.

665   The Court of Human Rights has upheld the Commission's rejection of all three complaints. In the *National Union of Belgian Police* case [11] the court said:

> " The court notes that while Article 11 (1) presents trade union freedom as one form or a special aspect of freedom of association, the Article does not guarantee any particular treatment of trade unions, or their members, by the State, such as the right to be consulted by it. Not only is this latter right not mentioned in Article 11 (1), but neither can it be said that all the Contracting States in general incorporate it in their national law or practice, or that it is indispensable for the effective enjoyment of trade union freedom. It is thus not an element necessarily inherent in a right guaranteed by the Convention. . . .
>
> . . . In the opinion of the court . . . the members of a trade union have a right, in order to protect their interests, that the trade union should be heard. Article 11 (1) certainly leaves each State a free choice of the means to be used towards this end. While consultation is one of these means, there are others. What the Convention requires is that under national law trade unions should be enabled, in conditions not at variance with Article 11, to strive for the protection of their members' interests.
>
> No one disputes the fact that the applicant union can engage in various kinds of activity *vis-à-vis* the Government. It is open to it, for instance, to present claims and to make representations for the protection of the interests of its members or certain of them. Nor does the applicant union in any way allege that the steps it takes are ignored by the Government. In these circumstances, the fact alone that the Minister of the Interior does not consult the applicant under the Act of July 27, 1961, does not constitute a breach of Article 11 (1) considered on its own." [12]

European Social Charter

666   The European Social Charter is more relevant to our main theme than the European Convention. The Charter came into force between a number

---

[10] Case No. 5614/72. A fourth complaint, *Swedish Airline Pilots* v. *Sweden* (case No. 5614/72), essentially based on the same facts as the Swedish Engine Drivers' Union complaint, was declared inadmissible on technical grounds.

[11] European Court of Human Rights, *National Union of Belgian Police Case: Judgment,* (Strasbourg, October 27, 1975).

[12] *Judgment,* paras. 38–40.

of member states of the Council of Europe [13] including the United Kingdom in 1965. Part 1 contains a number of objectives which member states agree to accept, such as the right of workers to " safe and healthy working conditions." Of more direct application are the rights embodied in Part 2.[14] These include a wide range of obligations on the member states to provide proper standards for those who work. Two examples must suffice, taken from the detailed provisions of the Charter.

Article 8

667   With a view to ensuring the effective exercise of the right of employed women to protection, the Contracting Parties undertake:

" (1) to provide either by paid leave, by adequate social security benefits or by benefits from public social funds for women to take leave before and after childbirth up to a total of at least twelve weeks;

(2) to consider it as unlawful for an employer to give a woman notice of dismissal during her absence on maternity leave or to give her notice of dismissal at such a time that the notice would expire during such absence;

(3) to provide that mothers who are nursing their infants shall be entitled to sufficient time off for this purpose;

(4) (a) to regulate the employment of women workers on night work in industrial employment;

(b) to prohibit the employment of women workers in underground mining, and, as appropriate, on all other work which is unsuitable for them by reason of its dangerous, unhealthy, or arduous nature." [15]

Article 10

668   With a view to ensuring the effective exercise of the right to vocational training, the Contracting Parties undertake:

" (1) to provide or promote, as necessary, the technical and vocational training of all persons, including the handicapped, in consultation with employers' and workers' organisations, and to grant facilities for access to higher technical and university education, based solely on individual aptitude;

(2) to provide or promote a system of apprenticeship and other systematic arrangements for training young boys and girls in their various employments;

(3) to provide or promote, as necessary:

(a) adequate and readily available training facilities for adult workers;

---

[13] The Social Charter is only one of a series of conventions drafted or in process of being drafted under the auspices of the Council of Europe relating to the conditions of workers. The Charter is the most important of these.

[14] States which become party to the Charter are free to choose to be bound by only 10 Articles (or 45 numbered paragraphs) out of the total of 19 Articles in Part II. A state need not accept the whole of Part II. The United Kingdom has accepted the following Articles in Part II: 1, 2 (not para. 1), 3, 4 (not para. 3), 5, 6, 7 (not paras. 1, 4 and 7), 8 (not paras. 2 and 3), 9, 10, 11, 12 (not para. 1), 13, 14, 15, 16, 17, 18 and 19.

[15] Note that the United Kingdom has not accepted paras. 2 and 3.

     (b) special facilities for the re-training of adult workers needed as a result of technological development or new trends in employment;

  (4) to encourage the full utilisation of the facilities provided by appropriate measures such as

     (a) reducing or abolishing any fees or charges;

     (b) granting financial assistance in appropriate cases;

     (c) including in the normal working hours time spent on supplementary training taken by the worker, at the request of his employer, during employment;

     (d) ensuring, through adequate supervision, in consultation with the employers' and workers' organisations, the efficiency of apprenticeship and other training arrangements for young workers, and the adequate protection of young workers generally."

669   There is no machinery for enforcement of the Charter open to individuals. The basic element in the enforcement machinery is an examination every two years of the law and practice of the states who are parties to the Charter, to determine how far such states are fulfilling their obligations under the Charter. The examination is conducted by an independent committee of experts based upon reports from the governments of the states concerned: these reports are sent for comment to the employers' organisations and trade unions in the states concerned. The committee draws up a report which is sent to the organs of the Council of Europe. The threat of publicity being given to a state's being in breach of its obligations is to be seen as the main sanction for non-compliance with the Charter. At the end of 1969 the first report of the Committee of Experts was published.[16] The Committee found Britain to be in breach of the following obligations (as at December 31, 1967)[17]:

670   (a) Article 1, para. 2. The right of the worker to earn his living freely in an occupation freely entered upon. The violation consisted in the fact that discrimination based on sex still existed in Britain. The Equal Pay Act 1970[18] and Sex Discrimination Act 1975 should go some way towards remedying this.

671   (b) Article 10, para. 3. Right to vocational training and retraining of adult workers.[19] The Committee said: "The United Kingdom does not fulfil the undertaking deriving from the provision since the facilities supplied for the vocational training and retraining of adults are still too modest in relation to the size of the population."[20]

672   (c) Article 18, paras. 1, 2 and 3. The right of migrant workers moving between states party to the Charter to engage in gainful occupation in the territory of other contracting parties. The Committee said: "The

---

[16] *Council of Europe, Committee of Independent Experts on the European Social Charter: Conclusions* (Strasbourg, 1969/70) (hereafter referred to as *Conclusions*).

[17] The Report covers only the first two years of the Charter's operation, up to December 31, 1967. What the Committee said therefore relates only to the position as it existed on that date. Since then there may have been changes which would now lead the Committee to different conclusions.

[18] See above, Chap. 11.

[19] *Ibid.*

[20] *Conclusions*, p. 139.

United Kingdom has not given proof in the existing regulations in this field [the immigration of workers] that there has been any trend towards the liberalisation and simplification of formalities . . ." [21]

This comment is particularly significant because the obligation in these Articles of the Charter designed to encourage free movement of workers between states parties to the Social Charter is not dissimilar to the obligation which arises in case of member states of the European Economic Community in the field of free movement of labour.[22]

673   (d) Article 19, para. 3. Co-operation between social services in emigration and immigration countries parties to the Charter. The Committee said that the United Kingdom has not done enough to promote co-operation between the social services of the different member states. This again is something which membership of the EEC would render necessary.

674   (e) Article 19, para. 2. Reunion of families of migrant workers. The Committee said:

" British [immigration] regulations cannot be regarded as compatible with the Charter so far as the following two points are concerned:
(a) that foreigners employed for domestic work are not entitled to have their wives and children join them;
(b) that permission to stay in the country may be refused in the case of a child of a migrant worker suffering from a disability requiring special care and treatment if the financial position of the parents is such as to render necessary recourse to a public institution for the care and treatment in question." [23]

675   It is worth adding also that the conclusion of the Committee of Experts, that the Republic of Ireland was in breach of its obligation [24] (an obligation which the United Kingdom has also accepted) to recognise a right to strike because the Irish protective legislation which has the effect of giving such a right in the Irish Republic does not apply to civil servants or workers who are employed under contracts other than contracts of employment meant that the United Kingdom was also in breach of this obligation. The rules governing British civil servants expressly stated that strikes by civil servants are disciplinary offences.[25]

In 1971 a second report of the Committee of Experts was published.[26] This covered the period up to December 31, 1969. This confirmed that the United Kingdom continued to be in breach of its obligations; only in respect of Article 17 (protection of mothers and children) had there been some progress. The Committee said that there were still categories of workers " for whom the periods of notice are certainly not reasonable (*e.g.,* one week for workers with nearly two years' seniority; two weeks if they have up to five years' seniority . . ." [27] (Article 4 (4) requires that every employee shall receive reasonable periods of notice for termination of

---

[21] *Ibid.*
[22] See below.
[23] *Conclusions*, p. 138.
[24] Art. 6, para. 4; *Conclusions*, p. 243.
[25] Estacode, N. 32 in force until 1976 said specifically that striking by a civil servant was a disciplinary offence.
[26] *Council of Europe, Committee of Independent Experts on the European Social Charter: Conclusions II* (Strasbourg, 1971).
[27] *Ibid.* p. 21.

employment.) The Committee also felt reservations as to the adequacy of provision for maternity leave in Britain and as to the protection of wages against deductions.

676   In 1973 the third report of the Committee of Experts was published.[28] Progress was reported in that the Committee concluded that Britain had fulfilled its obligations under Article 10, para. 3 (right to vocational training). However it is still found to be in breach of a number of its obligations:

677   (a) Article 1, para. 2. *Prohibition of forced or compulsory labour.* The Merchant Shipping Act 1970 in permitting fines for breach of a contract of employment, even when not endangering life, limb or property, and the forced return of deserting seamen to the ship from which they had deserted also involved a violation of this Article.

678   (b) Article 4, para. 4. *Reasonable periods of notice.* Despite some improvement in Great Britain the fact that a worker with nearly two years' service was entitled as a minimum to only one week's notice involved a violation.[29] The position in Northern Ireland was found to be even less satisfactory.

679   (c) Article 4, para. 5. *Limitation of deductions from wages.* The protection given by the Truck Acts was confined to workers engaged in manual labour; the absence of similar protection for non-manual workers involved a violation of the Charter. The Committee reported:

> " In its third report the United Kingdom Government explained that there had been no change in the situation and that *it had no intention of altering it since no deductions were in fact made from non-manual workers' wages and that their interests were well protected by the practice and activities of a powerful workers' association. In the light of the imprecise nature of this statement the Committee had to uphold its previous decision, while hoping for additional information in the fourth British report.*" [30]

680   (d) Article 5. *The right to organise.* Restrictions on the right of the police to organise was a violation of the Charter.[31]

681   (e) Article 6, para. 4. *Right to strike.* The Committee being misled into believing that the Industrial Relations Act 1971 meant that " in case of strike or lock-out the maintenance of contracts of employment was now formally guaranteed " [32] said that there was compliance with the Charter in Great Britain, although this right continued to be violated in Northern Ireland and the Isle of Man, to which the 1971 Act had no application.

682   (f) Article 8, para. 1. *Maternity leave.* The Committee solemnly recorded the following:

> " While drawing attention to the affirmation by the third British

---

[28] *Council of Europe, Committee of Independent Experts on the European Social Charter: Conclusions III* (Strasbourg, 1973).

[29] This still remains true under the Contracts of Employment Act 1972, after its amendment by the Employment Protection Act 1975.

[30] Italics added.

[31] Police Act 1964, s. 44.

[32] *Cf.* P. O'Higgins, " The Right to Strike—Some International Reflections," in J. R. Carby-Hall (ed.), *Studies in Labour Law* (Bradford, 1976), pp. 110–118.

report that *the right of all women workers to* 12 *weeks' maternity leave was firmly established in the United Kingdom*,[33] the Committee felt that, in any event, a right of such fundamental importance required to be guaranteed by legislation. Accordingly, the Committee found that the United Kingdom was still not fulfilling in all respects its undertakings under this provision of the Charter . . ."

The Committee reiterated its finding of breach by the United Kingdom of Articles 18 and 19 in its first Report.[34] They also found that in the Isle of Man there were breaches of Article 13, para. 1 (social and medical assistance for those in need) and of Article 17 (social and economic protection of mothers and children). They found that the latter article was also violated in Northern Ireland.

United Nations Covenant on Economic, Social and Cultural Rights [35]

683   This Covenant (1966) embodies a number of social rights very similar to those in the European Social Charter, including the right to strike, and the right to work, " which includes the right of everyone to the opportunity to gain his living by work which he freely chooses or accepts." Such enforcement machinery as envisaged follows the pattern adopted under the Social Charter, rather than giving a right to an individual to make an individual complaint as is the case with the European Convention on Human Rights. The Covenant, which has been ratified by the United Kingdom, is now in force, 10 years after it was first opened for ratification.

International Labour Organisation

684   The International Labour Organisation, set up in 1919, has produced over the years a very large number of Conventions and Recommendations, embodying standards covering most aspects of the employment relationship. There is no obligation upon any member state, of which the United Kingdom is one, to adopt any particular Convention or Recommendation produced by the ILO, but there is a gentle pressure put upon member states to give effect to such instruments. If a state accepts a Convention by ratifying it, that state is then under a legal obligation to bring its law or practice [36] into line with the terms of the Convention. In the case of a Recommendation this merely sets a desirable standard to be achieved and is not open for ratification in the same way as a Convention. In relation both to unratified Conventions and Recommendations member states send reports to the International Labour Office in Geneva, which are examined and commented upon by a committee of experts. In the case of ratified Conventions there are a number of means of enforcement, including

---

[33] Italics added. At the period to which the British Government's statement referred there was no legal right to maternity pay and no right to return. Even under the Employment Protection Act there will be a right to only six weeks' maternity pay, and that only in 1977.

[34] See paras. 672 to 674 above.

[35] This is only one of many relevant United Nations instruments. Others include the Universal Declaration on Human Rights (1948); the UN Covenant on Civil and Political Rights (1966); the UN Convention on the Elimination of all Forms of Racial Discrimination (1966); and the Declaration on Elimination of Discrimination against Women (1967).

[36] ILO Conventions do not necessarily require legislation. Often the obligations are satisfied if, as a result of collective bargaining in the state concerned, the standards embodied in the Convention have been attained in practice.

scrutiny by a Committee of Experts. In the case of Convention No. 87 on Freedom of Association (1948), Convention No. 98 on the Right to Organise and Collective Bargaining (1949) and Convention No. 135 Concerning Protection and Facilities to be Afforded to Workers' Representatives in the Undertaking (1972) there is special enforcement machinery in the form of the ILO Governing Body's Committee of Freedom of Association, which can interpret the provisions of these three conventions if a complaint is received from a workers' organisation that in a state which has ratified these conventions there has been an interference with the right of workers to join trade unions, to participate in collective bargaining or to function effectively as workplace representatives. The Conventions are designed to protect workers against interferences with these rights by governments or by employers. In the case of other Conventions which have been ratified by states there is provision for the receipt of complaints from organisations of employers or workers or from states.

European Economic Community [37]

685 The Rome Treaty,[38] the Constitution of the European Economic Community, contains a number of provisions relevant to the employment relationship. Article 48 provides for the freedom of movement within the Community for workers [39] belonging to Community countries.[40] This includes the right to enter a member country for the purpose of looking for work, the right not to be discriminated against in selection for employment on the grounds of nationality, the right of workers to settle with their families in any member state where employment has been found; the right to participate on equal terms with local workers in representative bodies in the workplace; the right to be governed by the same tax and social security rules as local workers; the right to be joined without formality by their family and dependants, and the right to have equal access to housing; the right in case of temporary unemployment to remain in the country where their last employment was for a year. Article 49, *inter alia,* provides for close collaboration between the employment services of the member countries. Article 51 protects the right to social security benefit of migrant workers by providing for the accumulation of qualifying periods where a worker has paid contributions in more than one state. Article 117 provides for the harmonisation of social security systems, but owing to the infinite variety and complexity of the different systems little progress has been made or is likely to be made in the foreseeable future. Article 118 provides, *inter alia,* that it is an aim of the Community to produce close collaboration between member states in the social field, particularly in matters relating to " employment, labour law and working conditions, basic and advanced vocational training, social security, protection against occupational accidents and diseases, occupational hygiene,

---

[37] See B. A. Hepple, " The Effect of Community Law on Employment Rights " (1975) 1 *Poly Law Review,* 50–57, on which this section is based.

[38] The best account of this whole area is Lyon-Caen, *Droit Social Européen* (Paris, 3me ed., 1974).

[39] Workers in this context means primarily persons employed under a contract of employment. Article 52 of the Rome Treaty provides for the freedom of self-employed persons to move freely, and to take up their occupations in the territory of member states.

[40] Migrant workers from non-member states are not entitled to the same protection as workers from EEC countries.

the law of trade unions and collective bargaining between workers and employers."

Since in so many of these areas Britain is the odd man out, it is likely that British membership of the EEC will involve her moving more into line with EEC practice.

686 Perhaps the most striking contrast between the position in many EEC countries and the United Kingdom is that there is a wider and higher floor of basic rights than is often the case in Britain. There is also much greater legal provision for account to be taken of the workers' opinions inside the enterprise. Without prejudice to the desirability or not of continued membership on other grounds, membership must add to the pressure which already exists inside Britain for a wider range of minimum labour standards to be embodied in British Labour law than is the case at present.

Equal pay

Article 119 provides that member states are to apply the principles of "equal remuneration for the same work as between male and female workers." [41]

Social Action Programme

The Commission and other organs of the Communities have given their approval to a number of measures in the field of labour relations, most but not all of which, were first enunciated in the *Social Action Programme* drawn up by the Commission in October 1973.[42] Principal amongst these are an agreement, in the form of a Recommendation to member states to adopt the principle of a normal working week of forty hours, and four calendar weeks to be introduced as a minimum for paid annual holidays by December 31, 1978. In addition, a Directive on mass dismissals was adopted by the Council of Ministers on February 17, 1975.[43] This Directive had been delayed in order to allow the United Kingdom time to consider its position in relation to the reform of the law of dismissal.

Employment Protection Act and Collective Redundancies Directive

687 The provisions of sections 99 to 107 of the Employment Protection Act 1975, are intended to give effect to the Directive on Collective Redundancies. It is interesting to inquire into the question, how far do the provisions of the Act fall short of the requirements of the Directive? [44] First of all there is the question of the coverage of the two instruments. The Directive is intended to lay down certain standards and procedures to be applied by employers in cases of " collective redundancies " which are defined (Art. 1) as " dismissals effected by an employer for one or more reasons not related to the individual workers concerned." This is a much broader concept than the one used in the Employment Protection Act, which, while it refers to redundancies, intends them to mean redundancies as

---

[41] For a discussion of Art. 119, see Chap. 11.

[42] For a comprehensive, but short, account of the *Social Action Programme*, as well as the draft directives referred to in this paragraph, see Dewi-Davies Jones, *Europe: Social Action Programme* (London, 1974).

[43] O.J. 1975, L48/29.

[44] See M. Freedland, " Employment Protection: Redundancy Procedures and the EEC " (1976) 5 I.L.J. 24–34.

defined in the Redundancy Payments Act 1965, s. 1, where " redundancy " is restricted to a situation where there is a cessation or reduction of business or a decline in demand for work of a particular kind. It is easy enough to give an example of a situation which would be covered by the Directive, but which is not covered by the provisions of the Employment Protection Act. In *Chapman and Others* v. *Goonvean and Rostowrack China Clay Co. Ltd.*[45] it was held that workers who lost employment, when their employer withdrew a free bus which had taken them to and from their work, because the men were unable, or were unwilling, to make arrangements at their own expense to travel a considerable distance to work. The employer's reason for withdrawing the bus was economic. The men concerned were held not to have lost their employment due to redundancy. In *Johnson* v. *Nottinghamshire Combined Police Authority*[46] two clerks lost their employment because they were unable to continue to do the same number of hours' work per week when their employer radically altered the working arrangements by introducing an alternating shift system. Again it was held that this was not a redundancy situation. In both these kinds of cases the provisions of the Employment Protection Act would have no application, although clearly dismissal for these kinds of reasons are within the coverage of the Directive.

688 Article 2 of the Directive requires the employer to consult workers' representatives " with a view to reaching agreement." This may involve a duty close to the North American duty of bargaining in good faith. The equivalent provisions in the Employment Protection Act do not require the employer to consult with the aim of reaching agreement. It is sufficient that he should consider representations made to him on behalf of the workers and state why he chooses to reject any of these representations. Furthermore, Article 2 of the Directive indicates that consultations are to cover " ways and means of avoiding collective redundancies or reducing the numbers of workers affected." There is no equivalent obligation in the Employment Protection Act. Under the Employment Protection Act, as under the Directive, a public authority has to be notified of the impending redundancies. The Directive states that " the workers' representatives may send any comments they may have to the competent public authority." There is no equivalent provision in the Act. The Act obliges the employer to consult only the representatives of " recognised " trade unions. Where he does not recognise any union, in apparent contrast to the Directive, he does not have to consult anyone.

689 The significance of any variation between the provisions of the Directive and those of the Employment Protection Act may not be merely of academic interest. Directives were assumed not to be directly enforceable inside the national legal systems of member countries of the EEC. It was assumed that there had to be an act of the local legislature to make the Directive part of the national law of the country concerned. This may not always be the case in fact. This is due to the recent expansive mood of the Court of Justice of the European Communities. This mood is apparent from the controversial decision in the case of *Van Duyn* v. *Home Office*[47]

---

[45] [1973] I.C.R. 50.
[46] [1974] I.C.R. 170.
[47] [1974] E.C.R. 1337.

in which the court ruled that Directive 64/221 (concerning public policy restrictions on the movement of foreign nationals) is directly applicable so as to confer individual rights enforceable in the courts of member states. This is remarkable because, unlike regulations which are said by Article 189 of the Treaty to be binding in their entirety and directly applicable, Directives are binding only on member states and then only as to the results to be achieved. Notwithstanding this, the Court of Justice has now enunciated the principle that in every case " the nature, general scheme and wording of the provisions " of the Directive in question must be examined.[48] If these " lay down an obligation not subject to any exception or condition and which, by its very nature does not require the intervention of any act either of the institutions of the Community or of member states " they are directly applicable and must be protected by national courts.[49]

690   Amongst draft Directives which are likely to be adopted in due course brief mention should be made of the draft fifth Directive,[50] on the structure of companies, which would require British companies to have worker directors. There is also the draft Directive on the retention of workers' rights in cases of mergers and takeovers.

Retention of rights on mergers and takeovers

691   The proposed Directive [51] in this field has its origin in the aim of harmonisation, and is likely soon to become effective. Its purpose is to protect workers in the case of mergers and takeovers. The worker is to be maintained in the legal position he would have been in had no change of employer taken place. This is to be achieved by the introduction of protective provisions and guarantees. Since these protective devices are specified in the draft Directive itself, it is arguable that the criteria of *Van Duyn* are satisfied and that accordingly national courts will have to protect the rights created.

So far as British labour law is concerned the protective devices envisaged are revolutionary. They go qualitatively beyond the collective redundancies Directive because they intervene not simply in the procedural aspects of the bargaining process (by requiring consultation and advance notice) but they are *primarily* concerned with the rights of individual workers, and go further than other Commission proposals in this field.[52]

The draft Directive is not restricted to the limited company, nor simply to mergers between companies and firms and takeovers where individual businesses or other organised work units are transferred so that one person replaces another person in the capacity of employer, but it also covers concentrations between undertakings where " a person or undertaking, a group of persons or undertakings, acquire the *control* of one or several undertakings." [53] This is particularly important because it is not limited

---

[48] At p. 1348 (12).
[49] At p. 1348 (13).
[50] Bull.E.C. 8, 1970, Supp. and Bull.E.C. Supp. 10/72.
[51] O.J. 1974 C104/1.
[52] In particular Art. 6. of the proposal for a third directive on mergers of joint stock companies, and Art. 30 of the draft convention on international mergers of joint stock companies.
[53] Art. 12 as read in the light of a proposed Council Regulation on competition policy.

to the transfer of the ownership of a business as a going concern—the concept which is the basis of existing British redundancy and seniority law [54] —but extends protection to cases where there is no transfer of ownership but simply a change in the degree of control exercised by the old employer over his company's future development. The security enjoyed by a worker may be affected by a change in control. The draft Directive is designed to cover this situation.

692 The most important provisions of the draft Directive are those which aim to ensure the automatic transfer of the old employment relationship with all its rights and obligations to the new employer. This transfer applies as well to rights and obligations from " customary industrial practice " which, in the British context, means above all the collective agreement operating as codified custom. This at a stroke will not simply overturn the common law doctrine of the personal non-transferable nature of the contract of employment,[55] but it will render otiose the absurdly complicated provisions of the Redundancy Payments Act 1965 and the Contracts of Employment Act 1972 dealing with changes of ownership. Instead of a series of elaborate fictions of re-engagement or reinstatement, fine distinctions between changes of ownership and sales of assets, and curious lines between oral and written offers of employment, the Directive adopts the simple remedy of automatic transfer.[56]

693 Recognising that the automatic transfer rule in itself is insufficient because the new employer might simply make the transfer the occasion for redundancies, the draft Directive aims at bringing the laws of member states into line with German, French and Italian law, by providing that " mergers and takeovers shall not constitute in themselves a reason for termination of the employment relationship on the part of the transferor or the transferee." [57] Nor does the merger or takeover or concentration provide a right unilaterally to alter the terms of the employment relationship, since the concept of " dismissal " includes a unilateral change in terms. There is, however, one exceptional circumstance in which termination, or unilateral change in employment terms, is permitted. This is what the draft calls dismissal necessitated by " pressing business reasons." Unless given a narrow interpretation by the courts this may constitute the weak link in the draft Directive. The nearest equivalent in British law is " redundancy " but there may well be a gap between this concept and the notion of " pressing business reasons." Properly construed it could result in a sensible demarcation of the limits of reorganisation of the workforce which flows from mergers, takeovers and concentrations.

Conclusion

694 The changing social face of the Community and the judicial activism apparent in recent decisions of the E.C.J. mean that individual employment rights are being expanded. Incidentally, through the process of

---

[54] *i.e.* Redundancy Payments Act 1965, s. 13, and Contracts of Employment Act 1972, Sched. 1, para. 9 (2).
[55] *Nokes* v. *Doncaster Amalgamated Collieries Ltd.* [1940] A.C. 1014, 1018, 1020.
[56] Arts. 1 and 2.
[57] Art. 4.

" harmonisation upwards," this is introducing into British labour law concepts of Continental labour law. The practical implication is that no student or practitioner of labour relations will, in future, be able to ignore Community law nor to neglect the comparative study of his subject.

[The next paragraph is 701.]

CHAPTER 21

INTERNATIONAL EMPLOYMENT CONTRACTS

701 THE international migration of workers has the result that contracts of employment which are to be performed in a state other than the state of origin of the worker may be governed by the labour laws of several states. Moreover, multi-national corporations may transfer workers, either permanently or temporarily, from the seat of the corporation to subsidiary establishments or from one establishment to another across national frontiers. This is a phenomenon of increasing importance on an international scale, particularly so within the European Economic Community because of the freedom of movement guaranteed by Article 48 and the freedom of establishment guaranteed by Article 51 of the Treaty of Rome.[1]

702 The question arises as to which national labour law should apply to employment relationships of an international character. The answer depends on (1) the English and Scottish conflict of law rules, which determine whether a contract or a tort is governed by the national law of England and Wales,[2] or Scotland,[3] or by the law of another state; and (2) the express or implied territorial scope of Acts of the United Kingdom[4] Parliament and of subordinate legislation. These are matters which have received little attention from the courts and legal writers.[5]

Conflict of laws and the choice of law

703 The English and Scottish courts apply to contracts of employment, like other contracts, the " proper law of the contract." By this is meant the law by which the parties intended the contract to be governed. Where their intention has not been expressed and cannot be implied from the circumstances, the " proper law " is the legal system with which the contract is most closely connected. The reader must consult specialist works on the conflict of laws for a full examination of these rules.[6] The point which needs to be observed here is that the principle of the autonomy of the parties to select the proper law has been accepted, and problems of a capricious or fraudulent choice of a law totally unconnected with the contract of employment have not been encountered in practice.[7]

---

[1] See Chap. 20 above.

[2] References to the " English " common law include Wales, but under the Welsh Language Act 1967, s. 4, references to " England " in Acts of Parliament no longer include Wales.

[3] Scotland has its own legal system and courts, but nearly all labour legislation extends to the whole of Great Britain, including Scotland. In a few exceptional cases (*e.g.* agricultural wages) there is separate Scottish legislation.

[4] Most labour legislation does not extend to the whole of the United Kingdom (*i.e.* it does not cover Northern Ireland and the Channel Islands and Isle of Man). The application of legislation to the territorial waters of the U.K. is discussed below.

[5] The only notable exception is O. Kahn-Freund, " Notes on the conflict of laws in relation to employment in English and Scottish law " (1960) 3 *Rivista di Diritto Int. e. Comp. del Lavoro* 307. For an international survey see F. Gamillscheg, *International Encyclopedia of Comparative Law* (1974), Vol III, Chap. 28.

[6] Esp. Dicey and Morris, *The Conflict of Laws* (9th ed., London, 1973), Pt. 6.

[7] Dicey and Morris, *op. cit.* pp. 729–734.

An implied choice may be inferred from the circumstances, such as an agreement that arbitration shall take place in a particular country which gives rise to an inference that the law of that country was intended to be the proper law.[8]

704   Where there is no express or implied choice, the judge puts himself in the place of the "reasonable man" in order to discover the law with which the contract has the "closest and most real connection." There is no rigid rule as to which connecting factors should be applied to contracts of employment. A very flexible approach has been adopted. In the case of high level management, advisory and specialist staff, the proper law (in the absence of express or implied choice) is likely to be the law of the place where the undertaking has its centre of control and management because such employees are an integral part of management of the organisation.[9] On the other hand, lower level employees are usually engaged in the state where they reside and where they are required to work and so the proper law (in the absence of express or implied choice) is likely to be the law of the place of residence of the worker or the law of the place where the work is to be performed.[10] But other factors, such as the law of the place of contracting, may also be relevant.[11]

705   Not all issues arising out of an employment relationship may be classified as contractual. In particular, it has been traditional to treat the question of liability for work accidents as arising in tort although, for some purposes, such liability may also be regarded as contractual.[12] As a general rule, a work accident in a foreign country is a tort and actionable as such in England only if it satisfies the so-called "double actionability" rule: the act must be both (a) actionable as a tort according to English law (had the act occurred in England), and (b) actionable according to the law of the foreign country where it was done.[13] But particular issues which arise out of a work accident may be treated as contractual. For example, in *Sayers* v. *International Drilling Co. N.V.*,[14] an Englishman entered into a contract of employment "in the American language" with a Dutch company to work on an oil rig as a derrickman in Nigerian territorial waters, his salary being payable in sterling. The contract contained what Lord Denning M.R. called "quite a good programme" for compensating the employee in the event of illness or accident. It also contained an exempting clause under which the employee accepted this compensation as his "exclusive remedy in lieu of any other claims . . .

---

[8] *Op. cit.* p. 736.
[9] *e.g. Re Anglo-Austrian Bank* [1920] 1 Ch. 69 (German manager of London branch of German bank under contract made in Germany: *held* German law applied).
[10] *e.g. South African Breweries* v. *King* [1899] 2 Ch. 173; [1900] 1 Ch. 273 (C.A.) (English employee under contract made in South African Republic with English company, to be performed entirely in South Africa: *held* law of South Africa applied); *M'Feetridge* v. *Stewarts & Lloyds Ltd.*, 1913 S.C. 773 (Irish domiciled minor under contract in Scotland to work there waived rights to sue employer for negligence: *held* Scottish law applied).
[11] See *e.g. De Bueger* v. *Ballantyne & Co. Ltd.* [1938] A.C. 452 (P.C.).
[12] *Matthews* v. *Kuwait Bechtel Corporation* [1959] 2 Q.B. 57 (English contract with Panamanian company to work in Kuwait: *held* claim arising out of work accident in Kuwait could be pleaded in contract or tort for purposes of obtaining leave to serve writ out of jurisdiction under R.S.C., Ord. 11, r. 1); comment by Jolowicz [1959] C.L.J. 163, and see Chap. 2, above.
[13] Dicey and Morris, *op. cit.* pp. 938 *et seq.*
[14] [1971] 1 W.L.R. 1176 (C.A.); comment by L. Collins (1972) 21 I.C.L.Q. 320.

whether at common law or under the statutes of the United Kingdom or any other nation." The case was argued on the basis that this exempting clause was void, under the Law Reform (Personal Injuries) Act 1948, s. 1 (3), if there was a contract governed by English law; but that the clause was valid if governed by the Dutch law applicable to international employment contracts. The Court of Appeal held that Dutch law was to apply, so validating the clause. Two members of the court applied " the proper law of the contract" approach and this led to Dutch law because the contract was in a standard form applicable to employees of many nationalities and to give it business efficacy it had to be governed by a single law, that of the " seat of the establishment" (i.e. the law of the employer) and also because the exclusion of rights under English law was said to indicate that English law did not apply. This latter reason, like the suggestion of Salmon L.J. that the system of law should apply which validated the contract rather than one which invalidated it (the " rule of validation" familiar in interpretation of contracts), appears to overlook the unequal bargaining positions of a multi-national employer and an individual employee. Accordingly it is submitted that the first reason given by the Lords Justices of Appeal is to be preferred. The third member of the court, Lord Denning M.R., regarded the claim as being in tort, the proper law of which was Dutch, while, he held, the proper law of the contract was English. To avoid a conflict between the proper laws, he favoured a " proper law of the issue" and this was Dutch law. Lord Denning's approach cannot, however, be reconciled with House of Lords' authority.[15]

706 What is particularly significant about the *Sayers* case is that none of the members of the Court of Appeal analysed the policy of the Act of the United Kingdom Parliament which invalidates exempting clauses of the kind found in that case. The Law Reform (Personal Injuries) Act 1948 was passed to abolish the doctrine of common employment which prevented an employee from suing his employer for damages arising from the negligence of a fellow employee. To prevent evasion of this provision, contracting-out was prohibited. Assuming that the negligent act which led to the employee's injury was an act which had it occurred in England would have been actionable in tort, and it was an act which was actionable according to the law of the place where it occurred (Nigeria), was there any reason for finding that this Act of Parliament did not apply? To classify the exempting clause as a matter of " contract" was, it is submitted, simply to confuse the issue because the question could equally have been classified as one of consent to the commission of a tort. The Court of Appeal ought to have approached the problem from the standpoint of the policy of the Act of Parliament in question, and not simply according to the conceptual classification of the issues.

Territorial scope of legislation

707 Another way of stating this last point about the *Sayers* case is to say that the Court of Appeal failed to analyse the oft-repeated principle that statutes have only territorial effect. The general rule has been said to be that Acts of Parliament apply only to transactions within the United

---

[15] *Boys* v. *Chaplin* [1971] A.C. 356; see Collins, *loc cit.*; and the critique in *Brodin* v. *A/R Seijan*, 1973 S.L.T. 198.

Kingdom (or such part of the United Kingdom as may be specified) and not to acts outside.[16] This is, however, a considerable over-simplification of the problem in relation to international employment contracts because it may mean that the Act applies to (1) contracts made in the United Kingdom; (2) contracts governed by the law of a part of the United Kingdom; (3) contracts where the work is to be done in the United Kingdom; (4) contracts where payment or some other act connected with the contract is to be effected in the United Kingdom. In each case it is necessary to examine the Act of Parliament in order to decide the precise territorial scope within one or more of these possible meanings.

A significant feature of judicial interpretation of labour legislation in England and Scotland has been the refusal to apply to these statutes the ordinary criteria of the conflict of laws.[17] Instead of regarding the scope of the legislation as being co-terminous with the proper law of the contract, labour legislation has generally been confined in its operation to work done within the territorial boundaries of Great Britain. For example the old Workmen's Compensation Acts were applied only to accidents arising out of and in the course of employment in Great Britain,[18] a policy continued by modern industrial injuries legislation.[19] The Factories Acts were judicially construed as being territorial in the sense that they applied only to work within the jurisdiction.[20] Statutes laying down the method of payment of wages (*e.g.* the Truck Acts) are applied to foreign contracts for the performance of work in Great Britain,[21] but, presumably, would not be applied to English or Scottish contracts for work abroad.[22] Even where awards or orders made under some statutory authority (*e.g.* an arbitration award) take effect as terms of individual contracts,[23] the courts are likely to limit their application to the country where the work under the contract is to be performed. The rationale is that the machinery for enforcement is territorially limited in extent.

708   In recent legislation the territorial scope of the legislation has usually been spelt out in express words. For example, the Equal Pay Act 1970 inserts an equality clause in the contracts of employment of men and women employed " at an establishment in Great Britain " [24] and Parliament has directed the courts to abandon conflict of law rules by providing that " for the purposes of this Act it is immaterial whether the law which . . . is the proper law of a contract is the law of any part of the United Kingdom or not." [25] The Contracts of Employment Act 1972 (minimum periods of notice and written statements) does not apply to any period when the employee is engaged in work " wholly or mainly outside Great Britain unless

---

[16] Maxwell, *Interpretation of Statutes* (12th ed., London, 1969), Chap. 8.
[17] Kahn-Freund, *loc. cit.*
[18] *Tomalin* v. *S. Pearson Ltd.* [1909] 2 K.B. 61.
[19] Social Security Act 1975, s. 131 and regulations made thereunder.
[20] *Yorke* v. *British & Continental Steamship Co.* (1945) 78 Ll.L.R. 181 (Accident in Gibraltar to employee under contract governed by English law: *held* dock regulations under Factories Act 1937 did not apply).
[21] *Duncan* v. *Motherwell Bridge & Engineering Co. Ltd.*, 1952 S.C. 131 (*held* by Inner House of Court of Session that provisions of Truck Act 1831, ss. 2, 3, applied if deductions made from wages in Scotland, irrespective of proper law).
[22] Kahn-Freund, *loc. cit.*
[23] See Chap. 8, above.
[24] s. 1 (1). See Chap. 11, above.
[25] s. 1 (11).

the employee ordinarily works in Great Britain and the work outside Great Britain is for the same employer." [26] At the same time periods of work outside Great Britain may be counted for the purposes of computing a period of continuous employment with the same employer (but not for any other purpose).[27] Subject to this the Act of 1972 applies whatever the law governing the contract of employment.[28]

709 The Redundancy Payments Act 1965 follows the somewhat curious scheme that an employee is not entitled to a redundancy payment if, on the " relevant date," he is outside Great Britain, unless under his contract of employment, he ordinarily worked in Great Britain.[29] At the same time, an employee who ordinarily works outside Great Britain is not entitled to a redundancy payment unless on the " relevant date " he is in Great Britain in accordance with instructions given to him by his employer.[30] Generally speaking, for the purpose of calculating the employee's period of continuous employment (on which his eligibility and the amount of payment depends) no account may be taken of weeks during all or part of which he was employed outside Great Britain and he was not an " employed earner " for the purposes of the Social Security Act 1975.[31] Section 56 (4) of the Act of 1965 provides that it is immaterial whether the law which governs any person's employment is the law of Great Britain, or a part of Great Britain, or not. It will be seen, therefore, that the Equal Pay Act, the Contracts of Employment Act and the Redundancy Payments Act, all exclude the ordinary rules of the conflict of laws. Instead, they provide, in general, for the exclusion of those who work abroad from the protection of the legislation.[32]

710 A similar policy is to be found in the Trade Union and Labour Relations Act 1974, Sched. 1, which excludes from the right to complain of unfair dismissal " any employment where under his contract of employment the employee ordinarily works outside Great Britain " [33]; the Sex Discrimination Act 1975, the employment provisions of which are limited to " employment at an establishment in Great Britain " [34]; and the Employment Protection Act 1975 which excludes from nearly all the new employment rights created by that Act an employment " where under his

---

[26] s. 12 (1).

[27] Sched. 1, para. 1 (2).

[28] s. 12 (2).

[29] s. 17 (1). See Chap. 14 for the meaning of " relevant date " (in general the date of termination), and Chap. 19 for the scope of the Act.

[30] s. 17 (2).

[31] s. 17 (3). An " employed earner " is defined in Social Security Act 1975, s. 2 (1) as a person who is " gainfully employed in Great Britain."

[32] The description of s. 56 (4) and similar provisions in other legislation as " particular choice of law clauses delimiting the scope of English domestic law " by Morris, *Conflict of Laws* (London, 1971), p. 235, is difficult to understand. The purpose of such provisions is to ensure that the question whether the legislation applies to contracts governed by the law of Great Britain is *not* answered in accordance with conflict of law rules. See Unger (1967) 83 L.Q.R. 427 at pp. 428–433; F. A. Mann (1966) 82 L.Q.R. 316; and A. D. Hughes (1967) 83 L.Q.R. 180.

[33] T.U.L.R.A., Sched. 1, para. 9 (2); and note that s. 30 (6) excludes conflict of law rules. *Cf.* T.U.L.R.A., s. 29 (3) which extends the territorial scope of the immunities in respect of " trade disputes " to matters occurring outside Great Britain; on the justification for this see Wedderburn (1972) 1 I.L.J. 12 at pp. 16–19. See also Chap. 1.

[34] S.D.A., s. 6; under s. 10 employment is regarded as being at an establishment in Great Britain unless the employee does his work " wholly or mainly outside Great Britain."

contract of employment the employee ordinarily works outside Great Britain." [35]

711   The primary importance attached to the place of work by these Acts can be justified on two main grounds. First, protective legislation is a part of the public policy of the United Kingdom, *i.e.*, the *lex fori*; secondly, there is a fear that employers may abuse their unequal bargaining power and circumvent the prohibition on contracting-out of the legislation by persuading the employee to agree to the application of a less socially advanced legal system. For these reasons labour legislation of the United Kingdom cannot be modified by agreement (*i.e.* the provisions are usually mandatory), and it is always and exclusively applicable in respect of work done in the United Kingdom. At the same time the international law principle of territorial supremacy of legislation means that Acts of the United Kingdom Parliament will generally not be applied as such to work done abroad although the contract is governed by the law of a part of the United Kingdom.

Ordinary place of work

712   The criterion used in legislation, whether the employee " ordinarily works outside Great Britain," has given rise to some difficulties of application. The words " ordinarily works " have no special meaning. As with the words " ordinarily resident " in tax legislation, it has been accepted that the converse of " ordinarily " is " extraordinarily " and that part of the regular order of a man's life, adopted voluntarily and for settled purposes, is not " extraordinary." [36]

713   In *Maulik* v. *Air India*,[37] an airline pilot employed by Air India and its predecessor had worked in a number of places, most of them outside Great Britain. The N.I.R.C. held that an industrial tribunal had been right in considering the whole period of the pilot's employment (not simply the last two years when he was based in London) and in finding that he ordinarily worked outside Great Britain. In *Portec (U.K.) Ltd.* v. *Mogensen*,[38] the Employment Appeal Tribunal approved this decision in *Maulik's* case, although pointing out that Mr. Maulik was also ordinarily working, during the last two years of his service, in Great Britain. In *Mogensen's* case, the employee was ordinarily working inside Great Britain while looking after the corporation's manufacturing establishment, and, at the same time, ordinarily working outside Great Britain, while selling its products in Europe. Since he ordinarily worked outside Great Britain for part of the time, he was not entitled to present a complaint of unfair dismissal. The Trade Union and Labour Relations Act 1974, Sched. 1, para. 9 (2), does not exclude only those who ordinarily work *only* outside Great Britain; it also excludes, from presenting a complaint of unfair dismissal those who ordinarily work outside Great Britain as well as ordinarily working inside.

---

[35] E.P.A., s. 119 (5) which excludes such workers from 14 of the rights created by E.P.A.

[36] *Portec (U.K.) Ltd.* v. *Mogensen*, L.S. Gaz., May 26, 1976 (E.A.T.) approving *Levene* v. *I.R.C.* [1928] A.C. 217 and *I.R.C.* v *Lysaght* [1928] A.C. 234.

[37] [1974] I.C.R. 528 (N.I.R.C.).

[38] L.S.Gaz., May 26, 1976 (E.A.T.).

714   The position is different under the Redundancy Payments Act 1965 because, as we have seen, entitlement depends upon whether or not the employee is inside Great Britain on the relevant date. So, in *Roux International Ltd.* v. *Licudi*,[39] a sales manager was required under his contract to spend half his time in Europe and half in Great Britain and Ireland. He was dismissed for redundancy in London. The N.I.R.C. held that the employee was in Great Britain in accordance with instructions given him by his employer when he was dismissed, so that even if he ordinarily worked outside Great Britain he was entitled to a redundancy payment under section 17 (2) of the Act of 1965. It appears, from the decision in *Mogensen's* case, that Mr. Licudi, the sales manager, would not have been entitled to present a complaint of unfair dismissal.

Offshore workers

715   Acts of Parliament are generally limited in scope to Great Britain and the territorial waters (that is, waters up to the three mile limit from shore). The Employment Protection (Offshore Employment) Order 1976 [40] has however extended certain legislation to particular employments in territorial waters and designated areas of the Continental Shelf. Most of the workers affected are working on rigs in British designated areas of the Continental Shelf (with certain exclusions); very few workers within territorial limits (*e.g.* diving or maintenance work beyond harbour limits) are affected because they are already covered by most employment legislation. The Order is designed to cover only employment in the designated areas beyond territorial waters which is connected with the exploration and exploitation of the seabed and subsoil. The main Acts [41] which are applied (in whole or part) with modifications are the Wages Councils Act 1959, Industrial Training Act 1964, Redundancy Payments Act 1965, Contracts of Employment Act 1972, Trade Union and Labour Relations Act 1974, and Employment Protection Act 1975.

Merchant seamen

716   The Merchant Shipping Act 1970 applies generally to those employed in ships registered in the United Kingdom but the reader must consult the Regulations made under the Act for the precise limits of particular provisions. Some employment legislation, such as the Trade Union and Labour Relations Act 1974, Sched. 1 (unfair dismissal) and parts of the Employment Protection Act 1975, exclude merchant seamen only if the employment is wholly outside Great Britain *or* the employee is not ordinarily resident in Great Britain.[42]

Proposals for reform in the EEC

717   At the present time there are under discussion within the EEC two proposals which, if adopted, will result in fairly extensive changes in the

---

[39] [1975] I.C.R. 424 (Q.B.D.).
[40] S.I. 1976 No. 766.
[41] In addition, S.D.A., s. 10 (5)–(7) permits the extension of that Act and the Equal Pay Act by Order to designated areas of the Continental Shelf.
[42] T.U.L.R.A., Sched. 1, para. 9 (3); E.P.A., s. 119 (6); *cf.* S.D.A., s. 10 (2) which treats employment on a U.K. registered ship as employment at an establishment in Great Britain unless the work is done wholly outside Great Britain. The S.D.A. expressly includes the territorial waters adjacent to Great Britain within its scope.

English and Scottish rules and practice relating to international employment contracts.[43] The first is a draft Regulation on the conflict of laws in employment relationships within the Community. This is to apply to relationships the obligations of which are to be fulfilled within the EEC. This adopts, as a general rule, subject to limited exceptions, the law of the place of work as the binding criterion. The second proposal is a draft Convention on the law applicable to contractual and non-contractual obligations, which appears to be intended to apply to employment relationships the obligations of which are to be fulfilled outside the Community. This applies the proper law of the contract as a general rule apart from so-called " mandatory rules for the protection of the employee " which are in force in the country where the worker habitually works or, the law of the seat of the business which engaged him, if the worker does not habitually work in any one country. These proposals are likely to undergo substantial changes before adoption, in the light of various criticisms which have been made.[44]

[The next paragraph is 721.]

---

[43] The first draft of the Regulation was published in O.J. 1972 C49/26; with comments by the Economic and Social Committee in O.J. 1972 C142/5; and the Parliament in O.J. 1973 C4/14. It has since been substantially amended but, at the time of writing, the revised draft is unpublished (V/622/75–E).

[44] *e.g.* F. Gamillscheg, *Intereuropäisches Arbeitsrecht* (1973) 37 *Rabels Z* 284 at pp. 289 *et seq.*

Part Five

PRACTICE AND PROCEDURE

CHAPTER 22

INDUSTRIAL TRIBUNALS

Sources

721 The industrial tribunals were established under section 12 of the Industrial Training Act 1964 and the rules governing the *constitution* of the tribunals will be found in regulations made under that Act.[1] The rules of *procedure* vary according to the particular statutory jurisdiction which the tribunal is exercising, but, in practice, the Industrial Tribunals (Labour Relations) Regulations 1974, as amended [2] (hereafter described as the 1974 Regulations) govern most proceedings, in particular those under the Redundancy Payments Act 1965, Docks and Harbours Act 1966, Equal Pay Act 1970, Contracts of Employment Act 1972, Trade Union and Labour Relations Act 1974, Sex Discrimination Act 1975 (but not appeals against non-discrimination notices), Employment Protection Act 1975, and compensation questions under certain other statutes. Separate regulations (not discussed here) govern (1) appeals under the Industrial Training Act 1964 [3]; (2) appeals under the Health and Safety at Work etc. Act 1974 [4] (3) appeals under the Sex Discrimination Act 1975 against non-discrimination notices.[5]

Aims

722 The Donovan Royal Commission on Trade Unions and Employers' Associations, described the purpose of industrial tribunals as being to provide for employers and workers " an easily accessible, speedy, informal and inexpensive procedure for the settlement of their disputes." [6] We shall see that these aims are reflected in the procedural rules. The method of getting a case before a tribunal is far simpler than the corresponding procedure for getting a case (even a small claim in the county court) before the ordinary courts; the average time it takes for a claim to come to hearing (in July 1976) is 10 weeks, compared with many months or even years in the ordinary courts; tribunals are relatively informal, not being bound by the rules of evidence which apply in the ordinary courts, interpreting procedural rules flexibly, and being designed to put the parties, particularly the unrepresented applicant or respondent, at ease; and they are inexpensive, in comparison with the ordinary courts because legal representation

---

[1] Industrial Tribunals (England and Wales) Regs. 1965, S.I. 1965 No. 1101; as amended by Industrial Tribunals (England and Wales) (Amendment) Regs. 1967, S.I. 1967 No. 301, Industrial Tribunals (England and Wales) (Amendment) Regs. 1970, S.I. 1970 No. 941; Industrial Tribunals (England and Wales) (Amendment) Regs. 1971, S.I. 1971 No. 1660 (hereafter referred to as the 1965, 1967, 1970 and 1971 Regs. respectively).

[2] S.I. 1974 No. 1386, as amended by Industrial Tribunals (Labour Relations) (Amendment) Regs. 1976, S.I. 1976 No. 661 (hereafter referred to as the 1976 Regs.). The 1974 Regs. replaced the Industrial Tribunals (Industrial Relations) Regs. 1972, S.I. 1972 No. 38.

[3] 1967 Regs. (above, n. 1).

[4] Industrial Tribunals (Improvement and Prohibition Notices Appeals) Regs. 1974, S.I. 1974 No. 1925.

[5] Industrial Tribunals (Non-Discrimination Notices Appeals) Regs. 1975, S.I. 1975 No. 2098.

[6] Cmnd. 3623 (1968) para. 577.

is the exception rather than the rule, with costs generally being awarded against a party only for frivolous or vexatious conduct.

The tribunals have had to try to uphold these aims despite the rapid growth in their case load. Having started, in 1965, with the single jurisdiction of hearing appeals against industrial training levies, they now have some 23 separate statutory jurisdictions (listed in Chapter 4). In 1965 they dealt with some 397 cases; by July 1976 claims were being presented (under all the jurisdictions then in force) at the rate of about 42,000 per annum; by 1977 it is expected that the case load will be between 55,000 and 60,000 a year.

Organisation

723   For administrative purposes, there are separate Central Offices of Industrial Tribunals (C.O.I.T.) in London (for England and Wales), Glasgow (Scotland) and Belfast (Northern Ireland). The C.O.I.T. organises the appointment of personnel and processes all applications. The principal administrative officer is the Secretary of the Tribunals. Regional Offices of Industrial Tribunals (R.O.I.T.) have been established at Ashford, Birmingham, Bristol, Bury St. Edmunds, Cardiff, Exeter, Liverpool, Manchester, Newcastle-upon-Tyne, Nottingham, Sheffield, and Southampton. The administration of applications, after they have been initially registered at the C.O.I.T., is delegated to the R.O.I.T.'s, each of which has an Assistant Secretary. Within each region hearings may take place at a number of centres and at 7 of these Offices of Industrial Tribunals (O.I.T.) have been established. The general aim in locating tribunals has been to minimise travelling time and expense while maintaining flexibility in the actual allocation of cases, depending on the availability of premises and personnel.

Personnel

724   There is a president of the Industrial Tribunals (for each C.O.I.T.) who must be a barrister or solicitor of not less than seven years' standing.[7] He is appointed (in England and Wales) by the Lord Chancellor and holds office for five years, but is eligible for reappointment. It is the president who exercises overall direction, playing a leading role in the shaping of procedure, determining the number of tribunals, and where and when they should sit, as well as sitting himself as chairman.

The tribunals are tripartite: there is a barrister or solicitor of at least seven years' standing as chairman; together with two lay members. The chairmen are appointed to a panel by the Lord Chancellor.[8] As at July 1976, there were 102 full-time chairmen and 62 part-time chairmen for England and Wales and more have been appointed since then. In each R.O.I.T. one of the full-time chairmen is appointed as regional chairman. For each hearing the chairman is selected by the president or the regional chairman (who may select himself). Part-time chairmen are generally expected to be available for hearings on at least 50 days each year, so that the essential continuity of experience can be maintained.

The lay members are appointed to panels by the Secretary of State for Employment " after consultation with such organisation or association of

---

[7] 1965 Regs., r. 3 (1).
[8] 1965 Regs. (as amended by 1967 Regs.), r. 5 (2).

organisations representative of employers or of employed persons as [he] considers to be appropriate." [9] As at July 1976 there were about 2,300 panel members for England Wales, and this number is expected to increase. Although there is no longer express provision for two separate panels of persons appointed after consultation with employers' organisations and trades councils, respectively, in practice the president (or regional chairman) will select members for a particular hearing so that one lay member is an employer's organisation nominee and the other a trades council nominee.[10] Members are paid a modest fee and expenses for each hearing. They are normally appointed for two years at a time.

Although applications must generally be heard by the chairman and two members, in the absence of one lay member, the application may, with the consent of the parties be heard in the absence of that member.[11] The president, or the chairman of the tribunal, or a chairman nominated for the purpose by the president (in practice all full-time chairmen) may sit alone for the purposes of dismissing proceedings where written notice of abandonment has been given by a party, allowing an appeal against training levy where the Industrial Training Board gives written notice that the appeal is not contested, deciding an application in accordance with the written agreement of the parties, dealing with any interlocutory matter or application, and making an order for costs in respect of any one of these matters.[12]

It needs to be emphasised that the three members of the tribunal are equal members, all participating in the decision-making process, although the tribunal's written decision is signed only by the chairman. In theory it is possible for the lay members to out-vote the lawyer-chairman on points of law, but this happens very rarely in practice. Members all have the opportunity to express their views not only as to the decision itself, but as to the reasons on which that decision is based. The practical responsibility for drafting the written decision, in the light of the lay members' views, rests with the chairman.

Attached to each tribunal is a clerk (who is not legally qualified) who advises the parties on points of procedure before the hearing begins, draws up a witness list, administers the oath or affirmation (unless the chairman otherwise directs), and generally assists the parties and the tribunal.

---

[9] 1971 Regs. This regulation was the result of the TUC boycott of the Industrial Relations Act 1971; previously there were separate panels of employer and union nominees. Although the " independent " lay members who were appointed under the 1971 Reg. to replace the union nominees who resigned have not been reappointed the regulation has not been changed. In practice one employer and one union nominee is nearly always selected; but there is nothing to prevent two employer nominees or two union nominees from sitting.

[10] In sex discrimination and equal pay cases, there is encouragement to select at least one person of each sex (Equality for Women, Cmnd. 5724 (1974), para. 83) and in racial discrimination cases, members of racial minorities (Racial Discrimination, Cmnd. 6234 (1975), para. 83).

[11] 1965 Regs. (as amended by 1967 Regs.), r. 5 (1).

[12] 1965 Regs. (as amended by 1967 Regs.), r. 5 (1A); under the 1974 Regs. the president, a nominated chairman or the chairman of the tribunal which heard the case, may do any act other than hear an originating application or review a decision (r. 11 (4)). Such a chairman may also refuse an application for a review if in his opinion it has no reasonable prospects of success (r. 9 (3)).

The originating application

725   Proceedings are commenced by the applicant sending to the Secretary of the Tribunals at C.O.I.T. an originating application containing the name and address of the applicant; the names and addresses of the persons against whom relief is sought; and the grounds on which that relief is sought.[13] There is no statutory requirement that form IT 1 should be used, although it is usually convenient to do so. The application need not specify the relief which is sought; provided the application contains the basic particulars mentioned, the tribunal may consider any appropriate relief unless a claim in respect of that relief is time-barred (see below). For example an applicant may specify that he is seeking a redundancy payment; unless the tribunal is deprived of jurisdiction because the application was presented too late for a claim in respect of unfair dismissal to be considered, the tribunal may award remedies in respect of unfair dismissal.[14]

Similarly, provided the application is presented timeously and the basic particulars are included in the application, the tribunal may amend the originating application by changing the basis of the claim or adding a respondent. In such cases, the tribunal should proceed as follows:

" (1) They should ask themselves whether the unamended originating application complied with [rule 1]. . . .

(2) If it did not, there is no power to amend and a new originating application must be presented.

(3) If it did, the tribunal should ask themselves whether the unamended originating application was presented to the Secretary of Tribunals within the time limit appropriate to the type of claim being put forward in the amended application.

(4) If it was not, the tribunal have no power to allow the proposed amendment.

(5) If it was, the tribunal have a discretion whether or not to allow the amendment.

(6) In deciding whether or not to exercise their discretion to allow an amendment, the tribunal should in every case have regard to all the circumstances of the case. In particular they should consider any injustice or hardship which may be caused to any of the parties, including those proposed to be added, if the proposed amendment were allowed or, as the case may be, refused. [Rule 10 of the Schedule to the 1974 Regulations] provides that a tribunal shall not normally award costs. If, however, the tribunal consider that the defect in the originating application has caused any party to incur unnecessary expense they could properly conclude that leave to amend should only be given if the party seeking to amend agrees to make some payment in respect of that expense and could order accordingly." [15]

Moreover, applications may be made at any time for the joinder of parties, and the tribunal may even join parties of its own motion.[16]

---

13 1974 Regs., r. 1 (1).

14 *Smith* v. *Automobile Pty. Ltd.* [1973] I.T.R. 376 (N.I.R.C.); *Coates* v. *C. J. Crispin Ltd.* [1973] I.T.R. 446 (N.I.R.C.).

15 *Cocking* v. *Sandhurst (Stationers) Ltd.* [1974] I.C.R. 650 (N.I.R.C.) at pp. 656–657; and see *Kapur* v. *Shields* [1975] I.T.R. 173 (Q.B.D.).

16 1974 Regs., r. 13; *A.S.T.M.S.* v. *Mucci* [1973] I.T.R. 118 (N.I.R.C.).

Time for presentation of claim

726   A summary of the qualifying periods and time limits for presenting claims under each of the main jurisdictions will be found in Appendix 3. The usual period is three months, but in some cases it is as short as six weeks (appeals against non-discrimination notices) and in others six months. These time limits go to the jurisdiction of the tribunal and so the point can be taken at any stage of the proceedings and will be taken by the tribunal itself even if not raised by the parties.[17]

In calculating the time, it must be borne in mind that " month " means calendar month,[18] and the time must be computed from the beginning of the day from which it is expressed in the relevant statute to run (*e.g.* from the beginning of the day which is the effective date of termination for a period of three calendar months, in the case of unfair dismissal).[19] The time is counted down to the date when the claim is " presented," and this means the day when it is received by C.O.I.T., or if it is closed, the next day when the C.O.I.T. is open.[20]

In some cases the tribunal has a discretion to extend the time limit. This is usually expressed (*e.g.* in regard to unfair dismissal) in the form that the application may be presented " within such further period as the tribunal considers reasonable in a case where it is satisfied that it was not reasonably practicable for the complaint to be presented within the period of three months." [21] This is a more liberal provision than was contained in the Regulations before 1974, but the Employment Appeal Tribunal has affirmed [22] that the operative principles for the application of the escape clause are still those laid down (in respect of the old Regulations) by the Court of Appeal in *Dedman* v. *British Building & Engineering Appliances Ltd.*[23] Lord Denning M.R. summed up the proper approach as follows:

> " If in the circumstances the man knew or was put on inquiry as to his rights, and as to the time limit, then it was ' practicable ' for him to have presented his complaint within the [time limit], and he ought to have done so. But if he did not know, and there was nothing to put him on inquiry, then it was ' not practicable ' and he should be excused.
>
> But what is the position if he goes to skilled advisers and they make a mistake? The English court has taken the view that the man must abide by their mistake . . . If a man engaged skilled advisers to act for him—and they mistake the time limit and present it too late— he is out. His remedy is against them.
>
> Summing up, I would suggest that in every case the tribunal should inquire into the circumstances and ask themselves whether the man

---

[17] *Westward Circuits Ltd.* v. *Read* [1973] I.T.R. 320 (N.I.R.C.); *Rogers* v. *Bodfari (Transport) Ltd.* [1973] I.C.R. 325 (N.I.R.C.).
[18] Interpretation Act 1889, s. 3.
[19] *Dorber* v. *London Brick Co. Ltd.* [1974] I.C.R. 270 (N.I.R.C.).
[20] *Hammond* v. *Haigh Castle & Co. Ltd.* [1973] I.T.R. 199, 201 (N.I.R.C.); *Anglo-Continental School of English Ltd.* v. *Gardiner* [1973] I.T.R. 251, 256 (N.I.R.C.).
[21] See Appendix 3 for the cases where this is used. Certain statutes use the formula that it must be " just and equitable " to extend the time.
[22] *Norgett* v. *Luton Industrial Co-operative Society Ltd.*, *The Times*, July 23, 1976 (E.A.T.).
[23] [1974] I.C.R. 53 (C.A.).

or his advisers were at fault in allowing the [time limit] to pass by without presenting the complaint. If he was not at fault, nor his advisers—so that he had just cause or excuse for not presenting his complaint within the [time limit]—then it was ' not practicable ' for him to present it within that time. The court then has a discretion to allow it to be presented out of time, if it thinks it right to do so. But, if he was at fault, or if his advisers were at fault, in allowing the [time limit] to slip by, he must take the consequences. By exercising reasonable diligence, the complaint could and should have been presented in time." [24]

In the context of this decision, it was held that the applicant was responsible for the fault of his solicitors; but an applicant will not be penalised for the fault of an employment exchange in misinforming him.[25]

A trap which needs to be avoided by an applicant is a delay in presenting an application while other proceedings are pending. For example, the N.I.R.C. held that time could not be extended for an employee who had awaited the outcome of a domestic appeals procedure before presenting a complaint of unfair dismissal.[26] However, it is submitted that in an appropriate case where the respondent has misled the applicant into delaying presentation of the application (e.g. to secure a settlement, or to complete a domestic appeal) a tribunal may develop and apply the equitable doctrine that fraud postpones the running of time in a case where the applicant might suffer real injustice by reason of the unconscionable behaviour of the respondent.[27] On the other hand, where the respondent has not misled the applicant, and the applicant or his skilled advisers have deliberately put the industrial tribunal application on one side pending completion of, say, criminal proceedings, the escape clause cannot be invoked.[28]

Service and appearance

727 The C.O.I.T. registers the originating application and serves a copy of it, by post, on the respondent,[29] informing him of the means and time for entering an appearance, the consequences of failure to do so, and his right to receive a copy of the decision. There are rules relating to the service of this and other notices.[30] In general, notices will be sent to the address given by a party on his originating application or appearance, or, if he names a representative, to that representative. The onus is on a party changing his address to notify the Secretary of Tribunals of that fact.

---

[24] At p. 61.

[25] *Harvey's Household Linens Ltd.* v. *Benson* [1974] I.C.R. 306 (N.I.R.C.); *Westward Circuits Ltd.* v. *Read* (above).

[26] *Macdonald* v. *South Cambridgeshire R.D.C.* [1973] I.C.R. 611 (N.I.R.C.); in view of this decision it seems difficult to support the decision in *Associated Tunnelling Co. Ltd.* v. *Wasilewski* [1973] I.T.R. 651 (N.I.R.C.) where the applicant was allowed to use the escape clause after delaying in presenting his claim because of union advice to take the matter to arbitration first. The basis of the latter decision may be that the applicant had not consulted the union for purposes of pursuing his statutory rights but for general help.

[27] *Cf. Grimes* v. *Sutton Borough Council* [1973] I.C.R. 240 (N.I.R.C.) (application out of time under C.E.A., s. 8).

[28] *Norgett* v. *Luton Industrial Co-operative Society Ltd.* (above).

[29] 1974 Regs., r. 2 (1). In redundancy payments cases, the Secretary of State must be notified, in sex discrimination and equal pay cases, the Equal Opportunities Commission.

[30] 1974 Regs., r. 14.

If no address is specified the last-known address may be used or, in the case of a corporation, its registered office. Recorded delivery is used only if a second set of documents is sent to a respondent who has not entered an appearance, and for the service of witness orders. Where service cannot be effected in any of the ways specified, the president or a chairman nominated by him may order substituted service (*e.g.* by publication in a newspaper circulating in the district).

The respondent may enter an appearance within 14 days of receiving the copy of the originating application.[31] The president, a chairman nominated by him, or the chairman of the tribunal hearing the case, has a general power to grant extensions of time; an application for an extension must set out the grounds on which the extension is sought.[32] A test of reasonableness (subject to an order for costs) is applied. So where a respondent delayed entering an appearance to an unfair dismissal application on the ground that the respondent was waiting to hear whether an article badly made by the applicant would be accepted by the customer, an application for an extension was rejected.[33]

The entry of appearance may be made on the standard form IT 3 but this is not obligatory. The apperance must, however, be in writing, setting out the respondent's full name and address and stating whether or not he intends to resist the application and if so on what grounds. On receipt of the appearance the Secretary of Tribunals sends a copy to any other party.[34]

If the respondent fails to enter an appearance, he may take no further part in the proceedings, except to apply for an extension of time, or to be called as a witness, or to apply for a review (see below) on the grounds that he did not receive notice of the proceedings leading to the decision. He is entitled to receive a copy of the decision.[35]

Conciliation

728   Conciliation Officers (C.O.) designated by the A.C.A.S.[36] are required to endeavour to promote a settlement of any complaint presented to an industrial tribunal in respect of unfair dismissal,[37] discrimination on grounds of sex or marital status or for breach of an equality clause,[38] discrimination on racial grounds,[39] and a variety of statutory claims under the Employment Protection Act 1975,[40] to which others may be added by Order.[41]

The 1974 Regulations [42] require the Secretary of Tribunals to keep the

---

[31] *Ibid.* r. 3 (1).

[32] r. 12. r. 3 (3) provides that an appearance sent in out of time is deemed to include an application under r. 12 for an extension; the tribunal may then grant an extension although the grounds are not stated and it may not refuse an application without giving the respondent an opportunity to show cause why an extension should be granted.

[33] *Cook* v. *Pardor Engineering Co. Ltd.* [1975] I.T.R. 28.

[34] 1974 Regs., r. 3 (1).

[35] r. 3 (2).

[36] See Chap. 4, above.

[37] T.U.L.R.A., Sched. 1, Pt. IV, para. 26.

[38] S.D.A., s. 64.

[39] Race Relations Bill 1976.

[40] E.P.A., s. 108 (2).

[41] E.P.A., s. 108 (2) (5).

[42] r. 2 (4).

C.O. informed of the proceedings, and to notify the parties that the services of a C.O. are available to them.[43] The C.O. may be requested to make his services available by *both* parties either before[44] or after[45] the application is presented. After the application has been presented, the C.O. may endeavour to promote a settlement even in the absence of a request from one or both the parties if he considers that he could act "with a reasonable prospect of success."[46] C.O.s are particularly charged with the duty, in dismissal cases, of seeking to promote re-engagement or reinstatement "on terms appearing to the C.O. to be equitable," or where the applicant does not wish to be re-engaged or reinstated or these remedies are not practicable and the parties desire him to act, to promote agreement as to the amount of compensation.[47] In practice, however, the C.O.s are not willing to assist parties in arriving at an agreed figure of compensation where a tribunal has heard a case and determined liability and then adjourned it for the purpose of allowing the parties to arrive at an agreed figure.

C.O.s are enjoined "where appropriate" to encourage the use of "other procedures available for the settlement of grievances.[48] This nod in the direction of voluntary procedures is consistent with the general philosophy of British industrial relations, but it is interesting to note that there is no *obligation* to exhaust domestic procedures. Indeed, it seems that it cannot even be held against a complainant in an unfair dismissal case that after dismissal he failed to exercise a right of domestic appeal, because only the circumstances at the time of the dismissal are relevant.[49] However, failure to utilise domestic procedures may, arguably, be relevant to the assessment of contributory fault on the part of the complainant.[50]

Evidence is not admissible in tribunal proceedings of anything communicated to a C.O. in connection with the performance of his functions, except with the consent of the person who communicated it to the C.O.[51] The aim of this provision is to preserve the confidentiality of conciliation in the hopes of promoting a settlement. Communications with legal advisers and other agents with an actual view to litigation in hand, and the conduct of that litigation are, in any event, privileged from disclosure.[52]

Further particulars, witness orders and discovery of documents

729   Further particulars of the grounds on which a party relies and the facts and contentions relevant thereto may be applied for.[53] In the past such applications have not been readily granted particularly where the burden of proof is on the employer. However, in *White* v. *The University of*

---

[43] r. 2 (1).
[44] T.U.L.R.A., Sched. 1, Pt. IV, para. 26 (4); S.D.A., s. 64 (2); E.P.A., s. 108 (4).
[45] T.U.L.R.A., Sched. 1, Pt. IV, para. 26 (2) (*a*); S.D.A., s. 64 (1) (*a*); E.P.A., s. 108 (3) (*a*).
[46] T.U.L.R.A., Sched. 1, Pt. IV, para. 26 (2) (*b*); S.D.A., s. 64 (1) (*b*); E.P.A., s. 108 (3) (*b*).
[47] T.U.L.R.A., Sched. 1, Pt. IV, para. 26 (3).
[48] T.U.L.R.A., Sched. 1, Pt. IV, para. 26 (4A); S.D.A., s. 64 (3); E.P.A., s. 108 (6).
[49] See Chap. 17 above.
[50] See Chap. 17 above.
[51] T.U.L.R.A., Sched. 1, Pt. IV, para. 26 (5); S.D.A., s. 64 (4); E.P.A., s. 108 (7).
[52] *M. & W. Grazebrook Ltd.* v. *Wallens* [1973] I.C.R. 256 (N.I.R.C.).
[53] 1974 Regs., r. 4 (1) (*a*).

Manchester,[54] the Employment Appeal Tribunal has indicated that in anything except the simplest cases, "commonsense and goodwill" may involve giving, when it is asked, reasonable detail about the nature of complaints which are going to be made at the hearing. In the words of Phillips J.:

> "It does not require any special forms; it does not require any special learning or knowledge. It is just a matter of straightforward sense. In one way or another the parties need to know the sort of thing which is going to be the subject of the hearing. Industrial tribunals know this very well and for the most part seek to ensure that it comes about. Of course, in the end, if there is surprise, they will ordinarily grant an adjournment to enable it to be dealt with but by and large it is much better if matters of this kind can be dealt with in advance so as to prevent adjournments taking place which are time-consuming, expensive and inconvenient to all concerned." [55]

In *White's* case itself the respondent's reply alleged that the reasons for the applicant's dismissal as a typist were, first that she was unable to cope with the duties associated with her job, and secondly that her attitude to and treatment of students and other university employees had caused ill-feeling and difficulty. The further and better particulars she sought were the respects in which it was alleged that she had been unable satisfactorily to cope with her duties and the way in which her attitude was said to be defective. The E.A.T. held that this was a classic case where particulars ought to be given. It was by no means a simple case and the applicant could not possibly prepare for the hearing unless she knew in reasonable details the allegations which would be made. If the particulars are not supplied as ordered all or part of the notice of appearance may be struck out, or the application may be dismissed.[56]

Witness orders, orders for the production of documents and orders for the discovery or inspection of documents may also be made.[57] Failure to comply with any such order may lead, on summary conviction, to a fine not exceeding £100.[58] In practice the tribunal Chairman and Secretary have to be careful to avoid giving an appearance of injustice to the applicant by discussing the evidence which the witness might give or other matters with the witness in the absence of the applicant.[59] It is for the applicant to satisfy the tribunal that a witness can give relevant evidence and that he will not attend without an order.[60]

The hearing

730   At least 14 days' notice of the hearing must be given unless the parties agree to a shorter time.[61] In practice postponements are not readily granted. The emphasis of the tribunals is on relatively speedy determination

---

[54] [1976] I.R.L.R. 218 (E.A.T.).
[55] At p. 220.
[56] 1974 Regs., r. 4 (5).
[57] *Ibid.* r. 4 (1) (*b*) (*c*). The rules for discovery are as in the county court.
[58] T.U.L.R.A., Sched. 1, Pt. IV, para. 21 (6); 1974 Regs., r. 4 (4).
[59] *H.G.S.* v. *Wilcox* [1976] I.R.L.R. 222 (C.A.).
[60] *Dada* v. *Metal Box Co. Ltd.* [1974] I.C.R. 559. It may be considered sufficient to show that the witness would find it easier to attend under order.
[61] 1974 Regs., r. 5 (1).

of disputes and the length of time between application and determination should not be prolonged without good reason. In unfair dismissal cases it is particularly important to have the question of liability determined as soon as possible because delay might prejudice the applicant's chances of reinstatement or re-engagement. Undue delay in making an application for a postponement may be a ground for refusing the application. Lengthy adjournments are to be avoided.[62]

Where two or more applications are brought against the same respondent it is often convenient to list these for hearing on the same day. Although the tribunal is entitled to hear all the applications together it is essential that each should be separately considered in order to see whether or not exactly similar circumstances apply to each case.[63] Moreover, in such cases, the tribunal has no power to order the evidence of the second or subsequent applicants to be heard before the evidence given on behalf of the respondent.[64]

It is the usual practice, in unfair dismissal cases, to determine liability and then hear evidence as to remedies as a separate issue.[65] Section 71 of the Employment Protection Act now appears to make this practice mandatory because when, on a complaint of unfair dismissal, the tribunal finds that the grounds of the complaint are well-founded it is under a duty, at that stage, to explain to the complainant what orders for reinstatement or re-engagement may be made and in what circumstances they may be made and to ask him whether he wishes the tribunal to make such an order. Sometimes preliminary points, as to jurisdiction, are set down for hearing as separate issues and in those cases a party should not be taken by surprise by having the substantive issue dealt with at that hearing without his consent.[66]

If a party fails to attend the hearing or to be represented, the tribunal may dispose of the application in his absence or may adjourn the hearing to a later date (after considering any written representations by that party).[67] There is a danger, if it subsequently transpires that a party was prevented from attending due to circumstances beyond his control when he had intended to attend, that the hearing in his absence may be a nullity.[68] Accordingly the party who is present should be warned of this danger by the chairman. If he elects to proceed, the tribunal may treat the originating application, or the appearance, as the case may be, as representations in writing and consider them accordingly. An absent party is entitled to seek a review of the decision.[69]

The hearing must be in public, unless it involves matters of national security, would involve disclosure of some matter contrary to an enactment, or of information communicated to a witness in confidence, or of information the disclosure of which would be seriously prejudicial to the interests of the undertaking other than in respect of collective bargaining.[70]

---

[62] *Barnes* v. *B.P.C. (Business Forms) Ltd.* [1975] I.C.R. 390 (Q.B.D.).
[63] *Green* v. *Southampton Corporation* [1973] I.C.R. 153 (N.I.R.C.).
[64] *Strowger* v. *David Rosenfield Ltd.* [1972] I.T.R. 375 (N.I.R.C.).
[65] *Copson* v. *Eversure Accessories Ltd.* [1974] I.T.R. 446 (N.I.R.C.).
[66] *Berkeley Garage (Southampton) Ltd.* v. *Edmunds* [1975] I.C.R. 228 (Q.B.D.).
[67] 1974 Regs., r. 7 (2).
[68] *Priddle* v. *Fisher & Sons* [1968] I.T.R. 358; *Murray (Turf Accountants)* v. *Laurie* [1972] I.T.R. 22.
[69] 1974 Regs., r. 9 (1) (c).   [70] r. 6 (1).

A party is entitled to submit representations in writing for consideration by the tribunal not less than seven days before the hearing.[71] That party must send copies to the other parties.[72] A " representation in writing " is in effect a written submission sent to a tribunal *in substitution* for evidence on oath and is usually resorted to where a party does not intend to appear at the hearing.[73]

Representation

731   A party and any person entitled to appear may present his case in person or be represented by counsel or by a solicitor or by a representative of a trade union or an employers' association or by any other person whom he desires to represent him.[74]

There is no legal aid available for representation before tribunals. However, the " Green Form " Legal Advice and Assistance Scheme may be used to give advice, write letters, conduct negotiations, obtain statements and counsel's opinion, and to prepare a " brief " for the tribunal. Where the cost is likely to exceed £25 the solicitor must apply to the Area Secretary of the Scheme for authority to exceed the limit.

Presentation of evidence

732   It is for the parties and not the tribunal to see that all relevant evidence is presented.[75] The general principle is that the parties must be allowed to have their say.[76] A party is entitled to make an opening statement, to give evidence, to call witnesses, to cross-examine and to address the tribunal.[77] An oath or affirmation is usually required.[78] Although no rules are laid down as to the weight to be attached to unsworn statements (including written representations), such statements may be described as " evidence " in the sense that they are material which the tribunal must take into consideration in determining the application. However, it is submitted that, where a fact is disputed, an unsworn statement can hardly vie with sworn evidence in cogency and weight.

The chairman of the tribunal should not dictate the order in which a party calls his witnesses,[79] nor should he place arbitrary limits on cross-examination.[80] This apart, the tribunal may in general regulate its own procedure and the aim is to achieve as great a degree of informality as possible. The ordinary rules of evidence are not applicable. For example, hearsay evidence may be admitted provided that it can fairly be regarded as reliable.[81] The tribunals may act on any matter which is logically

---

[71] r. 6 (3).
[72] *Ibid.*
[73] *Hardisty* v. *Lowton Construction Group Ltd.* [1973] I.T.R. 603. Accordingly there is no objection to a proof of evidence being read out by a party under oath without seven days advance notice.
[74] 1974 Regs., r. 6 (6). The fact that an applicant is unrepresented cannot *per se* be a ground for a rehearing: *Dalton* v. *Burton's Gold Medal Biscuits Ltd.* [1974] I.R.L.R. 45; nor is it in itself a ground for seeking an adjournment: *Singh* v. *London County Bus Services Ltd.* [1976] I.R.L.R. 176 (E.A.T.).
[75] *Craig* v. *British Railways* [1973] I.T.R. 636 (N.I.R.C.).
[76] *Kapur* v. *Shields* [1975] I.T.R. 173 (Q.B.D.).
[77] 1974 Regs., r. 7 (1).
[78] r. 7 (3).
[79] *Barnes* v. *B.P.C. (Business Forms) Ltd.* [1975] I.C.R. 390 (Q.B.D.).
[80] *Vickers* v. *Hudson Bros. (Midd.) Ltd.* [1970] I.T.R. 259 (Div. C.).
[81] *Etherington* v. *Henry J. Greenham (1929) Ltd.* [1969] I.T.R. 226 (Div. C.).

probative even though it would not be admissible as evidence in an ordinary court of law, provided that the other side is given a fair opportunity of commenting on it and contradicting it.[82] In practice, the tribunal will explain to an unrepresented party that relatively little weight can be attached to hearsay evidence and, in some cases, for example where letters or statements from a person not being called as a witness are produced only at the hearing, the chairman will not admit the evidence or will grant an adjournment (subject to an order for costs) to allow the other party to deal with the material.

Where a party is not represented by counsel or a solicitor, the chairman will attempt to help that party to present his evidence by explaining the law and procedure. He will also attempt to prevent unfairness by stopping an advocate or unrepresented party putting leading questions to his own witness on matters in dispute; and will stop a party who in the course of cross-examination gives evidence himself. A party may be allowed to read his proof of evidence by way of evidence in chief.[83] In England and Wales it is not the general practice to exclude witnesses from the hearing before giving their evidence unless a party specifically asks for their exclusion.

The party on whom the burden of proof rests should be asked to begin with the presentation of his evidence.[84] For example, if dismissal is admitted in an unfair dismissal case, the employer should begin. It is open to a tribunal to dismiss the case before hearing the other side,[85] but usually this will only be done where it is clear that, as a matter of law, even if the party who began proves his case he cannot succeed.

Decision

733 The tribunal's decision may be that of a majority.[86] The usual practice is that, after a short retirement, the tribunal's decision, with reasons, is given orally at the end of the hearing. This is recorded on to a tape and after it has been transcribed and edited by the chairman, he signs a fair copy of the decision. For administrative reasons this may take some weeks. It is only when the decision is formally entered in the register and copies have been sent to the parties that it is binding.[87] Before then, if it appears that there has been some mistake, the parties can be asked to come back for further argument and the decision already given orally can be varied. Once it has been promulgated (*i.e.* entered in the register), however, it cannot be altered except in one of three specific ways: (1) the chairman may by certificate under his hand correct clerical mistakes or errors arising from any accidental slip or omission; (2) the tribunal may review, revoke or vary its decision under the Rules, but only on application by a party (see below); and (3) a superior court or the Employment Appeal Tribunal may alter or vary or set aside the decision (see below).

In some cases it is not possible to announce the decision immediately

---

[82] *T. A. Miller Ltd.* v. *Min. of Housing* [1968] 1 W.L.R. 992, 995; and see generally, Wraith and Hutchesson, *Administrative Tribunals* (London, 1973) pp. 143 *et seq.*
[83] *Hardisty* v. *Lowton Construction Group* [1973] I.T.R. 603 (N.I.R.C.).
[84] *Gill* v. *Harold Andrews Sheepbridge Ltd.* [1974] I.T.R. 219, 220 (N.I.R.C.).
[85] *Brennan* v. *Lindley & Co.* [1974] I.R.L.R. 153 (N.I.R.C.).
[86] 1974 Regs., r. 8 (1). If the tribunal is composed of only two members, the chairman has a second or casting vote.
[87] r. 8 (3).

and the decision is reserved. In these cases as well it is only when the decision is promulgated that it is binding.

The superior courts have insisted that the industrial tribunals should state reasons for each part of a decision to show what influenced the tribunal in arriving at its decision.[88] This is to enable the parties to know why the tribunal has decided as it has and, secondly, because there is an appeal only on a point of law, it is desirable that the Appeal Tribunal should be able to determine precisely upon what grounds the tribunal arrived at its decision. It is not, however, necessary for the tribunal to make findings of fact on every peripheral matter in issue between the parties [89]; it is upon the major issues of fact that the tribunal must state what evidence it accepted and what it rejected, with its reasons.[90]

Agreed settlements

734   If the applicant at any time gives notice of the withdrawal of his originating application, the chairman [91] may make an order dismissing the proceedings.[92] Alternatively, all the parties may agree in writing upon the terms of a decision to be made by the tribunal, and the chairman may then decide accordingly.[93] The appropriate form of order (colloquially known as a "Tomlin" order) [94] is to stay all further proceedings upon the terms set out in the order except for the purpose of carrying such terms into effect, with liberty to apply for that purpose. It is wise to make the order in this form otherwise, in case of default, the party aggrieved may have no remedy except to commence fresh proceedings to enforce the terms. There is no reason why the terms of settlement should not include matters outside the tribunal's jurisdiction.

It will be noted that the tribunals possess no general power to dismiss applications for want of prosecution, but there is a power, sparingly used, to strike out or amend anything in an application or notice of appearance which is "scandalous, frivolous or vexatious." [95]

Costs

735   The normal rule is that costs will not be awarded.[96] The only exceptions are where: (1) a party has acted frivolously, that is knowing that the claim or defence has no substance (which will be inferred if it is manifestly misconceived), or vexatiously, that is the party has acted from some improper motive such as to harass the employer out of spite [97]; (2) the tribunal has postponed or adjourned the hearing on the application of a

---

[88] *Cooper* v. *British Steel Corporation* [1975] I.C.R. 454 (Q.B.D.).

[89] *Long & Hambly Ltd.* v. *Bryan* [1975] I.C.R. 200 (Q.B.D.).

[90] *Alexander Machinery (Dudley) Ltd.* v. *Crabtree* [1974] I.T.R. 182 (N.I.R.C.). Since it is the duty of the chairman to take a note of the substance of evidence placed before the tribunal (*Archbold Freightage Ltd.* v. *Wilson* [1974] I.T.R. 133 (N.I.R.C.)), it is not necessary for the substance of the evidence to be rehearsed in the decision.

[91] *i.e.* the president, a chairman nominated by him or the chairman of the tribunal hearing the case: 1974 Regs., r. 11 (4).

[92] r. 11 (2) (c).

[93] r. 11 (2) (d).

[94] From the similar practice of the Supreme Court: see Practice Note [1927] W.N. 290.

[95] 1974 Regs., r. 11 (2) (e).

[96] 1974 Regs., r. 10 (1).

[97] *E. T. Marler* v. *Robertson* [1974] I.C.R. 72 (N.I.R.C.).

party and the other party has incurred any costs[98]; or (3) any postponement or adjournment has been caused by the respondent where the employee has expressed a wish to be reinstated or re-engaged which has been communicated to the employer at least seven days before the hearing of the complaint, or the proceedings arise out of the employer's failure to permit the employee to return to work after an absence due to pregnancy or confinement.[99] In the first two situations the tribunal has a discretion whether or not to award costs; in the third situation the award of costs is mandatory, in the absence of a special reason.

When making an order for costs the tribunal has power to award either a specified sum (in practice, a figure between £35 and £50 is not uncommon), or the taxed amount of costs. The wording of the rule seems to suggest that a specified sum may be awarded only by agreement (although this is by no means clear) but parties are usually only too ready to accept a sum suggested by the tribunal rather than incur the further costs involved in taxing costs on the appropriate county court scale. Where taxed costs are awarded the tribunal must specify under which county court scale the taxation is to be made.[1]

Costs are to be distinguished from allowances. Allowances are paid out of public funds to litigants and witnesses, in respect of attendance at the hearing and are paid irrespective of the success or failure of a party. They are paid, on the authority of the clerk to the tribunal, on a scale fixed by the Secretary of State. Where costs are awarded against a party it is obviously just that no allowances should be paid to that party, and the tribunal may order such a party to repay all or part of the allowances to the Secretary of State.[2] It is also just that the successful party should not be paid both costs and allowances in respect of the same out-of-pocket expenses. Accordingly when an award of a specified sum is made this is usually stated to be in respect of costs only and not in respect of those matters which are covered by allowances.

Enforcement

736 One of the curiosities of the powers of industrial tribunals is that their ultimate sanction is the award of a sum of money. Even in cases of unfair dismissal where reinstatement or re-engagement is ordered, failure to comply with the order leads ultimately to an additional award of money and not to specific enforcement or the quasi-criminal sanctions of the ordinary courts in respect of contempt of court.[3] Any sum of money payable in pursuance of a decision of an industrial tribunal in England and Wales, which has been duly registered, is recoverable by execution issued from the county court after the making of an order for execution by that court. It is thereafter recovered as if it were payable under an order of the county court.[4]

Where an employer or employee has died, tribunal proceedings arising under the Redundancy Payments Act 1965, the Trade Union and Labour

---

98 1974 Regs., r. 10 (2) (a) as amended by 1976 Regs.
99 r. 10 (2) (b) as amended.
1 r. 10 (4).
2 r. 10 (1) (b)
3 See Chap. 17 above.
4 T.U.L.R.A., Sched. 1, Pt. III, para. 25 (5).

Relations Act 1974 and the Employment Protection Act 1975 may be instituted or continued or defended by a personal representative of the deceased, or, if there is no personal representative, by a person appointed by the tribunal.[5] An award may also be enforced by, or on behalf of, the estate of a deceased employee or employer.[6] Where a company is in liquidation under a winding-up order made by a court, the leave and directions of the court are required to commence or carry on proceedings against that company.[7] In cases under the Redundancy Payments Act 1965, however, the Secretary of State usually exercises his right to intervene where the respondent company is in liquidation and the liquidator does not contest the claim because once an award has been made the Secretary of State pays the employee the full amount under the provisions of section 32 of the 1965 Act. In cases under other jurisdictions, the Employment Protection Act 1975 allows the employee to obtain payment from the Secretary of State but only where the respondent company has become insolvent *after* the tribunal's award has been made.[8] The Act does not seem to help the employee whose former employer becomes insolvent *before* proceedings are commenced. In these cases, therefore, if the tribunal is satisfied that the company is under a compulsory winding-up order, the applicant cannot proceed without first obtaining the leave of the court.

Review

737 The tribunals have no general power to review their own decisions. The statutory power to review is limited to the following matters:

" (a) the decision was wrongly made as a result of an error on the part of the tribunal staff; or

(b) a party did not receive notice of the proceedings leading to the decision; or

(c) the decision was made in the absence of a party or person entitled to be heard; or

(d) new evidence has become available since the making of the decision provided that its existence could not have been reasonably known of or foreseen; or

(e) the interests of justice require such a review."

Although the last-mentioned ground confers a wide discretion it has been held that it does not cover a case where new evidence which it is now sought to place before the tribunal was available at the original hearing. Such a case must fall under paragraph (d).[9] Nor is it enough under paragraph (e) to allege surprise at the hearing; there must also be a miscarriage of justice.[10]

An application for a review may be made at the hearing. If it is not, it may be made to the Secretary of Tribunals at any time from the date of hearing until 14 days after the date of entry of a decision in the

5 E.P.A., Sched. 12 (which contains detailed provisions).
6 Industrial Tribunals Awards (Enforcement in Case of Death) Regs., S.I. 1976 No. 663.
7 Companies Act 1948, s. 231.
8 See Chap. 10, above.
9 *Flint* v. *Eastern Electricity Board* [1975] I.T.R. 152 (Q.B.D.).
10 *Hibbert* v. *Newling-Ward Hotels* [1975] 1 C.L. 103.

register.[11] The application in such a case must be in writing and must state the grounds in full.[12] The president, a nominated chairman or the chairman of the original tribunal may refuse the application himself if in his opinion it has no reasonable prospect of success.[13] If he does not refuse it, the full tribunal must hear it and may either vary or revoke its decision and order a rehearing.[14]

Appeals

738   The nature and composition of the Employment Appeal Tribunal was described in Chapter 4 where it was seen that, in general, appeals may be brought only on points of law. The Tribunal, like its predecessors (the N.I.R.C. and the Queen's Bench Division) has stressed that it will not interfere with tribunal decisions unless there is an error of law.[15] In particular the Appeal Tribunal cannot disturb a finding of primary facts, so long as there is evidence on which the industrial tribunal could reach that finding.[16] On the other hand, the question of what is a proper inference from the primary facts is a question of law with which the Tribunal can interfere.[17] But even in such cases the Appeal Tribunal will be reluctant to reach a different inference from that of the industrial tribunal which saw and heard the witnesses, on questions such as whether a dismissal was unfair, or whether an offer of suitable employment had been made by the employer.[18] In particular, the Appeal Tribunal will not interfere with awards of compensation unless the error is more than a trifling one. This is because tribunals have to assess compensation (and evaluate questions of the employee's contribution to his own dismissal) quickly and in a fairly rough and ready way.[19]

The Appeal Tribunal does not consider itself bound by decisions of the High Court, the Court of Session Outer House, or the N.I.R.C., although these are of considerable persuasive authority and the Appeal Tribunal will not lightly interfere with principles developed by those courts.[20] It is bound by decisions of the Court of Appeal, Court of Session Inner House, and House of Lords.

---

[11] 1974 Regs., r. 9 (2) as amended by 1976 Regs. A second application for a review, after the first has been refused is not possible: *Stevensons (Dyers) Ltd.* v. *Brennan* [1974] I.C.R. 194 (N.I.R.C.).

[12] r. 9 (2).

[13] r. 9 (3). Despite an *obiter dictum* to the contrary in *Coates* v. *C. J. Crispin* [1973] I.T.R. 446 (Sir John Donaldson) it seems that a tribunal with a different chairman cannot consider the review, because a tribunal is given power only to review its own decisions.

[14] r. 9 (4).

[15] *e.g. Smyth* v. *Autocar & Transporters Ltd.* [1975] I.C.R. 180 (Q.B.D.); *Hilti (Great Britain) Ltd.* v. *Windridge* [1974] I.C.R. 352 (N.I.R.C.); *Runham* v. *Wood Bros & Runham Ltd.* [1972] I.T.R. 277 (N.I.R.C.); *Watling* v. *William Bird & Son Contractors Ltd.* [1976] I.T.R. 70 (Q.B.D.).

[16] *John Brignell & Co. (Builders) Ltd.* v. *Bishop* [1973] I.T.R. 420 (N.I.R.C.); *Bricknell* v. *Thames Water Authority* [1975] I.C.R. 460 (Q.B.D.). The former N.I.R.C. issued a practice direction (July 24, 1973) that if an appeal which involved no question of law was instituted this might be considered unreasonable conduct justifying an award of costs.

[17] *John Brignell & Co. Ltd.* v. *Bishop* (above).

[18] *Winterhalter Gastronom Ltd.* v. *Webb* [1973] I.C.R. 245 (N.I.R.C.); *Harris* v. *E. Turner (Joinery) Ltd.* [1973] I.C.R. 31 (N.I.R.C.); *Wellman Alloys Ltd.* v. *Russell* [1973] I.C.R. 616 (N.I.R.C.).

[19] *Fougere* v. *Phoenix Motor Co. (Surrey) Ltd., The Times,* July 7, 1976 (E.A.T.); *Munif* v. *Cole & Kirby Ltd.* [1973] I.C.R. 486 (N.I.R.C.).

[20] *Portec (U.K.) Ltd.* v. *Mogensen,* L.S.Gaz. May 26, 1976 (E.A.T.).

The Appeal Tribunal will base itself primarily on the findings of fact recorded in the industrial tribunal's decision, but it is the practice to make available to the parties on request after the noting of an appeal, copies of the chairman's notes of evidence. Where there is a conflict between the notes of evidence taken by the chairman and the findings of fact as they appear in the tribunal's decision the Appeal Tribunal will generally be guided by the findings of fact in the decision unless compelling circumstances lead to the conclusion that the reasons may inaccurately state the substance of the evidence.[21] If a party wishes to allege on appeal that the chairman's notes are inaccurate he should give the chairman an opportunity to comment on the matters in respect of which the notes are said to be defective, bearing in mind that the chairman need record only the substance of the evidence and not all the details of it.

An appeal to the Appeal Tribunal is instituted by serving on the Tribunal within 42 days of the date on which the document recording the decision or order appealed from was sent to the appellant, a notice of appeal in accordance with a form prescribed under the Employment Appeal Tribunal Rules 1976.[22] The Registrar of the Appeal Tribunal is responsible for serving the notice of appeal on the other parties.[23] The respondent must deliver a reply in writing in the prescribed form within the time appointed by the Registrar, and may also note a cross-appeal.[24] The Registrar informs the parties of the date for hearing.[25] There is provision in the Rules for the holding of a meeting for directions where this would facilitate the future conduct of the proceedings.[26] The Tribunal may take such steps as it thinks fit to enable the parties to avail themselves of opportunities for conciliation.[27] Fresh evidence will be admitted only exceptionally where there is a reasonable explanation for it not having been put before the tribunal and it is credible and of a kind likely to have had a decisive effect on the tribunal.[28] For this purpose the Tribunal has power to order attendance of witnesses.[29] Hearings are held in public, save in the same exceptional circumstances in which an industrial tribunal may sit in private.[30] The rules as to representation are the same as in respect of industrial tribunals, but legal aid is available. Costs may be awarded against a party only where it appears to the Appeal Tribunal that any proceedings were unnecessary, improper or vexatious or that there has been unreasonable delay or other unreasonable conduct in bringing or conducting the proceedings.[31]

There is a further appeal on a point of law, with leave, to the Court of Appeal, and with further leave, to the House of Lords.[32]

---

[21] *Ogidu-Olu* v. *Guy's Hospital Board of Governors* [1973] I.C.R. 645 (N.I.R.C.).
[22] S.I. 1976 No. 322, r. 3 (1).
[23] r. 4.
[24] r. 6.
[25] r. 7.
[26] r. 13.
[27] r. 23.
[28] This was the practice of the N.I.R.C. and Q.B.D.: *e.g. Roux International Ltd.* v. *Licudi* [1975] I.C.R. 424 (Q.B.D.); *De Mars* v. *Gurr Johns & Angier Bird Ltd.* [1973] I.C.R. 35 (N.I.R.C.).
[29] r. 16.
[30] r. 18.
[31] r. 21.
[32] See Chap. 4 above.

Relationship with ordinary courts

739   We have seen that the Lord Chancellor has not yet exercised his power, under section 109 of the Employment Protection Act 1975, to confer jurisdiction on the tribunals in respect of claims for damages for breach of the contract of employment and other contracts connected with employment. Even when this is done, the tribunals' jurisdiction will be concurrent with that of the ordinary courts in these matters. So, while the tribunals have exclusive jurisdiction in respect of the matters assigned to them by statute, parties to contracts will retain the right to seek redress in the ordinary courts. Moreover, the tribunal's jurisdiction is to be limited to claims which arise or are outstanding on the termination of the employment, or arise in circumstances which give rise to proceedings already or simultaneously brought before a tribunal in respect of some other claim. (The Lord Chancellor may require one or both these conditions to be satisfied.)

The reasons advanced for these limitations [33] are the need to preserve the right to trial by jury (in the ordinary courts) and the argument that some contractual claims (*e.g.* in respect of inventions made by an employee) may raise complicated issues not really suitable for a tribunal which may not be full-time and is predominantly lay. These arguments are not, however, convincing when one remembers that the tribunals are in a sense " industrial juries " and civil cases in the ordinary courts are usually heard by a judge sitting alone; and that recent legislation already entrusts extremely complicated issues to the tribunals.

The multiplicity of courts and tribunals which may determine claims arising from the employment relationship has both procedural and substantive consequences. Procedurally, the same facts may lead to claims under different jurisdictions (*e.g.* during lay-off a worker may have claims before the tribunal for a guarantee payment, before a county court for sums due under his contract, and before a social security tribunal for unemployment benefit). Although industrial tribunals are not bound by the normal rules of evidence, it is submitted that where an issue has been raised and distinctly determined between the same parties in other civil proceedings, then, as a general rule the doctrine of " issue estoppel " should apply. This means that the same parties should not be allowed to fight that same issue all over again before an industrial tribunal. This applies to any assertion of fact, or the legal consequences of facts, which was an essential issue in a cause of action or defence between the same parties in previous county court or High Court proceedings. There may be an exception where further relevant material has since those proceedings become available. In practice, of course, tribunal proceedings may be concluded before proceedings in the ordinary courts and in those cases the ordinary courts may apply the doctrine of issue estoppel. An obvious example is a declaration by an industrial tribunal of the terms of a contract of employment at a particular date (see Chapter 7).

The effect of the multiplicity of jurisdictions on substantive law is shown by the different rules adopted by the N.I.R.C. and the High Court on the question of the deductibility of a redundancy payment from damages

---

[33] Royal Commission on Trade Unions and Employers' Associations, Cmnd. 3623, para. 579.

awarded for a dismissal which is unfair or wrongful.[34] Perhaps the most important consequence at the present time is that the law of unfair dismissal and the law of wrongful dismissal are entirely distinct (see Chapter 17). There is, however, a complex interaction between the law as developed by the tribunals and the law laid down in the ordinary courts. For example, many questions of statutory interpretation raise the question whether or not there has been a breach of the contract of employment (*e.g.* the definition of " dismissal," see Chapter 14), and the tribunals will be guided by the persuasive authority of decisions of the ordinary courts in such matters. Conversely, the Court of Appeal has on occasion allowed the law of unfair dimissal to influence equitable rules regarding the granting of injunctions.[35]

Relationship with domestic appeal proceedings

740 The doctrine of issue estoppel cannot arise in respect of a domestic disciplinary procedure because the decision of the domestic appeals body is not a " final " one in the legal sense. However, when an industrial tribunal comes to determine a complaint of unfair dismissal, the decision of the domestic appeals body in respect of that dismissal and the facts upon which it is based will obviously be admissible and relevant. In particular, if the domestic body has fully considered the facts this is one of the " circumstances " to which regard must be had in deciding whether the dismissal was fair or unfair.[36] At the same time, the Employment Appeal Tribunal has expressed the view that it is undesirable for a person who was a member of an appeal body which considered the employee's case to conduct the employer's case before the tribunal. It may be unavoidable to call such a person as a witness " though, perhaps, that, too, is not the best course." [37]

---

[34] See Chap. 16 above, para. 529.
[35] See Chap. 2 above, paras. 109 *et seq.*
[36] *James* v. *Waltham Holy Cross U.D.C.* [1973] I.T.R. 467, 473; see generally, S. D. Anderman, *Voluntary Dismissals Procedures and the Industrial Relations Act* (P.E.P., 1972).
[37] *Singh* v. *London County Bus Services Ltd.* [1976] I.R.L.R. 176 (E.A.T.).

APPENDICES

FURTHER READING

OUR object here is to give some indication of where students and others who wish to explore the area covered by this book further may find fuller information. This is not intended as a bibliography but is simply a guide to some of the more useful literature which may help to explain or illuminate the problems in the areas covered. It may be helpful to indicate first of all where fuller bibliographical material can be found. The definitive work is *A Bibliography of the Literature on British and Irish Labour Law* (London, 1975) by B. A. Hepple, J. M. Neeson and P. O'Higgins. A very useful short bibliography can be also found in K. W. Wedderburn, *The Worker and the Law* (2nd ed. Harmondsworth, 1971). The *Annual Survey of Commonwealth Law* (published every year since 1966, at Oxford) contains in its chapter on Labour Law bibliographical information on the more important books and articles published during the particular year under review. It includes material from the Commonwealth and is also useful with regard to British material. The *Industrial Law Journal* (London, four times a year) contains, once a year, a list of articles published on British labour law.

General. The following contain useful accounts, from differing points of view, of the basic principles of English labour law:

(a) The writing of Professor Sir Otto Kahn-Freund, who has exercised the most profound influence over the study of British labour law, in particular his contribution to A. Flanders and H. Clegg (ed.), *The System of Industrial Relations in Great Britain* (Oxford, 1954); his contribution to M. Ginsberg (ed.) *Law and Opinion in England in the Twentieth Century* (London, 1959), and his books, *Labour Law: Old Traditions and New Developments* (Toronto, 1968), and *Labour and the Law* (London, 1972).

(b) K. W. Wedderburn, *The Worker and the Law* (2nd ed. Harmondsworth, 1971), especially Chapter 1.

(c) P. O'Higgins, introductory part to " Collective Bargaining in Britain," in T. Mayer-Maly, *Kollectivverträge in Europa* (Munich and Salzburg, 1972).

Reference. Although it is now somewhat out of date G. H. L. Fridman, *The Modern Law of Employment* (London, 1963; supplements 1964, 1967 and 1972), contains an enormous amount of factual information.

Textbooks. Some modern textbooks will be found useful, especially O. Aiken and J. Reid, *Labour Law 1: Employment, Welfare and Safety* (Harmondsworth, 1971); K. W. Wedderburn, *The Worker and the Law* (Harmondsworth, 2nd ed. 1971) and *Cases and Materials on Labour Law* (Cambridge, 1967); R. W. Rideout, *Principles of Labour Law* (2nd ed. London, 1976); and *Chitty on Contracts,* Vol. 2.

Reports. There are four series of reports specialising in labour law. Two commenced publication in 1966. They are *Knight's Industrial Reports* (now called *Managerial Law*), and the *Industrial Tribunal Reports.* The latter is published by H.M. Stationery Office. The others commenced publication in 1972 and are the *Industrial Cases Reports* (Incorporated Council of Law Reporting; called *Industrial Court Reports* until December 1974) and the *Industrial Relations Law Reports.*

Periodicals. The leading journal is the quarterly *Industrial Law Journal* published in London for the Industrial Law Society. There is also the *Industrial Relations Review and Report,* which contains information and comment of legal interest, the publishers of which, Industrial Relations Services, London, also publish the *Industrial Relations Legal Information Bulletin,* which keeps readers up to date with current legal developments. Incomes Data Services, Ltd., London, publish the very valuable series *Incomes Data Briefs,* which contain good summaries and explanations of current legal developments. They also publish *Studies* on special topics.

Department of Employment Publications. The Department of Employment publishes some excellent free *Guides* on labour legislation, *e.g.* Equal Pay, Sex Discrimination, Contracts of Employment Act, the Redundancy Payments Scheme, etc. Even if these pamphlets were not free they would still deserve to be on anyone's list of " best-buys."

We list below some suggestions for reading on particular topics.

CHAPTER 1. *Collective Labour Relations.* Apart from books mentioned under *General* above, the following deserve particular attention. On the experience of the Industrial Relations Act, see B. Weekes, et al, *Industrial Relations and the Limits of Law* (Oxford, 1975) and A. W. J. Thomson & S. R. Engleman, *The Industrial Relations Act: A Review and Analysis* (London, 1975). On problems of the law in relation to industrial conflict, see O. Kahn-Freund & B. A. Hepple, *Laws Against Strikes* (London, 1972). A most important work on the comparative aspect of this topic is B. Aaron & K. W. Wedderburn, *Industrial Conflict: A Comparative Legal Survey* (London, 1972). On trade unions a work which is still useful, although out of date in some respects is C. Grunfeld, *Modern Trade Union Law* (London, 1966).

CHAPTER 2. *The Individual Employment Relationship.* For rather different views, compare O. Kahn-Freund, " Note on Status and Contract in British Labour Law " (1967) 30 M.L.R. 635, with R. W. Rideout, " The Contract of Employment " (1966) 19 *Current Legal Problems* 111.

CHAPTER 3. *The Contract of Employment.* A work of great value for all aspects of the contract of employment is M. R. Freedland, *The Contract of Employment* (Oxford, 1976). The tests for identifying the contract are discussed in depth by P. S. Atiyah, *Vicarious Liability in the Law of Tort* (London, 1967), Part II. A reading of the short note by Professor Kahn-Freund on *Cassidy* v. *Minister of Health* in (1951) 14 M.L.R. 504 is essential to an understanding of the " organisation " test. More recent developments are discussed by C. D. Drake, " Wage Slave or Entrepreneur " (1968) 31 M.L.R. 408, and in notes by G. de N. Clark (1968) 31 M.L.R.

450, Paul O'Higgins [1967] C.L.J. 27, and B. A. Hepple [1968] C.L.J. 2277. For a general survey of the problem of labour-only sub-contracting, see *Report of the Committee of Inquiry under Professor E. H. Phelps Brown into Certain Matters concerning Labour in Building and Civil Engineering* (Cmnd. 3714), esp. Appendix III (by R. W. Rideout); G. de N. Clark, "Industrial Law and the Labour-only Sub-contract" (1967) 30 M.L.R. 6, and P. O'Higgins, *The Listener*, April 27, 1967, p. 549. The position of public employees is dealt with in B. A. Hepple and Paul O'Higgins, *Public Employee Trade Unionism in the United Kingdom: the Legal Framework* (Ann Arbor, 1971) which contains a select bibliography of other works in this field.

CHAPTER 4. *Legal Machinery for Resolving Employment Claims.* The leading study is K. W. Wedderburn and P. L. Davies, *Employment Grievances and Disputes in Britain* (Berkeley, 1969) now overtaken by recent legislative developments, but still extremely valuable in regard to voluntary procedures (Part II) and arbitration, conciliation and inquiry (Part III). Among other special studies are: on voluntary procedures— A. I. Marsh, *Disputes Procedures in British Industry* (Royal Commission Paper No. 2, London, 1968). On Industrial Tribunals—C. E. McCormick, "Redundancy Payments Act in the Practice of the Industrial Tribunals," B.J.Ind.Rels., 8 (1970), 334; Sir D. Conroy, "Tribunals and the Courts," New L.J., 120 (1970) 1069; K. Whitesides and G. Hawker, *Industrial Tribunals* (London, 1975). On social security tribunals—H. Street, *Justice in the Welfare State* (2nd ed., London, 1975), Chapter 1, and K. Bell, *Tribunals in the Social Services* (London, 1970). On courts of inquiry— W. E. J. McCarthy and B. A. Clifford, "The Work of Industrial Courts of Inquiry," B.J.Ind.Rels., 4 (1964) 39.

CHAPTER 6. *Freedom of Association and the Right to Work.* The implications of *Nagle* v. *Feilden* have been considered by, among others, A. L. Goodhart (1966) 82 L.Q.R. 319; J. S. Hall (1967) 117 New L.J. 961; R. W. Rideout (1967) 30 M.L.R. 389; and J. A. Weir [1966] C.L.J. 165. For an earlier discussion of these problems, see D. Lloyd, "The Right to Work" (1957) 10 *Current Legal Problems* 36. All of these should be read, critically, in the light of W. E. J. McCarthy, *The Closed Shop in Britain* (Oxford, 1964).

CHAPTER 7. *Proof of Terms. Lister* v. *Romford Ice and Cold Storage Co. Ltd.* provoked a number of important articles, especially, G. L. Williams, "Vicarious Liability and the Master's Indemnity" (1957) 20 M.L.R. 200, 437; J. A. Jolowicz, "The Right to Indemnity between Master and Servant" [1956] C.L.J. 101; [1957] C.L.J. 21, and Lord Gardiner in (1959) 22 M.L.R. 652 on the Report of the Inter-departmental Committee. The leading sociological study of works rules is by E. O. Evans, "Works Rule Books in the Engineering Industry," *Ind. Rels. Journal,* 2 (1971) 54. On the Contracts of Employment Act, see D. W. Crump (ed.), *Dix on Contracts of Employment* (5th ed., London, 1976); C. Grunfeld (1964) 27 M.L.R. 70, and Paul O'Higgins [1964] C.L.J. 220.

CHAPTER 8. *Incorporation of Collective Terms, Awards and Orders.* On the legal status of collective agreements, see B. A. Hepple, "Intention to Create Legal Relations" [1970] C.L.J. 122; R. Lewis, "The Enforcement of Collective Agreements" (1970) 8 B.J.Ind.Rels. 313; J. Casey, "Collective Agreements: Some Scottish Footnotes," *Juridical Review* (1973), 22; Paul O'Higgins, "Legally Enforceable Agreements" (July, 1971) 12 *Industrial Relations Review & Report* 3, and N. Selwyn, "Collective Agreements and the Law" (1969) 32 M.L.R. 377 (correspondence in (1970) 33 M.L.R. 117 and 238).

CHAPTER 9. *Co-operation, Care and Fidelity.* There is only one general study of the implied duty of co-operation (J. L. Burrows, "Contractual Co-operation and the Implied Term" (1968) 31 M.L.R. 390) and this does not deal with the employment relationship. On care, the best work on the employer's duty is J. L. Munkman, *Employer's Liability at Common Law* (8th ed., 1975). On the employee's duty, see the reading listed under Chapter Six. Restraint of trade is dealt with in all the standard textbooks on contract. Breach of Confidence has provoked a fertile literature. See especially P. M. North [1965] *Journal of Business Law* 307; [1966] *ibid.* 31; and Gareth Jones (1970) 86 L.Q.R. 463. On inventions and patents, see the standard books, and Swan (1959) 75 L.Q.R. 77; and Morris (1959) 75 L.Q.R. 48; and Meinhardt [1971] J.B.L. 273.

CHAPTER 10. *Remuneration, Hours, Holidays and Time Off.* On apportionment, the leading study is by G. L. Williams (1941) 57 L.Q.R. 373. O. Kahn-Freund, "The Tangle of the Truck Acts" (1949) 4 Ind. Law Review 2, remains the most penetrating review of truck legislation. The *Report of the Committee on the Truck Acts* (1961) is discussed by O. Aiken (1962) 25 M.L.R. 220, and M. A. Hickling, *ibid.* 512.

CHAPTER 11. *Unfair Discrimination.* Race Relations: The best of the pamphlets written for management are D. Wainwright, *Race and Employment* (I.P.M., London, 1970), and M. Meth, *Here to Stay: A Study of Good Employment Practices in the Employment of Coloured Workers* (London, 1969). The Runnymede Trust (Industrial Unit) publishes teaching aids and gives advice to management, and the Race Relations Board itself publishes explanatory leaflets. For a detailed study of the role of the law in industrial race relations, reference may be had to Bob Hepple, *Race, Jobs and the Law in Britain* (2nd ed. Harmondsworth, 1970), and note on the Race Relations Acts in (1968) 32 M.L.R. 181. The *Street Report on Anti-Discrimination Legislation* (P.E.P., London, 1967), contains useful comparative material. Equal Pay: The Department of Employment has issued an explanatory booklet (1971). The background is discussed in a pamphlet by G. J. Mepham, *Problems of Equal Pay* (I.P.M., London, 1969). There are notes on the Act by B. Barrett in (1971) 34 M.L.R. 308; W. B. Creighton (1971) 22 N.I.L.Q. 533; B. N. Seear in (1971) 34 M.L.R. 312, and M. Freedland, *Bulletin of the Industrial Law Society*, No. 7 (1970), p. 3. On progress made before the Equal Pay Act came into force, see *Equal Pay*: First Report by the Office of Manpower Economics (H.M.S.O., 1972). See also P. Paterson and M. Armstrong, *An Employer's Guide to Equal Pay* (London, 1972).

CHAPTER 12. *Apprenticeship and Training.* There are studies of the Industrial Training Act by G. T. Page, *The Industrial Training Act and*

After (London, 1967), and G. B. Hansen, *Britain's Industrial Training Act* (Washington, 1967).

CHAPTER 13. *Disciplinary Action.* There has been little writing specifically on this subject from a legal point of view. Reference should be made to the writings of E. O. Evans (above, under Chapter Six), A. Avins (below, under Chapter Fourteen) and R. T. Ashdown and K. H. Baker, *In Working Order—A Study of Industrial Discipline* (H.M.S.O., Manpower Papers No. 6, 1973). On the legal nature of strike notice and strikes, see K. Foster, " Strikes and Employment Contracts " (1971) 34 M.L.R. 275; *ibid.* " Strike Notice: Section 147," (1973) I.L.J. 28; N. Lewis, " Strikes and the Contract of Employment " [1968] *Journal of Business Law* 24; P. O'Higgins, " Legal Effect of Strike Notice " [1968] C.L.J. 223 and *ibid.* " Strike Notices: Another Approach," (1973) I.L.J. 152.

CHAPTER 15. *Termination without Notice.* A monumental work containing a lot of information is A. Avins, *Employees' Misconduct* (Allahabad, 1968).

CHAPTER 16. *Termination by Notice.* A useful article on damages is C. D. Drake, " Wrongful Dismissal and Sitting in the Sun " [1967] *Journal of Business Law* 113.

CHAPTER 17. *Unfair Dismissal.* There is a growing literature on this new concept. See, in particular, S. D. Anderman, *Unfair Dismissals and the Law* (London, 1973) and Dudley Jackson, *Unfair Dismissals—How and Why the Law Works* (London, 1975). See also S. D. Anderman, *Voluntary Dismissals Procedures and the New Dismissals Legislation* (P.E.P., London, 1971) and *Voluntary Dismissals Procedure and the Industrial Relations Act* (P.E.P., 1972); and a series of contributions by G. de N. Clark: (i) " Unfair Dismissal and Reinstatement " (1969) 32 M.L.R. 532; (ii) *Remedies for Unjust Dismissal* (P.E.P., London, 1970), and (iii) " Remedies for Unfair Dismissal: A European Comparison " (1971) 20 *International & Comparative Law Quarterly* 397. A summarised account of decisions on unfair dismissal can be found in J. E. McGlyne, *Unfair Dismissal Cases* (London, 1976). A recent work discussing aspects of dismissals law in continental Europe is M. Panayotopoulos, *Le Contrôle Judicaire du Licenciement dans le Droit des Pays Membres de la C.E.E. et celui de la Grèce* (Paris, 1969).

CHAPTER 18. *Redundancy: Compensation and Consultation.* The basic work in this field is by Professor C. Grunfeld, *Law of Redundancy* (London, 1971). Quite useful is D. W. Crump (ed.) *Dix on Contracts of Employment* (5th ed., London, 1976). There is an illuminating discussion of the work of the industrial tribunals in redundancy cases in K. W. Wedderburn and P. L. Davies, *Employment Grievances and Disputes Procedures in Britain* (Berkeley, 1970). A number of useful articles should be referred to: M. Freedland, " Dismissal in the Redundancy Payments Act 1965 " (1970) 33 M.L.R. 93; C. E. McCormick, " The Redundancy Payments Act in the Practice of the Industrial Tribunals " (1970) 2 B.J.Ind.Rels. 334, and J. C. Wood, " Interpretation of the Redun-

APPENDICES

dancy Payments Act 1965 " (1968) 32 *Conveyancer* 343. An invaluable survey of the economic and social effects of the Act may be found in S. R. Parker, C. G. Thomas, N. D. Ellis and W. E. J. McCarthy, *Effects of the Redundancy Payments Act* (H.M.S.O., London, 1971).

CHAPTER 19. *Unemployment—Social Security Benefits.* The basic works are H. Calvert, *Social Security Law* (London, 1974) and C. Smith and D. C. Hoath, *Law and the Underprivileged* (London, 1975). The following will be found to be useful sources of information: E. O. F. Stocker and P. G. Milsson, *The Law relating to Supplementary Benefits and Family Income Supplements* (H.M.S.O., London, 1972); J. St. L. Brockman, *The Law Relating to Family Allowances and National Insurance* (2 vols., H.M.S.O., London, 1961); *ibid. The Law Relating to National Insurance (Industrial Injuries)* (2 vols., H.M.S.O., London, 1961), and E. Jenkins, *Index and Digest of Decisions under National Insurance Acts, the National Insurance (Industrial Injuries) Acts and the Family Allowances Acts* (2 vols., H.M.S.O., London, 1964). These are official compilations and contain no criticism and little explanatory material. Two non-legal works of value are V. N. George, *Social Security— Beveridge and After* (London, 1968), and G. D. Gilling-Smith, *The Complete Guide to Pensions and Superannuation* (Harmondsworth, 1967). The Supplementary Benefits Commission has published an outline of the law (and practice) of its administration of the system of supplementary benefits in the *Supplementary Benefits Handbook* (H.M.S.O., 4th ed., 1974). T. Lynes, *Penguin Guide to Supplementary Benefits* (2nd ed., Harmondsworth, 1974) is useful and critical. Three periodicals contain regular discussions of social security law: (i) *LAG Bulletin* (published by the Legal Action Group), and (ii) *Poverty* (published by the Child Poverty Action Group. The Child Poverty Action Group also publishes numerous useful pamphlets), and (iii) the *Industrial Law Journal.*

CHAPTER 20. *International Labour Standards.* There is no textbook in English covering the subject-matter of this chapter. Two French works however are the best available accounts. They are G. Lyon-Caen, *Droit Social International et Européen* (3me ed. Paris, 1974), and N. Valticos, *Droit International du Travail* (Paris, 1970). On labour migration in the EEC, see L. C. Hunter and G. L. Reid, *European Integration and the Movement of Labour* (Kingston, Ontario, 1970), and W. R. Böhning, *The Migration of Workers in the United Kingdom and the European Community* (London, 1972). On the Social Charter, see D. J. Harris, " The European Social Charter " (1964) 13 *International and Comparative Law Quarterly* 1076. On the I.L.O., reference should be made to E. A. Landy, *The Effectiveness of International Supervision—Thirty Years of ILO Experience* (London, 1966), G. A. Johnston, *The I.L.O.* (1971), *Freedom of Association: Digest of Decisions of the Freedom of Association Committee of the Governing body of the I.L.O.* (I.L.O., Geneva, 2nd ed., 1976), and to three books by C. W. Jenks: (i) *The International Protection of Trade Union Freedom* (London, 1957); (ii) *Human Rights and International Labour Standards* (London, 1960), and (iii) *Social Justice in the Law of Nations* (Oxford, 1970).

Keeping up to date with developments in the EEC poses special problems because of the sheer bulk of the materials involved. Apart from the *Official Journal* and *Bulletin* of the Communities the following works will be found useful: the monthly *European Industrial Relations Review* (published in London), and Sweet & Maxwell's *Encyclopedia of European Community Law*. On the Action Programme, Dewi-Davies Jones, *Europe : Social Action Programme* (London, 1974) will be found to contain a detailed summary of the most important aspects of the EEC's current social policy.

CHAPTER 21. *International Employment Contracts.* See O. Kahn-Freund, "Notes on the conflict of laws in relation to employment in English and Scottish law ": *Rivista di Diritto Int. e. Comparato del Lavoro* 3 (1960) 307; I. Szaszy, *International Labour Law* (Leyden, 1968); and F. Gamillscheg, Chap. 28 in Vol. III, *International Encyclopedia of Comparative Law* (1974).

CHAPTER 22. *Industrial Tribunals.* See reading under Chap. 4, above.

APPENDIX 2

EMPLOYMENT PROTECTION ACT 1975: COMMENCEMENT DATES

As at June 1, 1976, the following Commencement Orders had been made under this Act:

Commencement Order No. 1, S.I. 1975 No. 1938 (C.55).
Commencement Order No. 2, S.I. 1976 No. 144 (C.5).
Commencement Order No. 3, S.I. 1976 No. 321 (C.9).
Commencement Order No. 4, S.I. 1976 No. 530 (C.16).

These Orders bring into operation a substantial part of the Act on various dates between January 1, and June 1, 1976, but some of them (*e.g.* relating to maternity pay) will not be in operation until April 6, 1977. Further Commencement Orders will be made bringing the remaining sections into force. Where no date is indicated in the following Table, no Commencement Order had been made as at June 1, 1976.

Section of the Act	Order	Date of operation
1 to 16	1	February 1, 1976
17 to 24	—	—
25 (5)	4	June 1, 1976
25 (1) to (4)	—	—
26 to 28	—	—
29 (1), (2) and (4)	4	June 1, 1976
29 (3)	4	April 20, 1976
30 to 34	4	June 1, 1976
35 (1) (a)	4	April 6, 1977
35 (remainder)	4	June 1, 1976
36 to 41 and 42 (1), (2) and (3)	4	April 6, 1977
42 (4)	4	June 1, 1976
43 to 47	4	April 6, 1977
48 to 56	4	June 1, 1976
57 to 60	—	—
61	4	June 1, 1976
62 (in part)	4	June 1, 1976, so far as it relates to the purposes of section 61
62 (remainder)	—	—
63 (1) and (2) (d)	2	April 20, 1976
63 (2) (a)	—	—
63 (2) (b) and (c) (in part)	4	June 1, 1976, so far as it relates to payments under section 61 (3)
64 (part)	2	April 20, 1976, except (3) (d) and (6)
64 (3) (d) and (6)	4	June 1, 1976
65 to 69	2	April 20, 1976
70 to 80	4	June 1, 1976
81 to 84	—	—
85 (1) (part)	2	March 8, 1976, so far as it relates to section 102
85 (1) (remainder) and (2)	4	June 1, 1976

Section of the Act	Order	Date of operation
86	4	June 1, 1976
87 and 88	3	March 20, 1976
89 to 97	1	January 1, and February 1, 1976
98	—	—
99 to 108	2	March 8, 1976
109	1	January 1, 1976
110 (part)	2	March 8, 1976, so far as relates to sections 99 to 107
110 (remainder)	2 and 4	April 20, 1976
111	—	—
112	1	January 1, 1976
113 (part)	2	March 8, 1976, so far as relates to Protective Awards (section 101)
113 (remainder)	4	June 1, 1976
114 to 116	1	March 1, 1976
117 (part)	2	March 8, 1976, so far as relates to offences under section 105
117 (remainder)	2 and 4	April 20, 1976
118	1	January 1, 1976
119 (part)	2	March 8, 1976, so far as relates to sections 99 and 100
119 (part)	2	April 20, 1976, so far as relates to sections 64 and 65
119 (remainder)	4	June 1, 1976
120	4	June 1, 1976
121 to 123	1	January 1, 1976
124 (part)	1	January 1, 1976, subsections (1), (2) (*b*), (5) and (6) only
124 (4) (*a*)	4	April 20, 1976
124 (4) (*b*)	4	June 1, 1976
124 (2) (*a*) and (3)	4	April 6, 1977
125 (1) (part)	1 and 4	On or before June 1, 1976, so far as requisite for bringing into operation on the dates mentioned the various paragraphs of Schedule 16 set out below.
125 (2) (part)	1, 2 and 4	On or before June 1, 1976, so far as requisite for bringing into operation on the dates mentioned the various paragraphs of Schedule 17 set out below.
125 (3) (part)	1 and 4	On or before June 1, 1976, so far as requisite to bring into operation the whole of Schedule 18 EXCEPT so far as relates to the repeal in whole or part of: (a) The Terms and Conditions of Employment Act 1959; (b) The Payments of Wages Act 1960; (c) The Supplementary Benefits Act 1966; (d) Para. 9 (1) (*a*) of Schedule 1 to the T.U.L.R. Act 1974;

Section of the Act	Order	Date of operation
125 (3) (part) (*continued*)		(e) The Social Security Act 1975; and
		(f) The Social Security (Consequential Provisions) Act 1975
126 (part)	1, 2 and 4	On or before June 1, 1976, so far as requisite to bring into operation all the definitions in section 126
126 (part)	4	EXCEPT "guarantee payment" and "maternity benefit" April 6, 1977, to bring into operation the definition of "maternity benefit"
127 to 129	1	January 1, or February 1, 1976
Schedule 1	1	January 1, or February 1, 1976
Schedules 2 and 3	4	June 1, 1976
Schedule 4 (part)	2	March 8, 1976, so far as relates to section 102
Schedule 4 (remainder)	4	June 1, 1976
Schedule 5	4	June 1, 1976
Schedule 6	3	March 30, 1976
Schedules 7 to 10	1	January 1, 1976
Schedule 11	—	—
Schedule 12 (part)	2	March 8, 1976, so far as relates to sections 99 to 107
Schedules 13 and 14	1	January 1, 1976
Schedule 15	1 and 4	January 1, 1976 (paragraphs 2, 3 and 9) and March 1, 1976 (balance)
Schedule 16 Part I		
paras. 1 to 5	4	June 1, 1976
para. 6	—	—
paras. 7 to 16	4	June 1, 1976
para. 17	1	January 1, 1976
para. 18	4	June 1, 1976
Schedule 16 Part II		
paras. 1 to 6	4	June 1, 1976
paras. 7 and 8	—	—
paras. 9 and 10	4	June 1, 1976
para. 11	—	—
para. 12	4	June 1, 1976
paras. 13 and 14	—	—
paras. 15 to 19	4	June 1, 1976
Schedule 16 Part III		
paras. 1 to 6	1	January 1, or February 1, 1976
para. 7	1 and 4	January 1, or February 1, 1976, and (as to para. 7 (4)) 1 June, 1976
paras. 8 to 10	4	June 1, 1976
paras. 11 and 12	1	January 1, or February 1, 1976
para. 13	4	June 1, 1976
para. 14 (1) (*a*)	—	—
para. 14 (remainder)	4	June 1, 1976
para. 15	—	—
paras. 16 and 17	4	June 1, 1976
para. 18	1	January 1, 1976

Section of the Act	Order	Date of operation
Schedule 16 Part III		
(continued)		
para. 19	4	April 20, 1976
paras. 20 and 21	4	June 1, 1976
para. 22	4	April 20, 1976
para. 23	1	January 1, 1976
para. 24	4	June 1, 1976
para. 25	1	January 1, 1976
paras. 26 to 30	4	June 1, 1976
paras. 31 to 33	1	January 1, 1976
para. 34	4	June 1, 1976
para. 35	1	February 1, 1976
Schedule 16 Part IV		
paras. 1 to 8	1	January 1, or February 1, 1976
para. 9	4	June 1, 1976
paras. 10 to 17	1	January 1, or February 1, 1976
para. 18 (1) and (3)	1 and 4	January 1, or February 1, 1976
para. 18 (2)	4	June 1, 1976
Schedule 17		
paras. 1 to 6	1	January 1, or February 1, 1976
para. 7	4	June 1, 1976
para. 8	2	April 20, 1976
paras. 9 to 12	1	January 1, or February 1, 1976
para. 13	—	—
paras. 14 and 15	1	January 1, 1976
paras. 16 and 17	4	June 1, 1976
paras. 18 and 19	1	January 1, 1976
Schedule 18		
(in part)	1 and 4	January 1, February 1, March 1, or June 1, 1976, to the extent stated above under section 125 (3)
Remaining repeals	—	—

317

QUALIFYING PERIODS AND TIME LIMITS FOR PRESENTATION
OF CLAIMS

Explanatory note:

(1) *Qualifying period* means the period of continuous employment for the employee to be eligible to present a claim. For meaning of " continuous employment " see Chap. 5.

(2) *Time limit to "present" claim.* See the general discussion in Chap. 22.

(3) *E.D.T.* means the " effective date of termination " or, in redundancy payments claims, the " relevant date." Some statutes use the concept " when the employment ceased."

(4) *" Usual discretion to extend."* Means that the following formula (or similar words) is used: " within such further period as the tribunal considers reasonable in a case where it is satisfied that it was not reasonably practicable for the complaint to be presented within the period of [three] months."

Since the information is presented here in summary form, it is always necessary to consult the relevant statute for the precise qualifying period and time limit.

Jurisdiction	*Qualifying period* [1]	*Time limit to "present" claim* [2]
1. Written statement (C.E.A., s. 8)	13 weeks (s. 4 (1))	3 months from E.D.T.[3]
2. Redundancy payment (R.P.A., s. 9)	2 years (s. 8 (1))	6 months from E.D.T. (s. 21). " Just and equitable " extension if claims in next 6 months (E.P.A., Sched. 16, Pt. I, para. 9)
3. Unfair dismissal (T.U.L.R.A., Sched. 1, para. 4)	26 weeks (para. 10). None if " inadmissible reason " (paras. 6 (4), 11)	3 months from E.D.T. (para. 21 (4)) or before E.D.T. if dismissal with notice (E.P.A., Sched. 16, Pt. III, para. 21). Usual discretion to extend [4]
4. (a) Sex discrimination (S.D.A., s. 63)	—	3 months from act (s. 76 (1) (5)). " Just and equitable " extension
(b) Non-discrimination notice appeal (S.D.A., s. 68)	—	6 weeks from service (s. 68 (1))
(c) Breach of equality clause (Equal Pay Act, s. 2 (1))	—	6 months from E.D.T. (s. 2 (4))

Jurisdiction	Qualifying period [1]	Time limit to "present" claim [2]
4. (d) Discriminatory practices, adverts, incitement etc. (Commission complains under ss. 71–72, 73 and 38–40)	—	6 months from act (s. 76 (4)). "Just and equitable" extension (s. 76 (5))
5. Employment Protection Act—		
(a) Guarantee pay (s. 27)	4 weeks ending with last complete week before due (s. 22 (3))	3 months from due day. Usual discretion to extend (s. 27 (2))
(b) Medical suspension pay (s. 32)	Ditto (s. 30 (1)) 4 weeks to complain of dismissal (s. 29 (4))	Ditto (s. 32 (2))
(c) Maternity pay (s. 38)	2 years at beginning 11th week before expected week of confinement (s. 35 (2) (3))	Ditto (s. 38 (2))
(d) Failure to permit return after confinement (claim of unfair dismissal or for redundancy payment)	Ditto (subject to s. 50 (1) and Sched. 3) and as for redundancy payment	As for unfair dismissal and redundancy payment
(e) Employer's rebate from maternity fund (s. 46)	—	3 months from Sec. of State decision. Usual discretion to extend (s. 46 (5))
(f) Trade union membership and activity (s. 54)	—	3 months from act. Usual discretion to extend (s. 54 (2))
(g) Time off for union official (s. 57), or member (s. 58) and for public duties s. 59)	—	3 months from failure to give. Usual discretion to extend (s. 60 (1))
(h) Time off for redundant employee (s. 61)	2 years to date of expiry of notice (s. 61 (2))	Ditto (s. 61 (9))
(i) Payment of debts in insolvency by Sec. of State (s. 66)	—	3 months from Sec. of State decision. Usual discretion to extend (s. 61 (1) (2))
(j) Written statement of reasons for dismissal (s. 70)	26 weeks ending last complete week before E.D.T. (s. 70 (2))	3 months from E.D.T. Usual discretion to extend (s. 70 (5))

Jurisdiction	*Qualifying period* [1]	*Time limit to " present " claim* [2]
(k) Itemised pay statement (s. 84)	—	3 months from E.D.T. (s. 84 (4))
(l) T.U. complaint of breach of redundancy procedure (s. 101)	—	Before dismissal or 3 months from E.D.T. Usual discretion to extend (s. 101 (6))
(m) Claim for remuneration under protective award (s. 103)	—	3 months from E.D.T. Usual discretion to extend (s. 103 (2))

INDEX

321

Central Arbitration Committee,
  ad hoc arbitrator, 255
  award of, 59, 106, 173, 255
  composition of, 173
  disclosure of information, complaint
    concerning, 53
  discrimination, prevention of by, 415
  Fair Wages Resolution, 202, 256
  functions of, 173
  independence of, 173
  jurisdiction, 174
  procedure, 173
  trade dispute, as arbitrator in, 174
Certification Officer,
  breach of union rules, 26
  functions of, 172
  independent trade union, determina-
    tion by, 28
  lists of trade unions by, 27
  trade union amalgamations and, 44
Charities,
  discrimination by, 405
Chauffeur, 133
Checkweigher,
  functions of, 351
  wages, 348
Children. *See* Minors.
Civil court,
  exclusive jurisdiction, 159
  supervisory jurisdiction, 160
Civil servants. *See* Public employees.
Civil Service Arbitration Tribunal, 175
Codes of Practice,
  Advisory, Conciliation and Arbitra-
    tion Service, power of to issue, 169
  Code of Industrial Relations Practice,
    aim of, 95
    breach of, legal effect of, 96
    discipline, 462, 464
    dismissal, 462
    disputes, 153
    evidence, as, 95
    failure to observe, 95
    nature of, 95
    redundancy, 621
    time off work, concerning, 367
      et seq.
Collective agreements,
  agency, 244
  awards. *See* Awards.
  common law, 243
  confidential information, 292
  conflicts of, 252
  contract of employment and, 241,
    242, 245, 246
  discipline, breach of and, 442
  discrimination, 415
  discrimination against foreigners, 393
  employer's non-compliance with, 55
    et seq.
  enforceability of, 242 *et seq.*
  express terms, 234
  fair wages, 256, 257
  freedom of employer to contract out
    of, 55
  "guaranteed week," 327
  holidays, 365
  hours of work, 359

Collective agreements—*cont.*
  implied terms of contract, 221, 234,
    246, 247
  individual obligation, 249
  intention to create legal relations, 243
  nature of, 241
  "no-strike" clause, 253
  procedural, 241
  purposes of, 241
  remuneration, 302
  sick pay, 309
  substantive, 241
  terms and conditions, recognised, 55
    et seq.
  third parties and, 250, 251
  variation of, 245, 259
  written statements, as to, 245
Collective bargaining,
  collective agreements. *See* Collective
    agreements.
  comparison with U.S.A., 98
  contract and, 99
  definition of, 48, 241
  disclosure of information, in, 292
  historical importance of, 2
  individual and, 98
  preference for, 1
  recognition, right to, 46, 47, 50
Commission agent, 133
Common law,
  apprenticeship, 432
  breach of contract, remedies for, 108
  collective agreements, 243
  collective bargaining, 98
  deductions from wages, 454
  discipline, 453
  discrimination, 381
  duration of "employment," 137
  duty of court, 102
  forfeiture of wages, 454
  freedom of contract at, 201, 205
  implied terms, 224
  interpretation of statutes, and, 93
  minors, capacity to contract, 184
  notice to suspend, 460
  payment of wages, 344
  pro-rata remuneration, 307
  restraint of trade, 286 *et seq.*
  right to work, 201
  strike notice, 4, 460
  summary dismissal, 504
  termination of contract, 501
  training, 433
  wrongful dismissal, 504
Commonwealth citizens,
  restrictions on, 100
Companies,
  special register bodies, 29
  winding up, 475
Compensation,
  amount of, 582 *et seq.*
  benefits in kind, 584
  breach of contract, 108 *et seq.*
  calculation of, 581, 620
  confidential information, disclosure
    of, 289
  damages and, 597
  deductions from, 529, 584, 585, 597
  discrimination, for, 410

H.O.—11*

Discrimination—*cont.*
    statistical evidence, 387
    trade union by, 398, 403, 404
    training, 387, 398, 403
    Treaty of Rome, 422
    unfair dismissal and, 397
    U.S.A., comparison with, 386 *et seq.*
    victimisation, 392
Dismissal. *See also* Redundancy and Unfair dismissal.
    agreement, termination by, 491
    apprentices, of. *See* Apprenticeship.
    Code of Industrial Relations Practice, 462
    compensation. *See* Compensation.
    co-operate, refusal to, 275
    date of, 574
    declaration, 112
    definition, 484, 487
    E.E.C. Directive, 687
    industrial tribunal, complaint to. *See* Industrial tribunals.
    lay-off, 325
    lock-outs, during, 574
    misconduct, 503
    national security as reason for, 559
    notice. *See* Notice.
    pressure on employer, 574, 588
    procedures, 510, 589 *et seq.*
    proof of, 544
    property, for mishandling of, 282
    public employment, 113
    reason for, need for, 504, 545
    redundancy. *See* Redundancy
    re-engagement and. *See* Re-engagement.
    reinstatement and. *See* Reinstatement.
    summary. *See* Summary dismissal.
    unfair. *See* Unfair dismissal.
    variation of contract, effect of, 183, 491
    warning of, 463, 491
    written statement of reasons for, 506
    wrongful, unfair and, 504, 515, 547, 597
Disobedience, 554
Disputes. *See also* Industrial action.
    arbitration, use of, 153
    claims, 151 *et seq.*
    Code of Industrial Relations, Practice, under, 153
    contract of employment, arising from, 151
    of interest, 153
    of right, 153
    settlement of, 151, *et seq.*
Disqualification from driving, 557
Dock worker,
    " employee " as, 125, 126
    guarantee payment, 335
    registration, 100
    restrictions on employment of, 212
    status, 112
    unfair dismissal and, 573
Domestic servants, definition of, 124
    " employees " as, 126
Donovan Royal Commission on Trade Unions and Employers' Associations, 7

Drivers, hours of work, 362
    earnings. *See* Remuneration.
Duties. *See also* Employee; Employer.
    compulsory, 101 *et seq.*
    effect of classification as contractual, 101 *et seq.*
    extra-contractual, 102
    implied terms of contract, 101

Employee,
    absence from work. *See* Absence from work.
    agent, distinguished from, 133
    anaesthetist, as, 134
    au pairs, 130
    bad workmanship, effect of, 445, 446
    baker. *See* Bakeries.
    borrowed, 136, 139
    breach of contract, by, 531. *See also* Contract of employment.
    canvassing employers' customers, 285
    capability, dismissal concerning, 553
    casual, 125, 137, 653
    chauffeur, 133
    checkweigher. *See* Checkweigher.
    commission agent, 133
    collective agreement, knowledge of, 247
    conduct, dismissal for, 554
    control of, 133
    convicted offender. *See* Offender.
    cricket umpire, 130
    Crown. *See* Public employees.
    death of, 473
    definition of, 16, 122 *et seq.*, 601
    discipline. *See* Discipline.
    discrimination. *See* Discrimination.
    dismissal of. *See* Dismissal.
    disobedience, 554
    dock worker. *See* Dock worker.
    driver, 362
    duties,
        account, to, 282
        competition, 284 *et seq.*
        confidential information, concerning, 288, 290, 291
        co-operation, 274
        court, of, 278
        employer's property, handing, 282
        fidelity, 284
        indemnify employer, to, 278
        mitigation of loss of employment, 529
        notice. *See* Notice.
        obedience, 275
        performance of contract, 274
        spare-time work, concerning, 284
    employed, 414
    " employed earner," 709
    ex-employee, 285, 288
    factory. *See* Factories.
    fines, 447
    firemen, 141
    fishermen. *See* Fishermen.
    fixed term contract, under. *See* Contract of employment.